Sarah Raven's GARDEN COOKBOOK

Photography by Jonathan Buckley

BLOOMSBURY

LONDON · BERLIN · NEW YORK

To Tam, with love and thanks

Introduction

This book is all about the pleasures that fruit and vegetables can give you; its aim is to put them at the centre of every meal. It's also a practical guide to all that is wonderful in the edible plant kingdom, with more than 450 recipes using the vegetable garden – or a good seasonal market or greengrocer – as both their source and inspiration. It's not a vegetarian book – although it contains plenty of recipes that have nothing but vegetables in them.

For the past 150 years meat has dominated the British diet. In the nineteenth century the invention of the refrigerated ship meant that meat could be brought fresh from anywhere in the world, and it became increasingly cheap. The development of factory farming and the efficient networks of the global economy have meant that daily meat has become a possibility for everyone. In one way, that's a good thing, but a consequence has been that it is now as if a meal is no good unless it is built around a slab of flesh, which is a sad and reduced place to have arrived at.

Meat is hungry for resources. It uses land in the most profligate ways; it requires far more calories to produce meat than it eventually delivers. And, of course, it uses large amounts of energy in being shipped around the world. That is not how it used to be. Meat was once considered precious, a regular, delicious, but occasional visitor to the plate. The mainstays of your diet were vegetables and fruit. In a way, this book is advocating a return to an older habit, where these foods can reclaim their rightful place, not as a stand-in or supporting part, but at centre stage.

The world is thankfully turning in the right direction. Think of your local greengrocer twenty years ago. Its racks would have been dominated by apples, potatoes, carrots, floppy lettuce and cabbage. Today, if you have a local greengrocer, those things will still be there, but you'll find them among Florence fennel, celeriac, figs, pomegranates and a great array of mushrooms. Add to them the farmers' markets that are springing up all over the place, with their 'limited editions' of red Brussels sprouts, sweet tomatoes picked the night before, pumpkins and squash of all colours and sizes, and you will see that these are good times for fruit and veg.

Other parts of the world have kept faith with a more balanced approach in their cooking cultures. The Mediterranean has always been a wonderful source of inspiration for this way of eating. Traditionally, in France and even more so in Italy and Spain, where families would raise and slaughter their own animals, you'd eat meat or fish on high days and holidays, but by no means every day.

In these food cultures, vegetables are not the optional extras –
'the trimmings' – but the daily foundation of food itself.

When I was a child in the 1970s, we often went on holiday to
Asolo in the Veneto, a honey-coloured town in the foothills of the
Dolomites. Orchards and farmland ran up to its medieval walls, and
all the produce of garden and field was on sale in the market square
and under the shady stone arcades lining the streets. Day after day,
under the shopping and cooking guidance of Angelica, the cook in
the house where we stayed, we would feast on an abundance of
unfamiliar ingredients: globe artichokes, herby salads, wild greens,
borlotti beans, bitter chicory, sometimes with bread, sometimes
with pasta, sometimes with rice, but rarely with meat.

At university, like so many before me and since, I read Elizabeth
David over and over again, and I cooked with her books to hand in a
tiny house I used to rent in the mountains of the Auvergne. Then, to
support myself through medical school in London, I waitressed at the
River Cafe, which has done so much to bring the Italian culinary
tradition into the English mainstream. These influences moulded me
to a way of cooking that is based on really good ingredients and that
focuses on taste rather than appearance. Fruit and vegetables lend
themselves to simplicity; the less you do to them, the better. Food
cooked this way is alive with the flavour of its raw ingredients.

A great bonus of eating local, seasonal food is that your diet
will never be repetitive. As the seasons unfold, old favourites recur
and new opportunities present themselves. And, for the most
part, there's no need for it to have travelled from the other side of
the world. During the winter, there are almost as many delicious
possibilities as in summer.

I have poured enormous amounts of myself and my life into
this book. I think of it as a compendium of everything I've loved in
the garden and the kitchen over the last fifteen or twenty years. I'm
hoping that you will cook your way through it, and that over the years
you'll have a good time doing so. But I have a further ambition for
you, too. If you're lucky enough to have access to any outdoor space,
growing fruit and vegetables is a wonderful thing to do. It can't be
claimed that growing your own food is not time-consuming, but it is,
I think, a way to be happy, involving a little thinking, some physical
work and some creativity. Harvesting and cooking from the garden
is one of my greatest pleasures in life.

Sarah Raven   Perch Hill, East Sussex

January | February

Cabbages

When you are preparing cabbage, rip off the leaves one at a time and get rid of most of the central stem. It cooks at a different rate to the leaves, so chuck it away. With any green cabbage, if there's time, strip off the leaves a couple of hours before you want to eat and float them torn up in a sinkful of cold water. As with salad, this perks cabbage up and keeps it crisp. The plant cells absorb water by osmosis. The cell walls then bulge with the contained water. That's what gives them the crunch, which they retain when lightly cooked. Always cook cabbage with the lid off to keep it bright green.

Cabbage has a versatile flavour, which is delicious with butter and plenty of salt and pepper. For a simple lunch, have a plate of cabbage, yoghurt and some grated nutmeg. If on a diet, treat it like pasta: cut it up into fine spaghetti-like strands and serve it with a scattering of Parmesan cheese, or try it with finely grated root ginger, or dry-roasted caraway, sunflower or cumin seeds.

Cabbage is wonderful raw, either on its own or very finely sliced and mixed with carrot in a simple salad. Don't make it all slurpy like coleslaw, but dress it lightly with fruity olive oil, pulverised garlic, plenty of salt and pepper and lemon juice. Greek restaurants often serve this and it's good to eat with grilled meat or fish as a contrast to the ubiquitous tomato, cucumber and feta salad.

As well as green or white cabbage, at this time of year you must have a few meals of red. The virtues of red cabbage are its incredible colour and its texture, which is firmer than green. It will take more cooking, so is the ideal vegetable for rich, reduced, slow-cooked dishes like braised red cabbage and soup. With an added acid – vinegar or wine – the colour fixes as a brilliant magenta. Without this, it can turn an unappetising grey.

Fried cabbage
with juniper

A wonderfully healthy and delicious lunch. Have the cabbage on its own, or on top of a bowl of rice. For something more substantial, cut some seared steak, tuna or lambs' liver into thin strips and toss them in.

For 4–6:
- 1 small (or ½ large) Savoy cabbage (about 650g)
- 1 tablespoon dry-fried sesame seeds (you can mix in sunflower seeds too)
- 1 tablespoon juniper berries, crushed
- 2 garlic cloves, chopped
- Sea salt
- 2 tablespoons groundnut oil
- 1 red chilli, deseeded and thinly sliced (red is good for the colour)
- 2 teaspoons toasted sesame oil
- 1 tablespoon finely chopped fresh root ginger
- 1 tablespoon runny honey
- Splash of Japanese soy sauce
- Freshly ground black pepper
- Bunch of coriander, coarsely chopped

Chop up the cabbage – Savoy is best – into four and discard the hard white heart and leaf midribs before shredding it finely.

Dry-fry the sesame seeds on a gentle heat until they're golden brown. This will take about 5 minutes, but don't let them burn. Then put them to one side. Crush the juniper berries and garlic with the sea salt, using a pestle and mortar.

Heat a tablespoon of the groundnut oil in a wok or large frying pan. Add the chilli and cook for 1 minute on a medium heat. Scoop the chilli out of the oil, leaving the spicy oil in the pan, and add the sesame seeds. Add the rest of the groundnut oil and the sesame oil to the same pan and then the cabbage,

salt, juniper berries and garlic. Turn up the heat. Stir every minute or so for 5 minutes and then add all the other ingredients except the coriander. Stir for another couple of minutes and remove from the heat. The cabbage should still be crunchy. This tastes lovely with coriander leaves – add some chopped over the top.

Savoy cabbage
and coriander soup

This cabbage soup is based on a recipe by the Irish chef Denis Cotter. I often make my version for lunch in the winter, cooking it for a shorter time than he recommends. The cabbage is then crisp and bright. This soup has lots of different flavours, with a lovely after-bite.

For 6:
- 450g onions
- ½ Savoy cabbage (about 400g)
- 2 tablespoons olive oil
- 2 red or 4 green chillies, finely chopped
- 4 garlic cloves, finely chopped
- About 5cm fresh root ginger, peeled and chopped
- 2 tablespoons coriander seeds, crushed
- 800ml good vegetable stock
- 400ml tin of coconut milk
- Bunch of fresh coriander, chopped
- Juice of 3 limes
- Salt and black pepper

Finely chop the onions and very finely shred the cabbage, either by hand or by using the finest slicing disc on a food processor.

Heat the oil in a pan, add the onion and cabbage, and cook them over a moderate heat for a couple of minutes before adding the chillies, garlic, ginger and coriander seeds. Continue cooking for about 5 minutes, stirring regularly, until the onion and cabbage are tender but still have a bite to them.

Bring the stock to the boil in a separate pan and add it to the vegetables. Simmer for 5 minutes, then add the coconut milk, half of the fresh coriander, the lime juice and finally salt and pepper.

Serve the soup with extra coriander to taste.

Sweet-and-sour marinated cabbage

This pickle is northern European in origin and is good with warming, intense-tasting winter food. It goes well with smoked fish – trout or eel – and is ideal with a strong cheese. The key to this treatment is the fine shredding of the cabbage and the large quantities of fresh dill, and dill (or fennel) and mustard seed, in the marinade. This dish needs to be made at least the day before you want to eat it, so that the flavours of the seeds really come through.

For 6:
- ½ **white cabbage**
- 100ml **cider vinegar**
- 100g **caster sugar**
- **Large bunch of dill, finely chopped**
- 3 tablespoons **good sunflower oil**
- 1 **garlic clove, chopped**
- 2 teaspoons **dill or fennel seeds**
- 2 teaspoons **mustard seeds**
- **Salt and black pepper**

Cut your cabbage into quarters and remove the midrib, then slice the cabbage very finely. Use the green leaf only, not the stem.

Heat the vinegar in a small pan over a low heat and then stir in the sugar until it has dissolved. Allow this to cool.

Finely chop the dill. Add this and the oil, garlic, dill and mustard seeds, salt and pepper to the sweet vinegar and dress the cabbage with this marinade.

Leave in a jar or covered container at least overnight for the flavours to develop. This keeps very well in a screw-topped jar in the fridge and is still excellent after 2 or 3 weeks.

Bea's stuffed cabbage leaves

This is Bea Csap's recipe. She is from Hungary and is our gardener here on the farm. The stuffed cabbage leaves are excellent eaten on their own, dipped into natural yoghurt or with sauerkraut. The sauerkraut is not essential but it adds another flavour.

For 8–10 (about 20 rolls):
- 1 **cabbage**
- 4 **bay leaves**
- 150ml **white wine vinegar**
- **Bowl of iced water**
- 200g **smoked dry-cure bacon, chopped**
- 1 **chopped onion**
- 2 **garlic cloves, crushed**
- **Bunch of chopped mixed herbs (such as sweet marjoram, thyme and dill)**
- 1 teaspoon **smoked paprika**
- ¼ teaspoon **ground cumin seeds**
- **Salt and black pepper**
- 500g **minced pork**
- 500g **minced beef**
- 150g **cooked long-grain rice**
- 1 **egg**
- 1 **jar of sauerkraut (optional)**
- **Small bunch of dill**
- 570ml **chicken or vegetable stock**

Preheat a medium (180°C/gas mark 4) oven.

Choose the bright green outer leaves of the cabbage and blanch them whole for 2–3 minutes in a large pan of boiling salted water containing 3 of the bay leaves and the vinegar. Plunge the leaves into ice-cold water to cool and then remove the thickest part of the midrib. This makes them easier to roll.

Fry the bacon in a shallow pan until it's cooked, but not crisp, and put aside. In the same pan, add the onion to the bacon juices with the crushed garlic, chopped herbs, paprika, cumin, salt and pepper.

Mix the raw pork and beef together with the cooked rice and the

bacon (if using sauerkraut, reserve a little of the bacon to add to that) and onion mixture, adding a beaten egg to bind it and seasoning with salt and pepper (you can quickly fry a teaspoonful of the mixture in a dash of oil to test the seasoning). Take a small handful of this mixture and place on a cabbage leaf, then roll it up, starting from the stem end and tucking the edges inwards to make a neat roll.

If you're using sauerkraut, drain the jar, keeping the liquor to one side, and rinse under cold water in a sieve. Fluff it up and mix with the reserved bacon and a little more chopped dill. Place this mixture on the bottom of a casserole dish and arrange the cabbage rolls in quite a tight layer on top.

Cover with the stock plus a little of the sauerkraut liquor, add the remaining bay leaf and some more dill, and cook, covered, in the preheated oven for 1½ hours.

The ultimate minestrone

A great winter meal of a soup, based on a recipe from Marcella Hazan, the doyenne of Italian cookery writing.

For 4–6:
  3 tablespoons olive oil
  15g butter
  2 onions, chopped
  100g pancetta
  **1 large or 2 small carrot(s),
    chopped**
  1 celery stick, chopped
  2 courgettes, chopped
  100g red cabbage, shredded
  **450g fresh borlotti beans
    or 225g tinned cannellini beans**
  **3 large fresh tomatoes, chopped,
    or a 225g tin of chopped
    tomatoes**
  Salt and black pepper
  **450ml good chicken or
    vegetable stock**
  Remains of a bottle of red wine
  **Freshly grated Parmesan cheese,
    to serve**
  Crusty bread, to serve

Put the oil, butter, onion and pancetta into a large saucepan. Cook over a medium heat until the onion is a deep gold. Add the chopped vegetables, the shredded cabbage and the fresh borlotti beans. (If you are using tinned beans, do not add them at this stage.)

Add the chopped tomatoes and seasoning, and stir well. Then add the stock and the red wine, making sure that the liquid covers the vegetables. Cover the pan and simmer gently for at least an hour. If using tinned beans, add them after about 50 minutes.

When the liquid has significantly reduced and the soup looks rich and quite thick, taste and adjust the seasoning. Rest it for 10 minutes (the flavours are better when it is not scalding hot) and serve with freshly grated Parmesan and crusty bread.

Quick braised red cabbage

It is always said that the best red cabbage is cooked on a slow heat for a very long time. It's true that this deepens the flavour, but this simple recipe is delicious after just an hour of cooking. It's ideal with salted baked potatoes, game, roasted red meat or carbonnade of beef or venison.

For 6–8:
  1 large red cabbage
  50g butter
  Olive oil
  1 large onion, chopped
  **2 Bramley apples, peeled and
    roughly chopped**
  **100ml dark malt vinegar, and
    more if necessary**
  Grated zest of 1 large orange
  **2 heaped tablespoons soft
    brown sugar**
  Handful of raisins (optional)
  300g walnuts (optional)
  Salt and black pepper

Remove the core of the cabbage and slice it thinly or put it into a food processor using the finest slicing disc.

Put the butter and a splash of oil into a large pan, add the chopped onion and wait for it to soften before adding the red cabbage. Keep stirring to coat the cabbage well, then add the roughly chopped apple, malt vinegar, orange zest and soft brown sugar. Add the raisins and walnuts if you want to. Season with salt and pepper, and cook either over a gentle heat or in a moderate (190°C/gas mark 5) oven.

Check the cabbage regularly to make sure that it is not sticking and add more vinegar if necessary. Make this as sweet and sour as you like by adding more or less brown sugar and vinegar to taste.

The cabbage and apples will have softened after about an hour and should have cooked to a lovely glossy deep red, with nearly all the liquid absorbed. This freezes well.

Chicory

Chicory is an elegant and refined plant, at its most handsome in the winter, its harvesting time, when other things are rooty, earthy and rather cloddish. There are many different types and varieties: the crimson croquet ball of radicchio with its tightly packed leaves; the creamy-green and white pointed bullets of the Belgian Witloof; the larger, looser wine-red leaves of Treviso; the bright yellow-green, stippled crimson 'Variegata del Castelfranco'; and endive (or frisée).

Try to find several different chicories from a good winter market. They look beautiful and last well in a large shallow bowl in the middle of the table. They are all durable once harvested, slow to rot and relatively long-storing.

Chicory can be off-putting to the uninitiated, as it is bitter when raw, but when cooked it's delicious. To offset the bitterness of raw chicory, try combining it with sweet flavours. You can chop up a few leaves and add them to a mixed leaf salad; they have a complex flavour which is good as the odd surprise. The taste of raw chicory goes well with the sweet sharpness of any citrus fruit, and it's good with strong cheese.

I'm not so keen on endive, the large serrated, crinkly rosettes that possess a milder, less bitter flavour. Their texture is tough and they are hard work to eat – a bit like an organic Brillo pad – but you could add a few handfuls to your bitter leaf salad. Endive works well with crisp bacon or pancetta as one of the leaves in a classic French Grilled goats' cheese salad (see page 54). I have never eaten 'Variegata del Castelfranco' cooked, but the other varieties are very good roasted, griddled, sautéed or even deep-fried as tempura.

Treviso and Belgian chicories are more expensive. Belgian usually – and Treviso sometimes – are force-grown in the dark, which makes them more tender and less bitter. Radicchio and 'Variegata' are usually field-grown and therefore easier and cheaper to produce. Much of the chicory we buy in Britain comes from Italy and is sold as the heart of the plant only – the chicon – with the outer leaves removed. Many northern Italian households eat chicory almost every day from autumn until the late spring, when a wider selection of vegetables come into season, and it fills a good section of any Italian winter market stall. In Britain, Treviso may be difficult to find, so grab it when you can (although radicchio is fine as a replacement).

With all these chicories, if you can't buy them, consider growing them. Radicchio, 'Variegata del Castelfranco' and Treviso are hardy, easy-to-grow, invaluable winter plants ideal for a year-round productive patch.

Braised chicory

An excellent quick winter dish. It's delicious eaten on its own with crusty bread dipped in the lemony cream. It's also good with grilled, roasted or barbecued pork or veal.

For 6:
  1kg Belgian chicory
  200g prosciutto, chopped
  Salt and black pepper
  50g unsalted butter
  A little water or white wine
  Juice of 1 lemon
  275ml double cream

Butter an ovenproof dish which has a lid. Arrange the whole chicons in the dish, scattering over the chopped prosciutto. Season with salt and pepper, and dot with butter. Cover the dish with a sheet of greaseproof paper under the lid and either sweat over a low heat, turning from time to time, or bake in a low oven for 40 minutes until the chicory is tender and lightly browned. Check it from time to time to make sure there is enough moisture and add a little water or white wine if necessary.

Once it's cooked, add the lemon juice and cream – swirling them around the chicory – and serve with more coarsely ground black pepper.

Chicory and blue cheese salad

A very English version of a classic French salad, using Stilton, not Roquefort. With good hunks of cheese and some bread, it's quite enough for lunch, or you can make a smaller plate as a first course.

For 6:
  4 chicons of Belgian chicory
  3 pears – Conference are good,
    or any firm medium-ripe pear
  Squeeze of lemon juice
  50g walnuts

For the dressing:
  200g Stilton, Cashel Blue or any
    crumbly blue cheese
  Juice and grated zest of 1 lemon
  2 tablespoons single cream
  2 tablespoons olive oil
  Salt and black pepper

Break the chicory into individual leaves and peel the pears. Slice the pears longways, removing the core. To prevent them turning brown, quickly cover the cut surfaces of the chicory and pears with a squirt of lemon juice.

To make the dressing, whiz up two-thirds of the cheese with the lemon juice and zest, the cream and the olive oil. Add salt and pepper to taste.

Roast the walnuts for 3 minutes in a hot oven or a dry frying pan and break them into smaller pieces.

Using your hands, toss the leaves and pear slices with the dressing. Scatter the walnuts and the rest of the cheese crumbled over the top of the salad.

Chicory and
blood orange salad

Putting fruit in a salad may seem a bit retro but, don't worry, this salad looks beautiful and is ideal as a light winter first course when you're heading towards a rich meaty main. A squeeze of lemon with the orange juice in the dressing sharpens it up and gives it the strength to stand up to the bitterness of the leaves. To make the salad more substantial, add roasted walnuts.

For 4–6:
  2 small chicons of Belgian chicory
  1 small chicon of Treviso
    (if not available, use all
    Belgian chicory)
  Squeeze of lemon juice
  2 blood oranges

For the dressing:
  3 tablespoons olive oil
  1 tablespoon walnut oil
  Juice of ½ blood orange
  Juice and grated zest of ½ lemon
  Salt and black pepper
  1 heaped tablespoon walnuts,
    roughly chopped (optional)

If using small chicories, you can peel away the leaves one by one and eat them just as they are, without slicing. If you can only find big chicons, cut each frond in half long-ways and squirt immediately with lemon juice. Meanwhile, roast the roughly chopped walnuts, if using them, for 3 minutes in a hot oven or dry-fry them in a pan.

To end up with pith-free segments or slices of orange, cut a slice off both ends of the orange and then peel it as you would an apple: hold the orange with your non-preferred hand and, with a small serrated knife held with the blade pointing upwards, make short up and down sawing movements, going round and round the fruit until it is completely skinned. There should be no pith left on the orange. You can then follow each layer of skin down to the heart to cut the fruit into skinless segments, or slice the whole orange horizontally as thinly as you can, into cartwheels. Remove the pithy centre of each segment.

Make the dressing by mixing the olive and walnut oil, orange juice, lemon juice and zest, salt and pepper, making sure that it has a sharp enough taste. If you're using ordinary oranges – which have a sweeter flavour than blood oranges – add more lemon juice to make it good and tart. Scatter the walnuts, if using them, over the top.

Treviso al forno with griddled polenta

I had this slow-cooked vegetable at a simple restaurant in a beautiful arcaded walkway in Asolo, in the Veneto. Cooked chicory, and particularly Treviso, is on almost every menu there throughout the winter and this is one of the most adaptable ways to eat it. Treviso *al forno* – roasted in the oven – is delicious with almost anything: meat, fish or just polenta and a scattering of grated Parmesan. If you can't get Treviso, use Belgian Witloof.

For 10 as a starter or a side dish:
6 Treviso or Belgian chicories
Extra virgin olive oil, plus a bit
    extra for drizzling
Plenty of salt
Black pepper

For the polenta:
140g quick-cook polenta
50g butter
75g grated Parmesan cheese,
    plus a bit extra for scattering

Preheat the oven to 190°C/gas mark 5.

Cut the chicory in half longways. Drizzle the halves with olive oil, season with salt and pepper, and bake them, covered, in the preheated oven for 30 minutes.

To make the polenta, bring 1.5 litres salted water to the boil and then remove from the heat while you whisk in the polenta grains. Keep whisking until the mixture is quite smooth, and then put the pan back on the heat. It will start to bubble furiously, but keep stirring and turn the heat down.

Cook the polenta for a few minutes until it is thick and creamy. Add the butter and Parmesan, and season well. This really benefits from lots of salt and pepper. If you prefer 'wet' polenta, rather than griddled, add only 100g of polenta flour to the same amount of water, butter and Parmesan, and keep it warm until you want to eat. It won't be stiff enough to griddle.

To griddle the polenta, turn it out on to a large shallow plate or dish (ideally, the depth of the polenta should be about 1.5cm). Allow it to cool completely while you cook the chicory. When the polenta is cold, cut it into triangles or strips ready for cooking. Make sure the griddle is really hot and put the wedges of polenta on to char grill them for about 5 minutes on either side.

Put a dollop of polenta (or one or two slices if griddled) and one or two halves of roasted chicory on each plate. Drizzle with olive oil and scatter with coarsely grated Parmesan.

Treviso lasagne

I learnt how to make this Treviso lasagne, or *pasticcio*, in the house of some Italian friends – Daniella, Luciano and Silvia Piccolotto – just outside Asolo. The occasion was a bustling family affair, with several generations milling around in the kitchen. We ate it as a second course, after the antipasti and before the meat. It takes more preparation than everyday pasta, but does very well for a big family meal. We made our own pasta, rolling out the sheets until they were about 2mm thick, but you can, of course, use the ready-made variety.

This is one of my favourite winter meals. Add 200g chopped fried pancetta for a meatier dish.

For 8–10:
  600g Treviso or radicchio
  ½ onion
  1 garlic clove
  6 tablespoons extra virgin olive oil, plus a little more for the dish
  100g grated Parmesan cheese
  Salt and black pepper
  250g lasagne sheets – homemade or the packet variety
  A few knobs of butter, to finish

For the béchamel sauce:
  1 litre milk
  80g butter
  80g flour
  1 egg yolk
  250g tub of mascarpone cheese
  Freshly grated nutmeg, to taste
  200g (or to taste) grated cheese, such as Cheddar, pecorino or Parmesan

Preheat a medium (180°C/gas mark 4) oven.

Cut the Treviso or radicchio into 1–2cm slices. Slice the onion and peel the garlic clove, crushing it with the side of a knife but leaving it whole.

Heat the olive oil in a deep saucepan and cook the onion and garlic on a gentle heat until they are golden-brown. Remove the garlic and add the radicchio to the pan, stirring continuously to avoid it catching. Once it's wilted and brown – after 2–3 minutes – take it off the heat and season.

To make the béchamel sauce, bring the milk to the boil and, in a separate pan, melt the butter. Stir the flour into the butter, allow it to cook for a couple of minutes and then gradually add the hot milk. Add the egg yolk mixed with the mascarpone and plenty of nutmeg, stirring continuously as you add the ingredients. Season with plenty of salt and pepper.

Put one ladleful of the sauce to one side and mix the rest with the radicchio. Add almost all the grated cheese and stir until it melts.

If your pasta needs pre-cooking, boil the sheets in plenty of salted water and allow them to dry flat on a clean cloth. Lightly oil an ovenproof dish. Alternate the pasta with thin layers of the radicchio béchamel mixture in the dish. The layers of béchamel mixture should be quite thin so that the lovely bitterness of the radicchio is balanced with the flavour of the pasta.

Finish with the remaining béchamel, then the grated cheese and finally dot the top with the butter and a bit of extra nutmeg. Cook the lasagne in the preheated medium oven for 35–40 minutes.

Radicchio and lemon pasta

This is a simple chicory and pasta dish, quick to prepare. It's also delicious cold the next day, by which time the chicory has lost some of its bitterness.

For 4:
  100g chopped pancetta
  2–3 tablespoons extra virgin olive oil
  ½ onion, chopped
  1 garlic clove, finely chopped
  200g dried egg tagliatelle
  200g radicchio (or Treviso)
  3 tablespoons dry white wine
  50g butter
  Grated zest of 1 lemon
  100ml double cream
  Handful of flat-leaf parsley, chopped
  Grated Parmesan cheese, to serve
  Salt and black pepper

Bring a large pan of water to the boil. Put the chopped pancetta into a wide shallow pan over a moderate heat with half the olive oil. When the fat begins to run, add the chopped onion and garlic, and then cook with the pancetta for about 3–4 minutes, until the onion has softened.

Put the pasta into the pan of salted boiling water and cook until al dente.

Slice the radicchio into thin strips. Add the radicchio to the onion mixture with the wine and sauté until the radicchio begins to wilt. Add the butter and lemon zest; pour in the cream and season well.

Add this to the drained pasta with the remaining olive oil and the chopped flat-leaf parsley.

I love this pasta dish with a generous topping of Parmesan.

Citrus fruits

You can grow citrus trees in a greenhouse in the winter in Britain, and put them out in pots in a sheltered spot in the garden for the warmer months, but they won't produce enough fruit for you to cook. So having citrus in a garden cookbook is a bit of a cheat, but it's now, in the winter, that the main citrus season reaches its peak, and they're hard to resist. There are delicious imported lemons, limes, sweet and bitter Seville oranges and grapefruits. These make some of the best puddings at this time of year, when there isn't any native fruit to pick; and, of course, they are the essential ingredient in marmalade.

Bitter Seville oranges are a must and there's only a small window of opportunity in January and February to get them. Buy them when you can. You can always freeze them until you have time to make marmalade. The texture and taste of Sevilles isn't affected by a spell in the freezer.

When there are lots of small cheap oranges, buy them to squeeze for juice. Tart southern Italian blood oranges make the tastiest and they're around at the end of winter and for most of spring. What do you do with all the squeezed orange skins? You're not meant to put them in the compost or the worm bin – they're too acid. We went to stay with friends last winter who had the answer. Dry them out for a day or two in a slow oven or on top of a radiator, until they desiccate, but don't burn them. Their waxy skins mean they make effective firelighters and as they burn, they fill the room with a good marmaladey smell.

With all these recipes, you want to use unwaxed fruit, but they aren't always easy to find. Try to buy organic – the others may have preservative in the skin – and then de-wax them (you can do this with lemons, limes, oranges, grapefruits or clementines): drop the fruit whole into boiling water and swirl them around for a couple of minutes to melt the wax from the skin.

Amber marmalade

If you miss the Seville oranges, or if you have run out of marmalade halfway through the year, this is a delicious alternative, and it has a beautiful colour.

For about 3.5kg:
3 grapefruits
3 sweet oranges
3 large lemons
About 2.6kg granulated sugar

Wash the fruit and squeeze out the juice (an electric juicer is fantastic for this job, as it halves the time and makes the pithy membrane easier to remove). Pull out the thick white membrane and then slice the fruit thinly, keeping the pips.

Measure the fruit and juice and put them in a large bowl with three times their volume of water (about 3.6 litres). Put the pith that you have removed, together with the pips, into a muslin bag.

Pour the contents of the bowl into a preserving pan, and tie the muslin bag to the handle so that it hangs into the pan and steeps overnight. The next day, simmer, covered, over a low heat for about half an hour, and then remove the lid and cook for a further hour or so, until the fruit is soft. Warm the sugar in a very low oven for about half an hour.

Remove the muslin bag, squeezing out the liquid into the pan, and measure the fruit and juice. For every 600ml of juice add 450g of sugar. Put the pan back on a gentle heat and make sure that the sugar is completely dissolved before raising the heat and boiling rapidly until setting point is reached (to test, see right). Skim the scum from the surface with a spoon. Allow it to rest for at least 20 minutes – or the fruit peel will all float to the top. Stir once and pour into warm sterilised dry jars. Put a greaseproof disc on the top of each jar and cover immediately.

Seville marmalade

The best marmalade is quite chunkily cut and not too sweet, like the old-fashioned Oxford type.

For about 3.5kg:
1.4kg Seville oranges
1 teaspoon salt
Juice of 2 lemons
2.7kg granulated sugar

Scrub the oranges and put them whole into a large preserving pan, along with 2.4 litres of water and the salt. Cover with a lid and simmer the fruit gently until soft. This takes about 1 hour. Reserve the liquid and halve the fruit, scooping out the pith and pips with a spoon and putting this into a small saucepan. Add another 300ml of water to the pan of pith and pips and then simmer for 10 minutes.

Coarsely slice the orange peel and add to the reserved liquid in the preserving pan. Strain the liquid from the pith and pips, and add this liquid to the large pan. Add the lemon juice and sugar, and heat slowly to dissolve the sugar completely, stirring all the time. Increase the heat and bring to a rapid boil until the setting point is reached.

To test for the setting point, put a saucer in the fridge to cool. When you think the marmalade might be ready, put a spoonful of the boiling jam on to the saucer. Return the saucer to the fridge. Once it is cold, the jam should wrinkle when you push it with your finger.

After taking the marmalade off the heat, skim the scum from the surface with a spoon. Allow it to rest for at least 20 minutes – or the fruit peel will all float to the top. Stir once and pour into warm sterilised dry jars. Put a greaseproof disc on the top of each jar and cover immediately.

Marmalade ice cream with fresh oranges

Marmalade ice cream is one of the easiest you can make. We do it in our ice cream maker, but you don't need one. Just mix the marmalade with the cream, yoghurt and juice, pour it into a Tupperware box and put it into your freezer. You don't even need to stir it.

This ice cream is rich, so eat it with these tart, nutmeg-flavoured orange slices.

For 6–8:
For the ice cream:
350g Seville marmalade
300ml double cream
300ml full-fat natural yoghurt
3 tablespoons orange juice

For the oranges:
6 oranges
1 heaped tablespoon Seville marmalade
A little freshly grated nutmeg

To make the ice cream, put the marmalade, cream, yoghurt and orange juice into an ice cream machine and freeze/churn for 20 minutes. You might want to sieve out a bit of the orange peel beforehand. Pack into plastic containers and freeze. Allow 20 minutes in the fridge before serving the ice cream.

Meanwhile, peel the oranges, getting rid of every bit of pith (see page 26) and then cut them into segments. Collect as much of the juice as possible as you slice. Put the fruit and juice into a bowl and stir in the marmalade. Grate a little nutmeg over the bowl.

Tunisian orange and almond cake

This is an excellent cake to eat on its own or with baked fruit, such as rhubarb. It stores brilliantly.

For 8:
    45g slightly stale breadcrumbs
    200g caster sugar
    100g ground almonds
    1½ teaspoons baking powder
    200g melted butter
    4 eggs
    Finely grated zest of 1 large
        orange
    Finely grated zest of 1 lemon
    Whipped cream, thick Greek
        yoghurt or crème fraîche,
        to serve

For the syrup:
    Juice of 1 orange
    Juice of 1 lemon
    85g sugar
    2 cloves
    1 cinnamon stick

Mix the breadcrumbs with the sugar, almonds and baking powder in a food processor. Add the melted butter and eggs and beat well, then stir in the citrus zest. Pour into a greased and lined 20cm cake tin. Put into a cold oven and set the heat to 190°C/ gas mark 5. Bake for 40–50 minutes until the cake is a rich brown and a skewer inserted into the centre comes out clean. Allow to cool in the tin for 5 minutes, and then turn out on a plate.

While the cake is baking, make the syrup. Put all the ingredients into a pan and bring gently to the boil, stirring until all the sugar has dissolved. Simmer for 3 minutes. Remove the cloves and cinnamon stick.

While the cake is still warm, pierce holes in it with a skewer and pour over the syrup. Leave to cool, spooning the excess syrup back over the cake until it is all soaked up.

Serve with whipped cream, thick Greek yoghurt or crème fraîche.

Orange pasta

This is a surprising mix of things for a pasta sauce, but I remember enjoying it in a small restaurant in Rome. In fact I liked it so much that we went back three times in a five-day visit, until I'd worked out how to make it.

For 4:
    200g egg tagliatelle
    100ml double cream
    1 garlic clove, crushed and peeled
        but left whole
    Juice and grated zest of 1 orange
    Grated zest of ½ lemon
    Salt and black pepper
    2 tablespoons brandy
    50g butter
    150g Parmesan cheese, plus a
        little extra for scattering

Cook the pasta in salted boiling water until just al dente.

While it is cooking, heat the cream with the garlic and bring to the boil for a minute. Remove the garlic and add the orange and lemon zest, some salt and plenty of black pepper, then remove the pan from the heat to allow the cream to steep in these flavours for about 10 minutes.

Add the orange juice, brandy, butter and Parmesan, and toss with the drained hot pasta ribbons.

Scatter with a little more Parmesan cheese and add salt and plenty of pepper.

Sicilian orange and lemon salad

Antonio Carluccio told me about this salad, which is perfect with smoked fish, and eel in particular. You can just eat the citrus salad straight as you would in Sicily, where the fruit is at its absolute best, or mix it in with watercress.

For 8:
    4 oranges (blood oranges
        are lovely)
    2 lemons
    2 grapefruits
    2 bunches of watercress

For the dressing:
    Juice of 1 lime
    4 tablespoons extra virgin
        olive oil
    Sprigs of mint
    Salt and black pepper

Peel the oranges, lemons and grapefruits with a sharp serrated knife, removing all the white pith (see page 26). Cut out each segment from between the membranes and put into a ceramic bowl while you make the dressing. Whisk together the lime juice, olive oil, mint, salt and pepper, and pour it over the fruit.

Put a couple of bunches of watercress in a separate bowl. The fruit and watercress are lovely eaten together, but when dressed the watercress collapses within minutes, so keep them apart until you eat, and then just put a handful of watercress with a couple of spoonfuls of the citrus salad on each plate.

Preserved lemons

This recipe comes from John and Mary Stratton of Stratta, who sell infused oils, flavoured vinegars and pickles at our farmers' market.

Preserved lemons are used in North African tagines and make a wonderful addition to any lamb, chicken or fish stew. Just rinse one or two segments, chop them finely and throw them in about half an hour before the end of cooking. Try adding them to fish baked in an envelope of greaseproof paper or slicing some and adding them to oven-roasted vegetables. They are also good for seasoning rice or couscous. Lemons preserved in this way allow you to eat the entire fruit, including the pith, but rinse off the salt before using them and don't add any more salt until you have tasted what you have cooked.

For a 500ml jar:
4–6 organic lemons, depending on size
3 tablespoons sea salt
Boiling water to cover

Choose unwaxed lemons – ideally organic and with as few skin blemishes as possible, or de-wax your lemons (see page 30). Scrub them clean and cut into quarters. Remove the pips and pack firmly in a 500ml preserving jar, separating the layers with a sprinkling of salt.

Top with any remaining salt and fill the jar with boiling water, turning it to expel any air bubbles. Close firmly and store for a month before using. This allows the fruit to mellow and mature.

Once the jar has been opened it can be kept in the fridge with a layer of extra virgin olive oil floating on the surface to exclude the air.

Lemon cordial

You can use other citrus fruits for this cordial recipe. In Spain, you'll see a similar recipe made with clementines and it's delicious with limes.

For 2 x 750ml bottles:
3 unwaxed lemons
900ml boiling water
850g white sugar (granulated or caster)
30g citric or tartaric acid

With a swivel potato peeler, cut thick ribbons of rind from the fruit, leaving the white pith behind.

Put the rind into a heatproof bowl and pour over the boiling water. Stir in the sugar, keeping the water moving until the sugar has all dissolved.

Leave the mixture to cool and then add the juice from the lemons and the citric acid, and leave everything to steep overnight.

Next day, strain the rind away and bottle the cordial. Don't leave the rind in any longer or the cordial will become bitter.

Serve the cordial – just a little in the bottom of a glass – diluted with still or sparkling water.

This will store for about a month in the fridge, or you can pour it into clean plastic milk cartons and freeze it.

Homemade lemonade

You get a straightforward version of this – *citron pressé* – in every French and Italian café, where you add sugar to your own glass to taste, but I love this version of lemonade, which is frothed up in a blender with lots of ice.

For a jug for 6:
10 lemons
8 tablespoons caster sugar
4 tablespoons ice, plus some whole ice cubes to serve
20 mint or lemon balm leaves

Peel the lemons as instructed for oranges on page 26, making sure that you have removed all of the white bitter pith.

Then put the fruit in a blender with the sugar, ice, herbs and 1 litre of water, and whiz for 2 minutes. (It makes a terrible noise!)

Put a few mint or lemon balm leaves, some whole ice cubes and some lemon slices into a large jug and sieve the lemonade into it. This lemonade doesn't store (see left for one that does) and should be drunk straightaway. You can make this sort of drink with any citrus fruit.

Penne with preserved lemon and avocado

This too is John and Mary Stratton's recipe and it is a deliciously different way in which to use preserved lemons (see page 35). It makes the perfect weekday supper as it takes so little time to make. Cold, the next day – with a handful of mint, coriander and/or rocket – it also makes a great salad. My twin sister, Jane, said she wasn't tempted by the sound of this recipe when she read it. She is now a major convert.

For 4:
    2 skinless organic chicken breasts
    1 large glass of white wine
    30g butter
    200g penne
    220ml crème fraîche
    220ml double cream
    1 large avocado
    2 tablespoons pine nuts, toasted
    2 thinly sliced preserved lemon quarters
    Salt and plenty of black pepper

Put the chicken breasts in an ovenproof dish with a little wine, dot them with butter and then cover with foil. Cook the chicken in a moderate oven for 20 minutes.

Cook the pasta in salted boiling water until al dente. While it is cooking, heat the crème fraîche and double cream together in a small saucepan. Mash or cut up the avocado and cut the chicken into pieces.

Drain the pasta and add the avocado and chicken along with the cream mixture, toasted pine nuts and sliced preserved lemons. Stir gently to combine and season with salt and pepper.

Mrs Root's lemon soufflé

This is an extremely lemony mousse – tart and delicious – which was often made for us by a wonderful woman, Mrs Root or 'Rootie', my mother's housekeeper, when we were children. She used to make it in a bain-marie, but this is a quicker and simpler version. Note that it contains uncooked egg.

For 8:
    Grated zest and juice of 3 lemons
    15g gelatine (equals 4 large leaves of gelatine)
    3 large or 4 medium-sized eggs, separated
    115g caster sugar
    300ml double cream

In a small pan, mix the lemon zest and juice and soak the gelatine in this mixture, warming it a little to dissolve it completely.

Beat the egg yolks and caster sugar until foamy, then add to the gelatine and lemon mixture.

Whip the cream, then wash the beaters and beat the egg whites to stiff peaks.

Fold the egg yolk mixture and the whipped cream together, then gently fold in the egg whites.

Pour it into a shallow bowl and leave it to set for 4 hours, or overnight, before serving.

Lemon posset

A quick and easy alternative to Mrs Root's lemon soufflé from the Whitehouse Restaurant, run by my sister-in-law, Jane Stuart Smith, and Sarah Jones, in Lochaline on the west coast of Scotland.

They make this pudding through the year, serving it in champagne flutes and adding raspberries – picked wild – when they're in season.

For 8 champagne flutes:
   845ml double cream
   250g caster sugar
   Juice of 3 lemons and grated
      zest of 1 lemon

Bring the cream and sugar to the boil, stirring until the sugar has dissolved completely. Take this off the heat and whisk in the lemon juice and zest. Pour into moulds or glasses from a height. Allow them to cool and then refrigerate overnight.

Lemon and cumin biscuits

These are lovely on their own, or with ice cream or cheese. This comes from *The African Kitchen*, a fantastic book by Josie Stow and Jan Baldwin.

For 30 biscuits:
   300g caster sugar
   125g butter
   2 egg yolks
   Finely grated zest of 2 lemons
      and 4 tablespoons juice
   2 teaspoons freshly ground
      cumin seeds
   300g plain flour
   1 teaspoon bicarbonate of soda

Preheat the oven to 170°C/gas mark 3. Cream the sugar and butter together until light and fluffy. Gradually beat in the egg yolks, lemon zest and juice, and cumin. Sift together the flour and bicarbonate of soda, then fold into the butter mixture to form a soft dough.

Place the dough on a sheet of greaseproof paper and roll into a cylinder about 5cm in diameter, twisting the ends of the paper together and being very careful not to wrap any of the greaseproof paper into the dough. Place the dough in the freezer for 1½–2 hours until it is hard.

Line a baking sheet with a piece of greaseproof paper. Unwrap the dough and cut into 5mm slices. Place these on the baking sheet, leaving a very generous space between them to allow for spreading.

Bake the biscuits for 8–10 minutes or until just firm to the touch. Slide them on to a wire rack and then leave to cool.

Lemon and mint ice cream

Teresa Wallace is my twin sister's mother-in-law and this is her lemon ice cream recipe. She is a wonderful and impatient cook, so she has a good line in quick and easy tip-top recipes. This one is a doddle to make. The portions – once divided into six – may look a bit mean, but it's rich, although light because of the egg whites. Do note that this recipe uses uncooked eggs.

For 6:
   2 large eggs
   40g caster sugar
   150ml double cream
   Juice of 3 lemons
   1 teaspoon very finely chopped
      mint leaves

Separate the eggs and whisk the whites, adding the sugar when stiff. Whisk the egg yolks until they are foamy. Then whisk the cream until it is the same consistency as the egg whites. (If you whisk in this order you don't have to wash the beaters in between each ingredient.)

Fold the egg whites, yolks and cream together. Gently stir in the lemon juice and chopped mint. Put the mixture into a Tupperware box and freeze. There is no need to beat or churn.

Take it out of the freezer and put in the fridge about 20 minutes before serving.

Ceviche

The lovely flavour of fish with limes makes this one of the freshest-tasting salads. In the winter, eat it with crunchy salad leaves. I had it recently with Sicilian orange and lemon salad (see page 34) and it's also lovely in the summer with sliced tomato salad.

For 6:
500g fillets of salmon, skinned
500g fillets of sole, skinned
A few scallops (optional)
1 shallot, very finely chopped
Zest of 1 lime and 150ml lime juice
    (about 3–4 limes)
50ml white wine vinegar
Salt and black pepper
Flat-leaf parsley, finely chopped
Generous handful of rocket leaves
4 tomatoes, chopped and skinned
    (if in season)
Extra virgin olive oil

Cut the skinned fish roughly into slivers 1cm wide and put into a bowl with the scallops (if using), shallot, lime zest and juice, vinegar, salt and pepper, and leave for at least 3 hours, stirring from time to time. Drain well, mix in the parsley and pile into a shallow dish.

Serve with a small salad of rocket leaves and skinned chopped tomatoes (if in season), combined with a little extra virgin olive oil, salt and freshly ground pepper.

Pink grapefruit and Pimm's granita

This granita from Caroline Liddell and Robin Weir's book on ice creams is summer all over, so it doesn't really belong in a winter chapter, but grapefruits are at their best at this time of year. It is perfect when you want just a light sweet taste at the end of a meal.

For 6:
100g granulated sugar
8 tablespoons Pimm's No 1
Juice of 4–5 pink grapefruits
1 tablespoon lemon juice
8 mint leaves
1 egg white

Heating them together, dissolve the sugar in the Pimm's (this takes a few minutes). Stir in the strained grapefruit and lemon juice and 125ml water. Roll up the mint leaves and cut across the roll to make very thin strips. Add these to the liquid and chill in the fridge.

Break up the egg white gently with a fork, but do not whisk. Mix into the chilled liquid, pour into an ice cream maker and freeze/churn until firm enough to serve, making sure the mint leaves are well distributed. Either pack into a plastic box for freezing or serve immediately.

If you don't have a machine, this sorbet can be made by still-freezing. Pour the chilled mixture into a plastic container to give a depth of at least 4cm, cover with a lid and put into the freezer. Check after about 1½ hours, by which time it should have frozen around the edge with a slushy centre. Beat with a hand whisk, cover and return to the freezer. Do this a couple more times, leaving about 1½ hours in between. After you have done this a third time, leave it in the freezer for at least 3 hours before serving. (This method can be used for most sorbets, and those that do not contain alcohol freeze more quickly.)

Mandarin sorbet

All citrus sorbets are delicious. You can also use this recipe to make blood orange sorbet, which looks and tastes good, or make it with clementines, but mandarin is the best of all.

For 4:
8–10 unwaxed mandarins
¼ teaspoon glycerine
Juice of ½ lemon
1 egg white

For the sugar syrup:
150g sugar

To make the sugar syrup, dissolve the sugar in 200ml water over a low heat. Slowly bring to the boil. Boil for 2–3 minutes and then allow to cool. This stores very well in the fridge.

If you can't find unwaxed mandarins, drop the fruit into boiling water for a couple of minutes and dry them.

Pare away the zest with a potato peeler, put into a small saucepan with the sugar syrup and simmer for a couple of minutes. Allow to cool completely and then strain off the liquid.

Squeeze the juice from the mandarins and combine it with the cold syrup, glycerine and lemon juice. Break up the egg white with a fork to a froth and mix thoroughly with the syrup mixture. Add the glycerine, which will make the texture smooth and ungrainy.

Pour into an ice cream machine. Freeze/churn for 20–25 minutes and pack into a plastic container. Freeze for several hours. If you don't have an ice cream machine, see left. Take the sorbet out of the freezer and put it in the fridge 20 minutes before serving.

Evergreen herbs

Rosemary, sage, thyme and bay are stalwarts of the kitchen in the winter. If you choose one edible plant to grow, whatever the size of your garden, rosemary has to be a contender. It's easy, will be happy in a pot, is pickable fifty-two weeks of the year and has a delicious taste, much better fresh than dried. There are three varieties of rosemary in my garden, each with a slightly different character and use. *Rosmarinus officinalis* 'Sissinghurst Blue' is a shrubby variety with an unusually dark-blue flower. The bank outside the school is covered with a cascading, weeping form, *R.o.* 'Prostratus'. The plants, spaced 60cm apart, have now merged into a beautiful, gnarled waterfall of dark green. Around one of the beds in the veg garden is *R.o.* 'Miss Jessopp's Upright'. This is ideal for edging, as its very vertical habit means it doesn't fill much horizontal space, and it's also the best for flower arranging.

There are five varieties of sage in the garden here, but only three are good for cooking. The pretty smoky-crimson-leaved *Salvia officinalis* 'Purpurea' and the variegated, *S.o.* 'Tricolor', don't have much flavour. For the kitchen you want to grow one of three: the straight *S. officinalis*, with its bright silvery leaves, is excellent for cooking, as is *S. lavandulifolia*, with much greener leaves. I also grow the large, round-leaved *S.o.* 'Bergatten'. This last variety is excellent for tempura (see page 46) as it has leaves twice the size of those of ordinary sage, with plenty of flesh to get your teeth into. All are fine growing in a pot. Like rosemary, sage is easy to grow and to propagate by cuttings. It thrives in an open sunny position with well-drained soil. You can also grow it from seed. Treated as an annual, it never gets woody and produces new fresh leaves at a brisker rate.

Thyme is another wonderful herb for winter picking and is easily grown from seed or cuttings. I love lemon thyme in all its forms and that seems to do best for me on my heavy soil. It is one of the finest flavourings for pastry (see page 131), makes wonderful herb butter (see page 80), and is a good addition to burgers and meatballs (see page 49) as well as tapenade (see page 49).

As with rosemary, sage and thyme, there are so many dishes that need bay. It's the crucial ingredient in a classic béchamel sauce and few stocks or stews are complete without it. The flavour is also superb in mashed potato (see page 336). It's tempting to throw in lots of leaves whenever you use bay, but one bay leaf is usually all you'll need. It is evergreen, so you can pick it all year, but if you don't have a plant, the leathery texture of the leaves makes it a good herb for drying. Even crinkly and old, they lose little flavour.

Rosemary and anchovy crusted lamb

This is a dish that looks impressive but requires little effort, though it is worth finding really good lamb. The rosemary, anchovies and lemons give flavour to the crust. Eat this with a Potato and sage gratin (see page 48) and Fried cabbage with juniper (see page 17).

For 6:
2 best ends of lamb
   (2–3 cutlets per person)
Small bunch of thyme
2 sprigs of rosemary
100g fresh breadcrumbs
2 garlic cloves, finely chopped
1 tin of anchovy fillets
Grated zest of 1 lemon
Salt and black pepper
Seasoned flour
1 egg, beaten

For the sauce:
2 oranges
Glass of port
1 tablespoon redcurrant jelly

Cut away the chine bones from the lamb or ask your butcher to do it for you. Trim the lamb of all but a thin covering of the fat protecting the meat. Preheat the oven to 220°C/gas mark 7.

In a food processor, pulse the herbs, breadcrumbs, garlic and anchovy fillets until they are well combined and stir in the lemon zest. Season with a little salt and plenty of freshly ground pepper.

Dip the lamb into some seasoned flour, knock off the excess and then, with a pastry brush, cover with a layer of beaten egg. Pat on a thick layer of the breadcrumb mixture, pressing it firmly on to the surface of both joints.

Bake the lamb in the preheated oven for 45–50 minutes, depending on the size of the joints. (If they are becoming too brown, just cover them lightly with a sheet of foil.) Allow to rest for 10 minutes before serving.

While the lamb is cooking, make the sauce. Peel the rind of the oranges with a potato peeler and then shred it into fine strips. Cut the oranges into segments and put in a small saucepan with the shredded rind, port and redcurrant jelly, and bring to a simmer, making sure to whisk the jelly until it dissolves. Remove from the heat and keep warm until the lamb is ready.

Rosemary and pork farfalle

I love this meat pasta sauce and so do my children, particularly if I leave out the non-essential chilli and onion. It takes only 10 minutes to make and is one of our standard mid-week suppers. It has an unusual taste – a mix of rosemary with toasted sesame oil – which you never forget once you've tried it.

For 2–3:
1 onion, finely chopped (optional)
1 tablespoon olive oil
2 tablespoons toasted sesame oil
1 garlic clove, chopped
1 red chilli, finely chopped
   (optional)
500g lean pork mince, or
   tenderloin sliced into thin strips
10g sprigs of rosemary, the
   leaves stripped and quite
   finely chopped
100ml hot water
Salt and black pepper
200g pasta (penne or farfalle)
Freshly grated Parmesan cheese,
   to serve

Put your pasta water on to boil and meanwhile, if you are using it, fry the onion in the olive oil and toasted sesame oil for a few minutes until soft. Add the garlic, chilli if you are using it, pork mince and rosemary, and cook them together quickly to brown the mince. Then add the hot water and leave to cook gently with the lid on for another 5 minutes. Add plenty of salt and black pepper.

Cook the pasta until it is al dente. Drain it and mix with the sauce. Grate over lots of Parmesan.

Patmos chickpeas

There is a taverna – Flisvos – on the Greek island of Patmos where I had these chickpeas once, and I still remember them. It's taken several years and countless visits by a friend, Sofka Zinovieff-Papadimitriou, who lives in Greece, to get this recipe out of the cook. The keys to its deliciousness are plenty of onion and rosemary and, importantly, very long cooking.

The joy of chickpeas is that you can't over-cook them; they always keep their shape. The dish is even better heated up the next day. Eat this as one of a group of Greek starters, such as Ithaca pie (see page 74), wild greens, fried calamari and Saganaki (see page 273), as an accompaniment to meat or fish, or just with a big salad.

For 6–8:
500g dried chickpeas
4 onions, 2 left whole, 2 finely chopped
Salt and black pepper
4 tablespoons olive oil (Greeks are always generous with the oil)
2 tablespoons finely chopped rosemary
1 glass of white wine

Soak the chickpeas in cold water overnight and then boil them with the 2 whole onions and no salt. As the scum comes to the top of the liquid, remove it. Continue simmering the chickpeas gently, for about 40 minutes, until soft. Strain and season, reserving a little of the liquid and the onions.

Preheat the oven to 150°C/gas mark 2.

Gently fry the 2 finely chopped onions in the olive oil. Purée one-third of the chickpeas with the 2 boiled onions and a little of the reserved cooking liquid. I use a wand whizzer.

Put the remaining two-thirds of the chickpeas with the fried onion in an ovenproof dish with a lid. Throw in the rosemary, salt, pepper and white wine. Pour over the puréed onion and chickpea mix. Put into the preheated oven, covered, and cook slowly for about 2 hours. If the dish dries out, then just add a little of the reserved cooking juices.

You can use tinned chickpeas, but the flavour and texture is not so good. If you're using tinned, boil the onions separately for about 30 minutes. Mix with one-third of the chickpeas and follow the instructions as above, but cook them for only half the time.

Rosemary, olive and lemon chicken

This is a simple meal-in-one-pot. It's a classic Greek dish, often made with oregano rather than rosemary, and it's also lovely with bay. Eat this with a mound of spinach or Horta (see page 395). You can also use this recipe to roast a whole chicken.

For 5–6:
1 chicken, cut into 8 portions
Juice of 3 lemons
Leaves of 4 sprigs of rosemary (or 1 heaped tablespoon), coarsely chopped, plus a sprig or two for adding whole
Salt and black pepper
1kg waxy potatoes, such as Ratte, Belle de Fontenay or Charlotte, peeled and quartered longways
15 Kalamata black olives
5 tablespoons extra virgin olive oil

Preheat a medium (180°C/gas mark 4) oven.

Rinse the chicken pieces and pat them dry. Lay them out in a baking tray. Pour half the lemon juice over the chicken. Sprinkle with some of the chopped rosemary, salt and pepper.

Cut the potatoes like segments of a chocolate orange and arrange around the chicken. Add the olives, pour on the rest of the lemon juice and then sprinkle more rosemary over the potatoes. Using your hands, turn the potatoes to make sure they're coated well in the herbs and lemon juice.

Pour over the olive oil and add the sprigs of rosemary, plus a cup of water, and cook for 1½ hours in the preheated oven.

When the chicken is cooked, remove it and allow it to rest while you turn up the heat to crisp up the potatoes in a very hot (220°C/gas mark 7) oven for 15 minutes.

Rosemary flat bread

You can make flat bread standing on your head. The dough takes under 5 minutes to combine and about an hour to rise. This makes it ideal for whipping up quickly if you've got people coming to supper.

This rosemary version is lovely for dipping into hummus (see pages 85 and 305), Saganaki (see page 273) or White gazpacho (see page 330). Alternatively, you can smother the breads in dill or fennel seeds as you put them in the oven to bake.

For 6 medium-sized flat breads:
200g strong white flour
½ teaspoon dried yeast
150ml tepid water
1 tablespoon extra virgin olive oil
Salt
Rosemary, coarsely chopped

Put the flour into a large bowl and add the yeast. Add the warm water, olive oil and a pinch of salt, and start mixing it all together to a rather sloppy dough: if your mix is too dry, add a little more water; if the mix is too wet, add a little more flour.

Once you have a ball of dough, take it out of the bowl and knead on a floured surface for 5 minutes until it is elastic but slightly tacky. Leave the dough to rest under a damp tea towel for an hour. It will rise until it has about doubled in size.

Preheat a medium (180°C/gas mark 4) oven. Break off a 5cm-sized ball of dough and roll it out on a floured surface to a thickness of about 5mm. Repeat, until you have used all the dough. Brush each flat bread with olive oil. Sprinkle with a little salt and scatter with rosemary. Bake on baking trays for about 10 minutes, until the surface starts to bubble and turn a golden brown. Don't cook them too long or they'll turn into cardboard. Serve immediately.

Sage leaf tempura

Making tempura is easy. If you do it for just a few people who are happy to graze and chat, it's one of the greatest vegetable starters there is.

Use sage leaves as part of a winter garden tempura, with parsnips and Jerusalem artichokes, or in the summer with French beans and courgette flowers. Sage leaves are ideal for tempura as the batter sticks well to their wrinkly texture. Leave the stems on so that you have something to hold on to while you eat.

This makes perfect picnic food (see Summer garden tempura on page 207). Sage leaf tempura is also good on its own with a glass of wine, and the delicious oily, smoky flavour goes well with liver or beaten-out bread-crumbed pork. There is a wonderful recipe by Joyce Molyneaux (of the original Carved Angel restaurant in Dartmouth) for Escalope of pork with thyme tapenade (see page 49) and these tempura sage leaves are an ideal accompaniment to that.

For 8 as a snack or a side dish:
225g plain flour
Plenty of sea salt and black
  pepper
2 eggs
375ml iced sparkling water or
  cold lager
Groundnut oil, for frying
30–40 sage leaves, depending
  on size and variety

Sift the flour into a bowl with the salt and pepper and make a dip in the centre. Add the eggs and, with a balloon whisk, mix in the cold water or lager to make a not-too-smooth batter. It should be the thickness of double cream. Keep this in the fridge until you need it. The coldness of the batter hitting the hot oil gives a lighter, airier texture to the tempura leaves.

Pour the oil into a deep pan so that it reaches about one-third of the way up the side and have a lid or wire-mesh top on standby to prevent the oil spitting too much after you add each batch of leaves. Heat the oil until it reaches about 170°C. If you don't have an oil thermometer, it's easy to test. Drop a cube of bread into the oil. It should turn golden-brown in less than a minute.

Dip the herb leaves into the batter and then into the hot oil, and cook until pale gold and crisp. Fish them out with tongs and dry them on kitchen paper. These are at their best eaten hot and served sprinkled with sea salt and ground black pepper.

Potato and sage gratin

This is rich and absolutely delicious, and has a lovely flavour of sage. If you're worried about the amount of cream and milk, you can use a mixture of three-quarters good stock to a quarter cream.

For 6:

    4 or 5 large potatoes
    250ml milk
    284ml double cream
    2 garlic cloves
    75g butter, plus a bit more
        for the dish
    Salt and black pepper
    Freshly grated nutmeg
    80 small sage leaves, coarsely
        chopped
    100g Gruyère cheese

Preheat a medium (180°C/gas mark 4) oven.

Peel and thinly slice the potatoes. Mix the milk and cream together, then add the chopped garlic. Butter an ovenproof dish and arrange a layer of potato slices in the bottom. Season well and grate over some nutmeg. Cover this with a layer of sage and dot with butter.

Repeat the layers, seasoning as you go, until you have used up all the potatoes and sage leaves, and pour over the cream mixture. Cover with a layer of grated Gruyère and cook for about 1½ hours (at least: this dish takes ages to cook) until a deep gold on top. Test with a skewer to check that the potato is completely cooked. Cover the top if it is browning too quickly at any point.

This freezes well.

Matthew's confit of chicken

Matthew Rice is a devotee of the chicken, whether running around his garden or sitting on his plate. This is his recipe. Confit is best done with two chickens – cook too much for one meal, so that you can eat it from the fridge for the rest of the week. It is preserved in its own fat and lasts for days. Confit is a dish that requires long cooking, so buy a free-range bird. The bones of intensively farmed birds disintegrate easily and certainly won't stand up to the confit technique.

For 12:

    2 free-range organic chickens
    4 handfuls of sea salt
    40 cloves, crushed a bit using
        a pestle and mortar to release
        their fragrance
    20 fresh bay leaves
    Lots of ground black peppercorns

Portion up the chickens, taking off the breasts, wings and legs, so that you're left with two limbless bare carcasses. With their skins on, rub the meat pieces with the salt, cloves, torn-up bay leaves and ground peppercorns. Cover with cling film and put in a cold larder or fridge.

If you can, wait a couple of days for the meat to pick up the flavours of the herbs. If you can't, it will be fine to use the next day.

Preheat a fairly hot (200°C/gas mark 6) oven. Put the carcasses in a roasting tray and cook in the preheated oven for 20 minutes, then reduce the oven setting to 150°C/gas mark 2 and cook the chicken more slowly for 2 hours, draining off the fat into a bowl as you go. You need to render all the fat, and it's a surprising amount. With some birds, the fat is scarce. If this is the case, add a lump of butter. Throw away the bones and put the fat somewhere cool.

Wash the chicken pieces so that they are free of salt etc, and lay them in a clean earthenware or metal baking dish. Pour all the chicken fat over them and add a handful of fresh bay leaves. Cook very slowly at 150°C/gas mark 2, uncovered, for 2 hours or until the meat comes away from the bone easily. The pieces should be swimming in a shallow pool of fat. It sounds disgusting, but I promise it's not.

Eat the chicken there and then, or store it in the fridge. When you're ready to eat, warm it up thoroughly in a frying pan in a little of the fat. You won't really want anything else with it except a green salad and, perhaps, some mashed potato.

If you want to store it, neatly lay the cooked pieces in a bowl and cover them completely with fat. If one knuckle bone pokes out, the whole thing goes rotten.

Please note: the same confit technique can be used for duck, goose and guinea fowl, but beware of wild birds. Their fat, except that on a stubble mallard, can be rather disgusting and ruin things. However, fresh fat hen pheasant will also do very well.

Escalope of pork with thyme tapenade

I sometimes use thyme tapenade to spread over the pitta bread for Fattoush (see page 273) and I love it with Joyce Molyneaux's wonderful breadcrumbed escalope of pork recipe. She uses straight tapenade, but it is even tastier with the thyme addition.

For 4:
  575g trimmed pork fillet
  2 eggs, beaten
  2 handfuls of dried breadcrumbs
  Olive oil, for frying

For the tapenade:
  Small bunch of thyme
  250g olives (these must be really good ones – never buy the stoned kind)
  50g tinned anchovies in oil, drained
  1–2 garlic cloves
  25g capers, rinsed
  Olive oil

First, make the tapenade. Pull the leaves from the stalks of the thyme and stone the olives. Put all the ingredients into a blender and process for a few minutes. Add just enough olive oil in a stream to give you a thick, spreadable mixture. Put into small sterilised jars and cover.

This will make more tapenade than you need. You will have enough left over to fill a small jar, which will keep for about 3 months in the fridge.

Now for the pork. Cut the fillet at a slant across the grain into 12 slices. Spread one side of each slice with the tapenade. Dip the slices into the beaten egg and coat in the breadcrumbs. Leave in the fridge for about half an hour to firm up.

Heat some oil in a pan and fry the pork escalopes for 5 minutes on either side until nicely browned.

Lamb burgers with thyme and rosemary

Lean lamb shoulder, trimmed of excess fat, is excellent for this recipe as the meat is sweet and tender. You can also use fillet of lamb, but it will be more expensive. Serve with a large bowl of yoghurt, a crisp green salad and some flat bread (see page 46).

For 6 burgers or 12 canapés:
  2 small shallots
  500g lean minced lamb
  1 teaspoon chopped fresh rosemary
  1 tablespoon chopped fresh thyme
  1–2 garlic cloves, crushed and chopped
  ½ red chilli (optional)
  4cm piece of ginger, grated
  1 small egg, beaten
  Salt and black pepper
  Seasoned flour
  60–70g feta cheese
  Olive oil
  Large bowl of yoghurt, crisp green salad and some flat bread, to serve

Chop the shallots and add to the minced lamb in a large bowl. Chop the herbs, garlic and chilli (if using), and peel and chop the fresh ginger. Add these to the bowl, along with the beaten egg, and season well.

Generously sprinkle a large board with seasoned flour and have some more to one side for dusting your hands. Take a small handful of the lamb mixture and shape into a 6–7cm round, about 2.5cm thick. Put a small chunk of feta in the middle of the lamb and place another round of lamb, the same size, on top. Press down, lightly, using some extra seasoned flour to help shape a lamb burger about 9cm across. You can make these burgers as large or as small as you like – half this size makes a great little canapé.

Heat some oil in a frying pan or oil a barbecue grill and cook the lamb over a medium heat for about 3 minutes on each side. Alternatively, you can seal them quickly over a high heat and then finish them off on an oiled baking tray in a moderate oven for about 8 minutes.

Winter salad

The antioxidants in freshly picked salad leaves are one of the best guarantees against ill health, but try to avoid eating ready-washed packets, which have often been drenched in chlorine. There are many cut-and-come-again salad leaves and loose-leaf lettuce varieties which grow and produce well through the winter. Mizuna, mibuna, rocket, landcress, mâche or corn salad, winter purslane, any of the mustards and forced sea kale all make a delicious and interesting winter salad.

Rocket is good on its own and so is watercress, but mixing different punchy-flavoured leaves makes a delicious salad too. Add a bit of chervil or parsley, both good winter soft green herbs, as well as some gentler leaves – lettuce or corn salad – as background. With a boring supermarket lettuce, you need to make more of the dressing, but with tasty winter leaves, you don't always need to add the sharpness of vinegar or the fruitiness of oil.

If you like the idea of such a varied salad, try eating it without dressing. I love grabbing a good fistful of undressed salad from a central bowl and putting it on my plate to eat with my hands. You can then tear up or break in half a long spiky leaf of mizuna or a shred of horseradish-hot 'Red Giant' mustard, trying the flavours one by one. Without dressing, you don't get covered in oil and you can just sit and graze. Any leaves you don't eat, you can put back into a sealed plastic bag for the next meal. Without dressing or air, they last for days in the bottom of a fridge.

Whether you've bought the leaves or picked them, chuck the whole lot in a sink or bowl of cold water for a couple of hours before you eat. The salad benefits from a good long soak and stays perkier for longer. Drain and dry them gently – so as not to bruise the leaves. If you must leave them for any length of time, cover the bowl with a cold damp cloth or put them into a large plastic bag, secure the top and put them in the bottom of the fridge.

If you want your salad dressed, make the dressing in the bottom of the bowl. If you fancy something punchy, try shallot (see page 248) or garlic dressing (see page 54) but, on the whole, a simple dressing works best with the strong flavours of these winter leaves.

For a big bowl of salad to feed eight, use a generous splash (measured, about 4 tablespoons) of a good olive oil, the juice and grated zest of a half lemon and a generous twist of black pepper. Drop the herbs in on top of the dressing, and then the leaves. Finally, sprinkle sea salt – lots of it, salty salads are delicious – over the leaves, and toss well before serving.

Duck breast and peppery-leaf salad

Use a mix of leaves for this warm salad – Red Giant mustard, rocket, mizuna or watercress. Smoked duck breasts make this salad even easier to prepare.

For 6 as a starter:

3 fat duck breasts
1 tablespoon fennel seeds
Grated zest of 2 oranges
Pinch of sea salt
**6 small handfuls of mixed
    salad leaves**

For the dressing:

2 dessertspoons sesame oil
1 dessertspoon honey
**2 teaspoons Hoisin or plum sauce
    (see page 257)**
Juice of ½ lemon
Splash of sherry

Preheat a medium (180°C/gas mark 4) oven.

For perfectly cooked duck breasts – crisp on the outside and pink and juicy on the inside – make a criss-cross pattern with a serrated knife on the skin and rub in a mixture of fennel seed, orange zest and salt. Fry the breasts, skin side down, in a dry pan and cook on a medium heat until nearly all the fat is rendered – melted from beneath the skin – and the skin is golden brown. This will take about 10 minutes. Pour off the excess fat at least once and save it. It's delicious for cooking roast potatoes.

Transfer the breasts, in the same pan if you can, to the preheated medium oven for 8 minutes. Remove them from the oven; wrap them loosely on a plate with foil and leave to rest for at least 10 minutes. This is vital. It allows the flesh to relax and makes it deliciously tender.

While the duck is resting, mix the ingredients for the dressing. Slice the breasts thinly and add them to the salad just before you need them. Drizzle the dressing over the top.

Grilled goats' cheese salad

You'll find this as a standard dish on the set menu of simple French restaurants. Mix as many leaves into the salad as you can get your hands on – a few fronds of endive or frisée, some chicory and dandelion to give some bitterness, as well as some milder-tasting leaves.

For 6:

100g pancetta, chopped
1 garlic clove, crushed (not sliced)
1 small French baguette
200g small mature goats' cheese, with rind, rather than the fresh variety
2 tablespoons runny honey
6 sprigs of thyme
3 small handfuls of mixed mild salad leaves
3 small handfuls of bitter leaves, such as dandelion, any chicory and frisée
20–30 slow-roasted cherry tomatoes, if in season (see page 278)
2 tablespoons pine nuts, toasted

For the dressing:

1 garlic clove, finely chopped
1 tablespoon red wine vinegar or balsamic vinegar
4 tablespoons olive oil
1 teaspoon Dijon mustard
Salt and black pepper

Fry the pancetta in its own fat, with the garlic. Remove the pancetta once it begins to brown and let it cool. Discard the garlic.

Slice the French baguette into 1cm-thick ovals and toast these on one side. Heat the honey.

Cut the goats' cheese into thick slices and put one per piece of bread on the untoasted side. Season and drizzle over the warm honey. Put a sprig of thyme on the top and put the bread under the grill until the cheese begins to melt.

Tear up the salad leaves and make the dressing, combining all the ingredients together and whisking with a fork. Dress the leaves and put on individual plates. Scatter over the tomatoes, if you're using them, the pancetta and pine nuts, and add the toasted goats' cheese.

Winter flower and toasted seed salad

It's surprising how many edible flowers there are to pick, even in winter, but check they're not poisonous before you get stuck in. Winter-flowering pansies are all edible and, if picked regularly, will happily flower even in the coldest months, and in the south primroses appear in February on sunny banks. With the warmer winters, chervil and rocket – and even parsley – may start to flower. Pick a good handful of any of these for your salad. For a nutty taste, scatter some dry-toasted seeds over the top.

For 8:
> 3 heaped tablespoons mixed seeds, such as pumpkin, sunflower, poppy and sesame
> 30 mixed flowers
> 8 handfuls of leaves (at least 3 or 4 different varieties)
> 4 tablespoons good olive oil
> Juice and grated zest of ½ lemon
> 2 handfuls of any soft green herb (such as mint, parsley, coriander or chervil)
> Plenty of salt and black pepper

Dry-fry the seeds in a frying pan for 2–3 minutes with no oil, shaking them a couple of times as you do. You can toast them in the oven for a few minutes until they turn golden-brown (or silver in the case of mustard seeds), but, if they are hidden away in the oven, I tend to burn them.

Toss all the other salad ingredients together at the last moment, when you want to eat. Your hands are the best things for the job. Throw the toasted seeds over the top.

Fillet of beef with rocket

Thinly sliced raw fillet of beef, as used in the Italian dishes of carpaccio and *carne all'albese*, are excellent with the pepperiness of rocket. There are several types of rocket, but the two that you will see most often are wild and salad rocket.

For 8:
> 800g beef as a first course or 1.2kg as a main course, as a whole piece
> 3 tablespoons extra virgin olive oil
> A few coriander seeds, coarsely ground
> Salt and coarsely crushed black pepper
> 6 handfuls of rocket (wild or salad)
> 100g Parmesan cheese shavings
> 4 lemons, halved

Put the unsliced fillet into the freezer for 2 hours. This makes it easier to cut into very thin slices.

Slice the beef into slivers and put each slice in between two layers of greaseproof paper or cling film. Beat out as thinly as you can without breaking the flesh. Lay the slices out on a flat plate and drizzle with olive oil. Scatter the slices with the coarsely crushed black pepper and ground coriander seed.

Mix the rocket with a little olive oil, salt and more pepper and put a mound of leaves in the middle of the beef. Scatter over a few generous shavings of Parmesan. Serve with half a lemon on the side of each plate for your guests to squeeze over the meat. Don't do this in advance as the acidity will discolour the meat.

Rocket, beetroot and feta salad

I've been making this salad for years and it remains a stalwart. I sometimes mix mizuna in with the rocket if I don't have enough of that. Even in winter, you may be able to find fresh uncooked beetroot; but, if not, go for the vacuum-packed kind. Try to avoid the ones pickled in vinegar.

To make a refreshing summer lunch, the beetroot can be replaced with cubes of watermelon or, in the autumn, cubes of roasted squash. Roasted pumpkin seeds (see page 372) then make a delicious addition, along with a sweet balsamic sauce (see page 191).

For 8–10:
> 4 medium-sized beetroot (or 8 small), cooked and cut into chunks
> 8 handfuls of rocket (wild or salad)
> 2 handfuls of mint
> 200g feta cheese, crumbled

For the dressing:
> 3 tablespoons extra virgin olive oil
> Juice and grated zest of 1 lemon
> Salt and black pepper

Leaving their skins on, simmer or roast the beetroot in a pan until they're tender (20–30 minutes, depending on size). Let them cool slightly and rub off the skins, using your fingers. Cut them into chunks and allow them to cool. Combine the dressing ingredients.

Put all the other ingredients together in a salad bowl, reserving a sprinkling of mint leaves. Pour over the dressing, toss well and scatter over the reserved mint leaves just before serving.

Cauliflowers

A white cauliflower is a beautiful thing and quintessentially a cold climate plant. That's where many of the best recipes for it come from. Cauliflowers are widely used in Indian cooking, but it's rare to see them featuring in Italian, Spanish or even French food.

Cauliflowers are available all year, but are at their best in the spring and autumn. It's in the early spring – in March, the so-called famine month – that I find I use them most from the garden. Sown in late summer, the plants grow well through the winter, free from the usual brassica scourges of caterpillars and white fly, and they plump up at just the moment when there's very little else to pick.

The best variety I've grown is 'All Year Round' but, as with all cauliflowers, when its curds are fattening up you have to watch it. They can be still a bit small one day, and already shot and starting to run up to flower just a few days later. Keep checking and you'll cut it at the perfect moment.

I also love 'Limelight' and 'Romanesco' in lime-green, which you'll see in good greengrocers and which are also relatively easy to grow. Both mature quite quickly in early autumn from a late spring sowing. There are also orange cauliflowers and rich purple ones like the very old winter-hardy 'Purple Cape', worth buying or growing if you can find the seed. They are best summer-sown for harvesting in the early spring.

With all these fantastic-coloured cauliflowers, steam them and serve them just dusted with freshly ground cumin, or deep-fry them, but don't hide them with sauce. Alternatively, cut them up into small florets for eating raw as part of a plate of crudités, dipped into a spring *bagna cauda* or creamy anchovy dip (see page 422).

If you're in the mood, there's little better than a still slightly crunchy cauliflower cheese. You can add bacon or a scattering of crisped-up Parma ham, or smother it in a fluffy soufflé top (see page 61), which elevates it beyond family supper food.

As long as the florets are small, cauliflower is delicious raw. One of my favourite salads for this time of year is cauliflower in yoghurt, lime juice and toasted poppy seeds. Very fresh raw cauliflower takes on a creamy taste.

Vegetable korma

This is a dish for using up almost whatever you have in your vegetable basket, but cauliflower makes a good base. It's the perfect quick-and-easy weekday supper. Serve it with rice and one of your summer- or autumn-made chutneys.

For 6:
    1 onion, finely chopped
    2 tablespoons vegetable oil
    1 teaspoon good curry powder
    2 x 400ml tins of coconut milk
    1 cauliflower, chopped
    2 carrots, chopped
    1 parsnip, chopped
    2 good handfuls of chard
        or spinach, chopped
    French beans (good, but
        not essential)
    Bunch of coriander, roughly
        chopped
    Salt and black pepper

Fry the onion in the oil gently until soft. Add the curry powder and fry again for another minute or two. Then add the coconut milk and vegetables, except the beans, if you are using them.

Cook for about 10 minutes, until the veg are tender but not soft. If using beans, add them a couple of minutes before the end, as they take almost no cooking. Take off the heat and add the coriander.

Cauliflower cheese with Lord Dalrymple's top

This is a delicious Edwardian dish that was included in my aunt Fortune Stanley's 1974 cookery book, *English Country House Cooking*. With a crunchy salad of bitter leaves – chicory, dandelion and rocket – it is perfect for a light main course.

For 4:
    1 large cauliflower
    175g butter, plus a little more
        for the dish
    3 tablespoons flour
    6 tablespoons single cream
    250g strong Cheddar cheese
    Salt and black pepper
    1 tablespoon mustard
    6 eggs, separated

Preheat a moderate (180°C/gas mark 4) oven.

Divide the cauliflower into chunks and steam it for 3–4 minutes. Put the cauliflower in the bottom of a buttered soufflé dish.

Melt the butter, add the flour and stir over a gentle heat for 1–2 minutes. Add the cream and cheese. Season and add the mustard, and cook for 3–4 minutes, stirring continuously until the mixture thickens to the consistency of double cream. Take off the heat and stir in the egg yolks.

Whisk the egg whites and fold in. Pour the soufflé mixture over the cauliflower and bake in the preheated oven for about 15 minutes, until the top is browned and risen.

Cauliflower soup

This is a creamy gentle soup, with a lovely hint of almond.

For 6–8:
    1 medium-sized cauliflower
    25g butter
    1 large onion, chopped
    1 garlic clove, roughly chopped
    30g ground almonds
    1 litre good chicken or
        vegetable stock
    2 bay leaves
    450ml milk
    Salt and black pepper
    Freshly grated nutmeg
    Cayenne pepper
    Flaked almonds, toasted

Break the cauliflower florets into roughly even-sized pieces. Melt the butter in a frying pan and sweat the onion – without allowing it to colour – over a gentle heat for 5 minutes.

Add the garlic, cauliflower and ground almonds, and stir well. Pour in the stock, add the bay leaves, bring to the boil and simmer, covered, for 10 minutes until tender.

When slightly cooled, remove the bay leaves, liquidise in a food processor and put back into a clean pan. Add enough of the milk to give the consistency you want, grate in a little nutmeg, season carefully and bring to simmering point. Do not boil.

Serve dusted with cayenne pepper and scattered with toasted flaked almonds.

Purple sprouting broccoli, calabrese and spring greens

Purple sprouting broccoli, like rhubarb, appears when the garden and field harvest is sparse. It's iron-rich, packed with vitamins A, B and C, and delicious – somehow you know from the way that it tastes that it's good for you.

I grow three types of sprouting broccoli. The earliest is 'White Eye', a tasty, greeny-white variety, less prolific than its purple cousins. Next comes purple 'Rudolph', another early cropper which you can start to pick in February. I harvest these for a couple of months, picking little and often to encourage them to keep cropping. Pick the large central head first, which will then be followed by a profusion of tender side shoots. I also grow a mid-to-late season variety, 'Red Arrow', which crops in earnest from late March until May.

Ideally, pick your stems not long before you eat them. This is one of the quickest brassicas to flop. If you need to keep them, seal them in a plastic bag in the fridge. Picked or bought very fresh, you can steam finger-thick shoots and eat every scrap. But if you have chunkier stalks, don't discard them. When you're preparing them, press your thumbnail into the stalk. If it goes in easily, it's tender enough to eat; if not, peel the outer skin with a potato peeler, but don't chop the stalk off.

Lay the purple sprouting broccoli stems out in a single layer in a shallow pan, with about 8cm of boiling salted water. Steam or boil hard, uncovered, for a couple of minutes and then test with the tip of a knife. I love the idea – described by Lynda Brown in her brilliant book *The Cook's Garden* – of dipping the smallest shoots, like asparagus, into a soft-boiled egg.

Also try eating purple sprouting broccoli like asparagus with hollandaise sauce (see page 233). Tie ten thin shoots, trimmed right down, into neat little bundles with string. Stand them upright in 8cm of salted boiling water for about 7–8 minutes, until the stems are soft but the heads not collapsing. Put a bundle on each plate, season and add a dollop of hollandaise.

Many of these recipes can also be made with calabrese, which is available all year, but the flavour of purple sprouting is stronger and more interesting. It's more akin to that of spring greens.

At this time of year, there are also Brussels sprout tops. Freshly picked, these are delicious sautéed, or steamed and dressed in a slurp of olive oil or melted butter.

Purple sprouting broccoli with lemon and hazelnuts

This is almost too easy to call a recipe, but it's one of my favourite ways of eating purple sprouting broccoli. Serve this as a first course. People are always a bit surprised at the elevation of broccoli to a course on its own like asparagus, but they are soon converted.

For 4:
- 350g purple sprouting broccoli
- About 100g butter
- Juice and grated zest of ½ lemon
- Salt and black pepper
- 50g hazelnuts, halved and toasted

Trim the broccoli and steam until just tender, but retaining a good bite. Warm the butter and add the lemon zest and juice.

Arrange the broccoli stems on a large shallow dish or on individual plates (both warmed) and pour over the hot butter.

Season well with salt and pepper, and scatter over the toasted hazelnuts.

Purple sprouting broccoli pasta

This is a very familiar recipe, but so good that it would be a shame to miss it out. You can make this sauce with purple sprouting broccoli or the chunkier, greener calabrese.

For 4:
- 1 tin of anchovies in olive oil
- 1 garlic clove, chopped
- 1 red chilli, chopped (optional)
- 350g penne or farfalle
- 400g purple sprouting broccoli or calabrese
- Slurp of olive oil
- Black pepper
- Lots of grated Parmesan cheese

Pour the tin of anchovies with its oil into a frying pan over a gentle heat. The anchovies will gradually dissolve in the oil, in 2–3 minutes. Add the garlic and chilli (if using), and fry for another minute or two. Be careful not to let the garlic brown. Take the pan off the heat.

Meanwhile, cook the pasta in salted boiling water until al dente.

Trim the purple sprouting broccoli, retaining much of the stem as well as the heads. If the stems are tough, pare off the outer layer and then cut the stems into chunks. If using calabrese, separate the heads into small florets, breaking them off the main stem.

Steam the broccoli for about 5 minutes until soft. Purée one half, leaving the other in little chunks. Toss all together with the anchovies. Add a slurp of olive oil and black pepper to taste. Stir this into the pasta and add lots of Parmesan.

Broccoli soup with Gorgonzola

This is a classic soup, even better with Gorgonzola than Stilton.

For 4:
- 450g purple sprouting broccoli or calabrese
- 30g butter
- 1 onion, roughly chopped
- 2 small potatoes, cut into chunks
- 2 garlic cloves, roughly chopped
- 1.2 litres hot chicken stock
- 1 tablespoon lemon juice
- 200ml milk
- 115g Gorgonzola cheese
- Salt and black pepper
- 3 tablespoons double cream (optional)

Trim the purple sprouting broccoli, retaining much of the stem as well as the heads. If the stems are tough, pare off the outer layer and then cut the stems into chunks. If using calabrese, separate the heads into small florets, breaking them off the main stem.

Melt the butter in a large saucepan and put in the onion, chopped potato and garlic. Cook for 5 minutes without allowing to brown and add the broccoli. Stir well to combine and pour in the hot stock and lemon juice. Cover and simmer for 10–15 minutes until tender.

When the mixture has cooled a little, purée in a food processor and, if you want a very smooth soup, push it through a mouli or sieve into a clean pan.

Add the milk – more or less than the quantity given above, depending how thick you like it. Then add the crumbled cheese and season carefully (Gorgonzola is salty).

Reheat gently without bringing to the boil and add the cream, if using.

Double pepper broccoli

This is good as a vegetable side dish or, with rice, as a light supper. This recipe can be made with cavolo nero, but blanch it before adding to the wok.

For 4–6:
**600g purple sprouting broccoli
    or calabrese
1 sweet red pepper
2 tablespoons groundnut oil
1 tablespoon black mustard seeds
1 teaspoon dried chilli, crumbled
3 tablespoons good chicken or
    vegetable stock
Salt**

Trim the purple sprouting broccoli, retaining much of the stem as well as the heads. If the stems are tough, pare off the outer layer and then cut the stems into chunks. If using calabrese, separate the heads into small florets, breaking them off the main stem.

Deseed the pepper and then cut it into strips.

Heat the oil in a wok or deep frying pan and add the mustard seeds. Add the crumbled dried chilli and, when the mustard seeds begin to pop, add the broccoli and stir to combine. Add the strips of pepper and stock, and stir again.

Cover the pan, turn down the heat and cook for about 4–5 minutes, or until the broccoli is tender but crisp. If any liquid remains in the pan, raise the heat and boil it off. Season with salt before serving.

Spring greens risotto

This is a good, simple garden risotto. It is excellent with roast chicken.

For 4 as a side dish:
**180g spring greens
1 tablespoon extra virgin olive oil
30g unsalted butter
1 small onion, finely chopped
½ red chilli, finely chopped
225g Arborio rice
2 garlic cloves, chopped
Salt and black pepper
125ml red or white wine
About 750ml good chicken stock
Plenty of grated Parmesan
    cheese, plus more to serve**

Remove the stems from the spring greens, roll the leaves into cigar shapes and cut these across to produce long ribbons. Steam or blanch for 2–3 minutes. Drain.

Heat the oil and 20g of the butter in a heavy pan and add the onion. Sweat the onion and chilli until the onion begins to look translucent. To prevent it from colouring, cook it over a gentle heat under a piece of greaseproof paper.

Add the rice, garlic, salt, pepper and spring greens, and stir well. Add half of the wine and let it bubble up and evaporate.

In a separate pan, bring the stock to the boil. Add the hot stock to the rice by the ladleful, stirring constantly between additions and waiting until the stock has been absorbed before adding the next ladleful.

After about 20 minutes, test to see if the rice is cooked (it should still have a bite). Adjust the seasoning if necessary. Remove from the heat and beat in the remaining butter, wine and Parmesan. Serve with a bowl of extra Parmesan.

Rhubarb

Rhubarb is a miraculous plant. It crops when the garden and fields are at their barest. It is increasingly hailed as a 'superfood', rich in antioxidants, as well as being an excellent gentle purgative. It's also incredibly easy to grow, being one of the rare productive plants that will put up with shade and continue to produce despite almost total neglect. In fact, rhubarb is so extremely persistent that when archaeologists and historians spot it in the middle of nowhere, they assume people must have lived there once. There may be no architectural remains, but a good clump of rhubarb is a sure sign that the ground was once cultivated.

From early in the year, you'll find forced rhubarb – stems that have been grown with heat in the dark and are the sweetest and most tender. Exposure to light encourages them to become more fibrous and the taste to become sharp. Wakefield in West Yorkshire is still the heart of rhubarb forcing country and has been for over a hundred years. There it's picked by candlelight, which is less intense than day or electric light, and so less likely to affect the newly emergent stems.

By the middle of spring, field-grown rhubarb becomes available – a cheaper and still delicious thing. This has emerged naturally under its own steam and will need a little more cooking and sugar, but it's still invaluable for making delicious puddings.

I grow lots of rhubarb, cultivating three different varieties to give me maximum picking time. I start with 'Timperley Early', which has the least flavour, but in my garden crops from mid-March if covered. Then I move on to mid-season 'Stockbridge Arrow', and finish with the late 'Queen Victoria', which crops right into June.

If you want to blanch your plants for extra sweetness, allow the crown – the heart of the plant – to die back in the autumn and clear away any debris once the leaves are brown and withered. When the weather starts to get milder in February, water the plants well first and then cover the crowns with straw and a tall rhubarb forcing pot. A bucket is usually too short, but a chimney pot or old dustbin work well. Use bubble wrap or straw to clad the outside. This helps protect against frost, which will split the stems, making them translucent and not good to eat. Six to eight weeks is the usual forcing time. The stalks grow quickly once they get going, so after six weeks inspect every couple of days.

To pick the stems, pull them gently from the base, taking care not to break the secondary stems nestled right at the heart of the plant. To store, slice off the leaves, and put the stems in a plastic bag. Otherwise, they wilt quickly.

Rhubarb syllabub

One of my favourite spring puddings. It's easy and quick to make, as well as being light, frothy and delicious.

For 6–8:
    Juice and grated zest of 1 orange
    100g caster sugar
    6 stems of young pink rhubarb
        (about 500g)
    2 cardamom pods
    2 star anise

For the syllabub:
    284ml double cream
    Grated zest and juice of
        1 large lemon
    3–4 tablespoons Grand Marnier,
        dry sherry or white wine
    100g caster sugar

Preheat the oven to 190°C/gas mark 5. Warm the orange juice in a pan and dissolve the sugar in it.

Cut the rhubarb into sections the length of your thumb and cook in the orange juice with the zest, cardamom and star anise for 10 minutes. Then cool the fruit.

To make a syrupy juice, lift out the rhubarb pieces and boil up the juice until it thickens.

To make the syllabub, put the cream, lemon zest and juice, alcohol and sugar into a bowl and beat for several minutes, until the mixture becomes thick and light.

Remove the cardamom pods and star anise from the rhubarb. Put the rhubarb into individual glasses, spoon the syllabub mixture over the top and chill for a couple of hours.

Rhubarb sorbet

A wonderfully light sorbet with a really punchy taste. It's a good way of using up rhubarb when there's too much to keep up with in the garden.

For 6–8:
    600g rhubarb
    Juice of 1 orange
    1 teaspoon vanilla extract
    Juice of 1–2 lemons

For the sugar syrup:
    450g sugar

To make the sugar syrup, dissolve the sugar in 600ml water over a low heat. Slowly bring to the boil. Boil for 2–3 minutes and then allow to cool. This stores very well in the fridge.

Cut the rhubarb into short lengths and put them into a saucepan with the orange juice. Simmer, covered, until the rhubarb is tender, then put to one side to cool.

Add the sugar syrup to the rhubarb and blend in a food processor until smooth. Add the vanilla, lemon juice to taste and freeze/churn in an ice cream machine until nearly frozen. (Or pour into a plastic container with a lid, freeze and, after about 1½ hours, beat with a hand mixer or food processor. Put the mixture back into the freezer and repeat the process again a couple of times at intervals.)

Transfer to the fridge about 20 minutes before serving. You need to eat this within a couple of months.

Rhubarb upside-down cake

This treacly and delicious cake looks and tastes fantastic.

For 6–8:
    480g rhubarb
    60g soft brown sugar
    60g butter
    Grated zest of 1 orange
    125g unsalted butter
    175g caster sugar
    3 eggs
    175g flour
    1 teaspoon baking powder
    ½ teaspoon salt
    1 tablespoon milk
    Toasted flaked almonds
    Icing sugar, for dusting
    Crème fraîche and demerara
        sugar, to serve

Preheat the oven to 180°C/gas mark 4.

Cut the rhubarb at an angle into slices about 5cm long. Melt the brown sugar with the butter in a 26cm frying pan with an ovenproof or removable handle. Add the orange zest and remove from the heat. Cover the base of the pan with the rhubarb.

Cream the butter and sugar until whitish. Gradually add the eggs, one at a time, while still beating. Sift the flour, baking powder and salt, and fold into the mixture. Add the milk and mix well. Spread the mixture over the rhubarb with a spatula.

Bake in the preheated oven for about 30 minutes, until the cake mixture is firm to the touch. Leave to cool for about 20 minutes in the pan and then invert on to a large flat serving plate.

Sprinkle with the toasted flaked almonds and dust with icing sugar. Serve warm with crème fraîche.

To reheat, put on a large baking sheet, sprinkle with demerara sugar and bake for 15–20 minutes in an oven preheated to 180°C/gas mark 4.

Rhubarb tart

A lovely tart which has a fresh and sharp flavour.

For 4–6:
   3 eggs
   275ml double cream
   50g sugar
   Grated zest of 1 orange
   A few saffron strands
   450g rhubarb, cut into roughly
      3cm lengths
   50g toasted flaked almonds

For the shortcrust pastry:
   150g plain flour
   50g caster sugar
   75g unsalted butter, very cold
   1 egg yolk
   A little iced water

Make the pastry by processing the flour and sugar together for a minute or so. Chop the cold butter into chunks and add to the flour and sugar. Pulse carefully until the mixture resembles breadcrumbs, remove and put into a mixing bowl.

Mix the egg yolk with a little iced cold water, add to the bowl and mix until the pastry comes together in a soft ball. Roll out on a floured surface and use to line a 20cm flan tin, then chill for half an hour in the fridge.

Preheat the oven to 190°C/gas mark 5. Prick the bottom of the tart with a fork, cover with a round of greaseproof paper or foil and weight this down with some baking beans or rice. Bake the pastry case blind for about 15 minutes.

Take it out of the oven, but leave the oven on, and remove the beans or rice and the lining paper. Put it back in the oven to cook for another 10 minutes. Let it cool slightly.

Lightly beat the eggs and mix them with the cream, sugar, orange zest and saffron. Cut the rhubarb into lengths and arrange them in circles in the tin.

Pour over the cream mixture and bake in the oven for 15 minutes, then lower the temperature to 180°C/gas mark 4 and continue to bake for about 10 minutes, until the filling is firm and beginning to colour.

Allow to cool and scatter over the toasted almonds.

Poached rhubarb with stem ginger ice cream

This recipe is delicious with the sweet, tender early stems of rhubarb. Just a little treacly muscovado sugar is enough to retain the slight sourness in contrast to the sweet ice cream.

For 10:
   Juice and grated zest of 3 oranges
   2 tablespoons muscovado sugar
   3 star anise
   6 rhubarb stems (about 800g)
   4cm piece of ginger root, peeled
      and thinly sliced

For the ice cream:
   568ml milk
   100g caster sugar
   Few drops of good vanilla extract
   220g sweetened condensed milk
   Pinch of salt
   475ml whipping or double cream
   6 pieces of stem ginger, finely
      chopped
   2 tablespoons ginger syrup

First make the ice cream. Heat the milk with the sugar and vanilla, and bring to boiling point. Remove from the heat and cool. Add the condensed milk, salt, cream, chopped ginger and syrup.

If you have an ice cream maker, freeze/churn the mixture for 20 minutes; if you don't, put it into a plastic container and freeze, breaking up the ice particles a couple of times with a fork at 2-hour intervals.

Preheat the oven to 190°C/gas mark 5.

Warm the orange juice in a pan and melt the sugar, then add the star anise. Cut the rhubarb into sections the length of your thumb and lay them in a shallow heatproof dish, almost touching. Pour the warm liquid over the rhubarb and scatter over the orange zest and ginger.

Cover and bake in the preheated oven for about 10 minutes. The stems will then keep their shape. Serve with a couple of balls of the ice cream.

Spinach

If you were cast away on a temperate desert island, it would make sense to take a packet of spinach seed. With so many different ways to eat spinach, you'd be slow to get bored. The young leaves are as good raw as cooked; it is lovely wilted in a little water, butter or olive oil, and just as delicious slow-cooked in an Italian *pasticcio* or *spanakopitta* – Greek spinach pie (see page 74). Spinach makes good soup, good pasta and good risotto. Like potatoes, it goes with everything.

It's always been said to be particularly good for you, very rich in iron and easily absorbed. Pregnant women were told to eat it by the barrow-load to avoid anaemia; it was the source of Popeye's strength. In fact, spinach is rich in iron, but not in a form from which we can benefit; it is excreted from our bodies almost totally unabsorbed. However, spinach is an excellent source of vitamin A and folic acid. Spinach can protect against cancer of the prostate, breast, stomach, colon, lung, skin and cervix. Consumers of spinach also gain protection against osteoporosis, heart disease and arthritis.

Spinach is easy to grow and, as non-organic spinach is usually covered in more chemicals than most other veg, growing your own is a good idea. It does best in the garden in the spring and autumn. The northern European variety 'Giant of Winter' is hardier than the rest, and is said to crop right the way through the coldest months, but it doesn't come near Swiss chard's winter productivity. 'Trinidad', on the other hand, is slower to bolt in the summer and suits a hot climate. Most spinach varieties are happiest and crop for longest in cool temperatures, moderate light levels and plenty of rain.

My favourite variety is 'Dominant', with good mildew- and disease-resistance, and fantastic texture and taste. When I visited Raymond Blanc's vegetable garden at Le Manoir aux Quat' Saisons, I was glad to hear 'Dominant' had come top in their taste trials, as it had done at Perch Hill. It is now the only variety we grow.

So-called 'perpetual spinach' is a leaf beet, and will produce right the way through the winter, if not the entire year. It's tougher than spinach, easier to grow, slower to bolt, coarser in texture and taste, but still well worth it.

Spinach freezes well, so when you have plenty in the garden, freeze it for later. Remove the stems and tear the leaves into ribbons. Blanch for 2 minutes, plunge into ice-cold water and squeeze with your hands or twist in a clean tea towel to get it really dry before freezing in batches. When cooked, it reduces in volume by about three-quarters.

Spinach and lentil soup

Spinach is excellent with pulses – lentils, chickpeas or almost any bean. This is a delicious warm winter soup – very filling and perfect for a weekend lunch.

For 6:
  200g spinach
  200g red lentils
  2 tablespoons olive oil
  1 tablespoon ground cumin
  1 tablespoon ground coriander seeds
  1 tablespoon ground turmeric
  1 teaspoon ground cloves
  1 teaspoon ground cinnamon
  1 onion, finely chopped
  4 garlic cloves, finely chopped
  5 tomatoes, skinned and chopped (or a 400g tin of chopped tomatoes)
  1 teaspoon tomato purée
  400ml tin of coconut milk
  Large bunch of coriander, roughly chopped
  Lemon juice, to taste

Remove the stems from the spinach and finely shred the leaves.

Cook the lentils in 1.5 litres of water. Bring to the boil and simmer for 15–20 minutes, until just tender.

Heat the oil in a frying pan and stir-fry all the spices. Add the onion and garlic, and sweat until soft.

Add the spices and onions to the lentils in their cooking liquid, and then add the tomatoes, tomato purée and coconut milk. Cook for a further 15 minutes.

Add the spinach and cook just enough to wilt. Take off the heat and add the coriander and lemon juice to taste, then season.

Ithaca pie

This is a local Ithacan version of *spanakopitta* which we ate in a small taverna in Stavros. It was cooked with spinach mixed with *horta* – wild greens picked from the hillside. A combination of spinach, kale, chard, dill and mint gives almost the same rich and varied taste, but if you don't like the hint of bitterness, just use spinach, parsley, mint and dill. Serve this with a finely chopped cabbage and grated carrot salad, dressed with good Greek olive oil, salt and lemon juice.

For 12–15:
For the filling:
  1kg spinach, chard, kale (one, or a mixture of all, of these greens)
  Large bunch of dill, finely chopped
  4 tablespoons finely chopped mint
  4 tablespoons finely chopped parsley
  1 onion, finely chopped
  2 garlic cloves, finely chopped
  300ml olive oil
  4 spring onions, finely chopped
  2 leeks, finely chopped
  1 tea cup of long-grain rice
  200g feta (optional)
  Salt and black pepper

For the shortcrust pastry:
  750g plain flour
  1 teaspoon salt
  375g unsalted butter
  3 eggs, beaten
  Ice-cold water
  1 tablespoon sesame seeds

Remove tough stalks from the spinach, chard and kale. Coarsely chop the leaves and add the finely chopped herbs. Sauté the onion and garlic in a little oil in a large pan and add all the greens, including the spring onions and leeks. Mix well with most of the remaining oil. Add the uncooked rice and take off the heat. Season well.

To make the pastry, sift the flour with the salt and rub in the butter or pulse in a food processor until it has the consistency of breadcrumbs. Add enough beaten egg and iced water to bring the pastry together in a ball. Wrap it in cling film and leave it in the fridge for at least 30 minutes.

Preheat the oven to 180°C/gas mark 4. Divide the pastry into two, allow it to warm up for a minute or so and roll it out – on a floured surface – as thinly as you possibly can.

Roll one piece around a rolling pin to carry it and put it in the base of a baking tin about 40 x 50cm and 4cm deep. It is important that there's plenty of extra pastry hanging over the side of the tin.

Add the filling and then crumble over the feta, if you are using it. Cover with the other layer of pastry. Then crimp the two layers together by brushing with a little water and pinching around the edge.

Brush a little oil over the top, scatter with a few sesame seeds and prick the surface with a knife. Bake the pie in the preheated oven for just over an hour.

This is delicious once it has cooled a little and is, perhaps, even better eaten cold the next day. It's also excellent for feeding lots of people on a picnic.

Spinach and Gruyère tart

There are many delicious spinach tarts, but this very simple one is the best I have tried. Serve with a salad.

For 4–6:
300g spinach
100g sorrel
200ml double cream
100ml milk
3 eggs
1 teaspoon Dijon mustard
Freshly grated nutmeg
½ teaspoon cayenne pepper
200g Gruyère cheese, grated
Salt and black pepper
100g pine nuts

For the shortcrust pastry:
175g plain flour
½ teaspoon salt
75g unsalted butter
1 egg, beaten
Ice-cold water

To make the pastry, sift the flour with the salt and rub in the butter or pulse in a food processor until it has the consistency of breadcrumbs. Add enough beaten egg and iced water to bring the pastry together in a ball. Wrap it in cling film and leave it in the fridge for at least 30 minutes.

Preheat the oven to 200°C/gas mark 6. Roll out the chilled pastry and use to line a 26cm tart tin. Prick the bottom of the tart with a fork, cover with a round of greaseproof paper or foil and weight this down with some baking beans or rice.

Bake the pastry case blind for about 15–20 minutes. Take it out of the oven (leaving the oven on but turning the setting down to 180°C/gas mark 4) and let it cool slightly, and then remove the beans or rice and the lining paper.

Pick over the spinach and sorrel leaves, removing any tough ribs. Cook until tender and drain thoroughly. To remove excess liquid, squeeze the leaves out with your hands or twist them gently in a clean tea towel. Chop the greens very roughly.

Mix the cream, milk and eggs together and add the mustard, grated nutmeg, cayenne and cheese. Season with salt and pepper.

Spread out the greens on the pastry case. Scatter over the pine nuts and pour over the cream mixture.

Cook the tart for 30–35 minutes and serve warm.

Spinach and sorrel frittata

Frittatas make easy, quick substantial family food. I love this with a combination of spinach and sorrel, but spinach also works well on its own.

For 4–5:
300g spinach
200g sorrel
200g pancetta, cut into chunks
2 tablespoons olive oil
2 garlic cloves, chopped
6 eggs
Salt and black pepper
150g grated Parmesan cheese
200ml crème fraîche
Finely chopped parsley

Preheat the oven to 180°C/gas mark 4.

Remove tough stalks from the spinach and sorrel, and chop both leaves. In a frying pan with an ovenproof handle, fry the pancetta in the oil for 5 minutes. Add the garlic, spinach and sorrel, and allow the leaves to wilt.

Beat the eggs with the salt, pepper, cheese and crème fraîche, and pour over the veg.

Fry over a gentle heat for 7–8 minutes, and then put the pan in the preheated oven for a further 5 minutes.

Turn the frittata out on a flat plate and then flip it over again. Scatter with plenty of parsley.

Creamed spinach

There are many recipes for creamed spinach, but this one is quick, light and simple.

For 4 as a side dish:
 500g spinach
 1 tablespoon olive oil
 30g butter
 4 shallots, chopped
 2 garlic cloves, chopped
 100ml double cream
 A little freshly grated nutmeg
 Salt and black pepper

Wash the spinach leaves well and dry them off in a salad spinner.

Steam the spinach for 3 minutes and roughly chop.

In a deep frying pan, heat the oil and butter together, add the shallots and garlic, and gently sweat until they have softened and become translucent. Add the chopped spinach, raising the heat slightly to bubble away any excess liquid from the spinach. Lower the heat again and add the cream, grated nutmeg, salt and pepper, and stir to heat through. Serve immediately.

Spinach with split peas or lentils

Fave e foglie, as it is called in Italy, is a classic Roman dish. It is delicious yet virtuous-feeling, and is best eaten when just warm. You can use broad beans, lentils or split peas, but I prefer lentils. Chard or wild greens, such as nettles or chicory, can be substituted for spinach.

For 6 as a starter:
 250g Puy lentils, split peas
 or other pulses
 250ml white wine
 2 bay leaves
 2 whole garlic cloves
 Small bunch of thyme
 1 celery stick
 Salt and black pepper
 Extra virgin olive oil
 Large bunch of flat-leaf parsley,
 coarsely chopped
 500g spinach or chard
 Juice and grated zest of 1 lemon
 Salt and black pepper
 2 tablespoons capers, rinsed

Boil the lentils or split peas with the wine, bay leaves, garlic, thyme and celery stick (left whole), with enough water to cover. Cook for about 20 minutes, until just tender. Remove the bay, thyme, garlic and celery. Drain the lentils, pour over a little olive oil and season while still hot. Allow to cool a little and then add the parsley.

Steam the spinach or chard leaves. Dress with a little olive oil mixed with the lemon juice and zest. Season with salt and black pepper.

On each plate, serve a large spoonful of lentils, topped with a few capers, alongside a mound of leaves.

Sag aloo

Our own version of the Indian classic. Serve with a meat curry and rice.

For 4:
 500g waxy potatoes
 450g young spinach leaves
 1 teaspoon mustard seeds
 1 tablespoon sunflower oil
 1 teaspoon cumin seeds, toasted
 and ground
 ½ teaspoon chilli powder
 1 large onion, chopped
 3 garlic cloves, chopped
 5cm piece of root ginger, peeled
 and chopped
 275ml vegetable stock or water
 Salt and black pepper
 1 teaspoon garam masala
 1 tablespoon olive oil
 Natural yoghurt, to serve

Peel the potatoes and cut them into chunks about 2.5cm. Blanch the spinach or steam it for 2–3 minutes. Drain well and chop it coarsely.

Put the mustard seeds in a heavy-based pan with the sunflower oil and fry until the seeds begin to pop. Add the ground cumin and chilli powder, and cook for a minute or two. Add the onions, garlic and ginger, and cook gently for a further 4–5 minutes.

Stir in the chopped potatoes and 200ml of the stock with some salt and pepper. Cook for 8–10 minutes and then add the chopped spinach.

Cover the pan and cook until the potatoes are just tender. If it needs more liquid during the cooking, add the remaining stock or water.

Take off the heat, stir in the garam masala with the olive oil and adjust the seasoning.

This is lovely served warm with plenty of natural yoghurt.

Baby spinach, pancetta and roasted almond salad

Raw baby spinach makes one of the most mild and tender salad leaves. This simple mixture is delicious.

For 4:
75g pancetta, very thinly sliced (but not chopped)
75g almonds
220g baby spinach
Good handful of small sorrel leaves, stems removed
2 large avocados (optional)
50g Parmesan cheese

For the croutons:
2–3 thick slices from a wholemeal or granary loaf
Sunflower oil, for frying

For the dressing:
2 teaspoons Dijon mustard
1 teaspoon caster sugar
1 dessertspoon red wine vinegar
100ml sunflower oil
3 tablespoons extra virgin olive oil
Salt and black pepper

Preheat the oven to 180°C/gas mark 4.

First make the croutons: cut the slices of bread into large cubes. Heat some sunflower oil in a small frying pan and, when the oil is really hot, cook the bread cubes until golden and crisp. Dry on kitchen paper and season while hot.

Put the pancetta slices on an oiled baking sheet and bake in the preheated oven for about 10–15 minutes, until crisp.

Halve and toast the almonds in a frying pan for a few minutes, tossing them once or twice as they cook.

To make the dressing: whisk the mustard, sugar and vinegar together in a jug, using a wand or hand mixer. Gradually add the two oils in a stream while whisking and season carefully with salt and black pepper.

Put the spinach and sorrel leaves in a large shallow bowl and toss in just enough of the dressing to coat the leaves.

Peel the avocados if you are using them, slice into large pieces and season. Pare the Parmesan with a potato peeler.

Add the croutons, sorrel, avocado, Parmesan and herbs to the spinach, combining gently, and throw over the pancetta slices and almonds. Drizzle more dressing over the top.

Spinach malfatta

Spinach ravioli can be a fiddle to make. These lighter dumplings are just as good, and easier to prepare.

For 4:
500g spinach
1 garlic clove, finely chopped
1 egg white
50g Parmesan cheese, finely grated, plus more for serving
100g breadcrumbs
Plenty of freshly grated nutmeg, to taste
1 tablespoon spring herbs (parsley, chives or fennel), finely chopped
Salt and black pepper
1 tablespoon flour
Really rich tomato sauce (see page 277), to serve

Remove the stems from the spinach (if the leaves are large) and finely chop the leaves. Cook in a little salted water or steam until they are tender. Squeeze out the water. Combine the spinach with the garlic, egg white, Parmesan, breadcrumbs, nutmeg, herbs, salt and pepper.

Shape the mixture into small dumplings the size of walnuts. The easiest way to cook these is to steam them. You can then do two layers at once. Lay them out, spaced 2cm apart, in a steamer lined with layers of perforated greaseproof paper, with a little butter or olive oil on the sheets to prevent the dumplings sticking. Put the lid on and steam for 10 minutes.

Serve with melted butter or plenty of Really rich tomato sauce (see page 277), and a scattering of grated Parmesan.

Spring herbs

Herbs are productive plants that everyone can grow. They take up little space, are happy in a pot on a window ledge or doorstep, and are bountiful for months at a stretch. A handful of leaves, finely chopped, is often all that's required to transform a dish.

There are four stalwarts that are the first to emerge in early spring – chives, fennel, sorrel and lovage. These join parsley and chervil – both hardy biennials – that grow happily outside for most of the winter. By April, you'll also have coriander, which is best sown in the early spring or late summer. It runs up to flower too quickly in the hotter months, but grows well in the cool bright days of spring. Combine a few leaves of each of these herbs (using lovage sparingly) and make a spring salsa verde or green mayonnaise.

The first young leaves of all these herbs are also delicious chopped or torn and scattered over a salad. This is my favourite way of eating lovage – just a sprinkling, as it has a strong smoky celery taste. Once the leaves of lovage grow beyond the size of a child's hand, they're too strong to use raw, but are invaluable as flavouring in stews (see Hungarian goulash on page 88) and stocks. Lovage makes an ornamental plant when fully grown, so why not grow it?

If you keep picking chives, coriander, fennel and sorrel little and often, they'll remain succulent and tasty for longer. Left unpicked for weeks, they'll flower and then seed, and lose their flavour. Coriander is a short-lived annual and will need re-sowing, but the rest just need to be cut to the ground and fed with a potash-rich feed (Tomorite is ideal) around mid-June. They'll have sprouted again within a couple of weeks and will be there to harvest for the rest of the summer.

Pick your herbs as and when you want them, but if you need to store them, wash the leaves and wrap them in kitchen paper. Put them, still wrapped, in a plastic bag at the bottom of the fridge and most will last ten days. You can also freeze herbs in ice trays: finely chop them, mix them in a little water and fill the trays. You can add these cubes to soups and stews. Herb butters are also ideal if you have too much of any one herb. Take a handful of any soft herb and mix it with soft unsalted or lightly salted butter in a food processor. Place the herb butter on a length of cling film, roll it into a cylinder and freeze. Cut it off in discs with a warmed knife to melt over a steak or a bowl of vegetables.

The flavour of all these herbs comes from oils in the leaves. Parsley and lovage will take some cooking and still retain their flavour, but with chives, chervil, sorrel, fennel and coriander, the rule is 'less is more'. Add them just before taking the pan off the heat.

Spring salsa verde

A herb dressing that is wonderful with globe artichokes, chicken, fish, beef or lamb.

For 8–10:
1 large bunch of flat-leaf parsley
1 large bunch of mixed herbs
   (chives, fennel, chervil,
   coriander, sorrel and just one
   or two leaves of lovage or
   winter savory)
4 gherkins, rinsed
20–30 small capers, rinsed
250ml olive oil
Juice of ½ lemon
Salt and black pepper

Chop the herbs coarsely.
   Add the gherkins and capers with the olive oil and lemon juice. Blitz only briefly, or chop by hand, so that you have a coarse-textured sauce. Season to taste.

Green mayonnaise

I love green herb mayonnaise, particularly in spring, when the first chives and sorrel give a sharpness to the taste. It is lovely to eat with salmon, prawns and boiled potatoes or cold chicken and ham.
   There are a few things worth knowing about mayonnaise: the ingredients must be at the same temperature, so take your eggs out of the fridge a couple of hours before you start. To thin any mayonnaise, whisk in a little boiling water. Mayonnaise can be very successfully made in a food processor, but you will need to make a bigger quantity than that made by this recipe (at least 4 eggs).

For 8–10:
1 good handful of mixed green
   herbs (half parsley, with the
   other half made up from one
   or all of chives, fennel, chervil
   and sorrel)
1 egg yolk (use an egg that is
   at least 2 days old)
1 whole egg
2 tablespoons lemon juice
1 garlic clove
275ml sunflower oil (or 100ml olive
   oil and 175ml sunflower oil)
Salt and black pepper

Finely chop your herbs by hand or in a food processor. Add the egg yolk, whole egg, lemon juice and garlic, and whisk for a few seconds. While beating with a whisk, or with the motor running, add the oil in a slow stream and the mayonnaise will thicken. Season well.
   If your mayonnaise curdles, you can rescue it by putting another beaten egg yolk into a jug or bowl and, while whisking continuously, pouring the rogue mayonnaise into this in a thin stream.
   Mayonnaise will keep in the fridge for at least 5 days, stored in an airtight container.

Herb dumplings

Dumplings – not too big – can be the making of a stew. If they're flavoured with herbs, so much the better. Parsley, chives and lovage all make delicious flavoured dumplings.

For 12 small dumplings:
100g self-raising flour
60g suet
About 20g fresh herbs
Salt and black pepper

Sift the flour into a mixing bowl and add the suet and the chopped herbs. Season with salt and pepper. Add just enough water to make a lumpy, doughy mixture (about 3–4 tablespoons).
   Flour your hands and shape the mixture into small balls. Add these to a casserole for the last 20 minutes of the cooking time. Make sure they sit on top of the stew and are not submerged.
   Continue to cook your casserole, covered. About 10 minutes before the end, if cooking in the oven, remove the lid and allow the dumplings to brown a little on top. If cooking on the hob, take the lid off and place the casserole in a hot oven (200°C/gas mark 6) for the final 10 minutes.

Spring herb and wild greens pasta

This Provençal pasta dish is never quite the same each time you make it, as it depends on what you can find growing at the time. Young dandelions, purslane and any other wild salad greens are good additions. In spring, when the young shoots are tender, a discreet amount of winter savory is also good, but basil, cultivated marjoram flower buds and leaves, lemon balm, rocket, hyssop, parsley, sorrel, celery leaves and spring onions are all possible candidates.

For 4:
Pinch of salt
60g mixed fresh herbs and salad greens, plus a small handful of herbs to finish
250g pasta flour, plus more for dusting
2 eggs plus 1 egg yolk, beaten
1 tablespoon olive oil
Extra virgin olive oil or unsalted butter, to serve
Parmesan cheese, to serve

Pound together the salt, herbs and greens, either using a pestle and mortar or in a food processor, to form a paste.

Put 250g of the flour into a mixing bowl and make a well in the centre. Pour the herb mixture and the eggs into the well and stir with a fork, moving outwards to bring in the flour gradually and adding, if necessary, a splash of warm water or more flour to form a soft but sticky dough.

Thickly flour a work surface and turn the dough on to it. Knead repeatedly and turn it in the flour. Push with the heel of your hand to stretch it, fold it, turn it in the flour and repeat. The greens will release their liquid and absorb more flour.

When the dough feels silky and no longer sticky, form it into a ball, cover it with a tea towel and leave it to rest for 1 hour.

Scrape the work surface clean, flour it again and roll out the dough as thin as you can. Cut it into strips about 4cm wide and cut the strips across into squares.

Bring a large saucepan filled with salted water to the boil. Add the oil. Toss the squares loosely in your hands (or in a sieve) to rid them of excess flour and drop them in the boiling water. When the water returns to the boil, adjust the heat to maintain a gentle boil and cook, stirring regularly, until tender, for about 12–15 minutes.

Drain and serve in warmed soup plates. Sprinkle over extra virgin olive oil or unsalted butter, the remaining herbs and plenty of grated Parmesan.

Chervil butter

With mixed leaves, anchovy and capers, this is more than just a herb butter. It is wonderful with fresh tuna, lamb or pork chops.

For 6–8:
15g chervil
15g baby spinach
15g watercress
150g unsalted butter
1 teaspoon capers
1 garlic clove
1 anchovy fillet
2 teaspoons lemon juice
Salt and black pepper

Blanch the herbs by dropping them into boiling water for 30 seconds and then refresh them in very cold water. Dry them on kitchen paper or twist them gently in a clean tea towel.

Put the herbs, butter, capers, garlic, anchovy and lemon juice into a food processor, and blend until smooth. Season and put the mixture on a sheet of cling film. Roll up into a tube shape and then roll in the film. Put in the fridge or freezer until firm and then wrap in another layer of film or greaseproof paper.

With a knife dipped into boiling water, cut slices from the roll when you need them for meat or fish.

Smoked salmon pâté with chervil

A light and delicious pâté, which is excellent on white or brown bread. I particularly love chervil with salmon, but later in the year I make this with chives or dill. All three are delicious.

For 8:
- 170g smoked salmon (you can use trimmings)
- 510g cream cheese
- 300ml double cream
- 60g unsalted butter, softened
- Lemon juice to taste, plus slivers of lemon to serve
- 1 teaspoon cayenne pepper
- 2 tablespoons chopped fresh chervil, chives or dill
- Black pepper
- Warm toast, to serve

Put the salmon, cream cheese and double cream into a blender. Whiz briefly.

Add the butter, lemon juice, cayenne pepper, herbs and black pepper. Whiz until the mixture forms a paste consistency. Check the seasoning and adjust if necessary.

Pack into a pâté dish and put in the fridge for an hour or two to set.

Serve with warm toast and a sliver of lemon.

Hummus with coriander

I love hummus anyway, but with the extra brightness of coriander this is one of my favourite lunches. Eat it with flat bread (see page 46) or chunks of cucumber, radish, cauliflower, bulb fennel, carrots and celery for a healthy and delicious meal.

For 6:
- 125g chickpeas
- 1 head of garlic
- 1 tablespoon tahini
- 200g Greek yoghurt
- Handful of fresh coriander, chopped
- Salt and black pepper

Soak the chickpeas overnight.

Preheat the oven to 180°C/gas mark 4. Drain the chickpeas and pour over more water to cover generously, bring to the boil, cover and cook for about 30 minutes, until tender but still intact.

Meanwhile, roast the head of garlic in the oven for about 20 minutes, until the cloves feel very soft.

Drain the chickpeas, reserving a little of the liquid and allow to cool for 5–10 minutes before putting into a food processor with the tahini, Greek yoghurt, chopped coriander and salt and pepper to taste.

Crush the roasted garlic cloves to release the sweet soft garlic pulp and add as much or as little as you like to the hummus.

Pork fillet with coriander

A pork dish with a bright and sparky flavour. It's very quick to make and an ideal mid-week supper. Eat it with rice or, even better, Spinach with split peas or lentils (see page 78).

For 2:
- 350g pork fillet
- 1 onion
- 30g butter
- 1 tablespoon olive oil
- 2 teaspoons coriander seeds, crushed
- 100g chestnut mushrooms, halved
- 1 large garlic clove, crushed and chopped
- 70ml ginger wine
- 1 heaped teaspoon soft brown sugar
- 1 tablespoon lemon juice
- 200ml crème fraîche
- Salt and black pepper
- 20g fresh coriander, chopped

Trim the tenderloin and slice it across into slices 2–3cm thick.

Slice the onion and sauté in the butter and oil with the crushed coriander seeds for a few minutes until translucent. Lift out with a slotted spoon, put to one side and keep warm.

Sauté the mushrooms in the same pan for 2–3 minutes with the garlic and add them to the onions.

If necessary, heat a little more oil in the pan and add the pork. Turn it in the butter and oil for 3–4 minutes and return the vegetables to the pan.

Add the ginger wine, brown sugar and lemon juice, and allow it all to bubble for about 5–6 minutes, until the ginger wine begins to go syrupy.

Add the crème fraîche, season with salt and pepper and finally stir in the chopped coriander.

Alastair Little's stuffed chicken with coriander pesto

This is excellent for a spring or summer lunch, eaten outside or, even better, for a picnic. You can make it the day before, and the taste will intensify as the chicken sits in the coriander juices. It slices brilliantly for putting between hunks of bread or eating with new potatoes and green salad.

For 6:

**1.5kg boned chicken, plus
    2 large chicken breasts,
    ideally free-range
4 thin slices of pancetta
Large bunch of tarragon
Sprig of lemon thyme
2 garlic cloves
1 glass of dry white wine
1 tablespoon olive oil
Salt and black pepper
Coriander and flat-leaf parsley
    leaves, to serve
Lemon wedges, to serve**

For the coriander pesto:

**2 large bunches of coriander
    leaves
Large bunch of flat-leaf parsley
2 large garlic cloves
12 chive stalks
150g Parmesan cheese
85g pine nuts
Salt and black pepper
300ml extra virgin olive oil, plus
    more for drizzling**

First, make the pesto. Take the stalks off the coriander and the parsley. Peel and chop the garlic. Cut up the chives thinly. Grate the Parmesan by hand or with the grating disc of a food processor. Add the garlic and pine nuts to the Parmesan, and process to incorporate. Add the coriander, chives and parsley, and process until combined. Season carefully with salt and black pepper. Add the olive oil to the mixture in the processor by adding it in a thin stream while the motor is running.

Preheat the oven to 200°C/gas mark 6. Spread half of the pesto on the inside of the flattened carcass of the boned bird. Wrap the chicken breasts in 2 of the pancetta slices and place these centrally on the pesto. Spread the remaining pesto on top of them and wrap the boned bird around these to make a neat joint.

I've eaten this with my friend Caroline Owen-Lloyd. She sews it up at this stage, using a darning needle and string – separated into strands so that you can thread it. This keeps most of the stuffing in.

Put the herbs and unpeeled garlic in a suitable ovenproof dish (or loaf tin) into which the chicken joint will fit snugly and pour in the wine.

Brush the breasts of the bird with the olive oil and season with salt and pepper. Put the remaining pancetta slices on top and cover loosely with foil.

Roast for 1½ hours, removing the foil and basting after 1 hour. Baste again 20 minutes later.

Remove from the tin, place on a board and wrap in tin foil to rest for 10 minutes, then cut across into slices about 2.5cm thick.

Drizzle with a little extra virgin olive oil and scatter over fresh coriander and flat-leaf parsley. Serve with wedges of lemon.

Lettuce and lovage soup

The flavour of lovage is at its best when it's young and fresh, as it is when it first appears – as a perennial herb – in early spring. With this soup, the smokiness of the lovage offsets the mildness of the cooked lettuce. It's delicious.

For 6:

**6 Little Gem or other small
    lettuces
Handful of young lovage leaves
30g butter
4 spring onions, chopped
2 tablespoons plain flour
475ml milk
475ml good vegetable stock
Freshly grated nutmeg
Salt and black pepper
Cream or Greek yoghurt, to serve**

Pull the lettuce apart and steam with the lovage until just tender. Allow to cool for 5 minutes and then liquidise.

Melt the butter in a saucepan and sweat the onions without allowing them to brown. Stir in the flour and allow it to cook but not brown. Add the milk and stock bit by bit, whisking all the time. Simmer for a couple of minutes and then add the lettuce mixture. Season well with nutmeg, salt and pepper.

Eat this hot or cold with a dollop of cream or Greek yoghurt.

Hungarian goulash with lovage

I had this dish at the twenty-first birthday party of my friend Caroline Frapwell, and still remember it! It is excellent party food, and the flavour improves if you cook it the day before. If there are no dumplings, serve with rice and steamed broccoli.

For 6–8:
  1 large onion, chopped
  2 tablespoons sunflower oil
  1 red pepper, cut into strips
  350g button mushrooms, whole
    or halved
  1 garlic clove, chopped
  600g pork fillet
  Plain flour
  Salt and black pepper
  ½ teaspoon cayenne pepper
  2 teaspoons paprika
  1 bay leaf
  4 tablespoons finely chopped
    lovage
  400ml good vegetable stock
  400ml tin of chopped tomatoes
  3 tablespoons tomato purée
  250ml crème fraîche
  Large bunch of flat-leaf parsley,
    finely chopped
  1 teaspoon white sugar

Fry the onion in a little sunflower oil in a casserole dish until soft. Add the red pepper and mushrooms, and cook for 5 minutes. Then add the garlic and set aside off the heat.

Cut the pork into strips, roll in seasoned flour and fry in a little sunflower oil to seal. Add to the casserole dish.

Add the spices, bay leaf and some of the lovage, followed by the stock, tinned tomatoes and tomato purée. Cook gently, covered, for at least 2 hours. You can add herb dumplings for the last half an hour (see page 83). Allow the goulash to cool a little and then add the crème fraîche with plenty of parsley and more lovage.

Jane's Thai chicken curry

There are a great many Thai chicken curry recipes, but I like this one from my sister Jane as it includes lots of vegetables and tastes delicious. Coriander – added in large quantities at the end – is central to its flavour.

For 6:
  4 medium-sized to large organic
    skinless chicken breasts
  About ½ thumb-size piece of
    ginger, coarsely chopped
  Stick of lemon grass, cut into 3
  500g mixed vegetables (to include,
    depending on the time of year,
    broad beans, peas, French
    beans, runner beans, spring
    onions, courgettes, Swiss
    chard, spinach, cabbage or
    cavolo nero)
  Splash or two of olive oil
  1–2 tablespoons Thai red
    or green curry paste
    (or to taste)
  400ml tin of coconut milk
  Juice of 2 limes
  Splash of soy sauce
  Splash of Thai fish sauce
  Large bunch of coriander,
    coarsely chopped

You can cook this in the oven or on the hob. If you are using the oven, preheat to 180°C/gas mark 4.

Put the chicken breasts in a saucepan – and halve them if they are really large. Just cover with water. Add the ginger and lemon grass and poach for 10 minutes. Strain, reserving the liquid. Cut the chicken breasts into walnut-sized pieces.

Cut the vegetables into chunks, not too small. Fry them gently in olive oil in a wide-based saucepan for 10 minutes, turning regularly. Add the chicken to the pan.

In another small pan, fry the curry paste for 3 minutes in a little olive oil. Add the coconut milk and lime juice to taste, and heat for 5 minutes.

Pour the sauce over the chicken and vegetables, and cook in the preheated oven or on the hob for 20 minutes.

Add a splash each of soy and fish sauce, and serve scattered with lots of coriander. Serve with rice. (The liquid you have reserved can be drunk separately, like miso, or used as stock for risotto.)

Parsley soup

A wonderfully clean-tasting, fresh
spring soup.

For 6:
- **2 leeks**
- **2 potatoes**
- **80g curly or flat-leaf parsley,
  leaves and stems**
- **1 onion, sliced**
- **25g butter**
- **800ml good stock**
- **Salt and black pepper**
- **200ml milk**
- **100ml single cream (optional)**
- **Deep-fried parsley (see page 90),
  to finish**

Rinse the leeks and slice them, making
sure that you use at least some of
the green tops. Peel and chop the
potatoes. Separate the tops from the
stems of the parsley and then chop up
the stems.

Fry the onion in the butter and,
when soft, add the potatoes, parsley
stems and sliced leeks. Cook for
about 5 minutes without allowing the
vegetables to colour.

Add the stock and cook for
about 10 minutes, until the potatoes
are tender. Allow to cool for a few
minutes. Pulse the parsley leaves
or chop them by hand (these won't
liquidise) and add to the mixture.
Liquidise and season carefully.

Return to the rinsed pan and
add the milk. Reheat, adding the
cream, if using, but without allowing
the soup to boil.

Scatter with deep-fried parsley.

Parsley sauce

This is a béchamel sauce with lots of
parsley. Parsley sauce is, of course,
traditional with fish and new potatoes,
but it's also the best thing to eat with a
clove-flavoured ham, baked potatoes
and carrots. Cook your ham in hay
– this keeps it succulent and gives it a
distinctive sweet, grassy taste. To do
this, choose a casserole that snugly
fits your ham joint. Put a little water
in the bottom and pack the hay in all
around the edges of the ham. Cover
and bake it.

For 8:
- **1 litre milk**
- **1 onion, stuck with a few cloves**
- **A few black peppercorns**
- **2 bay leaves**
- **80g butter**
- **80g flour**
- **Large bunch of curly or flat-leaf
  parsley, stems removed,
  finely chopped**
- **Plenty of salt and black pepper**

Bring the milk to the boil with the
clove-studded onion, peppercorns and
bay leaves.

In a separate pan, melt the
butter and stir in the flour, allowing it
to cook for a couple of minutes. Then
gradually add the strained hot milk.
Add the parsley, stirring continuously.
Season with salt and pepper.

Deep-fried parsley

The spring alternative to deep-fried kale, with a softer, gentler and more fragrant taste. Eat it with an aperitif, or scatter it on top of almost any soup. Curly-leaved parsley is better for this than the flat-leafed form.

For 8–10:
   200g curly-leaf parsley, stems and
      any coarse midribs removed
   Groundnut oil for deep-frying
   1 teaspoon soft brown sugar
   2 good pinches of sea salt,
      finely crumbled
   25g crushed cashew nuts or
      flaked almonds (optional)

Wash the parsley and dry thoroughly in a clean tea towel or salad spinner.

Heat some oil for deep-frying to 170ºC. Use a deep-fat fryer if you have one. If you don't have a fryer, use a saucepan, but fill it only one-third full of oil and fry in small batches to keep the temperature constant.

Drop a handful of parsley into the oil. Fry for just a few seconds, remove with a slotted spoon and drain on kitchen paper. Repeat with the rest of the parsley.

Scatter the soft brown sugar and salt over the top, adding crushed cashew nuts or flaked toasted almonds if you like.

Serve the parsley straight away. It tastes nicest when it's hot.

Warm chickpea and parsley salad

All you need is a pile of crunchy lettuce on the side of this lovely spring salad.

For 4:
   250g chickpeas
   ½ onion, stuck with a couple
      of cloves
   ½ carrot
   2 bay leaves
   Sprig of thyme
   2 tablespoons extra virgin olive oil
   Sea salt and black pepper
   Very large handful of chopped
      parsley
   1 sweet white onion, thinly sliced
   2 garlic cloves, finely chopped
   Lemon juice (optional)

Soak the chickpeas in cold water to cover overnight.

Drain and pour over fresh water, covering the chickpeas well. Add the onion, carrot, bay and thyme. Bring to the boil and cook, covered, for about 30 minutes, or until tender but still intact. Check from time to time that there is enough water, and top up if necessary. Remove the onion, carrot and herbs and drain the chickpeas.

Pour over the extra virgin olive oil while the chickpeas are still hot, season with plenty of sea salt and black pepper, and stir in the chopped parsley, sliced onion and finely chopped garlic. Add lemon juice if you want a sharper taste.

Jane Grigson's sorrel sauce with fish

The best ever sauce to eat with fish. Serve it with a whole turbot or use it to transform a common-or-garden salmon steak.

For 4–6:
  1.5kg whole fish
  250ml white wine
  1 onion, sliced
  1 garlic clove, coarsely chopped

For the sauce:
  **2 handfuls of sorrel leaves
    (French or wild)**
  250ml double cream
  Salt and black pepper

Cook your fish in the oven in the white wine, along with the onion and garlic.

Prepare your sorrel purée. Sorrel cooks very quickly, wilting down to virtually nothing in the pan and turning a cow-pat olive colour. (To keep its freshness and colour, you only want it to touch the heat.) Remove the central leaf midrib and chop it finely. Bring the cream to the boil, add the sorrel and immediately take the pan off the heat.

Add 4 tablespoons of the fish juices and season to taste.

Sorrel soup

Another spring classic. We tried many sorrel soups, and this simple recipe made the tastiest.

For 6:
  25g unsalted butter
  1 tablespoon olive oil
  3 shallots, finely chopped
  2 leeks, finely chopped
  300g potatoes, chopped
  1 litre good vegetable stock
  **250g sorrel, ribs and stems
    removed, and sliced**
  150ml double or single cream
  Salt and black pepper

Warm the butter and olive oil in a pan, and sweat the shallots and the leeks without allowing them to brown.

Add the potatoes and stir in the stock. Simmer the vegetables, covered, for about 25 minutes. Add the sorrel for the last 2 minutes.

Take off the heat and then blend in a liquidiser. Add the cream and season well.

Warm before serving, but do not allow to boil. Thin the soup with a little milk or stock, if necessary.

Potato gratin with sorrel

The flavour of sorrel is excellent with potatoes, which absorb some of its citrus taste. This is delicious with salmon or chicken.

For 4–6:
  **30g unsalted butter, plus more
    for the dish**
  1kg potatoes
  150g young sorrel leaves
  250g sweet white onions
  Salt
  175ml double cream

Preheat the oven to 180°C/gas mark 4 and butter a 2-litre gratin dish.

Peel the potatoes and slice them lengthwise as thinly as possible – a mandoline is useful for this. Remove the stem from the sorrel, roll it up tightly and cut across to make thin strips. Thinly slice the onions.

Melt a tablespoon of the butter in a sauté pan over a low heat. Add the sorrel, sprinkle with a little salt and cook for a minute, stirring with a wooden spoon, until the sorrel just begins to wilt. Add the cream and simmer for a minute. Remove from the heat.

Put the potatoes and onions in a saucepan. Add a good pinch of salt and pour over just enough water to cover them. Bring to the boil, cooking for 8–10 minutes, shaking the pan regularly to make sure they don't stick to the bottom. Take off the heat and drain. Pour a layer into the gratin dish, spread some sorrel mixture evenly over the top, and repeat.

Place in the preheated oven and bake for about an hour.

Watercress and wild garlic

Watercress makes a particularly delicious salad. It has the pepperiness of mature rocket, but not the bitter overlay. It's also very good for you, with a high concentration of vitamin C, as well as beta-carotene and vitamin A equivalents. These are important antioxidants, needed for healthy skin and eyes.

You'll find wild watercress in fast-running shallow chalk streams such as the Itchen and Bourne in Hampshire, which both have a long association with commercially grown watercress. Because of the risk of liver fluke – a gut parasite we share with sheep – it's not a good idea to eat wild watercress uncooked. If you find it, make it into soup, where the stems as well as the leaves give fantastic flavour.

Watercress doesn't like either cold or hot, preferring a temperature somewhere in between, so it flourishes in the spring and we traditionally eat most of it at Easter. It seems to have a spring detox association, at a time when we crave strong acerbic flavours.

Buy it when it's looking perky and emerald-green, and when you get it home slice off the ends of the stalks, pick the rest over, rinse it and put it in a plastic bag. Squeeze out the air and then store it in the salad drawer at the bottom of the fridge for up to a couple of days.

Like watercress, wild garlic is good for you. It's particularly effective in reducing high blood pressure and blood cholesterol levels. Where I live in Sussex, walk into a damp part of almost any wood in late spring, and you're greeted by an amazing carpet of wild garlic. It flowers at the same time as bluebells, which colonise the dryer ground. The smell is particularly strong when the flowers go over and the plants run to seed.

You can dig up and eat the bulbs, but they can give you a stomach upset, so you're better off sticking to the flowers, seed heads and leaves. Scatter the flowers over salads and soups. Break up the fresh green seed pods and do the same. Just a few leaves – picked when young and quite finely chopped – will give an extra punch. Use the leaves and flowers as a base for pesto to eat with starchy potatoes or pasta (see page 95). The leaves are best blanched first.

Watercress soup

A peppery, fresh and delicious soup.

For 4:
  1 tablespoon sunflower oil
  20g butter
  1 onion, chopped
  1 large potato, peeled
  400g watercress, plus a few
    sprigs for decoration
  350ml vegetable or chicken stock
  Salt and black pepper
  300ml milk
  Lemon juice
  Dollop of cream

Heat the oil and butter and sweat the onion in this gently until translucent. Add the potato and cook for 3 or 4 minutes, without allowing it to brown. Take the leaves from the stalks of the watercress and then chop up the stalks roughly.

Add these to the pan and then add the stock. Season, cover the pan and simmer gently until the potatoes are tender.

Chop the watercress leaves coarsely and add them to the saucepan. Pull off the heat and allow to cool a little before transferring to a food processor to blend.

Return the soup to the rinsed pan and add enough milk to give a creamy consistency. Bring to simmering point.

Remove from the heat, add a little lemon juice to taste and season. Serve with a dollop of cream and sprigs of watercress.

Fried watercress

A tasty base on which to put baked fish, fish cakes and grilled chicken. The leaves are just wilted, but the stalks retain their crunch and tasty hot flavour.

For 4 as a base, 2 as a side dish:
  100g watercress
  1 teaspoon hazelnut
    (or other nut oil)
  2 garlic cloves, crushed
    and chopped
  Sea salt

Wash the watercress thoroughly and dry in a salad spinner.

Heat the nut oil in a non-stick frying pan, add the garlic and cook for a few seconds.

Throw in the watercress and turn in the oil and garlic for not more than a few seconds.

Remove from the heat and toss with plenty of sea salt.

Watercress hollandaise

This delicious peppery sauce is fantastic with any fish or chicken.

For 6–8:
  3 tablespoons white wine vinegar
  6 black peppercorns
  1 bay leaf
  3 egg yolks
  175g unsalted butter, cut into
    small chunks
  Salt and black pepper
  2 bunches of watercress
  1 tablespoon vegetable stock or
    white wine

Boil the vinegar with 1 tablespoon of water and the peppercorns and bay leaf, until it is reduced to 1 tablespoon, and allow to cool.

Half-fill a wide shallow pan with water and bring to simmering point. Put the yolks in a heatproof bowl, sit this in the pan of water and whisk well. Add the butter bit by bit, whisking all the time. Gradually as it warms, the mixture will become thick and shiny. Remove from the heat and stir in the cooled reduced vinegar and salt and pepper (see page 233 for more hollandaise tips).

Take the leaves from the watercress and liquidise them with a tablespoon of stock or white wine in a food processor (or use a wand blender if you are making a small quantity).

Stir this into the warm hollandaise.

Watercress and smoked trout salad with horseradish

You can throw this simple spring salad together quickly. The watercress and horseradish are ideal with the rich, oily fish.

For 4:
  4 leeks
  Bunch of chives, chopped
  200g watercress
  4 smoked trout fillets (or hot-smoked salmon)

For the dressing:
  2 tablespoons freshly grated horseradish
  1 tablespoon Dijon mustard
  2 tablespoons white wine vinegar
  120ml groundnut oil
  Salt and black pepper

Cut the leeks into quarters lengthways, wash and boil or steam for 8–10 minutes. Drain well.

Make a dressing by mixing together the grated horseradish, mustard, vinegar and 1 tablespoon of water, then add the groundnut oil. Season well.

Add the dressing to the leeks and leave for a few minutes. Add the chopped chives.

Lift the leeks out of the dressing and put them into a large shallow dish, toss the watercress in the dressing and add to the dish. Finish with the smoked trout.

Wild garlic pesto

I make lots of this in the spring, using it as pasta sauce and to stuff baked potatoes (see page 339). It freezes well for use right through the year, but if freezing leave out the cultivated bulb garlic.

For a large jar:
  2 handfuls (about 100g) of wild garlic leaves with flowers
  200ml extra virgin olive oil, plus a bit more for sealing
  50g pine nuts or walnuts
  2 garlic cloves
  50g Parmesan cheese, grated
  Salt and black pepper

Blanch the wild garlic leaves in boiling water for about 10 seconds. Refresh in cold water and pat dry on kitchen paper.

Put the wild garlic, olive oil, pine nuts or walnuts, together with the garlic cloves, into a food processor and blend to a purée. Transfer to a bowl and mix in the grated Parmesan. Season carefully and put into a sterilised jar.

Pour over a little extra olive oil to seal and cover tightly.

Wild garlic soup

A traditional spring soup from the south of France, which deserves to be more of a staple here in Britain, where wild garlic thrives.

For 4:
  About 50 wild garlic leaves, plus a few flowers, to serve
  500ml milk
  25g butter
  2 shallots, finely chopped
  ½ red chilli, finely chopped
  100g potatoes, peeled and chopped
  4–6 garlic cloves, chopped
  200ml single cream
  Salt and black pepper

Blanch the wild garlic leaves for a few seconds in boiling water. Refresh in cold water, drain and dry.

Bring the milk to boiling point, take off the heat and add the wild garlic leaves. Leave to infuse until cold.

Heat the butter and sweat the shallots and chilli without allowing them to colour. Add the potatoes and the garlic cloves, and turn in the butter. Add the milk mixture and cook until the potatoes are tender.

Purée in a food processor and return to the pan. Add the cream and season with salt and pepper. Reheat without boiling.

Serve the soup with chopped garlic flowers.

May | June

Asparagus

I've never met anyone who doesn't relish asparagus. Freshly picked, it's the caviar of the productive plant world, with a powerful and unique taste. There is endless debate as to how you should cook it. Some say just lay it flat in a pan; others swear by cooking the stems upright in a tall, narrow steamer, with the boiling water coming up to about a third of their height. Cooked in either of these ways, asparagus is perfect after 7 or 8 minutes. Then there are those who say you get the best flavour if you toss it in olive oil, sprinkle it with salt and pepper, and roast it for 15–20 minutes, and even a few who vote for cooking it on the griddle or barbecue, scattering over pecorino or Parmesan as you eat. I don't think it makes much difference. If you've got very fresh asparagus, it's magnificent however you cook it.

It's the 'fresh as a daisy' factor, picking it that day or at a pinch the day before, that really makes the difference. After a day, both the texture and taste deteriorate. The newly emerged stems are full of sugars, which gradually convert to starch after picking, and the flavour will acquire a slightly bitter undertone.

If you live in an asparagus area, such as Evesham or Norfolk, you can get hold of just-picked bundles from beside the road. If you don't, and you have the space, this is one of the most life-enhancing plants to grow. It may only crop for six to eight weeks, but over that time, you will have several truly delicious meals a week.

All asparagus needs is some salt and, perhaps, lemon butter or hollandaise. Last spring I had a supper with Hugh Fearnley-Whittingstall of a few spears of asparagus served with a soft-boiled egg, instead of bread soldiers. That was as good as it gets.

Asparagus is a perennial and with a bit of planning you can put in a few plants of several forms, all cropping at slightly different times. 'Connover's Colossal' is the earliest to produce and the most popular choice in Britain. Next in line are 'Franklim', and 'Gijnlim', a new Dutch variety, both mid-season May croppers, which produce lots of spears once they have settled in, with famously good flavour. I also have 'Dariana', a highly recommended French mid-season form that crops in May. My last is an American variety, 'Martha Washington', which produces lots of long spears into early June.

The unblanched green spears have a stronger yet sweeter flavour than the white so popular in Italy and France. The latter is achieved by earthing up the spears, so that they grow in the dark. This makes for a more tender spear and a subtler flavour, making them ideal for canning. I'd rather eat them strong and fresh.

Asparagus with almonds

This is simple and delicious, the perfect May first course.

For 4:

1kg English asparagus
About 100g butter
Grated zest of 1 lemon and juice
 of ½ lemon
Plenty of toasted slivered almonds
Flaky salt

Break off the bottom tough or bendy ends of the asparagus. Cook your asparagus in loose bundles, standing the stems upright in the pan, or steaming them lying on their side.

Meanwhile, melt the butter. Once it is melted, add the lemon juice.

Remove the asparagus from the pan as soon as the thickest bit of the stalk is only just cooked and still has a bite to it. Drain and lay the spears out on a warm flattish dish. Pour over the lemon and butter mix, and scatter over the lemon zest, almonds and salt.

Asparagus omelette

We eat this all the time in late spring. It's the perfect mid-week supper, and lovely eaten with slices of brown toast or some small minty new potatoes.

For 2:

250g asparagus
3 tablespoons olive oil
4 eggs
1 tablespoon cold unsalted butter,
 cut in small pieces or grated
Salt and black pepper

Break off the bottom tough or bendy ends of the asparagus. If the stems are quite chunky, pare off a thin layer of stalk at the stem end with a potato peeler. Cut the spear end at an angle into 2 or 3 slices and the stalks into smaller slices, as they take longer to cook. Drop these into a pan of boiling water for 1 minute. Drain and dry.

Heat some oil in a pan and sauté the asparagus for half a minute or so, then remove from the pan.

Break the eggs into a bowl, add the butter, salt and pepper and beat with a fork. Add the asparagus. Season well.

In an omelette pan set over a good heat, swirl the oil around until it's practically smoking, and pour in the egg mixture, shaking the pan to distribute it. As soon as you see it beginning to cook, lift the edge of the omelette, allowing more of the uncooked egg to reach the hot base of the pan. When it begins to set, roll the omelette over and over itself into a loose tube shape and tip it on to a warm serving plate.

Asparagus pasta with lemon

Simple lemon pasta is always delicious, and with the addition of asparagus it's magnificent.

For 4:

240g asparagus
350g penne or egg tagliatelle
Salt and black pepper
50g unsalted butter
100ml double cream
Grated zest and juice of 1 lemon
2 tablespoons extra virgin olive oil
1 tablespoon finely chopped flat-
 leaf parsley, to serve
Grated Parmesan cheese, to serve

Snap off the bottom tough or bendy ends of the asparagus. If the stems are quite chunky, pare off a thin layer of stalk at the stem end with a potato peeler. Cut the stalks at an angle, leaving the tips whole. Steam or boil the asparagus for 7–8 minutes, until tender but still crisp. Rinse in cold water and drain.

Cook the pasta in salted boiling water until al dente.

While you're cooking the pasta, warm the butter and cream in a pan over a gentle heat and simmer for a couple of minutes. Add the cooked asparagus and the lemon juice and zest. Take off the heat and leave for 5 minutes for the flavours to blend.

When the pasta is cooked, drain all but a tablespoon of the cooking liquid, add the olive oil and combine with the asparagus and lemon sauce.

Stir, season and serve with plenty of chopped flat-leaf parsley scattered on top and a bowl of grated Parmesan.

Primavera risotto

A Venetian classic which always looks as good as it tastes, with the first, tender mini beans, asparagus and mangetouts of the season.

For 4–5:
About 450g selection of new vegetables, such as asparagus, broad beans, peas, mangetouts
About 1.5 litres good vegetable or chicken stock
100g unsalted butter
1 large onion, chopped
500g Arborio or Carnaroli rice
2 glasses of white wine
130g grated Parmesan cheese, plus more to serve

Blanch the vegetables for 2 minutes in a large pan of boiling vegetable or chicken stock. To stop them cooking, plunge them into cold water and put to one side. Reserve the stock and keep it warm.

Melt half the butter in a heavy-based pan and fry the onion, without allowing it to colour, for about 5–6 minutes. Add the rice and stir to coat it with the butter. Add the wine, letting it bubble up and evaporate.

Gradually add the hot stock, a ladleful at a time, stirring continuously. Allow each ladleful of stock to be absorbed before adding the next. The rice will reach the al dente stage after about 18 minutes. If you like your risotto softer, cook for another 5 minutes.

Take off the heat and beat in the remaining butter. Add the blanched vegetables and the Parmesan, and heat through.

Check the seasoning and serve immediately with an extra bowl of Parmesan.

Salad of asparagus, broad beans, rocket and peas

A wonderful fresh, delicate salad using young spring veg. When they're small and very fresh, asparagus spears are delicious just briefly blanched.

For 4:
Bunch of new asparagus
Handful of peas
Handful of small broad beans
Bunch of rocket (or milder spinach)
Salt
2 tablespoons extra virgin olive oil
A little chopped flat-leaf parsley
Few curls of pecorino cheese
Balsamic vinegar

Break off the tips of the asparagus and blanch for 2 minutes. Remove any coarse bits from the asparagus stalks with a potato peeler and slice thinly at an angle. Blanch these too.

Pod the peas and blanch for 2 minutes. Do the same with the broad beans and, if they're larger than a thumbnail, remove their skins, revealing the bright green beans inside.

Dress the rocket with salt and olive oil and put to one side.

Lightly dress the beans, peas and asparagus with olive oil and salt, and pile on a plate.

Put the rocket on the top and toss a little, adding the parsley, curls of pecorino and a drizzle of the balsamic vinegar.

Broad beans

I think broad beans want eating at about the size of a thumbnail, but they're often twice that size when you buy them – leathery-skinned and starchy. So it's really worthwhile growing your own, as you can then eat them at every stage. In Italy and France, you'll be served the pods cooked whole, when they are only a few centimetres long. In Italy, you'll eat the beans raw, when they're small, with pecorino cheese. The saltiness of the cheese is perfect with the young beans, washed down with plenty of red wine.

When the beans themselves have reached the size of a ten-pence piece, they're better cooked, and bigger than that, they're best cooked *and* skinned. Pop out the bright green beans from their skins by pinching between your thumb and forefinger. Put them into a bowl and dress them (while still warm) with lemon juice and a good fruity olive oil. They're also delicious at this mature stage when puréed with a little olive oil, garlic and herbs (see page 109) and piled on crostini.

Broad bean tips – the top section of the young plant – are also quite tasty. You need to pinch out the tips anyway to prevent black fly infestation, but as long as they're not already plastered with flies, don't chuck them – eat them! Chop them up small and wilt them into a Primavera risotto (see page 102), or make a pasta with the beans and their tips, mixed with pancetta, crème fraîche and some grated Parmesan cheese.

If you have a glut of beans, freeze them while still small. Blanch them in boiling water for 2 minutes. Drain and plunge them into ice-cold water and freeze.

The best all-round, early-autumn- or late-winter-sown broad bean is 'Super Aquadulce Claudia', and if you're going for only one variety, it should probably be this. It has good flavour, is highly prolific and is hardy. I also love 'Stereo', a variety for spring sowing. This produces large numbers of petite pods containing small tender green-white beans. It's my favourite variety as far as flavour goes. 'The Sutton' is another worthwhile small variety which only reaches 45cm and yet produces a good crop of beans. It's ideal for little, exposed gardens. 'Red Epicure' is an unusual form, producing lovely rich crimson beans with good flavour. The colour fades on cooking, so eat them small and raw. I usually grow this for its colour, but it's not a heavy cropper.

It's worth knowing that 1kg broad beans in their pods give about 300g shelled beans.

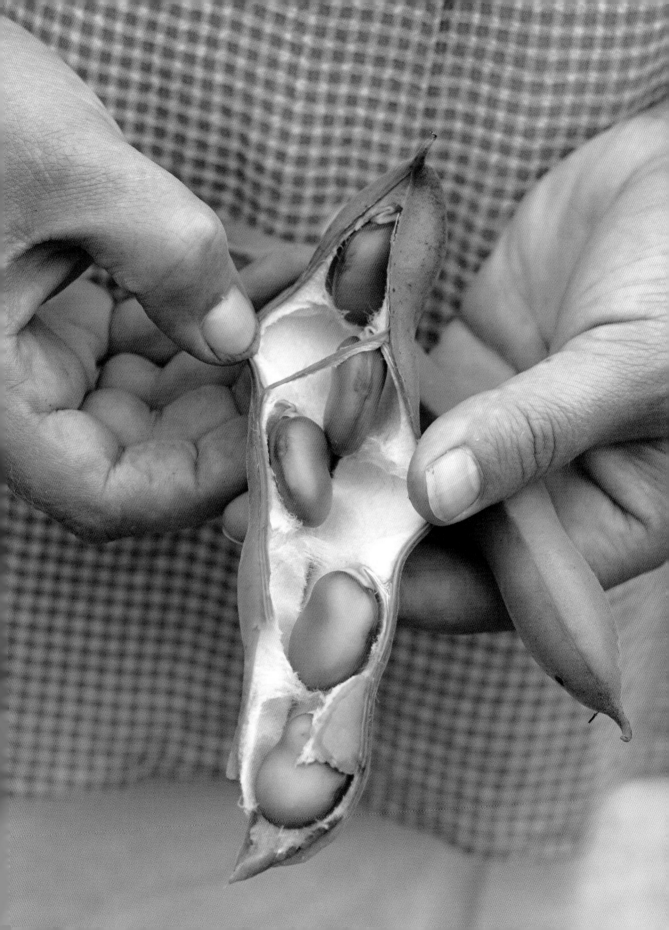

Broad beans with olive tapenade

Here is a quick and delicious way of cooking beans if you've had a surfeit. This dish has a strong taste that's good with roast chicken or Quick tomato tart (see page 279), or even just warm crusty bread. It keeps well for a day or two in the fridge.

For 6:
    400g broad beans, shelled weight

For the olive tapenade:
    1 tablespoon good olive oil
    Handful of flat-leaf parsley,
        chopped
    1 garlic clove
    Handful of mint, chopped
    1 tin of anchovies in oil, drained
    3 tablespoons pitted black olives
    1 tablespoon capers
    Juice and grated zest of 1 lemon

Cook the broad beans for 5–8 minutes, depending on size, until they're just tender. Immediately cool them under cold running water for a few seconds to stop them cooking and drain again.

To make the tapenade, put all the ingredients into a food processor and whiz for 30 seconds, no more, so that the herbs don't turn to mush.

Pour this over the cooked beans when they're still warm.

Spring vegetable soup

This is a lovely fresh light soup which – with all the baby veg – looks as good as it tastes.

For 6–8:
    150g spring onions
    300g new potatoes
    2 tablespoons olive oil
    3 or 4 baby artichokes, halved
        with the chokes removed and
        thinly sliced
    250g Swiss chard or spinach,
        thinly sliced
    Good bunch of chervil or parsley
    1 garlic clove, crushed and
        chopped
    2 litres good vegetable stock
    Salt and black pepper
    300g broad beans, shelled weight
    Plenty of grated Parmesan cheese
    Crusty bread, to serve

Thinly slice the spring onions. Peel the new potatoes and chop them into small chunks. Heat the oil and gently sauté the spring onions. Add the artichoke heart slices, potatoes, chard, herbs and garlic, and cook for a further few minutes.

Add the stock and a little salt and bring to the boil. Simmer covered for about 15–20 minutes.

Add the broad beans and cook for about 5 minutes, until they are tender but still intact.

Serve with plenty of grated Parmesan and crusty bread.

Warm broad bean salad

A very simple salad of broad beans with a handful of herbs.

For 6:
    400g broad beans, shelled weight
    1 tablespoon chopped mint
    2 tablespoons chopped chervil
    ½ teaspoon chopped tarragon
    2 spring onions, finely chopped
    2 tablespoons tarragon or white
        wine vinegar
    100ml extra virgin olive oil
    Salt and black pepper
    1 tablespoon chopped parsley,
        to serve

Bring a pan of water to the boil and cook the broad beans for about 5 minutes, depending on their size, until tender. Drain and immediately cool them under cold running water for a few seconds to stop them cooking. If the beans are large, skin them (see page 104); but, if they're tiny, don't bother.

Make a dressing by adding all the herbs except the parsley to the spring onions and vinegar in a bowl and whisking in all but 1 tablespoon of the olive oil.

Heat the remaining olive oil and toss in the cooked beans just to warm them through before tipping into a serving bowl.

Toss the beans in the dressing. Season and serve with the parsley.

Tagliolini with broad beans and beurre blanc

This recipe is at its very best when the beans are still tender and small.

For 4:

 250g broad beans, shelled weight
 350g tagliolini or fine spaghetti
 75g fried pancetta or prosciutto
 2 tablespoons finely chopped
  summer savory or thyme,
  to serve
 Grated Parmesan cheese, to serve

For the beurre blanc:

 4 tablespoons white wine
 4 tablespoons white wine vinegar
 1 heaped tablespoon finely
  chopped shallots
 Salt and black pepper
 175g unsalted butter,
  cold and diced

To make the beurre blanc, reduce the wine, vinegar, shallots, salt and pepper in a small saucepan until you have only a tablespoon of liquid left. Whisk in the cold butter bit by bit over a very low heat or using a bain-marie, until thick and creamy. Season. Keep it warm in a vacuum flask or bain-marie.

Bring a pan of water to the boil. Cook the beans in the water for 4 minutes. Remove them, reserving some of the cooking liquid, and cool them quickly in a sieve under cold running water.

Pop some of the bright green beans out of their skin by pinching them with your thumb and forefinger; this adds a wonderful colour. Discard the skins and purée half the beans with a tablespoon of the cooking water.

Cook the pasta in salted boiling water until just al dente, leaving a tablespoon or two of the cooking liquid in the pan. Add the bean purée, pancetta or prosciutto and the beurre blanc, and stir. Season carefully.

Lastly throw in the remaining beans and stir. Serve with summer savory or thyme and grated Parmesan.

Young broad beans in cream

Soft, comforting and delicious, this is one of my favourite ways of eating broad beans. It's good with chicken and new potatoes, and makes a delicious sauce for fettuccine.

For 8 as a side dish:

 600g small broad beans,
  shelled weight
 30g butter
 ½ tablespoon plain flour
 250ml double cream or crème
  fraîche
 Salt and black pepper
 1 garlic clove, finely chopped
 Good bunch of fresh summer
  savory
 6 slices of smoked bacon or thinly
  sliced pancetta
 Small bunch of parsley, chopped

Use young small beans if you can. Cook them for 5 minutes and, if they are large, skin them as described on page 104.

Melt the butter in a shallow pan and add a little flour. Then pour in the cream and add salt, the garlic and savory. Bring to the boil and put aside to steep for 10 minutes.

Fry or roast the bacon or pancetta until crisp and break into small pieces.

Add the beans to the flavoured cream and then boil, uncovered, for 5 minutes. Remove the savory. Add more salt and pepper to taste, and scatter with the broken-up bacon or pancetta and chopped parsley.

Broad bean crostini

Once broad beans get big and leathery, or they've been in the freezer for more than two or three months, don't eat them on their own. Turn them into a sort of lemony hummus, delicious dolloped on crostini, or dipped into with pieces of toasted pitta bread, with fresh shredded mint scattered over the top.

For 6–8:

 150g broad beans, shelled weight
 3 tablespoons extra virgin olive oil
 Juice and grated zest of 1 lemon
 Handful of finely chopped mint,
  plus more for finishing
 Salt and black pepper
 A few slivers of pecorino cheese

For the crostini:

 Fresh good-quality white bread
  (a baguette works well)
 Extra virgin olive oil
 2 garlic cloves, peeled and
  cut in half
 Salt

To make the crostini, cut the bread into finger-thick slices and drizzle the olive oil over them, then toast them on a medium-hot barbecue, grill or griddle pan until brown and crisp. Lightly scrape one side with the cut side of the garlic and sprinkle with salt.

Boil the broad beans for 5 minutes or so until they're tender. If you have time, squeeze them out of their skins. Purée them with most of the olive oil, the lemon juice and zest, mint and plenty of salt and black pepper. Without skins, the beans make a smoother purée.

Spread the crostini with the topping and sprinkle with olive oil, slivers of salty pecorino and a scattering of mint.

Crunchy lettuces

A crunchy, sweetish lettuce is essential for a good summer salad. Soft-textured, strong-flavoured leaves – rocket, mustard and watercress – are fine in the winter and spring, but once it starts getting hot, you want leaves that you can break in half.

There are plenty of salads with crunchy lettuce at their heart. I love a Caesar salad with grilled chicken (see page 112) and Salad niçoise (see page 210), but perhaps best of all is the perfect green salad. For this, it's worth remembering several things. First, buy or grow a good lettuce. It's hard to beat 'Cos', 'Romaine' or 'Little Gem', all of which are widely available. Steer well clear of any commercially grown 'Iceberg', which have zero (or worse, a chemical) flavour.

In the trials here at Perch Hill, there are four front runners in the crunchy lettuce brigade. The American variety 'Black Seeded Simpson' came top this year, with a lovely sweet taste, huge hearts the size of a Savoy cabbage – it needs to be spaced 45cm apart – and every leaf having that all-important crunch. 'Reine de Glace' is another front runner, as good cooked as raw. It's lovely in a salad and its crunchy stem also stands up well to cooking, with a hint of bitterness to its flavour. You can also never go wrong with 'Cos Lobjoits' and 'Little Gem'.

All lettuces benefit from being broken up and submerged in a sink of cold water for a couple of hours. This perks up any floppy leaves. Then it's important to dry them well. Add good-quality olive oil to lemon juice or red wine vinegar, stir and pour over the leaves at the last minute. As an alternative to an oil-and-vinegar dressing, try coating lettuce hearts in garlic-flavoured butter or oil, still hot from the pan (see page 112).

You can do more with crunchy lettuce than just make a salad. Use it as you would Belgian chicory in the winter, as a scoop for Hummus with coriander (see page 85) or spicy pork mince. It's also good with lovage in soup (see page 87) and as a vegetable. I love it sautéed with bacon and peas, or with the stems still crunchy but the leaves wilted in a lamb fricassée (see page 115).

Caesar salad

The combination of lettuce, anchovies and Parmesan is quite delicious. Serve it with grilled chicken breast or slices of smoked chicken.

For 6:

**450ml homemade mayonnaise
(see page 124)
2 garlic cloves
20 anchovy fillets
Sunflower or groundnut oil,
for deep-frying
3 slices of white or brown bread,
cut into large cubes
Salt and black pepper
2 tablespoons grated Parmesan
cheese
Mixture of Cos lettuce and rocket
About 5 or 6 slices crisp-fried
pancetta, cut into strips**

Put the mayonnaise, garlic and half the anchovy fillets into a food processor and blend until smooth. If the mayonnaise is too thick, thin by whisking in a little boiled water. Chop the rest of the anchovy fillets and fold these into the mixture.

Fill a small saucepan one-third full of oil and heat. Drop in one bread cube and if it immediately sizzles, put in half the pieces of bread. Lift them out when they are crisp and golden, and put them on kitchen paper to drain. Fry the second batch and season well. While they are hot, sprinkle with some of the Parmesan. Keep warm.

Tear the larger Cos leaves into pieces and mix them with the rocket. Toss with just enough of the mayonnaise to coat the leaves, scatter with the remaining Parmesan and throw over the croutons and crisp pancetta.

Lettuce hearts with hot butter dressing

Children who don't like lettuce often love it prepared this way. Roughly chopped chives and new radishes are good with this. You can also serve crunchy lettuce hearts dressed with olive oil quickly heated with a clove of garlic, a squeeze of lemon and some finely chopped red chilli.

For 4:

**4 small crisp lettuce hearts, such
as Cos or Reine de Glace
100ml unsalted butter
Sea salt and freshly ground
black pepper**

Discard the outer darker-green leaves and quarter the lettuces longways, and wash and dry them.

Warm the butter in a small pan. Arrange the lettuce in a shallow bowl.

Just before serving, pour over the hot butter with plenty of sea salt and black pepper.

Sauté of peas and lettuce

Serve this as a side dish with chicken or fish, or eat it as a meal on its own with a bowl of rice.

For 4–6:
  80g unsalted butter
  A little caster sugar
  Salt and black pepper
  500g fresh peas, shelled weight
  1 garlic clove, finely chopped
  6 thin slices of pancetta or prosciutto, cut into strips
  2 Little Gem lettuces, torn or sliced
  Bunch of parsley, finely chopped, to serve

Heat 500ml water with 20g of the butter, a little sugar and a good pinch of salt. Bring it to the boil and plunge in the peas for 3–5 minutes, depending on the size, and then drain and refresh under cold running water.

In a sauté pan, heat the rest of the butter and gently fry the garlic without allowing it to brown. Add the pancetta or prosciutto, lettuce and peas, and cook together for just 2 minutes.

Season with salt and freshly ground black pepper, and serve with a knob of butter and plenty of chopped flat-leaf parsley.

Lamb fricassée with Cos lettuce and lemon juice

Scatter plenty of toasted almonds and herbs over the top of this wonderful Greek classic, and eat with rice and a Grated carrot and poppy seed salad (see page 430).

For 4–6:
  900g boned shoulder or neck fillet of lamb
  1 large onion, or bunch of spring onions, finely chopped
  3 tablespoons olive oil
  Salt and black pepper
  220ml dry white wine
  220ml chicken stock
  1 large Cos lettuce, cut into ribbons
  Handful of dill, flat-leaf parsley or mint, roughly chopped
  2 tablespoons flaked almonds, toasted

For the egg and lemon sauce:
  2 large eggs
  Juice of 2 lemons

Trim the fat from the lamb and cut it into bite-sized chunks. Sauté the meat gently in the olive oil in a large saucepan with the onions for about 10 minutes. Add salt and pepper, the wine and the stock. Cover and simmer gently for about 1½ hours, or until the meat is tender. Add a little water if it becomes too dry.

Add the lettuce and three-quarters of the herbs right at the end, cooking them only very briefly (1–2 minutes), so that they remain slightly crisp and green.

Just before you eat, make the egg and lemon sauce by whisking the eggs with the lemon juice. Remove from the heat and stir this into the stew, beating vigorously. This will thicken the sauce.

Add the remaining herbs and scatter toasted almonds over the top.

Globe artichokes

I love the unique acrid smell when you're cooking artichokes. You walk into the room and you know what you're having for supper. If you're feeding lots of people, start cooking early, as they take ages. Cook four or five at a time in two huge pans. Find a lid or a plate that is just too small to cover the pan and use it as a weight to prevent those at the top from floating and thus taking longer to cook. Put half a lemon in the water for a brighter green colour and cook them for 30–40 minutes, depending on size. They will start to smell strongly when nearly done. Test them by pulling off one of the bottom leaves. If it comes off easily, the artichoke is ready.

If you've grown your own artichokes, it's always worth soaking them in very salty water for an hour or so before cooking. The earwigs and insect life nestling amongst the leaves will then float to the top. If you're buying them, only go for the ones that are fresh greeny-grey, with no dryness at the leaf tips. Also hold them up by the stem and jiggle them about; if they're really fresh, they don't flop around and when you cut the stem, it slices easily in one go. If the stems are tough and stringy – needing a serrated knife to cut them – they won't be quite as soft and tender.

You can prolong your picking season with artichokes, which are perennials, by growing a few different varieties that crop in succession. This is an imprecise science, but I find that the beautiful, neat 'Violetta' crops first, followed by 'Green Globe' and then the hugely fat-hearted French 'Gros de Laon'. This one has been bred for its hearts alone and if that's the bit you like best, seek it out.

The best way to introduce artichokes into your garden is from plants begged from a friend with a good variety. You can grow artichokes from seed, but they don't always come true. To build up more, you can start taking offsets – side chunks of root – from the mother plant in her second spring.

Artichokes have an extraordinarily sweet aftertaste and so make any wine taste strange. In Italy, you'll usually be offered a glass of water to have with them, not wine.

Globe artichokes with Angelica's sauce

My favourite recipe in the book – it reminds me of Angelica, the cook in the house my parents used to rent in Asolo, in the foothills of the Dolomites. I love the whole palaver of artichokes: pulling the leaves off and dipping them into the rich sauce, until you get to the soft heart, which you dunk and eat all in one go.

For 6–8:
1–2 small artichokes per person
Salt

For the sauce:
4 eggs, hard-boiled and shelled
1 very large bunch of soft green herbs (half flat-leaf parsley and the rest a mixture of chives, fennel, dill and/or coriander, or one of these)
2 tins of anchovy fillets, drained and finely chopped
About 300ml extra virgin olive oil
3 tablespoons red wine vinegar
Black pepper

Cook your artichokes in boiling salted water for about 40 minutes. Drain them in the sink, face down, for 5 minutes and, when they've cooled a bit, give each a squeeze to get rid of any remaining water.

You can roughly chop the ingredients for the sauce in a food processor, but you want a coarse texture, not a purée, so it's best done by hand. I break up the eggs roughly with the back of a fork and chop the herbs and anchovies with a sharp knife. Mix the whole lot together with the oil and vinegar in a large bowl. You won't need much salt because of the anchovies, but add plenty of pepper.

Give everyone an artichoke on a plate with enough room for a good dollop of sauce.

You'll need a large bowl on the table for the discarded leaves (these make great mulch for the garden).

Griddled mini globe artichokes

A recipe for young tender artichokes when they first appear in the spring or, if you're growing them, the small side ones which form on the stem below the main large king. This is also an excellent recipe for using just the hearts later in the year, when the artichokes have got too big and tough. You can eat them on their own, as a meze with a few fresh herbs chopped over the top, or make them into a lovely first course with some slabs of buffalo mozzarella and slices of a good sweet-tasting tomato such as Brandywine.

For 4:
8 small artichokes (buy those with the longest stems, or pick with at least 4cm stalk)
Juice of ½ lemon
400ml white wine
200ml extra virgin olive oil
2 garlic cloves, peeled, but left whole
Sprigs of thyme

Strip down the artichoke by removing the outer, tougher scales until you get to the soft white ones. Then cut the top off the whole thing and pare off the stringy outer third of the long stem with a sharp knife. Cut the artichokes in half and, with a spoon, scrape out the choke – the nascent flower – if it has started to form. Drop them straight into a bowl of water acidulated with the lemon juice.

When they're all prepared, poach them gently for 20 minutes in the white wine and olive oil with the garlic and thyme added to the cooking liquid.

The artichokes are delicious eaten just like that, still warm. Or you can store them in olive oil in the fridge for griddling later. They will last a couple of weeks there.

Raw globe artichoke heart salad

If you're abroad and find artichokes cheap, or you have a glut in the garden, this is a wonderfully glamorous and wasteful recipe. You eat slivers of just the heart, raw and marinated in lemon juice with garlic, parsley and olive oil. Antonio Carluccio showed me this dish, which can be out of the garden and on the plate in 10 minutes. I like that. Again, this is best with young tender early artichokes or small ones from a side stem.

You need:
2 artichokes per person
Juice of 1 lemon
Extra virgin olive oil
Garlic, very finely chopped
Plenty of flat-leaf parsley, finely chopped
Salt and black pepper

Pick or buy your artichokes with long stems as these, as well as the hearts, are delicious if you skin them and you then double your salad.

Prepare the artichokes as for Griddled mini globe artichokes (see left).

Slice the artichoke hearts lengthways into fine slivers and lay the slices out on a flat plate. Squeeze the lemon juice over them and then add some olive oil, a little garlic and a good pinch of finely chopped parsley, and salt and pepper.

You can eat them straight away, or alternatively leave them marinating for a couple of hours, which will make them more tender.

Globe artichoke heart tempura

This recipe was given to me by Matthew Rice, who grows groves of globe artichokes. You prepare the artichokes in the same way as you do when eating them raw, but rather than marinating them, you blanch them and dip them in tempura batter. This brings out the incredible nutty flavour of the artichokes, and they're even more delicious dipped in a Green mayonnaise (see page 83). You can use artichokes of any size, but the bigger the hearts the better.

For 6 as a starter:
6 large globe artichokes
Juice of ½ lemon
Olive oil, for deep-frying

For the tempura batter:
225g plain flour
Plenty of sea salt and black pepper
2 eggs
375ml iced water or cold lager

Prepare slices of artichoke heart by stripping all the leaves and scraping out the choke (the fluff within the heart). Slice the heart into 2cm strips and drop immediately into a bowl of water acidulated with the lemon juice.

To make the batter, sift the flour into a bowl with the salt and pepper and make a dip in the centre. Add the eggs and, with a balloon whisk, mix in the iced water or lager to make a not-too-smooth batter. It should be the thickness of double cream. Keep this in the fridge until you need it.

Pour the oil into a deep pan so that it reaches one-third of the way up the side. Heat the oil until it reaches about 170ºC. If you don't have an oil thermometer, it is easy to test: just drop a cube of bread into the oil, and it should turn golden brown in less than a minute.

Dry and dip the slices of artichoke heart into the batter and then put them into the hot oil until they turn pale gold and crisp. Dry them on kitchen paper.

These are at their best eaten hot, sprinkled with sea salt and ground black pepper. If you have enough of them, you can eat globe artichokes like this on their own, but I love mixing them with other shapes and flavours, so I add other early summer herbs and veg, sage and basil leaves and mangetouts (all fried in a tempura batter), as well as some baby carrots and radishes, straight from the garden, to eat raw as a contrast to the hot crunchy tempura.

Globe artichoke tart

Braised globe artichokes

This recipe uses the young leaves and hearts of small artichokes, or just the artichoke hearts when they have reached full size. You can make one large tart or several small tartlets.

For 4–6 as a starter:
   5 new small globe artichokes
   or 5 artichoke hearts
   100ml olive oil
   100ml dry white wine
   100ml vegetable stock or water
   3 garlic cloves, unpeeled
   A few parsley stalks
   1 small pack of puff pastry
   200g tub of ricotta cheese
   1 large egg, beaten
   1 tablespoon milk
   Salt and black pepper
   75g grated Parmesan cheese

Trim and cut away only the outer leaves of the artichokes (see Griddled mini globe artichokes, page 118), and put them into a heavy-based pan. Cover with equal parts of olive oil, white wine and stock or water. Put in the garlic cloves and parsley, and bring to the boil. Cover and simmer gently for about 30–40 minutes. Then remove the lid and cook further to reduce the liquid until it is treacly.

Preheat the oven to 200°C/gas mark 6.

Roll out the puff pastry as thinly as you can and use to line a 23cm tart tin. Fan out and separate the artichokes, or cut the hearts into thin slices, and spread them in a layer over the pastry.

Mix the ricotta with the beaten egg and milk to thin the mixture. Season well. Spread this in a thin layer over the artichokes and scatter over the Parmesan.

Put into the preheated oven and bake for about 15 minutes, until the pastry is cooked. Then reduce the oven setting to 180°C/gas mark 4 and cook for a further 10 minutes.

This is a wonderfully luxurious way of eating artichokes as a side vegetable. The sweet flavour of the artichokes is excellent with chicken or fish.

For 4:
   6 good fresh young artichokes
   4 tablespoons olive oil
   2 garlic cloves, peeled and
      chopped
   Handful of freshly picked herbs,
      such as summer savory,
      parsley, mint and/or marjoram,
      all finely chopped
   1 red chilli, chopped and
      deseeded (optional)
   100ml white wine or vermouth
   Salt and black pepper

This is good with fresh young artichokes, prepared as for griddling (see page 118).

Heat the olive oil in a pan large enough to allow the hearts to lie next to each other, stem upwards. Add the artichokes to the heated oil and allow to cook until slightly brown. Add the chopped garlic, let it colour a little and then add half the herbs, turning the artichokes in the mix.

Add a little chilli, if you are using it, and the wine or vermouth. Cook gently for 20–30 minutes, until the artichokes are soft when they are tested with a knife.

Add the remaining herbs and season.

New/waxy potatoes

You can buy what look like new potatoes in the winter, but they will have been long lifted and cold-stored. It's only in the summer that they have that memorable sweetness. The sugars quickly convert to starch on storing, so the real bonus of growing your own is that you can eat them within minutes of lifting them from the soil.

Potatoes divide in their consistency between floury ('Maris Piper' and 'Desiree') and waxy ('International Kidney', 'Charlotte', 'Belle de Fontenay', 'Ratte' and the late-season 'Pink Fir Apple'). The floury ones – those with a high water content – are good for chips, baked potatoes, roast and mash. The flesh 'collapses' when cooked, creating a rough surface that crisps up well in oil, while the insides become fluffy. Floury potatoes tend to be maincrops, which are harvested towards the end of the year (see pages 334–41). Waxy potatoes, on the other hand, have a low water content and so hold up well to boiling and slicing, making them ideal in salads, and for sautéing and dauphinoise. Most of these are earlies, although a few come later in the summer for eating in the autumn.

The best way to eat really fresh new potatoes is simply to boil them in salty water with mint and serve them with a knob of butter, some mayonnaise or a drizzle of extra virgin olive oil. Alternatively, try scattering them with finely chopped summer savory and soft summer thyme, including the herb flowers. There are some lovely new potato combinations for salads, and do also try eating them parboiled and then roasted in a hot oven for an hour in good olive oil.

Opinions vary as to whether you should leave the skins on new potatoes or peel them. I cook them in the skins – to improve their end flavour – but remove them before eating. The skins may be good for you, but they spoil the softness and sweetness of the potato flesh.

New potatoes are easy to grow and you don't even need a garden to do so. I grow my earliest potatoes in empty compost bags. Roll the plastic down to halfway and in February or March, half-fill the bags with soil mixed with a few handfuls of manure and bury a couple of seed potatoes. Put the sacks somewhere light but frost-free and the potatoes will start to sprout. As the tops grow, roll up the bag's plastic and add a little soil to cover them. They'll have reached the top of the bag in May and lots of tasty baby potatoes will be ready. Turn the whole thing upside down or, if you want to eat them bit by bit, cut a slit in the side of the bag and rummage around.

New potatoes in saffron dressing

These are lovely either warm or cold, and look and taste magnificent.

For 4:

450g new potatoes
100ml light olive oil
3 tablespoons sherry
A few strands of good-quality
  saffron
1 garlic clove
½ red chilli, finely chopped
½ teaspoon paprika (optional)
1 tablespoon Dijon mustard
3 tablespoons white wine vinegar
Salt and black pepper

Cook the potatoes in boiling salted water for about 15 minutes, depending on size, and peel.

Warm the oil and sherry in a small pan and put in the strands of saffron to infuse for a few minutes.

Combine the remaining ingredients in a food processor, adding the oil mixture slowly in a thin drizzle until it makes a thickish emulsion.

Pour over the cooked potatoes and season.

Potato salad with capers and anchovies

My all-time favourite potato salad for a picnic or big summer lunch, best served with a bowl of Red onion marmalade (see page 249). All you need is a green salad. Chive flowers look and taste good with potatoes.

For 4:

600g small waxy potatoes,
  such as International Kidney,
  Charlotte, Pink Fir Apple,
  Ratte, Nicola, Anya or Winston
1 medium-sized red onion, halved
  and very thinly sliced (optional)
2 tablespoons capers, rinsed
  and roughly chopped
1 tin of anchovies, drained
  and roughly chopped
Good handful of herbs (all or some
  of dill, basil, thyme, coriander,
  parsley, fennel, chives and
  mint), roughly chopped

For the homemade mayonnaise:

1 whole egg and 1 extra yolk
1 level teaspoon mustard powder
1 garlic clove (optional)
Good pinch of salt and black
  pepper
200ml good sunflower oil
100ml olive oil
Lemon juice or white wine
  vinegar to taste

Cook the potatoes in salted boiling water for about 15 minutes, until they're just done. Drain them in a colander and leave them to cool.

Meanwhile, make the mayonnaise. Put the egg and yolk, mustard powder, garlic (if using), salt and pepper into a liquidiser or bowl. Whisk until frothy. Add the sunflower oil and then the olive oil in a stream, while still processing or whisking, until the mixture thickens. Add the lemon juice or vinegar to taste and season. If the mayonnaise curdles at any point, start the whole process again with a third egg yolk, whisking it in a clean bowl and adding the curdled mixture in a slow stream while processing or whisking. This makes just over 300ml and can be stored in the fridge for a few days. If you want to lighten the mayonnaise, you can mix it with an equal volume of natural yoghurt.

Peel the potatoes and put them with the red onion (if you're including it), capers and anchovies into a salad bowl. Add the mayonnaise and mix together gently. Scatter with the herbs.

Chorizo with potatoes

Originally a Nigella Lawson recipe championed by Nigel Slater in *Real Food,* this is a quick, cheap and easy dish, perfect for a mid-week supper. Morcilla sausage (Spanish black pudding) makes an interesting addition. Just replace 100g chorizo with 100g morcilla. The morcilla will break up during the cooking, thereby enriching the sauce. This dish can be either a soupy or a dryish stew. The quantities below will make it veer towards dryness – if you prefer, add just a little more water with the potatoes.

It is delicious served with crusty bread and a green salad. Cucumber raita (see page 196) also makes a tasty, tangy accompaniment.

For 4:
 1 tablespoon oil
 1 small to medium-sized onion, finely chopped
 100g bacon or pancetta
 400g semi-dried chorizo
 3 garlic cloves, finely chopped
 1 bay leaf
 150ml dry sherry
 750g small waxy potatoes
 Salt and black pepper
 Chopped fresh coriander

Preheat the oven to 200°C/gas mark 6.

Put the oil in a wide rather than deep pan that can go in the oven and put on the hob over a medium-to-low heat. Add the onion and cook for 5 minutes or so, until it begins to soften.

While these are cooking, cut the bacon or pancetta into matchsticks and skin and slice the chorizo into fat coins (if using morcilla, skin it but leave it whole, as it will disintegrate during cooking).

Add the garlic to the pan and cook, stirring, for another couple of minutes. Add the sausage and cook for 5 minutes, stirring regularly. Then add the bay leaf and sherry, and stir.

Slice the potatoes in half or quarters, depending on the size, and add to the pot. Then pour over boiling water to cover, but not too much – don't worry about the odd potato sticking out. Stir and simmer for 10 minutes, and check the seasoning.

Put the dish, uncovered, in the preheated oven and cook for 30–40 minutes. Check it halfway through that time to make sure it hasn't dried out too much, and give it a stir.

Ladle into bowls, and scatter over some chopped fresh coriander.

French beans with new potatoes

The squeaky texture of fresh French beans combines beautifully with the softness of potatoes, and there are many ways of using these two in a salad. You can toss them both in a little truffle oil and add a few rocket leaves, or serve them like this with nut oil, toasted almonds and lots of dill.

For 6:
 450g new potatoes
 450g French beans
 1 tablespoon walnut or hazelnut oil
 4 tablespoons chopped dill
 1 garlic clove, finely chopped
 230ml sour cream
 1 teaspoon caster sugar
 Salt and black pepper
 2 tablespoons flaked or halved almonds, toasted

Cook the new potatoes in boiling salted water, then cut them in half and peel if you want to. Next, cook the beans for 4 minutes (the beans must be crisp).

Drain the beans and potatoes, plunge the beans into cold water and drain again. Pour the oil over both while they are still warm. Toss to coat.

Combine the chopped dill and garlic with the sour cream, sugar and seasoning, and carefully fold into the potatoes and beans.

Scatter over the almonds.

Smashed roast new potatoes with garlic and rosemary

My children call out for this as soon as they see new potatoes coming in from the garden.

For 6:
  1 head of garlic
  1kg new potatoes
  1 tablespoon finely chopped
    rosemary
  50g butter
  3 tablespoons olive oil
  Sea salt and black pepper
  Grated pecorino (optional)

Preheat the oven to 200°C/gas mark 6.

Put the head of garlic on to a piece of foil and roast in the preheated oven for about 40 minutes, until soft.

Meanwhile, scrub the potatoes and put them into a saucepan. Pour over boiling water, add salt and cook them for 15 minutes.

Melt the butter in a small saucepan. Drain the potatoes and crush them roughly. Squeeze out the soft garlic from the cloves and add it to the melted butter with the finely chopped rosemary.

Toss the crushed potatoes in the garlic butter mixture and season well. Drizzle with the olive oil.

Place in an ovenproof dish and roast until golden brown and crisp on the top. Scatter a layer of freshly grated pecorino (if using) over the top before serving.

New potato salad with quails' eggs and black pudding

An interesting and robust summer salad that is ideal as a first course or as a light lunch.

For 6–8:
  900g new potatoes, scrubbed
  ½ red onion, finely chopped
  ½ red chilli, finely chopped
  12 quails' eggs
  Celery salt
  225g black pudding
  Sunflower oil for frying
  2 good handfuls of rocket leaves
  Black pepper
  Bunch of flat-leaf parsley,
    finely chopped

For the dressing:
  2 tablespoons olive
    or sunflower oil
  Lemon juice to taste
  1 teaspoon caster sugar
  Salt and black pepper

Whisk together all the ingredients for the dressing.

Bring a pan of salted water to the boil and cook the potatoes for about 15 minutes, until tender but not soft. Drain and pour a little of the dressing into the pan and add the finely chopped onion and chilli. Boil the quails' eggs for about 3 minutes and plunge into cold water. Peel and dust with a little celery salt.

Cut the black pudding into slices and then cut these in half, and fry them in a little sunflower oil. Put to one side and keep warm.

Arrange the rocket in a large shallow bowl. Toss the potatoes and black pudding in the dressing and season with pepper. Place on the rocket and scatter over the quails' eggs and plenty of parsley.

Peas

Peas eaten raw, straight from pods just picked from the plant, are as good as it comes. They taste completely different from shop-bought fresh peas – sweet, tender and delicious. If you have a party in the summer, pick a bowlful of pods and leave them around for people to shell and eat.

As soon as you harvest them, peas start to lose sugar as it converts to starch. If you can't eat the peas within hours, they are best quickly blanched (2 minutes in boiling water) and frozen, rather than left in the fridge. I've tried several different varieties and, after two or three days, they taste more like a lentil than a pea – dense in texture and starchy in taste.

Young, fresh peas are so sweet that all they need is a sprig of mint in the cooking water and a knob of butter when you eat them. If you're growing peas, don't forget to pick and eat lots of pea tips – the growth tips and side shoots, 3–4cm long – covering the plant as it climbs. These are fantastic, called 'green gold' by the Japanese. They have the sweetness of peas, with the succulence of the heart of a 'Cos' lettuce. Add them to a crunchy-leaved salad, quick-fry them in a stir-fry, wilt them over a risotto (see page 131) or, if you have plenty, blanch and eat them as a vegetable.

There are various types of pea to choose from and they're easy to grow. I sow mine like radishes into a gutter pipe (see page 134). Sowing under cover ensures rapid and good germination, as well as giving some protection from mice and pigeons, both of which can be a scourge outside.

You can grow straightforward peas, such as the long and heavy-cropping 'Hurst Green Shaft', or go for mangetout varieties, which you eat as flat unfilled pods, before the peas have formed. I grow the purple-podded mangetout 'Carouby de Mausanne', which looks magnificent, but the pods are only good when small. There are, of course, also sugar snaps – succulent pods filled with peas, which you eat in their entirety.

Sugar snaps and mangetouts are heavy producers over a short season, so grow only a few plants or you'll be overwhelmed. If the pods are left on the plant to fatten up and toughen, they become much less good. Their quick growth curve makes them difficult to keep up with, but it also makes them ideal varieties for pea tips. Inevitably, stealing many of the growing tips will compromise the harvest of shelling peas. That's a shame with slower-growing forms, but it is a real blessing with these.

Pea purée

A simple and delicious purée which is at its sweetest and best with the peas that are just picked, although frozen peas are also fine. Don't over-purée the peas; in fact, they are nicer with two-thirds puréed and one-third left barely blitzed, to retain some texture. The purée is lovely with chicken or any roast meat.

For 4:
450g shelled peas, fresh or frozen
½ teaspoon sugar
Small bunch of mint leaves,
    finely chopped, apart from
    a sprig
20g butter
125ml single cream
Salt and black pepper

Put the peas into boiling salted water with the sugar and a sprig of mint. With frozen peas, cook for only a minute or so; with fresh peas, cook for 4–5 minutes, until just tender but still with a bite, and then drain, removing the mint.

Liquidise in a food processor or roughly mash by hand with the butter and cream.

Season with black pepper and serve with a scattering of finely chopped mint.

Crushed peas

This is a Raymond Blanc recipe, in which peas are flavoured with marjoram, lemon and olive oil. It's perfect with lamb, fish or chicken.

For 4:
600g fresh shelled
    or thawed frozen peas
85ml extra virgin olive oil
2 tablespoons finely chopped
    marjoram
2 tablespoons finely chopped
    fresh mint
Salt and white pepper
Juice of ½ lemon

Crush the peas in a food processor, using the pulse button. Do not purée them, as it is important to retain much of the texture.

Transfer the peas to a medium saucepan and stir in the olive oil, chopped herbs, plenty of salt and a pinch of white pepper.

Cook the crushed peas on a medium heat with the lid on for 4 minutes. Stir in the lemon juice, then taste and correct the seasoning if you need to.

Peas with cucumber and mint

The taste and texture of peas mixed with crunchy – just cooked – cucumbers are good with chicken and fish.

For 4:
500g shelled peas
½ large cucumber, skinned
    and with the seeds removed
30g butter or 2 tablespoons
    olive oil
Bunch of spring onions, chopped
2 tablespoons dry sherry
250ml crème fraîche
1 teaspoon caster sugar
2 tablespoons chopped mint

Add the peas to a pan of boiling water and cook until just tender. Drain and plunge into cold water.

Cut the cucumber at an angle into 1cm slices.

Heat the butter or olive oil in a sauté pan and add the spring onions, cucumber and dry sherry, and bubble up for a couple of minutes.

Add the peas, crème fraîche, sugar and chopped mint. Just warm through and serve.

Pea and ricotta tart with thyme pastry

My great friends Aurea Carpenter and Andrew Palmer first cooked me this Alastair Little recipe about 15 years ago, and I've cooked it every summer since. Eat it with a tomato salad.

For 4–6:
For the thyme pastry:
  200g plain flour
  Pinch of salt
  50g cold butter, cut into chunks
  50g cold lard, cut into chunks
  1 heaped tablespoon finely chopped thyme

For the filling:
  350g shelled peas
  225g ricotta cheese
  200ml crème fraîche
  2 eggs
  3 tablespoons coarsely chopped mixed herbs (basil, mint and chives)
  5 tablespoons grated Parmesan cheese
  Salt and black pepper

First make the pastry. Sift the flour and salt and rub in the butter and lard or process until the mixture resembles breadcrumbs. Put into a mixing bowl, add the thyme and just enough cold water to bring the pastry together in a ball. Roll out the pastry and use to line a 23cm flan tin. Rest it in the fridge for 30 minutes.

Preheat the oven to 200°C/gas mark 6. Prick the bottom of the tart with a fork, cover with a round of greaseproof paper or foil and weight this down with some baking beans or rice. Bake the pastry case blind for about 20–25 minutes. Take it out of the oven, reducing the oven setting to 180°C/gas mark 4, and let it cool slightly, then remove the beans or rice and the lining paper.

Boil the peas for 3 minutes, drain, plunge into cold water and put to one side.

To make the filling, mix the ricotta with the crème fraîche and the eggs, and season well. Stir in the chopped herbs and Parmesan.

Put the peas into the pastry case and pour over the mixture. Bake in the oven for 25 minutes. Serve warm.

Mint and pea tip risotto

Another quick garden supper for when peas and mint are at their most abundant and best.

For 6–8:
  300g shelled peas
  Handful of fresh mint leaves, stalks removed, plus more to finish
  100g unsalted butter
  About 2 tablespoons olive oil
  1 onion, finely chopped
  2 garlic cloves, finely chopped
  500g Arborio or Carnaroli rice
  2 glasses of white wine
  About 1.5 litres hot vegetable or chicken stock
  175g Parmesan cheese, grated, plus more for serving
  1 handful of pea tips, sugar snaps or mangetouts

Cook the peas with most of the mint. If they're home-grown, pick them at the last minute so that they retain their sweetness. Once soft, pulse them quickly in a food processor to a rough purée. Keep the purée warm.

Melt half the butter with the olive oil in a heavy-based pan and fry the onion, without allowing it to colour, for about 5–6 minutes. Then add the garlic and rice, and turn to coat these with the butter and oil. Add the wine, letting it bubble up and evaporate.

Gradually add the hot stock, a ladleful at a time, stirring continuously. Allow each addition of stock to be absorbed before adding the next. It will reach al dente stage after 18 minutes.

Take off the heat and beat in the extra butter. Add the mint and pea purée and most of the Parmesan.

Blanch the sugar snaps/ mangetouts for 2 minutes and add them and the pea tips to the risotto and warm through, stirring for a couple of minutes. Add more finely chopped mint and serve with more Parmesan.

Chilled pea soup with roasted garlic

This adaptation of Nigella Lawson's recipe is one of my favourite early summer soups. It's also delicious with frozen peas, just thawed in the hot stock and whizzed.

For 4–6:

1 head of garlic
1 litre good vegetable stock
2 tablespoons olive oil
1 small bunch of spring onions, chopped
1kg shelled peas, fresh or frozen
Bunch of mint
150ml single cream
Salt and black pepper

Preheat the oven to 180°C/gas mark 4 and roast the whole head of garlic for half an hour until sweet and caramel-like inside (see page 253). Scrape the garlic flesh from the skin and put to one side.

Heat the stock.

In a large saucepan, heat the olive oil and cook the spring onions in it gently, until softened but not browned. Add the peas and mint, and cook for a few minutes. Add the hot stock and cook until the peas are just tender. Remove the mint and drain the peas, reserving the stock.

Liquidise the peas with the garlic and a little of the stock, and return to a large mixing bowl. Add enough of the reserved stock to give the consistency you want (the soup will thicken slightly when it is chilled) and add the single cream. Season.

Cover the bowl and chill for at least 2 hours before serving.

Pea and pancetta farfalle

A classic pasta dish that will be loved by both children and adults alike.

For 4:

10 rashers of bacon, smoked and streaky, or pancetta
1 large onion, finely chopped
1 tablespoon olive oil
30g butter
350g farfalle
Salt and black pepper
1 garlic clove, finely chopped
400g fresh shelled peas, or frozen peas (cooked for 2 minutes in boiling water)
250g crème fraîche
Freshly grated nutmeg
Good handful of grated Parmesan cheese

Roast or fry the bacon or pancetta until it is crisp. Let it cool for a couple of minutes and then cut it into 2–3cm lengths with scissors.

Cook the onion very gently in the olive oil and butter for 6–8 minutes.

Meanwhile cook your pasta in salted boiling water until al dente.

Add the garlic to the onion and cook for another minute or two before adding the crisp bacon or pancetta and peas.

Add the crème fraîche, and seasoning and nutmeg to taste, and stir around in the pan for a couple of minutes.

Combine the sauce and the pasta. Add plenty of Parmesan.

Squid, pea and chorizo stew

My sister Jane gave me this recipe. In the summer serve it with rice and a green salad. It's also good in the winter made with frozen peas, eaten with crusty bread and Cucumber raita (see page 196).

For 6:

300g chorizo, skinned
1 medium-sized onion, finely chopped
3 tablespoons olive oil
680g tomato passata
100ml red wine
300g squid, cleaned
250g fresh shelled or thawed frozen peas
Bunch of parsley, finely chopped

Cut the chorizo into discs about as thick as a pound coin and then cut these in half if you don't want them to be too chunky.

Fry the onion in the oil over a gentle heat for 6–8 minutes.

Add the chorizo and cook for about 5 minutes until the fat runs. Add the passata and red wine. Reduce the sauce for 10 minutes on a gentle heat.

Cut the squid into rings and cut up the tentacles a bit. Add to the stew and cook for about 10–15 minutes, until the squid is tender.

Add the peas about 5 minutes before the end of the cooking time.

Serve sprinkled with the parsley.

Radishes

There is a brilliant way of growing radishes in which you don't even need a garden, and you'll be picking them at least a month earlier than if they were growing outside. Sow the seeds, spaced 3cm apart, in plastic guttering – the half-moon section pipe you get from any builder's yard. You don't need to drill holes for drainage: just fill the pipe with compost and keep the compost moist. Put it somewhere warm. The seeds don't need light until they germinate, which they will do within a few days.

As soon as they show green, put the pipe outside or on a window ledge or doorstep, or in the garden, and wait a month. You'll then have perfect plump crunchy radishes. We are quite efficient about this now and try always to have at least one pipe on the go. Radishes are almost always better fresh and home-grown. All too often the bought ones are a bit flaccid, and don't possess the all-important crunch.

There are various long, winter-hardy tap-rooted radishes which are good grated in salad, but my favourites are the gobstopper-sized spring and summer forms. The best variety is the round, pink and white 'Cherry Belle', which knocks the socks off the widely available 'French Breakfast'. 'Cherry Belle' is hot, but not too hot, with an excellent texture. I also grow 'Sparkler', which is slower than any other variety to form a woolly heart. Even quite big, these still make lovely eating and are ideal for cooking, sliced in half or braised whole with other summer veg (see page 137).

To eat them raw, just wash the roots and have them with sea salt. To help the salt stick, smear the radishes in some softened unsalted butter or some ice-cold water before dipping them. This is a great nibble with a glass of wine before dinner, with some quails' eggs and celery salt and a big bowl of just-picked peas.

If you grow your own radishes, you can also eat the leaves. Picked small and fresh, they have a good peppery flavour and make a punchy addition to any mixed leaf salad. When the leaves are larger, they get a bit coarse and hairy, but you can still use them, cut into ribbons and wilted, for extra flavour in a stir-fry, and they make a surprisingly delicious pasta sauce (see page 137).

Early summer crudités on ice with aïoli

Fill a large flat bowl with ice and pile on all the youngest, most tender veg you can buy or pick. Serve them with aïoli and perhaps some crème fraîche with a handful of dill. The ice will keep the veg fresh and crunchy and the whole thing looks and tastes fantastic.
This makes great simple party food, ideal for serving lots of people.

For 6:
Crushed ice
Mixture of early summer
vegetables, such as radishes,
mini carrots, peas and
purple-podded mangetouts

For the aïoli:
2 garlic cloves
Sea salt
1 whole egg plus 1 extra yolk
½ teaspoon mustard powder
Pepper
2 tablespoons balsamic vinegar
275ml oil (I usually use two-thirds
sunflower, one-third olive oil)

To make the aïoli, crush the garlic with a pinch of sea salt, using a pestle and mortar. Put the egg and yolk into the bowl and add mustard, pepper and half the vinegar.

Whisk these together with a hand mixer or in a food processor, then carefully add the oil in a stream while stirring continuously, until the oil emulsifies and makes a thick smooth mayonnaise. Adjust the seasoning and stir in more vinegar to taste.

Half-fill a large shallow bowl with ice and lay out the veg on top, with a bowl of aïoli in the middle.

Glazed summer veg

Serve this delicious mix of mini early summer vegetables with meat or fish.

For 8–10:
600g small new potatoes,
scrubbed
600g small new carrots
600g large radishes
600g small new turnips
3 or 4 garlic cloves, peeled
Fresh thyme sprigs
100ml olive oil
30g unsalted butter
Salt and black pepper

Cut the potatoes in half lengthwise and trim the tops of the carrots, radishes and turnips to about 1cm, but keep the roots whole.

Combine the vegetables, garlic and thyme in a heavy-based pan and coat with the olive oil. Add 300ml water and bring to the boil. Cover the pan with a sheet of greaseproof paper and then the lid, and simmer, stirring occasionally, for about 15 minutes, until all the vegetables are tender. Transfer the vegetables to a serving dish and keep warm.

Remove the thyme and boil the remaining juices for a minute or two to emulsify the oil. Take off the heat and add the butter, stir well and pour over the vegetables.

Season well.

Radish top pasta

If you grow your own radishes, try this peppery pasta sauce, particularly when some of the radishes are too big and woolly to be good raw.

For 4:
About 25 radishes with
their leaves
Salt and black pepper
350g pasta
3 tablespoons extra virgin olive oil
1 onion, chopped
1 garlic clove, finely chopped
75g pine nuts, toasted
75g Parmesan cheese,
plus more to serve
Bunch of flat-leaf parsley,
chopped

Cut the tops off the radishes and wash and dry them. Slice the radishes and chop their leaves.

Bring a large pan of salted water to the boil and add the pasta.

Meanwhile heat the oil in a pan and sweat the onion for 3–4 minutes. Add the garlic, pine nuts, radish tops and the sliced radishes, and cook until the tops wilt and soften.

Remove from the heat, season and keep warm.

When the pasta is al dente, drain, leaving a couple of tablespoons of the pasta water in the pan. Add the radishes and the Parmesan, and stir them together.

Serve the pasta with a bowl of more Parmesan and plenty of flat-leaf parsley.

Samphire and elderflowers

I love picking wild food. To engage with a particular place in the moment is absorbing, and any delicious things you find to eat are a bonus. In March and April, look for watercress and wild garlic (see page 92) and wild sorrel (see page 80). In May and June, it's samphire and elderflowers. Later in the year, you mustn't miss the blackberries and sloes (see page 320) and mushrooms (see page 342).

Samphire grows on mud flats around much of our coast and you tend to find it in vast carpets as far as the eye can see. It's best picked as it first emerges in early summer, when the fronds are about 15cm long. It forms a bushy plant, which you can pull up by the roots, or snip off at the base with scissors so that it will shoot again. It needs to be washed several times, and picked over so as to discard the base of the stalks, but that's quick and easy to do. You can also buy it at this time of year from fishmongers.

Samphire is good for you: rich in vitamins and with excellent digestive and anti-flatulent properties. It was given to sailors to protect them against scurvy. It's not only healthy but also delicious.

If it is young, you can eat it raw with a dressing, or sauté it quickly in butter with lime juice, parsley, garlic, salt and pepper. I love it eaten like asparagus as a first course, just simply boiled for about 10 minutes in plenty of water, and then smothered with melted butter. It's also fantastic with fish, meat or chicken. As the plants grow, the stems develop a tougher interior structure. Samphire is still delicious at this stage, but once it is cooked, you need to pull the exterior flesh off with your teeth as you eat it.

Elderflowers are also at their best in May and June. Pick the flowers in full sun, ideally a few days after they first come out. Every flower in the spray will then be open and rich in pollen, and will therefore have the cleanest, freshest flavour. Once the petals have gone flat white and lost the creamy hue, the pollen has dropped and the flavour is less strong. Don't pick the flowers once they have begun to brown, as the flavour takes on a nasty hint of cat's pee.

Use them to make the classic cordial, or make flower fritters by dipping them in batter and dusting them with icing sugar to eat with a squirt of lemon juice. The unusual flavour of elderflowers combines well with sharp tastes, so mix them with lemons, rhubarb, blackcurrants or the first of the gooseberries.

Samphire with fresh peas and young broad beans

One up from straight samphire, this makes an excellent first course. Samphire needs thorough rinsing as it can be very muddy.

For 8–10 as a starter:
80g unsalted butter
1 teaspoon caster sugar
1kg samphire
400g fresh peas, shelled weight
400g small broad beans
1 garlic clove, chopped
6 thin slices of pancetta
   or prosciutto, cut into strips
Black pepper

Rinse the samphire thoroughly in a colander under cold running water. Heat 500ml water with 20g of butter and the sugar. Bring to the boil, plunge in the samphire and cook for 10 minutes. Add the peas and broad beans, and cook for another 3–5 minutes, depending on size. Drain and refresh under cold running water.

Melt all but a knob of the remaining butter in a frying pan and gently fry the garlic without allowing it to brown. Add the pancetta or prosciutto, samphire, peas and broad beans, and cook together for just 2 minutes.

Season with black pepper and serve with the reserved knob of butter. You don't need salt as samphire is so naturally salty.

Samphire sauce

This makes a good accompaniment to any fish, but is particularly good with cold salmon and trout.

For 6:
2–3 big handfuls of young and
   tender samphire fronds
3 tablespoons extra virgin olive oil
Salt and black pepper
250ml crème fraîche
Grated lemon zest and juice
   to taste

Rinse the samphire thoroughly in a colander under cold running water. Chop very roughly, put into a food processor and pulse to a purée.

Slowly add the oil and season.

Put the samphire purée into a bowl and then fold in the crème fraîche, lemon zest and a little lemon juice to taste.

Elderflower cordial

This excellent, not too sweet, version of the classic cordial will keep for a very long time.

For 2 x 750ml bottles:
    1.35kg granulated sugar
    Flowers from 15–20 elderflower heads
    2 oranges, thinly sliced
    2 lemons, thinly sliced
    2 limes, thinly sliced
    30g tartaric (or citric) acid

Put 1.15 litres water and the sugar in a saucepan, and dissolve the sugar completely before bringing to the boil. Add the flowers and return the water to the boil. Remove from the heat immediately.

Thinly slice the fruit into a large bowl or jug. Add the tartaric acid and pour over the hot syrup and flowers. Stir well and cover loosely. Leave for 24 hours.

Strain into warm sterilised bottles and seals. This keeps for a couple of months in the fridge. If you make plenty, pour some into plastic bottles and freeze. It will last for years.

Elderflower fritters

I first made these from Roger Phillip's book on wild food. They are lovely on their own and fantastic with Elderflower and gooseberry ice cream (see page 143).

For 6–8:
    100g plain flour
    Pinch of salt
    1 egg, lightly beaten
    150ml tepid water
    12 elderflower heads, unwashed but picked over
    Groundnut oil, for deep-frying
    Icing sugar, for sprinkling

Sift the flour with the salt into a bowl. Make a dip in the centre and add the egg. Whisk while adding the water, until you have a smooth batter.

Hold the flower heads by their stalks and dip them into the batter. Deep-fry them in very hot oil, about 170ºC, until golden and drain on kitchen paper. Trim the excess stalk and serve warm, sprinkled with icing sugar.

Elderflower and gooseberry jam

This is one of the most delicious jams – typically British, and a taste that reminds one immediately of summer.

For 10–12 jars:
    2.7kg gooseberries
    2.7kg sugar, still in its packets
    15g butter
    A few elderflower heads, tied in a muslin bag

Top and tail the gooseberries and put them into a preserving pan with 1.1 litres of water. Warm the sugar in its packets or a bowl in a very low oven for about half an hour.

Simmer the fruit gently, with the muslin bag of elderflower heads tied to the pan handle, until it is soft. Pour in the warm sugar, stirring to make sure that it is dissolved.

Add the butter, raise the heat and boil rapidly until the setting point is reached (see page 170).

Pour into clean, warm jars, cover with wax discs and seal.

Elderflower and gooseberry sauce

A wonderful sauce for oily fish, such as mackerel, which is also very good with goose.

For 4–6:
   450g gooseberries
   100ml white wine
   2–3 elderflower heads
   25–50g sugar, depending
      how sharp you like the sauce
   50g butter
   Freshly grated nutmeg

Top and tail the gooseberries and put them into a pan with the wine, elderflower heads and sugar. Simmer until the gooseberries are soft.

Add the butter and nutmeg and then mouli, or liquidise in a food processor and sieve.

Elderflower and gooseberry ice cream

This recipe for one of the best early summer ice creams was given to me by Teresa Wallace. She tends to cook more purée than she needs and freezes it in 75g and 150g blocks for making more ice cream through the year.

For 6:
   2 large eggs, separated
   50g caster sugar
   200ml double cream

For the purée:
   75g gooseberries
   2–3 elderflower heads
   50g sugar

To make the purée, put the elderflowers and gooseberries in a pan with just enough water to stop them catching on the bottom of the saucepan – you want a good concentrated flavour. Cook very gently until the fruit is reduced to a mush.

Push this mixture through a fine sieve or mouli and let it cool. Add the sugar. You can use more, but 50g gives a lovely sharp taste.

To make the ice cream, whip the egg yolks with the sugar until they are pale yellow and foamy. Whip the cream and then in a separate bowl beat the egg whites to firm peaks. Mix together the gooseberry purée and the whipped egg yolk with the sugar, then add the cream, and finally fold in the beaten egg whites.

Spoon the mixture into individual pots or glasses and freeze.

There is no need to beat or churn this ice cream. The egg white stops it forming too many ice crystals and it will be a perfect consistency to eat after 20 minutes out of the freezer in the fridge.

Please don't ever buy out-of-season strawberries again. They are tasteless and likely to have been covered in chemicals and produced in a city of polytunnels by cheap exploited labour. They're all looks and no substance. Everything that the strawberry should give you – sweet-scented, enveloping lusciousness – is missing from these fakes. What you want is the real thing, and the best way to get that is to go to a local pick-your-own fruit farm, where you can see for yourself how the strawberries are being produced, or, even better, grow your own. There is something magically gratifying about picking them from outside your door.

They're at their best eaten straight from the plant, still warm from the sunshine, which helps release their subtler flavours. Sprinkle vanilla sugar over them and leave them to bleed their juices for an hour or two before eating them with a mound of thick cream.

If you have too many to cope with, make ice cream. My children love nothing better than this – just 450g strawberries, the juice of one orange and one lemon, 300ml double cream and 150g caster sugar. For grown-ups, I like the surprising addition of black pepper (see page 147) or alternatively a dash of balsamic vinegar, which cuts through the sweetness.

If you want to grow your own, which are the strawberry varieties with supreme flavour? My early summer strawberry is 'Royal Sovereign', which gives giant-sized fruit, packed with taste. This variety is ideal for forcing – that is, for picking from under glass cloches from the beginning of May. You can't go wrong with 'Cambridge Favourite', which has medium-sized fruit and good taste and disease-resistance. Also try 'Honoeye' and 'Florence'. 'Honoeye' is early and has excellent flavour, but is not very vigorous, so you only want to keep plants for a couple of years. 'Florence' is also delicious, with dark-red berries, but in contrast it is both late and vigorous, needing no drip-feeding to keep it cropping well, so it's ideal for the organic grower.

I am also fanatical about the perpetual 'Mara des Bois'. If you visit almost any French market during July or August, there will be whole stalls devoted to this deep-red fruit alone. It has a fantastic woodland flavour and is easy to grow, with good resistance to disease – including the dreaded powdery mildew. It's ideal for the domestic garden as it fruits lightly over two or three months.

Alpine strawberries are delicious. I grow 'Mignonette', which lines the paths down my south-facing vegetable bank. We start picking in April, and go on right until the frosts in November.

Strawberry and black pepper ice cream

This is wonderful with fresh strawberries and gooey meringues (see page 148). Leave the pepper out if you're making this for children.

For 6–8:
450g strawberries
Juice of 1 orange
Juice of 1 lemon
300ml double cream
150g caster sugar
Black pepper

Hull the strawberries and purée them with the fruit juice in a food processor. Add the cream and sugar until well mixed. Season with pepper to taste – remember, the flavour is milder when frozen than at room temperature – and blitz a few more times to mix the pepper in.

Put the mixture in an ice cream maker and freeze/churn for 20 minutes. Serve immediately or pack in plastic containers for the freezer.

If you don't have an ice cream maker, place the mixture in a shallow container and freeze until half frozen. Put the mixture back into the food processor and blitz again until smooth, before putting it back in the freezer to freeze completely.

Take the ice cream out of the freezer and put in the fridge for half an hour before serving.

Strawberry sauce for ice cream

This makes an excellent sauce for good vanilla or strawberry ice cream.

For 4–6:
450g strawberries
350g blueberries
1 tablespoon lime juice
100ml honey
3 tablespoons dark rum
75g unsalted butter
2 tablespoons soft brown sugar

Hull the strawberries and cut into quarters. Combine the two fruits and pour over the lime juice.

Heat the honey, rum, butter and sugar in a small saucepan over a gentle heat until the butter is melted. Allow the mixture to cool.

Toss the berries in the sauce and pour over ice cream.

Marinated strawberries

This is the simplest way of serving strawberries – one up from eating them straight from the punnet. Do this when you want strawberries on top of ice cream or meringue, when you want to hull them a few hours before you eat. Adding the lemon and orange juice preserves them for several hours.

For 6:
   2kg strawberries
   Juice of 1 orange
   Juice of 1 lemon
   Caster or vanilla sugar

Hull the strawberries and slice them in half. Drizzle with the orange and lemon juice, and enough caster sugar to taste. Chill for an hour or until you are ready for them, stirring from time to time.

Strawberries with meringues

These slightly gooey-centred meringues, served with strawberries, remain one of the best ever puddings. My daughter Rosie has her birthday in the summer and we almost always have this then. Strawberries are, of course, also delicious with pavlova (see page 353).

For 12–14 large meringues:
   Sunflower oil
   4 egg whites, room temperature
   110g granulated sugar
   110g caster sugar
   1.5–2kg hulled strawberries
   Double cream or ice cream,
      to serve

Cover a baking tray with a layer of greaseproof paper and rub a little sunflower oil over the surface or, if you have one, use a silicon mat.

Whisk the egg whites until very stiff and dry. Add the granulated sugar, one tablespoon at a time. Keep whisking and continue until the egg white regains its stiffness. Then carefully fold in the caster sugar with a large metal spoon.

Put tablespoonfuls of this mixture on the prepared paper or mat and cook in a very low oven to dry out at 110°C/gas mark ¼ for 2 hours. Leave in the oven until cold before taking them off the paper or mat.

Serve with strawberries and cream or ice cream.

Strawberries Romanoff

A more sophisticated version of a fruit sundae. Children may prefer sweet wine instead of Cointreau.

For 4–6:
- **700g strawberries**
- **80g caster sugar, or to taste**
- **200ml double cream**
- **3 tablespoons Cointreau**
- **250ml homemade vanilla ice cream (see page 201, Quick lavender ice cream, but leave out the lavender)**

Hull the strawberries, halving the large ones, and sprinkle with the sugar. Chill well and, just before serving, transfer the strawberries to a glass serving dish (or individual glasses).

Beat the cream with the Cointreau and then beat the ice cream and fold the two together. Spoon the mixture over the strawberries.

Fresh strawberry and shortbread tart

I love this orange-flavoured shortbread base from Claire MacDonald with almost any fruit. You can ring the changes with it and use cinnamon instead of orange – particularly good topped with raspberries.

For 6–8:
For the base:
- **175g softened unsalted butter, cut into little chunks**
- **175g plain flour**
- **50g semolina**
- **50g caster sugar**
- **Grated zest of 2 oranges**

For the topping:
- **250ml double cream**
- **1 tablespoon caster sugar**
- **Juice of ½ lemon**
- **1kg strawberries, hulled**
- **Icing sugar or caster sugar, for sprinkling**

Preheat the oven to 160ºC/gas mark 3. Grease a loose-based 20cm tart tin.

Combine the base ingredients in a food processor and blend for a minute, or mix together in a bowl, rubbing the butter into the dry ingredients. Press the shortbread mixture into the tin to cover the base. Prick with a fork and bake in the preheated oven for 40–45 minutes. Cover with foil if it begins to brown too soon. It should be a light biscuit colour.

Let it cool for 10 minutes, then remove from the tin and leave on a wire rack to cool further.

Meanwhile, whip the cream, adding the caster sugar and lemon juice to taste.

Pile this on to the cooled shortbread base and add as many strawberries as you can.

Sprinkle icing sugar or more caster sugar over the top.

Strawberries with rosé wine

You'll find this pudding all over southern France, where it's eaten with a bottle of ice-cold rosé wine.

For 4:
- **1kg strawberries, hulled**
- **100g caster sugar**
- **150ml rosé wine**

Put the strawberries (halving the large ones) into a large serving bowl. Sprinkle with the sugar and drizzle over the wine. Stir them from time to time.

Prepare this about an hour before you want to eat.

Champagne cocktail with alpine strawberries

Alpine strawberries are delicious, but tiny. This is a luxurious summer drink that will make a little go a long way, as you don't need a lot of fruit.

For 8 glasses:
8 sugar lumps
8 dashes of Angostura Bitters
125g alpine strawberries, mushed
1 bottle of chilled champagne
or sparkling wine

Put one sugar lump flavoured with a dash of Angostura Bitters in each glass.

Divide the strawberry mush between the glasses and fill up with champagne or sparkling wine.

French strawberry jam

An excellent runny jam that is not too sweet, perfect with scones and cream or added to yoghurt or porridge.

For about 5 jars:
1kg strawberries (if you are not adding wild strawberries, use 1.25kg)
250g wild or alpine strawberries (optional)
850g sugar
Juice of 1 lemon

Hull the strawberries and cut them in half or quarters, if very large. (Leave the wild strawberries whole, if using, and put them to one side.)

Put the halved strawberries into a large heavy-based pan with the sugar and lemon juice. Warm the pan over a very low heat, stirring until the sugar has completely dissolved, and then raise the heat and bring to the boil, stirring continuously. Allow the fruit to boil for 5 minutes, add the wild strawberries, if using, and boil for a further 2 minutes.

Remove from the heat, skim off the scum with a large metal spoon and allow the jam to stand for at least 20 minutes before putting into warm sterilised jars. Cover with wax discs and seal.

This keeps well but is better kept in the fridge after opening.

Alpine strawberry gratin

A gratin usually implies cooking, but not here. This needs to sit in the fridge for a while, but only takes 10 minutes to make and everyone always loves it.

For 6:
300ml double cream
300ml natural yoghurt
225g alpine strawberries
Grated zest of 1 lemon
Caster sugar, to taste
Lemon juice, to taste
115g demerara sugar

Whip the double cream to soft peaks and fold in the yoghurt, a few of the alpine strawberries, and the lemon zest with enough caster sugar and lemon juice to taste.

Fill the bottom of 6 ramekin dishes – or a large dish if you prefer – with the remaining strawberries and cover with the cream mixture. Over this carefully spread the demerara sugar, smoothing it with the back of a spoon. Put into the fridge for at least 2 hours to form a crust. Add lots of extra strawberries on the plate around each ramekin.

Apricots, peaches and nectarines

There are few things I love more for breakfast than a slice of fluffy white bread with sweet unsalted butter and golden-yellow apricot jam.

Apricots don't grow and ripen reliably in the open in Britain as they need plenty of warmth and shelter. They are most successful with the trees fanned out against a south-facing wall or, better still, grown in a greenhouse. Although they are self-fertilising, the blossom comes in March, before many bees are around, so to ensure a good crop they need hand-pollination. Few of us bother with this, so you'll almost certainly end up buying apricots from France, Italy, Turkey or Greece.

I love the taste of apricots, but picked abroad before they're fully ripe, they vary hugely in flavour and texture, and are almost always best cooked. Use the less interesting and slightly under-ripe ones for poaching. Keep the best for tarts and, of course, making jam.

If you can get your hands on them, it's a crime to cook ripe peaches or nectarines. They are best eaten just as they are. As children, if we were very lucky, we'd be given a prized white peach from a ramshackle Victorian greenhouse where we went on holiday on the west coast of Scotland. Peaches and nectarines grew surprisingly well there. I still remember those wonderfully juicy fruits as some of the best things I've ever eaten.

In this country, peaches are most successfully grown in East Anglia and the south-east. 'Peregrine' is a good and popular variety, again best grown against a south- or south-west-facing wall, giving the tree and its blossom protection from the wind. Nectarines, the peaches' smooth-skinned and more delicate relations, are trickier, with a lower yield. In Britain, they really need to be grown under glass.

If you buy furry-skinned peaches and want to peel them, drop them into boiling water for 30 seconds. Lift them out with a slotted spoon, and plunge them straight into very cold water to stop them cooking. The skins then slip off easily. To stone them, slice them in half around the stone and carefully twist until they separate. Lever the stone out with a pointed knife.

The most luxurious way of using peaches is to make them into Bellinis, with a purée of skinned white peaches and a good Prosecco, one to five being the correct ratio. Just pour the peach purée into a champagne glass and top up with Prosecco, champagne or sparkling wine. If you like your Bellini sweeter, whisk a little sugar syrup into the peach purée. If you want to give it more of a kick, add a splash of peach brandy instead.

French apricot jam

Apricot jam is one of the best. The French are excellent at making jam that is not too set and not too sweet.

For about 3–4 jars:
1.5kg fresh apricots
800g sugar
1 vanilla pod
Juice of 1 lemon

Halve and stone the fruit, reserving a handful of the stones.

Put the fruit with the sugar into a preserving pan. Score the vanilla pod down its length and cut into three. Add to the fruit and sugar with the lemon juice, stir together and leave to steep for several hours.

If you have the patience, crack the stones with a nutcracker, or wrap them in a tea towel and whack them with a hammer, and remove the kernels. Blanch them in boiling water for 1 minute, plunge into cold water and remove the skins. Split the kernels in two and add to the fruit. They add a lovely extra taste.

When the sugar and apricots have softened, put over a low heat and stir until the sugar has completely dissolved. Turn up the heat and boil for 20–25 minutes, until the mixture is thick.

Allow to stand for 20 minutes and bottle in warm sterilised jars, ensuring that the vanilla and kernels are divided between the bottles. Cover and seal while still hot.

Once open, store in the fridge.

Apricot tart

Amaretti biscuits sprinkled on the base of this tart absorb the juice from the apricots, giving another layer of texture and taste. The tart is delicious served warm with cream, and fantastic with a chunk of Stilton or any blue cheese.

For 6:
675g apricots
50g soft brown sugar
6–8 Amaretti biscuits
2 whole eggs
75g sugar
200ml double cream
1 teaspoon vanilla extract
Cream or a chunk of Stilton
or any blue cheese, to serve

For the pastry:
75g cold unsalted butter
175g plain flour
1 dessertspoon caster sugar
1 egg, beaten
A little ice-cold water

Preheat the oven to 200°C/gas mark 6. Halve the apricots and remove the stones. Unless they are very ripe, sprinkle them with a little light brown sugar and roast them in the oven for about 20 minutes.

To make the pastry, using a food processor or by hand, rub the cold unsalted butter into the sifted flour until it resembles breadcrumbs and stir in the sugar. Add the egg mixed with a very little ice-cold water and bring the mixture together in a ball with your hand. Roll out and use to line a 25cm flan tin, then put in the fridge to chill for 30 minutes or so.

Prick the bottom of the tart all over with a fork, cover with a round of greaseproof paper or foil and weight it down with some baking beans or rice. Bake the tart case blind in the preheated oven for about 15 minutes, until the base is pale golden.

Take from the oven, but leave the oven on. Remove the beans or rice and the paper or foil, and let the tart base cool.

Crush the biscuits and spread over the pastry. Put the apricots, cut-side up, on the crumbs in one tight layer. Whisk the eggs with the sugar until pale and thick. Add the cream and the vanilla extract. Pour this over the apricots and bake the tart for 15 minutes in the preheated oven. Lower the heat to 180°C/gas mark 4 and cook for a further 20 minutes or until the custard is set and lightly coloured.

Peaches with Bourbon

This is an American recipe, one step up from eating peaches just as they are, that makes a wonderful summer pudding.

For 4:
  5 peaches, peeled and sliced
  100ml Bourbon whiskey
  1 teaspoon almond extract
  **3 tablespoons soft light brown
    sugar**
  Whipped cream, to serve

Put the peaches in a bowl with the Bourbon, almond extract and sugar, and stir them all together carefully, trying not to bruise the fruit. Cover and steep for a couple of hours.
      Serve with whipped cream.

Peach or nectarine zabaglione

Fluffy, light zabaglione is delicious with peaches and nectarines, or a mixture of the two.

For 4:
  4 egg yolks
  50g caster sugar
  **¾ tablespoon Marsala or
    dessert wine**
  **6 peaches or nectarines,
    skinned and sliced**

Lightly whisk the egg yolks and sugar together, and add the Marsala or wine.
      Put the mixture into a metal bowl and sit it in a wide shallow saucepan half-filled with simmering water. Whisk constantly until the mixture has swollen into a soft foam that nearly holds its shape.
      Arrange the peaches or nectarines in individual gratin dishes or one large shallow dish, and pour over the zabaglione.

Peach melba

A simple combination of vanilla ice cream, fresh peaches and raspberry coulis. It's not sophisticated, but it is delicious. You will probably make more of the coulis than you need, but it will keep in the fridge for a day or two and can be used on ice cream. Some toasted almonds or praline (see page 357) make a tasty addition to this pudding.
      For a recipe for vanilla ice cream, see Quick lavender ice cream on page 201, but leave out the lavender.

You need:
For each glass:
  2 scoops of vanilla ice cream
  1 white peach, peeled and sliced
  A few raspberries

For the raspberry coulis:
  500g raspberries
  **2–3 tablespoons icing or caster
    sugar to taste**

To make the coulis, put the raspberries and sugar into a food processor. Purée and then push the purée through a coarse sieve or mouli.
      In each fluted glass, pile in a couple of scoops of good vanilla ice cream. Scatter over the peach slices, pour over some raspberry coulis and finally add a few fresh raspberries.

Beetroot

You either love beetroot – it's one of my favourite vegetables – or you loathe it and, like my father, won't let it anywhere near your plate. I think he'd been forced to eat too much of it at school. It's true you don't want the purple juice bleeding all over other things, but as long as you keep it segregated, there's nothing prettier than a few chunks of beetroot. If the purple really puts you off, go for white or the lovely orange 'Burpees Golden', or choose the roots with pink and white stripes ('Chioggia').

As far as purple varieties go, my favourite is 'Pronto'. It is excellent whether eaten small or large, is slow to bolt (run up to flower before the root swells) and seldom forms that horrid black woolly heart.

Beetroot has a very dense texture, so the roots take much longer to cook than one expects. A fair-sized root needs well over half an hour before it's properly soft. Boil the roots, leaving 2–3cm of their tops, as well as tails and skins on, and then peel them once they've cooled. You can also bake or roast them. Wrap them in foil and bake for about an hour, or intersperse them with a couple of whole heads of garlic for a delicious smoky mild garlic taste. My favourite way of cooking beetroot is to lay them on top of a base of rock salt, mixed with different herbs and spices, and then roast them (see page 162).

Beetroot are emerging as another 'superfood', with the maximum health benefits gained from eating them raw. Grate them for salads (see page 163) or steam them to retain much of their rich vitamin and mineral content. You can cut them in half or quarter them to reduce the cooking time.

When beetroot are tiny, the tops are also good. Try them as a sweet-tasting addition to a mixed leaf salad. A good tip Christopher Lloyd gave me when I first started growing veg is to leave a few of your beetroot roots in the ground through the winter. In the early spring, they start to sprout tasty tender leaves with a vivid purple midrib, which look beautiful. You can treat these as cut-and-come-again leaves to add to your early spring salads.

If you grow your own – or buy really fresh beetroot, say from a farmers' market – the roots will sometimes come with their fully grown tops. Try cooking these in a little water and apple juice. This draws out the flavour and sweetness of the leaves, and they are delicious.

Roast beetroot with lentils and goats' cheese

The mixture of the texture of the lentils with the creamy sharpness of the cheese and the sweetness of the beetroot is wonderful. Eat this for lunch with a green salad or have it as a first course for supper.

For 6 as a starter:
  Coarse sea salt
  1 tablespoon cardamom pods, lightly crushed
  1 tablespoon juniper berries
  1 tablespoon caraway seeds
  1 tablespoon cumin seeds
  1 tablespoon star anise
  8 small to medium-sized beetroot
  3 tablespoons olive oil
  200g Puy lentils
  About 200ml white wine
  2 small garlic cloves, thinly sliced
  10 cherry tomatoes, halved (optional)
  Small bunch of flat-leaf parsley, finely chopped
  Small bunch of mint, finely chopped
  15–20 mint leaves, left whole
  Salt and black pepper
  200g goats' cheese, soft curd or cream cheese

For the dressing:
  Juice and grated zest of 1 lemon
  3 tablespoons olive oil

Preheat a medium (180°C/gas mark 4) oven. Scatter the salt and spices over the base of a baking tray and lay the beetroot whole on top, then drizzle over a tablespoon of the olive oil. Cook in the preheated oven for just under an hour, until the beetroot are completely soft to the tip of a sharp knife. Take them out of the oven and let them cool enough for you to peel. Peel and cut into small chunks. Cover to keep warm.

While the beetroot are roasting and cooling, cook the lentils in equal parts white wine and water, with the garlic and the remaining olive oil. Cover the lentils with about an inch of liquid in a pan and then add more if they need it. Once the lentils are soft but not mushy – this usually takes about 20 minutes – take them off the heat and drain off any excess liquid. Allow to cool for 5 minutes, add the tomatoes (if using), parsley and chopped mint, and season.

Lay out some lentils on each plate. Add a few whole mint leaves, then crumble the goats' cheese (or curd or cream cheese) over the top. Finish with the warm, fragrant beetroot cubes.

Make the dressing by whisking the ingredients together, drizzle it over the salad and eat while still warm.

Pantzarosalata

This is a dish that I've had with my friend Kate Hubbard. It's a delicious purée with a very strong flavour, using walnuts and beetroot, best served as a dip with pitta bread or with boiled salad potatoes and a green salad.

For 6:
   1 large beetroot (about 180g)
   4 tablespoons chopped walnuts
   30g stale white bread, crumbled
   1 garlic clove
   6 tablespoons olive oil
   2 tablespoons red wine vinegar
   ½ teaspoon salt

Cook the beetroot in boiling water for 30–40 minutes, depending on size. Once cooked and cool enough to handle, peel it and chop it coarsely.

Blend this and the other ingredients together until smooth.

Grated beetroot salad with toasted mustard seeds and orange

This lovely nutty-flavoured salad is a fantastic-looking dish with any beetroot, and sensational with the stripy variety Chioggia. Once cooked the colours of this merge into a pretty overall pink, but raw the stripes remain.

For 4–6:
   3 tablespoons mustard seeds
   4–5 medium-sized beetroot (ideally an unusual-coloured variety such as Chioggia)
   1 tablespoon hazelnut oil
   Grated zest and juice of 1 orange
   Salt and black pepper

Toast the mustard seeds in a dry frying pan for 2–3 minutes, stirring all the time.

Peel the raw beetroot, grate it and put it into a large shallow bowl. Pour over the hazelnut oil and toss together with the orange zest and juice, toasted mustard seeds, salt and pepper.

Nadah Saleh's Lebanese beetroot salad

Nadah Saleh – the great Lebanese cook – came to our cookery school last year and demonstrated lots of vegetable-based eastern Mediterranean dishes suited to the summer and autumn. This was my favourite. It's delicious eaten as one of many meze, and lovely with grilled meat and kebabs.

For 4:
   4 medium-sized beetroot
   1 garlic clove
   1 teaspoon salt
   2 tablespoons tahini
   500ml natural yoghurt
   Handful of fresh mint leaves, coarsely chopped

Cut the beetroot into 4 and steam for 30–40 minutes until tender. When cool enough to handle, peel them.

In a bowl, pound the garlic with the salt and stir in the tahini and yoghurt, mixing thoroughly.

Cut the beetroot into chunks and put in a shallow dish. Spread the yoghurt mixture over the top of the beetroot and scatter with lots of mint.

Beetroot relish

This relish is delicious with smoked fish, ham and cold turkey.

For a large jar:
 300g raw beetroot
 1 teaspoon cumin seeds
 Olive oil
 **1 tablespoon grated fresh
  horseradish**
 **About ¾cm piece of fresh root
  ginger, peeled and grated**
 100ml red wine
 100ml red wine vinegar
 **Grated zest and juice
  of 1 orange**
 **1½ tablespoons light soft
  brown sugar**
 Salt

Peel and grate the beetroot. In a dry frying pan, toast the cumin seeds and set aside.

Over a gentle heat, add a splash of oil to the pan, then the grated beetroot, horseradish and ginger, and stir together.

Add the toasted cumin seeds and the remaining ingredients, with salt to taste, and cook for 2–3 minutes. Lift out the beetroot with a draining spoon and put into a clean warm jar.

The relish will last a good 2–3 weeks in the fridge.

Roast beetroot soup

There are many beetroot soup recipes, but this is my favourite. The secret here is first roasting the beetroot in the oven.

For 4–6:
 500g beetroot
 **2–3 large Swiss chard or
  beetroot leaves**
 **1.5 litres homemade chicken
  stock**
 1 tablespoon olive oil
 **4 shallots or 1 onion, finely
  chopped**
 2 carrots, chopped
 2 celery sticks, chopped
 2 garlic cloves, crushed
 Salt and black pepper
 **150g plain yoghurt or sour cream,
  to serve**
 Chopped tarragon, to serve

Preheat a medium (180°C/gas mark 4) oven. Tear the leaves off the beetroot, but do not cut its roots off. Scrub the roots clean and roast in the oven for an hour or so. The beetroot are cooked when the skin looks wrinkled and can be easily pushed off.

If using chard, separate the green part of the chard from the stalk. Chop up the stalk and boil in half the stock for 5 minutes. Then add the shredded leaf and cook for a further 10 minutes. If using beetroot leaves, just cook the shredded leaves in half the stock for 5–7 minutes.

In a frying pan, gently fry in the olive oil the shallots, chopped carrots, chopped celery and crushed garlic, being careful not to burn them. Add all of these to the saucepan with the stock and chard or beetroot leaves, cover with the rest of the stock and simmer for 8 minutes.

Rub the skin off the beetroot and chop it up. Put in a processor or blender together with a small amount of the stock mixture. As you blend, gradually add the rest of the stock mixture. You can do this in two batches, if necessary.

Sieve or mouli the soup to remove any fibrous threads.

Add a little water if the soup is too thick. Check the seasoning and serve either hot or chilled, with a swirl of yoghurt or sour cream and a scattering of chopped tarragon.

Beetroot and mini onions in béchamel

This is fantastic comfort food, sweet and creamy, and wonderful with any roast meat and roast potatoes, especially roast lamb.

For 4:
- **4 medium-sized beetroot**
- **8 large spring onions/small onions or shallots**
- **1 tablespoon olive oil**

For the béchamel sauce:
- **300–400ml milk**
- **1 bay leaf**
- **30g butter**
- **1 tablespoon plain flour**
- **Salt and black pepper**

Boil the beetroot for 40 minutes with their skins left on, until you can slide a fine-tipped knife straight into the flesh to the centre. Leave them to cool for 10 minutes, then remove the skin with your fingers – it comes off easily. Depending on size, halve or even quarter the beetroot.

At the same time, peel the onions or shallots. These are best left whole, so go for small. Blanch them for 5 minutes in boiling water, then sauté them gently in a tablespoon of olive oil for another 5 minutes until they are slightly coloured and soft.

To make the béchamel sauce, bring the milk to the boil with the bay leaf and, in a separate pan, melt the butter. Stir the flour into the butter, allow it to cook for a couple of minutes and then gradually add the hot milk, stirring continuously. Season with plenty of salt and pepper.

Pour the sauce over the onions and beetroot, and leave the flavours to steep for 10 minutes before serving.

Risotto of beetroot, dill and Florence fennel

Make this when you feel like something with full-on colour and flavour. Serve it on a large white plate and eat it with a bright green Cos lettuce salad on the side.

For 6 as a main course, 8 as a starter:
- **500g beetroot, washed but not peeled**
- **3 tablespoons olive oil**
- **1 onion, finely chopped**
- **300g Florence fennel, finely chopped**
- **2 garlic cloves, finely chopped**
- **460g risotto rice**
- **1.75 litres vegetable stock, heated**
- **Small bunch of dill, chopped**
- **80g goats' cheese**
- **Salt and black pepper**

Wrap the beetroot in foil and bake in an oven preheated to 200°C/gas mark 6 for an hour. Leave them to cool. Peel them and then dice them into 1–2cm pieces.

Put the oil in a pan and cook the onion, fennel and garlic very gently until softened. Add the rice and coat it well in the oil. Then add the hot stock gradually a ladleful at a time, stirring all the time, as the liquid is absorbed. Cook it until the rice is al dente. This usually takes 15–20 minutes.

Add the beetroot and cook for a further 5 minutes, then add the dill and the cheese.

Allow to stand, covered, for 5 minutes. Then season with salt and pepper to taste.

Stir-fried beetroot tops with chilli and ginger

I first saw this Indian way of cooking beetroot greens in Madhur Jaffrey's book *World Vegetarian*, and I now cook them this way when I want a change from chard or spinach.

For 4:
- **450g beetroot greens**
- **3 tablespoons vegetable oil**
- **1 fresh green chilli, cut into long thin slivers**
- **3cm piece of fresh ginger, peeled and cut into long thin slivers**
- **½ teaspoon salt**

Strip the beetroot greens from the stalks and cut them into fine ribbons.

Put the oil in a large pan and warm over a high heat. When the oil is hot, put in the chilli and ginger. Stir them around for a minute and then add the greens.

Cover the pan, turn the heat to low and cook until the leaves have wilted. Add the salt and stir, then add 4 tablespoons of water and bring to a simmer.

Cover again and cook on a low heat, stirring occasionally, until the greens are tender.

Blackcurrants, white currants and redcurrants

Currants are an expensive rarity in the greengrocer. To find them in abundance, you need to visit a pick-your-own or grow your own. Apart from a cherry in full fruit, there's nothing more perfect in a productive garden than a white or redcurrant bush covered in chains of glassy berries. Every branch looks as though it was made in a Venetian glass factory, with each bead shining as if it were lit from inside.

The more sultry blackcurrants can look wonderful too. The best method of pruning a blackcurrant is to cut out complete branches – the older third – while they are still dripping with fruit in July and bring them in to the house to harvest. Put them in a vase to admire for a couple of days and then strip them. An early pruning allows the new wood to mature before winter and, if the pruning is done in time, to produce fruit the following year.

With redcurrants and white currants, you see their fruit most clearly when they're trained against a wall. As with most plants, they prefer an open sunny site with plenty of organic matter in the soil, but will still produce good yields in a less-than-perfect situation. Cordon-trained, they are ideal for a smaller garden, as they take up a quarter of the space of a bush. Netting them at fruiting time is also easier, with batons attached to the wall.

With currants, as with all the fruit in my garden, I aim to prolong the cropping time for as long as possible, so I select varieties which fruit in succession. For reds, 'Junifer' starts me off, followed by the classic 'Laxton's No 1', which produces huge strings of brilliant red berries from mid-July, with 'Red Start' to end the season. This has excellent disease-resistance and its late flowering helps to avoid frost damage, so it's ideal if you garden in a frost pocket or on a cold site in the north. For their translucent beauty and added sweetness, it's also worth having a white currant bush or two. I've put in 'White Versailles', an early-season heavy cropper with large sweet, juicy berries and good disease-resistance.

Blackcurrants are tougher and more tolerant, and they love a rich, heavy clay soil like mine, with plenty of organic material added. I grow 'Ben Hope', a mid-season, exceptionally heavy cropper, with tasty medium-sized berries.

A couple of other currant tips: always pick them when it's hot and dry – wet currants will go mouldy in a trice – and use a fork to remove the berries from the stalks. It's much quicker and easier than doing it by hand.

Blackcurrant and almond cake

This makes a good pudding, served warm with cream, crème fraîche or Greek yoghurt. You can make it in advance and reheat it gently, covered with a piece of foil.

For 6–8:
    200g butter, plus a little more
        for the flan tin
    200g caster sugar
    3 eggs
    200g ground almonds
    1 teaspoon vanilla extract
    200g blackcurrants, topped
        and tailed
    Icing sugar

Preheat the oven to 180°C/gas mark 4. Butter a 25cm loose-bottomed flan tin and line the base with a circle of baking parchment.

Cream the butter and sugar in a food processor or with a hand beater until the mixture is pale. Add the eggs, one at a time, beating well and, after each addition, fold in some of the ground almonds and a few drops of vanilla extract.

Put the mixture into the flan tin and scatter over the blackcurrants. Their flavour is intense, so don't be tempted to use more fruit.

Cook for 30 minutes until golden and just firm and, before serving, sieve over some icing sugar.

Blackcurrant cup cakes

Use blackcurrants, not imported blueberries, to flavour your cup cakes. They are fantastic in cakes, where their intense flavour is perfectly offset by the sweet softness of the sponge.

For 12 cup cakes:
    100g blackcurrants, topped
        and tailed, and a few more for
        decoration, plus a few drops
        of blackcurrant juice
    1 tablespoon light brown sugar
    100g butter
    100g caster sugar
    2 eggs
    100g self-raising flour
    1 teaspoon baking powder
    100g icing sugar
    A little lemon juice

Preheat the oven to 200°C/gas mark 6.

Pick over the blackcurrants, then rinse them and toss them in the brown sugar.

Cream the butter and caster sugar until pale and fluffy, and beat in the eggs. Then gradually add the flour, sifted with the baking powder. Stir the blackcurrants into the mixture.

Spoon the mixture quite meanly into fairy cake cases (remember that they will rise and you will need room for the icing once they are cooked).

Bake them for 15–20 minutes and then allow them to cool in their cases on a wire tray.

Mix the icing sugar with a little lemon juice and a few drops of blackcurrant juice to create pink icing. Ice the cupcakes and finally drop one blackcurrant on top of each.

Philippa's blackcurrant leaf sorbet

This is an approximation of a recipe that my husband, Adam, remembers his mother making. It's delicious – fresh and delicate.

For 4–6:
    3 handfuls of blackcurrant leaves
        (young ones have more flavour)
    Grated zest of 2 lemons and juice
        of 3 lemons
    175g sugar
    1 egg white, lightly whisked with
        a fork

Bruise the blackcurrant leaves with a rolling pin to help release their flavour.

Make the sorbet base by putting the lemon zest, sugar and 575ml water into a pan and gently stirring over a low heat until the sugar is dissolved.

Bring to the boil and add the blackcurrant leaves. Take the pan off the heat. Let it cool and add the lemon juice, then leave the whole thing to infuse for a couple of hours until the flavour is strong enough.

Strain and put the liquid in an ice cream maker and freeze/churn.

After 10 minutes, add the egg white, mixing it in well. Continue to freeze/churn for a further 10 minutes or until frozen.

You can do this without an ice cream maker (see page 69), adding the egg white just before you pour the liquid into the Tupperware.

Take the sorbet out of the freezer and put in the fridge for half an hour before serving.

Cassis

Cassis, blackcurrant brandy, is traditional for making kir with white wine. If stored somewhere cool and dark, this will last for at least a year.

For about 1.5 litres:
450g blackcurrants, crushed
450g white granulated sugar
570ml brandy
A few tips of new blackcurrant leaves

Strip the berries from the stalks and crush them (no need to top and tail). Put them and the other ingredients into a large kilner or screw-top jar. Leave on a sunny windowsill. Stir the mixture and turn the jars twice a week.

Leave for one month, strain and then bottle the liqueur.

Blackcurrant jam

This wonderful jam, with a powerful taste, is good on fluffy white bread.

For 5–6 jars:
1.2kg granulated sugar, still in its packets
900g blackcurrants
Juice of 1 lemon (optional, as the fruit is high in pectin, but good for flavour)

Warm the sugar in its packets or a bowl in a very low oven for about half an hour.

Strip the berries from the stalks – no need to top and tail – and put them into a heavy-based pan with 600ml water. Bring to the boil and simmer gently until the fruit is tender.

Add the warmed sugar and lemon juice (if using), and stir until the sugar is completely dissolved. Bring to the boil again and boil rapidly for about 20 minutes.

Draw off the heat whenever you test for set. Have a cold saucer ready and test by putting a teaspoonful of jam on the saucer and leaving it to cool in the fridge. If the jam wrinkles when you push it with your finger, that means it's ready.

Spoon off any scum from around the edge of the pan and allow the jam to stand for 15 minutes before stirring once and pouring it into warm sterilised jars.

Cover with wax discs and seal while hot. It will store unopened for about a year. Once opened, keep it in the fridge.

Redcurrant jelly

The classic jelly to eat with lamb, this is also invaluable for puddings (see right) and glazes.

For 10–12 jars:
    2.5kg redcurrants
    Sugar (for exact quantity
        see below)

Put the redcurrants, stalks and all, into a preserving pan with 1.7 litres of water and bring to the boil. Simmer gently until the currants are soft.

Put the pulp into a jelly bag and leave it to drip to extract the juice.

Put the juice into a clean preserving pan and for every 600ml juice add 550g sugar. Stir over a gentle heat to dissolve the sugar and bring to the boil.

Boil rapidly until it reaches setting point (see left) and then pour into warm sterilised jars. Cover with wax discs and seal. The jelly will store unopened for about a year. Once opened, keep it in the fridge.

Russian redcurrant and raspberry pudding

This is an adaptation of Margaret Costa's recipe for raspberries in her *Four Seasons Cookery Book*. The addition of redcurrants gives an excellent sourness to this summer classic.

For 4:
    250g redcurrants
    250g raspberries
    4 tablespoons caster sugar,
        plus more to serve
    275ml sour cream
    2 eggs
    1 tablespoon flour

Preheat a slow (150°C/gas mark 2) oven.

Put the redcurrants and raspberries into a shallow oval gratin dish, scatter over 3 tablespoons of sugar and place in the middle of the preheated oven, until the fruit are hot through.

Beat the sour cream with the eggs, flour and remaining tablespoon of sugar.

Pour the mixture over the redcurrants and raspberries and put the dish back in the oven at the same temperature but nearer the top.

Cook for about 45 minutes, until the topping turns a pale golden brown and becomes firm.

Sprinkle with a little more sugar before serving. This is best served hot or warm.

Emma's redcurrant steamed pudding

A lovely old-fashioned pudding cooked for me by Emma Bridgewater.

For 4–6:
    110g unsalted butter, plus more
        for the basin
    110g caster sugar, plus extra
        for the redcurrants
    2 eggs
    1 teaspoon vanilla extract
    175g self-raising flour
    ½ tablespoon baking powder
    200g redcurrants, stripped and
        rolled in a tablespoonful of
        sugar, plus more to serve
    1 small jar of redcurrant jelly
    Cream, to serve

Cream the butter and sugar together and then beat in the eggs, followed by the vanilla extract.

Sift the flour and baking powder together into another bowl, and lightly fold into the creamed mixture. Gently mix the redcurrants in.

Grease a small pudding basin with a little butter and spoon the mixture into it. Cover with 2 layers of greaseproof paper and then with a layer of foil, pleated to allow for expansion, and tied loosely with string. Stand the bowl in a large pan one-third filled with simmering water, cover and boil for 3 hours, topping up the water level with boiling water when necessary.

Heat the redcurrant jelly in a small pan. Turn out the pudding and surround it with more fresh redcurrants. Pour the redcurrant jelly over the pudding and serve with cream.

Frosted redcurrants with Chantilly cream

Make your redcurrants sparkle, and then dip them into this delicious flavoured cream. This dish is good with Almond meringues (see right). Note that the recipe includes uncooked egg whites.

For 4–6:
  2 egg whites
  450g redcurrants, in clusters on their stalks
  Caster sugar, for coating

For the Chantilly cream:
  275ml double cream
  1 level tablespoon vanilla sugar, caster or icing sugar
  ½ teaspoon vanilla extract
  1 egg white

Lightly beat the egg whites and use it to coat the redcurrants, using a pastry brush. Dip the clusters into a bowl of caster sugar to frost them and allow to dry on a rack or on kitchen paper.

To make the Chantilly cream, whip the double cream with the sugar and vanilla until it reaches the soft-peak stage.

Whip the egg white until it just holds its shape and fold carefully into the cream. Do this just before you serve the redcurrants, as it won't hold its shape for long.

Arrange 5 or 6 redcurrant chains and a dollop of cream on each plate.

Almond meringues

These are the most wonderful nutty meringues, and they taste fantastic with Frosted redcurrants (see left).

For about 20 small meringues:
  Groundnut oil for the baking sheet
  4 egg whites
  110g granulated sugar
  110g caster sugar
  Pinch of salt
  Grated zest of 1 lemon
  45g almonds, blanched, chopped and toasted until golden
  275ml double cream

Preheat the oven to 110°C/gas mark ¼. Rub a trace of oil over a sheet of greaseproof paper and use to line a baking tray. Alternatively use 'Lift-Off' paper or a silicone sheet.

Whisk the egg whites until stiff and dry. Continue whisking while you add the granulated sugar, one tablespoonful at a time, until the egg white regains its former stiffness. Lightly fold in the caster sugar, lemon zest and almonds with a metal spoon, being careful not to knock out the air. Put spoonfuls of the mixture on to the baking sheet and cook in the very low oven for about a couple of hours until crisp. Turn off the oven and, with the door open, leave the meringues until completely cold.

Sandwich the meringues together with whipped double cream, lightly sweetened to taste.

Cherries

There can be few things more beautiful than a fifty-foot cherry tree, with a forty-foot canopy in full blossom, surrounded by clouds of cow parsley. Fifty years ago, that would have been a common sight in much of Britain. There were extensive cherry orchards in Kent, Herefordshire, Hertfordshire, Suffolk, Devon and Buckinghamshire. Even five years ago, there were spring auctions in the village halls around Faversham and Sittingbourne in Kent, with orchard owners selling off the right to pick their fruit.

In the last twenty years, though, swathes of large-scale cherry orchards have been grubbed out. They couldn't compete against cheaper fruit imported by supermarkets. Huge trees are also difficult to pick and almost impossible to net against birds. What commercial cherry trees there are now are almost always grafted on to dwarf rootstock. These can be easily grown under nets, or even under plastic, to protect them from the rain. Gone is that majestic vision of cherry trees as far as the eye can see.

To add to their problems, cherries have a short fruiting season and do not store for long. They first appear in June, when French and Spanish cherries flood the market. These are good, but on the whole not as plump and juicy as the slower-to-develop Kent-grown fruit.

The best thing to do with a sweet dessert cherry is just to eat it as it is, grazing from a brimming bowl in the middle of the table. Sweet cherries make a good sauce for ice cream and are lovely in a fresh fruit salad.

Sour cooking cherries, the 'Morello' and 'Nabella' varieties, are ideal for bottling and pickling, and they make delicious jam. The good thing about a self-fertilising 'Morello' is that the birds tend to leave the sour fruit on the branch for you to pick. It has beautiful single blossom and is one of the few fruiting plants that will thrive against a north wall.

When you next visit a French market, look out for a cherry stoner. Hard to find here, this is a brilliantly simple tool for effortlessly stoning cherries or olives.

Cherry clafoutis

A classic no-pastry tart, which keeps the flavour of the fresh cherries, this must be served warm. It is a brilliant and easy recipe for other fruit too – I also love it with plums.

For 6:

Butter for the dish or pan
50g flour, plus more for the dish or pan
3 eggs
100g sugar
1 tablespoon vanilla extract
¼ teaspoon salt
250ml milk
450g sweet dessert cherries, stoned or not as you wish
Icing sugar
Crème fraîche, to serve

Preheat the oven to 190°C/gas mark 5. Butter and flour an ovenproof dish or a frying pan (about 23cm) with a metal or detachable handle.

Whisk the eggs in a large mixing bowl, add the sugar, vanilla and salt, and then sift in the flour. When the mixture is quite smooth, mix in the milk. This can be done in advance and rested for 2–3 hours, but is not essential.

Pour about 1cm of batter into the ovenproof dish or pan, cover with the cherries and then pour over the remaining batter.

Bake in the middle of the preheated oven for about 40 minutes, until it is puffed and golden-brown.

Remove the clafoutis from the oven and allow it to cool a little. If you've used a frying pan, turn it out on to a plate. Sprinkle the clafoutis with icing sugar. Serve it warm with crème fraîche.

Cherry compote for ice cream

This is the simplest way of eating sweet dessert cherries, almost as they are off the tree. Serve on top of good vanilla ice cream.

For 6–8:

100g unsalted butter
1 bay leaf
70g light soft brown sugar
2 tablespoons lemon juice
150ml orange juice
Pinch of salt
500g fresh sweet dessert cherries, stoned

Melt the butter in a pan and cook until it is beginning to brown. Add the bay leaf. Reduce the heat, add the sugar and make sure it has dissolved completely before adding the lemon and orange juices and the salt. Whisk while cooking, until the sauce has reduced by half.

Add the cherries and leave on the heat until the cherries have warmed through.

Morello cherry jam

Cherry jam can be very sweet and, certainly in France, it is often mixed with redcurrants to make the jam less sweet. Pulped and sieved redcurrant juice (500ml) can be added to the quantities below before boiling. Crack some of the cherry stones to reveal the kernels and add these – they give it a really lovely flavour. Do this with a nut cracker or wrap them in a tea towel and whack them with a hammer.

For about 6 jars:

About 1.35kg sugar, still in its packets
2.7kg Morello cherries, weighed before stoning
Juice of 3 lemons

Warm the sugar in its packets or a bowl in a very low oven for about half an hour.

Stone the cherries and tie the stones in a muslin bag. Put the cherries into a pan with the lemon juice and the muslin bag, and cook very gently until the juices begin to run and the fruit softens. Remove the bag. Stir in the warm sugar and make sure it is completely dissolved before raising the heat and boiling until setting point is reached (see page 170).

Remove from the heat. Skim the scum from the surface and allow the jam to stand for at least 20 minutes. Stir once before pouring into warm sterilised jars. Cover with wax discs and seal. It will keep unopened for up to a year, but refrigerate after opening.

Caroline's cherry tart

A good friend of mine, Caroline Owen-Lloyd, has a huge cherry tree and, in occasional bumper years, the birds fail to strip it bare. Then she uses the sweet black cherries to make lots of these tarts.

For 6–8:
   **About 600g stoned and halved
      cherries**
   Crème fraîche or cream, to serve

For the orange pastry:
   **75g butter, plus more for the
      flan dish**
   **170g plain flour, plus lots more
      for dusting**
   50g icing sugar
   Grated zest and juice of 1 orange

For the frangipane:
   110g butter
   110g caster sugar
   2 eggs
   25g plain flour
   110g ground almonds

Preheat the oven to 180°C/gas mark 4.
   To make the pastry, mix all the ingredients together in a food processor, or by hand. The mixture will look quite wet and sticky, but don't worry. Mould it into a ball and put it in the fridge for 30 minutes.
   Butter a 22cm flan dish or tart tin and roll out the chilled pastry, using masses of flour on your rolling surface so that it doesn't stick. The secret is to roll the pastry very, very thin. This recipe makes slightly too much pastry, which saves the usual anxiety of not quite having enough to line the base. Use any leftovers to make jam tarts.
   Pierce the bottom of the tart base with a fork and cover with greaseproof paper and rice or baking beans and bake blind for 10 minutes. Take from the oven, leaving the oven on, remove the rice or beans and paper, and allow it to cool slightly.

To make the frangipane, cream the butter and sugar, and add the eggs one by one, then the flour and almonds. Put the frangipane mixture into the pastry case and then fill to the brim with the cherries.
   Cook for 20–30 minutes in the oven until the frangipane has turned slightly golden.
   Allow to cool on a wire rack and then ease out of the case.
   Serve warm or cold with crème fraîche or cream.

Courgettes

So many people say they're bored with courgettes. They get oppressed by the huge quantities that even a couple of plants produce, and complain there aren't enough things you can do with them. I love them and think they're one of the most versatile vegetables you can grow or buy.

I grow the pale-green-skinned 'White Defender', dark green 'Defender' and bright yellow 'Taxi', all varieties bred for good flavour and disease-resistance. They last for ages in the vegetable rack, not losing much in terms of flavour or texture. With three different colours, they also look good together.

Particularly when they grow large, it's worth bleeding courgettes. Slice or grate them, sprinkle with salt and then let them sit in a colander for half an hour before squeezing them out with your hands or by putting them in a tea towel and twisting either end. You'll get loads of liquid out of them.

I try not to let my courgettes turn into marrows, but inevitably a few get away. I love the generous fatness of marrows, particularly the brilliant yellow ones, and so I often pick them to make an arrangement in the middle of the table. It's harvest festival time.

That uses up a few, but it's also worth having some recipes up your sleeve for eating marrows through the summer and into the autumn. Stuffed marrow can be watery and insipid, but it can be delicious too – and there are many more ways to use them.

Then there are glamorous courgette flowers. These aren't easy to buy in Britain, although you may find them at a good farmers' market, but if you grow your own courgettes, you'll have plenty opening in your garden every day. It's tempting to pick squash and pumpkin flowers too, but these tend to have a bitter flavour and are not as nice. If you've got only a few plants, harvest the male flowers only, but if you have a glut, then use the female flowers as well. These always have a courgette forming behind the flower. As you pick, lay them in a single layer in the bottom of a basket or trug and use them as soon as possible. Courgette flowers are delicious stuffed (see page 189) or simply dipped in batter, fried and then served with lemon juice and Parmesan.

Courgette risotto

This risotto looks good with different-coloured courgettes and plenty of courgette flowers. It has a delicious, creamy and gentle taste.

For 6–8:
   **About 1.5 litres good vegetable
      or chicken stock**
   2 shallots, finely chopped
   1 garlic clove, chopped
   2 tablespoons olive oil
   **6 small to medium-sized
      courgettes**
   **A few strands of good-quality
      saffron**
   Small bunch of tarragon
   500g Arborio rice
   1 glass of white wine
   Salt and black pepper
   30g unsalted butter
   **150g Parmesan cheese, plus more
      to serve**
   **Some courgette flowers (if you
      can find them)**

Put the stock on to heat.

Gently fry the shallots and garlic in the olive oil.

Slice the courgettes and add to the pan with the saffron and most of the tarragon, coarsely chopped.

Add the rice, making sure that it is well coated with the oil before you add any liquid.

Pour in the glass of wine and allow it to bubble up and evaporate before you season with salt and pepper and begin to add the stock, a ladleful at a time, while stirring continuously. The rice must absorb each addition of liquid before you add the next.

Keep adding more stock and stirring it in until the rice is al dente, which may take up to 20 minutes.

When the rice is ready, stir in the unsalted butter and Parmesan, and adjust the seasoning, adding a little more wine if necessary. Tear the courgette flowers into strands and scatter most of them over and through the rice. Allow to stand for 5 minutes or so.

Scatter with the remaining tarragon leaves and more courgette flower strands, and serve with plenty of extra Parmesan.

Courgette and dill farfalle

When we're not eating courgette risotto, we're often enjoying courgettes in a pasta sauce. You can make this with tarragon or sweet cicely, but I like it best with lots of fresh dill.

For 4:
   **6 small to medium-sized
      courgettes, thinly sliced**
   Salt and black pepper
   1 onion, finely chopped
   2 garlic cloves, chopped
   30g butter
   2 tablespoons olive oil
   **150ml sour cream or crème
      fraîche**
   Small bunch of dill, finely chopped
   350g farfalle
   **Plenty of Parmesan cheese,
      grated**

Put the courgettes in a colander, sprinkle with a little salt and let them drain. Dry on kitchen paper.

Sweat the onion and garlic in the butter and oil over a low heat for about 10 minutes.

When the onions are soft, add the courgettes and cook them gently together for 5 minutes without allowing them to colour. Add the sour cream or crème fraîche, and season to taste.

Let this bubble up and then add the chopped dill and immediately turn off the heat.

Meanwhile, cook the farfalle in a large pan of salted boiling water until al dente.

Drain the pasta and combine with the courgette sauce. Add more salt and pepper to taste, and plenty of Parmesan.

Courgette soufflé

Delicate and subtle, this is Teresa Wallace's adapted version of Elizabeth David's recipe. It's also nice cooked in individual ramekins, in which case reduce the cooking time to 20 minutes.

For 3–4:
- 30g butter, plus more for the dish
- 450g courgettes
- Salt and black pepper
- 25g Parmesan cheese or 50g Gruyère cheese
- 2 eggs, separated, plus 1 extra egg white

For the béchamel sauce:
- About 150ml warmed milk
- 25g butter
- 1 tablespoon plain flour

Preheat the oven to 180°C/gas mark 4 and butter a medium soufflé dish.

Grate the courgettes, salt them and leave in a colander for 10 minutes or so. Squeeze out any juices and dry on kitchen paper.

While the courgettes are draining, make the béchamel sauce. Bring the milk to the boil and, in a separate pan, melt the butter. Stir the flour into the butter, allow it to cook for a couple of minutes and then gradually add the hot milk, stirring continuously. Season with plenty of salt and pepper.

Cook the courgettes gently in the butter until soft, then mix with the béchamel sauce. Add the cheese, remove from the heat and allow to cool slightly. Add the egg yolks and plenty of black pepper, stirring all the time.

Whisk the egg whites to stiff peaks and fold them in. The secret with any soufflé is to have the basic mixture roughly the same consistency as the beaten egg whites.

Spoon into the prepared soufflé dish and cook in the oven for 30–40 minutes until risen and slightly firm on top, but still wobbly in the middle.

Courgette soufflé tart

This is a wonderful light fluffy tart of Tam's, which she has made for years using every veg imaginable. Her very favourite version is with courgettes. It sounds a bit of a palaver, but I promise you it's worth it, and it's as good cold as it is hot. Serve it with a tomato salad.

For 6:
For the pastry:
- 175g plain flour
- Pinch of salt
- 75g unsalted butter
- A little paprika
- 1 tablespoon grated Parmesan cheese
- 1 egg yolk
- A little iced water

For the filling:
- 2 onions, sliced
- 1 garlic clove, finely chopped
- 50g butter or 2 tablespoons olive oil, plus more butter for cooking the onions, garlic and courgettes
- 450g courgettes, sliced at an angle
- 2 tablespoons plain flour
- 175ml hot milk
- 175g Cheddar cheese
- Dijon mustard, to taste
- Grated zest of ½ lemon and 2 teaspoons lemon juice
- Small bunch of sweet cicely or tarragon
- Salt and black pepper
- 3 eggs, separated
- 142ml natural yoghurt

Make the pastry by combining the flour, salt and butter, and pulsing in a processor or rubbing the flour and salt into the butter by hand, until it resembles breadcrumbs. Add the paprika and grated Parmesan, and mix well. Beat the egg yolk with a little iced water, and then add this to the flour mixture. Use just enough to make a soft smooth dough that will hold together in a ball.

Roll out the pastry on a floured surface and use to line a 26cm tart tin. Put it in the fridge for 30 minutes to rest.

Preheat the oven to 200°C/gas mark 6. Prick the bottom of the tart all over with a fork, cover with a round of greaseproof paper or foil and weight it down with some baking beans or rice. Bake the tart case blind in the preheated oven for about 15 minutes. Take from the oven, but leave the oven on at 180°C/gas mark 4. Remove the beans or rice and the paper or foil and let the tart base cool.

To make the filling, fry the onions and garlic in a little butter or oil for 3–4 minutes and then add the courgette, and cook together for a minute or two until they're soft.

In a saucepan, melt the butter or oil and stir in the flour. Cook for a minute and gradually add the milk, whisking continuously until smooth. Add the grated cheese, mustard, lemon zest and juice, herbs, salt and pepper. Fold in the courgette mixture and put to one side to cool slightly.

Mix the egg yolks with the yoghurt and add to the cooled mixture.

In a clean bowl, whisk the egg whites until stiff and fold them carefully into the mixture, using a metal spoon. Pour into the pastry case.

Cook in the oven for about 25 minutes, or until set and golden.

Courgette and lemon salad

Courgettes are tasty eaten raw, fresh and simple. This salad looks lovely with different coloured courgettes, golden-yellow and deep- and pale-green. It is good just as it is, or with a handful of toasted pine nuts or quartered almonds scattered over the top. It's ideal with a rich creamy pasta sauce or risotto.

For 6–8:

3–4 courgettes
Grated zest of 1 lemon
**   and juice of ½ lemon**
Grated zest of 1 lime
**   and juice of ½ lime**
2 tablespoons olive oil
2 tablespoons chopped summer
**   savory or tarragon**
1 teaspoon runny honey
Salt and black pepper

Cut the courgettes very thinly lengthways with a potato peeler and put the slices in a shallow dish. Grate over the zest of the lemon and lime.

Make a dressing with the olive oil, lime and lemon juice, together with the herbs, honey and salt and pepper.

Pour the dressing over the courgettes and toss gently.

Greek courgette pie

This is delicious warm and almost as good cold. The Greeks make it at the weekend and then eat it cold for breakfast or lunch for the rest of the week. It's good with a tomato and onion salad.

For 10–12:

1kg courgettes
Salt
1 large onion, chopped
4 spring onions, chopped
150ml olive oil
1 pack of filo pastry
300g feta cheese
3 eggs
120ml double cream
Small bunch of dill
Small bunch of parsley
Mint leaves stripped from
　　2–3 stems
Milk, for glazing
Sesame seeds for scattering

Grate the courgettes and salt them, allowing them to drain for 30 minutes. Squeeze out any excess juice.

Fry both types of onions in a little of the olive oil until they're soft and then add the courgettes. Fry them together gently for 15 minutes until the excess liquid evaporates.

Meanwhile, preheat the oven to 200°C/gas mark 6. Separate out 6 filo pastry sheets and brush them with oil on both sides. If the pastry seems to be a bit dry, lay it between two damp clean tea towels.

Place 3 of the sheets in the base of a 30 x 40cm oven tray, one oiled sheet layered on top of the next.

Pour in the courgette mixture and crumble the feta over it. Beat the eggs and cream together and drizzle them on top. Add the herbs, pepper and salt, and fork the cheese and egg mixture lightly into the courgettes.

Fold in the filo sheets enclosing the courgette mix and brush with oil. Then place another filo sheet on top and brush with oil, and repeat with 2 more sheets. Brush lightly with oil and snip most of the excess pastry around the edges, leaving just enough to tuck in right the way around the tin. Glaze the pie with a little milk and scatter sesame seeds over the top. Prick the pastry all over with a fork.

Put the pie in the preheated oven and cook it for about an hour. You can shake it in the pan to see if there's much movement. Remove from the oven when the pie is set and the pastry golden. Put a tea towel over the top and leave it to cool for half an hour before you eat.

Crisp courgette wedges with anchovy mayonnaise

I first had this dish at the restaurant De Kas in Amsterdam, and I've been making it every summer since. The triple layer of coating – flour, egg, breadcrumbs – gives these the most delicious crunch. If you're not one for anchovies, try the wedges dipped into Green mayonnaise (see page 83).

You'll probably have some of the mayonnaise left over, but it keeps well in the fridge.

For 4:

4 tinned anchovy fillets, drained
200g bread for crumbs
Grated zest of 1 lemon
1 tablespoon grated Parmesan cheese
1 egg, beaten
A little seasoned flour (salt, pepper and some English mustard powder)
400g courgettes, cut into wedges about 7–8cm long
Groundnut or sunflower oil, for frying

For the anchovy mayonnaise:

1 whole egg, plus 1 extra egg yolk
1 garlic clove
6 tinned anchovy fillets, drained
½ teaspoon English mustard powder
Salt and black pepper
275ml sunflower oil (or one part olive oil to two parts sunflower oil)
2 tablespoons lemon juice

First make the anchovy mayonnaise. Put the whole egg and the egg yolk in a food processor or bowl and mix them with the garlic, anchovy fillets, mustard, salt and pepper.

When the mixture is quite smooth, carefully add the oil in a stream while blending continuously, until the oil emulsifies and makes a thick and smooth mayonnaise. Finally stir in the lemon juice to taste.

Make the breadcrumbs by combining the anchovy fillets with the bread in a food processor. Add the lemon zest and Parmesan to the breadcrumbs.

You need 3 shallow bowls, one containing the seasoned flour, a second with the beaten egg and the third the breadcrumb mixture. Dip the courgette wedges into first the flour, then the egg and finally the breadcrumbs. Then shallow-fry them in the oil, with 5 or 6 only in the oil at one time, until they're golden, but still with a good bite.

These can easily be made in advance and heated briefly in a hot oven to crisp them up.

Serve as soon as they are all cooked, with the mayonnaise.

Matthew's stuffed courgette flowers

Matthew Rice grows lots of courgette plants, as much for the flowers as for the fruit. This dish is rich, filling and delicious.

For 8:
16 courgette flowers
200g podded peas (frozen is fine)
300g Philadelphia or other cream cheese
Salt and black pepper
Small bunch of parsley, coarsely chopped
1 tablespoon olive oil
Olive oil, for frying

For the tempura batter:
225g plain flour
Plenty of salt and black pepper
2 eggs
375ml cold lager

First make the tempura batter. Sift the flour into a bowl with the salt and pepper and make a dip in the centre. Add the eggs and, with a balloon whisk, mix in the cold lager to make a batter the thickness of double cream that is not too smooth. Keep this in the fridge until you need it.

Shake the courgette flowers to dislodge ants and earwigs and remove the stigma from the centre. Cook the peas in plenty of salted boiling water for 3 minutes. In a mixing bowl, combine the peas, cream cheese, salt, pepper, parsley and a little olive oil.

With your fingers, gently part the flower petals, leaving one finger inside to keep it open. Take a teaspoon of the mixture and carefully stuff the flower. The stickiness of the mixture will mean that you can seal the pointed end easily with a little twist.

Heat about 10cm of olive oil (the oil is an important component of the taste) in a deep pan, making sure the oil doesn't come more than one-third of the way up the sides of the pan, until it reaches about 170°C. If you don't have an oil thermometer, it's easy to test the temperature. Drop a cube of bread into the oil. It should turn golden brown in less than a minute. Dip each stuffed flower in the tempura batter, then fry them in the hot oil.

Turn them after 30 seconds and again after 2 minutes. When they're golden, remove them from the oil and drain them on kitchen paper.

These are at their best eaten hot, sprinkled with sea salt and ground black pepper.

Tam's stuffed courgette flowers

This makes a lighter stuffing. Sometimes I do some flowers stuffed with Matthew's mix and some with Tam's. One of each per person makes a good first course.

For 8:
1 tablespoon olive oil
½ teaspoon chopped fresh red chilli
Good sprig of marjoram or thyme, stripped and chopped
12 stoned olives, chopped
175g cooked couscous
100g fresh goats' cheese
100g cooked baby broad beans or peas
Salt and black pepper
16 courgette flowers
Olive oil, for frying

For the tempura batter:
225g plain flour
Plenty of salt and black pepper
2 eggs
375ml cold lager

First make the tempura batter. Sift the flour into a bowl with the salt and pepper and make a dip in the centre. Add the eggs and, with a balloon whisk, mix in the cold lager to make a batter the thickness of double cream that is not too smooth. Keep this in the fridge until you need it.

Pour a little olive oil into a saucepan and, over a gentle heat, add the chilli, chopped herbs and olives. Cook for 2 minutes or so.

Remove from the heat and combine with the cooked couscous. Crumble in the fresh goats' cheese and the broad beans or peas, and season well.

Stuff the flowers with this mixture and then dip them into the batter and fry in olive oil until golden. Drain on kitchen paper.

These are at their best eaten hot, sprinkled with salt.

Courgette chutney

Sometimes you feel as if you're sinking under a garden full of courgettes. You can leave them to grow into marrows, but this stops the plants producing so much small fruit. This chutney is a good way of using them up. The recipe was given to me by the chef Paul Burton, taught to him by his grandmother.

For 3–4 jars:
Pickling spices (coriander seeds, yellow mustard seeds, dried chillies, allspice, ginger, black peppercorns and a couple of bay leaves)
700g courgettes
250g raisins
250g dried apricots
1 small green apple
250g sugar
¾ tablespoon salt
500ml white wine vinegar

Tie the spices in a muslin bag.

Cut the courgettes into cubes. In a large preserving pan, combine with all the other ingredients and tie the muslin bag on to the handle so that it dangles into the mixture. Leave it for 24 hours.

Stir over a low heat to dissolve the sugar gently.

Cover and simmer for at least an hour, pressing the bag of spices from time to time, until the pieces of courgette are translucent and the liquid is golden and syrupy.

Pour into warm sterilised jars and cover or use the woollen jumper technique (see page 304).

Marrow and coconut soup

You can make this fantastic soup with courgettes, and it's a delicious way of using the bigger, fatter and more abundant marrow, but only if deseeded and salted.

My godmother, Marni Hodgkin, cuts this recipe right down to softened onion, courgette or marrow, some good stock and a tin of coconut milk. Try this if you want something really simple.

For 4–6:
1kg medium-sized marrow or about 8 courgettes
Salt
1 large onion, chopped
1 tablespoon olive oil
1 teaspoon grated fresh ginger
2 garlic cloves, crushed
2 tablespoons chopped basil, plus more to serve
2 tablespoons chopped mint, plus more to serve
1 litre chicken or vegetable stock
250ml coconut milk

Peel and deseed the marrow and cut it, or the courgettes, if using instead, into 2cm chunks. Put them into a colander, sprinkle with salt and let them drain for 30 minutes to get rid of the excess water. Pat them dry.

Fry the onion gently in the oil. Add the grated ginger and garlic, plus the marrow or courgette chunks. Add the basil and mint with half the stock and cook for 10 minutes.

Blend in a food processor and then put the liquid back in the pan with the rest of the stock and the coconut milk. Simmer for about 5 minutes.

Throw in another tablespoon of mint and basil leaves as you eat.

Marrow and ginger jam

This is an Edwardian recipe. The lemon jelly and pineapple may sound like bizarre additions, but this makes a heavenly syrupy compote.

For 4–5 jars:
  1kg marrow
  Juice and grated zest of
    2–3 unwaxed lemons
  8cm piece of fresh root ginger
  750g granulated sugar
  1 packet of lemon jelly
  1 small tin of pineapple, thinly
    cut, drained

Peel the marrow, remove the seeds and cut the flesh into cubes. This is long-cooked, so there's no need to salt and bleed.

Bruise the piece of ginger and tie it in a muslin bag.

In a large bowl, layer the marrow with the sugar, lemon juice and zest, and put the bag of ginger in so that it hangs over the side of the bowl. Leave the whole mixture steeping for 24 hours.

Place it all in a preserving pan with the ginger again tied to the handle and stir to dissolve the sugar gently over a low heat. Add the lemon jelly and pineapple, cover and simmer gently (unlike the rolling boil usually used for jam or jelly). Press the bag of ginger from time to time.

Simmer until the pieces of marrow are translucent and the liquid is golden and syrupy. (It will have the finished consistency of a compote, not a set jam.) Pour into warmed sterilised jars, cover and seal. You can use this straight away, but it will store, unopened, for years.

Roasted marrow, aubergine and onion with balsamic sauce

When you feel like something virtuous and simple, this is a good supper, eaten with a dollop of Cucumber raita (see page 196) or minty yoghurt. Alternatively, serve it as a side vegetable with almost any meat or fish.

For 6–8:
  1 medium-sized marrow
  Salt and black pepper
  A little olive oil
  2 red onions, quartered
  2 aubergines, cubed
  100ml apple juice
  100ml balsamic vinegar
  2 tablespoons sunflower oil
  Small bunch of herbs, such as
    summer savory, tarragon and
    parsley, chopped

Peel the marrow, deseed it and cut it into chunks about 1cm thick. Put in a colander and sprinkle well with salt, then leave to drain. If you have something halfway between a marrow and a courgette about 25cm long, you shouldn't need to peel it.

Lay the chunks out in a single layer on a baking tray in a low (150°C/gas mark 2) oven for about an hour. This will dry them out further. Then pour over a little olive oil and whack up the heat to 220°C/gas mark 7 for another 15 minutes. This will brown the chunks around the edges.

Meanwhile, put the onions and aubergines on another baking tray. Pour over a little bit of olive oil and roast in a medium (180°C/gas mark 4) oven for 45 minutes.

In a pan, mix the apple juice with the balsamic vinegar and reduce it by three-quarters over a gentle heat. Add the sunflower oil.

Mix the roasted vegetables together and dress them with this mixture. Scatter the herbs over the top.

Cucumbers

It's the fresh, cool crunchiness of a cucumber's flesh that makes it so delicious. Unlike tomatoes, cucumbers – and almost everything made with them – are best served as cold as possible. They are also usually best peeled. Particularly when home-grown, towards the end of the season the skins can be tough. And for many recipes, it is worth salting them once they are sliced. You'll be amazed by the amount of liquid that they produce.

If you're growing your own cucumbers, choose a modern hybrid such as 'Burpless Tasty Green'. With modern varieties you have none of the bother of removing male flowers to prevent bitterness: this problem has been bred out of almost all cucumbers now. I've grown 'Burpless Tasty Green' for years. It's incredibly reliable and heavy-cropping, grown both inside in a greenhouse and out, producing medium-sized, smooth-skinned cucumbers with sweet tender flesh.

Sometimes I also grow a mini cucumber variety such as 'Zeina', which produces large amounts of 'Lebanese' cucumbers, the size of a large cigar. These are so prolific that it's difficult to eat enough, but keep picking: don't leave them to yellow on the plant or they'll stop producing. Make soup and pickles if you have a glut (see pages 195 and 197). Mini cucumbers are fantastic eaten freshly picked, topped and tailed, and cut lengthways to dip into hummus (see page 85) or creamy herby goats' cheese. I also like the old-fashioned round, so-called 'melon cucumbers' such as 'Crystal Apples', which are sweet and very juicy.

Much more popular almost everywhere in Europe – north and south – than here is the gherkin or cornichon, a mini cucumber pickled for eating through the winter with a plate of antipasti. A sweet dill pickle – not too acrid and vinegary – makes gherkins delicious and, for the first time this year, I made lots. They are wonderful with salami and cold meat, and I love them sliced over the top of Lamb burgers with thyme and rosemary (see page 49).

Mint and cucumber soup

This is an easy soup to make; refreshing and light, it is ideal for lunch on a hot day or as an almost-instant first course for a summer dinner. It's also a useful way of using cucumbers when there's a surplus. You can make a big batch and freeze it, but if you do, leave the garlic out to be added when you eat.

For 6:
  1 head of garlic
  2 large cucumbers
  Good bunch of mint
  30ml olive oil
  500g tub of full-fat milk, natural yoghurt or fromage frais
  Salt and black pepper

Roast the garlic (see page 253) to give the soup a delicious smoky background taste. Peel the cucumbers, slice them in half longways and scoop out the seeds with a teaspoon.

Strip the mint leaves off their stems and coarsely chop them.

Blend the garlic, cucumbers and mint in a food processor, then add the olive oil in a stream, with the machine still running. Stir in the yoghurt and add plenty of black pepper and salt.

Like all cucumber soups, this should be served really cold, with perhaps a flower-studded ice cube floating in the top of each bowl.

Cucumber and garlic soup with chives

Made with a stock base and plenty of yoghurt, this soup is a meal in itself if eaten with bread. It has a lovely sharp taste from the chives, fresh garlic and lemon juice.

For 4–6:
  1 large cucumber
  400ml Greek yoghurt
  200ml crème fraîche
  175ml cold vegetable or chicken stock
  1–2 garlic cloves, mashed to a very fine paste using a pestle and mortar
  2 tablespoons chopped chives, plus more to finish
  Salt and black pepper
  Juice of 1 lemon
  Purple chive flowers, to finish (optional)

Grate the cucumber. If the outer peel is tough, remove it; but if the cucumber is young and fresh it grates easily.

Mix together the yoghurt, crème fraîche and stock, and then add the cucumber, garlic and chives. Give the mixture a quick blitz in a food processor to combine.

Season the soup with salt and pepper and a little lemon juice, then chill it for at least 1 hour.

Ladle the soup into bowls and finish with chopped chives and, if you like, dismembered purple chive flowers.

Marinated cucumber and dill salad

This is a recipe from my friend Lucinda Fraser, and it's fantastic for making in large quantities when you have lots of people to lunch. It's at its most delicious eaten fresh, but it's fine made the day before.

For 4–6:
  1 large cucumber
  100ml rice wine vinegar
  110g caster sugar
  Good bunch of dill
  Salt and black pepper

Peel the cucumber and slice it as thinly as possible. (If you have one, use a mandoline or the slicing disc on a food processor.) Remove the seeds only if there are lots of large ones, but you must remove the skin.

Heat the vinegar in a small pan over a low heat and stir in the sugar until it has dissolved. Allow to cool.

Finely chop the dill. Layer a quarter of the cucumber in a small high-sided dish and season. Sprinkle a quarter of the dill over the cucumber. Repeat the layers.

Pour over the vinegar, cover and leave for at least an hour.

Drain the liquid (of which there will be lots) before you eat.

Cucumber raita

This is a very basic dish, but I make it all the time. It's a good meze to eat alongside falafels, olives, baby broad beans and bacon, or to have on its own with flat, pitta-style bread (see page 46). Without the turmeric, it's Greek tzatziki. The Greeks up the garlic to two cloves and add a tablespoon of olive oil.

For 4–6:
½ cucumber
¼ teaspoon fine salt
200g mild whole-milk natural
   yoghurt
Small bunch of mint
1 garlic clove, finely chopped
Small pinch of ground turmeric
   or paprika

Grate the cucumber – you don't need to skin – and put it in a sieve over a bowl. Sprinkle it with the fine salt and leave it to drain for half an hour. Pat the cucumber dry with kitchen paper. Mix with the yoghurt, mint, garlic and just enough water to give you the consistency you want, usually in the region of 100ml.

Add a pinch of turmeric for extra flavour and pale yellow colouring or sprinkle paprika over the top.

Fresh horseradish and cucumber sauce

Horseradish is delicious mixed with all sorts of things. It's excellent with beetroot (see page 164) and with sour cream and new potatoes. I love it with cucumber, to eat with almost any fish, and it's famously good with smoked fish, but also superb with fresh salmon and sea bass.

For 8:
5–6cm fresh horseradish root
1 cucumber
Salt and black pepper
4 tablespoons white wine vinegar
½ teaspoon caster sugar
230ml double cream, whisked to
   hold its shape, or crème fraîche
200ml single cream

Wash the horseradish and peel it, then grate it either by hand or with the grating disc in a food processor.

Peel the cucumber, slice it in half lengthways and scrape out the seeds. Grate or chop the flesh, sprinkle with salt and leave in a colander for about 20 minutes.

Put the grated horseradish into a bowl with the vinegar, sugar and black pepper. Stir in the double cream, followed by the single cream.

Dry the grated cucumber with kitchen paper. Fold it into the cream and season.

Surinam pickled cucumber

This is a recipe from Fanny Lichtveld, who lived for a while in Surinam. It's a wonderful way of storing cucumber for several weeks and it tastes delicious with ham and cold meat.

For about 500ml:
  1½ cucumbers
  1 tablespoon salt
  150ml cider vinegar
  1 onion, thinly sliced in rings or half rings
  2½ tablespoons sugar
  3 star anise
  1 tablespoon pickling spice
  1 red chilli, pricked or chopped into large bits

Peel the cucumber, cut in half lengthways and deseed, then cut up into large chip-like strips. Put in a colander, sprinkle with most of the salt and leave to drain for at least half an hour.

Slowly heat 275ml water with the vinegar, onion, sugar, spices, chilli and a pinch of salt until boiling. Warm the sterilised jars.

Fill the jars with the cucumber chunks and pour over the boiling liquid.

Seal the jars and keep them somewhere cold and dark, but eat within a few weeks. Keep in the fridge once open.

Sweet cucumber pickle

This recipe is excellent for the long-term storing of cucumbers. It's sweet and tangy, with a good crunch, and is delicious eaten with potato salad, cold meat and pâtés and in Cheddar cheese sandwiches. I am addicted to this and make loads. It stores for up to a year.

For 5 small jars:
  3 large cucumbers
  2 onions
  50g salt
  600ml white wine vinegar or distilled white vinegar
  450g granulated sugar
  1 tablespoon mustard seeds
  1 teaspoon celery seeds
  5 cloves
  ½ teaspoon ground turmeric

Peel the cucumbers and cut lengthways into thinnish sticks about 6–7cm long and about 0.5cm deep and 1.5cm wide.

Thinly slice the onions into half moons. Put the cucumber and onions into a large mixing bowl and sprinkle with salt. Cover this with a weighted plate and leave for 2–3 hours.

Rinse the cucumber and onion in cold water, and then let stand to drain. While they are draining, put all the remaining ingredients into a saucepan and stir over a low heat until the sugar has dissolved. Add the cucumber and onion, bring to the boil and simmer for 1 minute.

Remove from the heat and lift the cucumber and onion out of the liquid. Put into warm sterilised jars.

Return the liquid to the heat and boil rapidly for at least 10 minutes to reduce it. Pour the liquid over the cucumber in the jars and cover. Keep in the fridge once open.

Dill-pickled cornichons

These mini cucumbers should be pickled and then eaten with char-grilled burgers or salami and cold ham.

For 4–5 jars:
  1kg tiny gherkin cucumbers, about 5cm long
  3 tablespoons coarse sea salt
  4 garlic cloves, peeled
  3–4 sprigs of thyme
  3–4 sprigs of tarragon
  1 tablespoon black peppercorns
  2 bay leaves, cut into strips
  2 dried chillies, crumbled
  White wine vinegar or cider vinegar, to cover

If they're small, leave the cornichons whole; if they're large, slice them. Wash and rub them gently to remove the spiny bits. Put them into a colander.

Mix them with the salt and allow them to stand and drain for 24 hours.

Either rinse and dry or rub with a cloth, and put into sterilised jars along with the garlic, herbs, peppercorns, strips of bay and dried chilli pepper.

Fill to the top with the vinegar and cover tightly, ideally with a plastic lid. These are best stored in a cool and dark place, and will be ready after one month. After opening, store them in the fridge.

Edible flowers

I love edible flowers. They may be perceived as a bit fussy, but so what? I like bright colour in my food.

If you're patient, and I'm not, you can crystallise edible flowers and add them to cakes, but more realistic for most of us is to use them as they are, studding ice cubes or scattered in salads. Pointy, star-shaped rubber ice makers look the best, with blue and white borage flowers or delicate pansies frozen in the cubes. These look pretty in any summer drinks or floating in a cold soup.

English marigolds (calendulas) look lovely in a salad, as do dandelions and chicory, with their distinct tart taste. As soon as the summer gets hot, lots of your herbs will start to flower. Salad rocket is usually the first and once the flowers begin to form, the leaves turn inedibly hot. Don't chuck your plants until you've stripped all the flowers for adding to a bowl of salad. These taste similar to the leaves, but milder. Do the same with parsley, coriander, fennel and dill – all tasty and colourful. You can also scatter the flowers of borage, chives and any dianthus, rose or pansy, but with the larger flowers, pull the petals off the flower base first – don't add the whole thing.

Nasturtiums in salads have become so popular they're almost a cliché, but there are other ways of using these tasty, peppery flowers, and their buds and leaves. Add them to mashed potato or, even better, use them instead of black pepper in haddock fish cakes (see page 202).

My favourite variety of nasturtium is 'Tip Top Mahogany', with deep crimson flowers, contrasting with the acid-green leaves. There's also a new variety, 'Black Velvet', with even richer, darker flowers in off-black. Use these dipped in batter and fried for a Summer garden tempura (see page 207).

We think of lavender as a beautiful and fragrant ornamental plant, but it's also a lovely, unusual taste in puddings, biscuits, cakes and ice cream. Put a sprig into the custard when you're making crème brûlée (see page 202) and quiz everyone as to what they think the flavouring is. Rather than vanilla sugar, make lavender sugar for introducing this flavour to your food through the winter.

Stuffed lamb
with lavender

The flavour of lavender is wonderful
with meat, particularly lamb. To
make the most of the fragrant taste,
puncture the skin of the lamb with a
sharp knife and push some lavender
flowers into the meat, and also add
plenty to the stuffing.

For 6–8:
   1 boned leg of lamb
   Olive oil
   Bunch of lavender
   2 garlic cloves, sliced
   Good bunch of hay, washed under
      cold running water
   2 glasses of white wine
   Salt and black pepper

For the stuffing:
   150g medium couscous
   250ml good lamb or vegetable
      stock, boiling
   2 shallots, chopped
   50g raisins, soaked for a
      few minutes in warm water
   50g toasted pine nuts
   5–6 lavender heads, finely
      chopped
   Flat-leaf parsley, chopped
   Grated zest of 1 lemon
   Salt and black pepper

Preheat the oven to 200°C/gas mark 6.
      To make the stuffing, put the
couscous into a mixing bowl and pour
over the boiling stock, whisking with
a fork to break up any lumps. Cover
with a tea towel and put to one side for
about 15 minutes, stirring occasionally.
      Sweat the shallots until soft
and translucent. Once the couscous
is ready, add the shallots and the
remaining ingredients, mix well
and season with salt and freshly
ground pepper.
      Stuff the cavity of the boned leg
with the couscous mixture and tie it
into a good shape.
      Smear the surface of the lamb
with olive oil, season really well and

then make a dozen or so cuts in the
skin of the lamb with a sharp knife
and push into each incision a short
lavender head and a sliver of garlic.
      Make a nest of the washed hay
in a casserole dish and put in the lamb.
      Pour over the wine, cover and
roast the lamb for 20–25 minutes per
450g plus 25 minutes, and remove the
cover for the last 15 minutes to brown
the joint.
      Lift the lamb out of the
casserole, cover with foil and then a
tea towel, and allow to rest while you
strain the juices into a small saucepan
and boil to reduce a little.
      Check the seasoning and
serve with the lamb and some Rowan
jelly (see page 324), Redcurrant jelly
(see page 171) or Mint and apple jelly
(see page 231).

Quick lavender
ice cream

A delicately flavoured lavender
vanilla ice cream.

For 4–6:
   375ml milk
   65ml honey (lavender honey,
      if possible)
   4–6 stalks and heads of fresh
      lavender, plus a few more
      to serve
   1 vanilla pod, split
   Pinch of salt
   125ml condensed milk
   284ml double cream
   Strips of lemon zest, to serve

Heat the milk with the honey, lavender
and vanilla pod until just below boiling
point and stir gently. Allow to cool
completely, then pour through a
sieve to remove the lavender and
vanilla, and put in the fridge for half
an hour or so.
      Add the salt, condensed milk
and double cream to the chilled
mixture and freeze/churn in an ice
cream maker for about 20 minutes.
      Put into a plastic container and
freeze for at least 4 hours.
      To serve, remove from the
freezer and put in the fridge for about
15–20 minutes to soften slightly.
Decorate with fresh lavender and strips
of lemon zest.

Lavender crème brûlée

Crème brûlée is ubiquitous, as it's so easy to prepare in advance, but the subtle addition of lavender gives it a whole new lease of life.

For 6:
  6 egg yolks
  1 level tablespoon caster sugar
  2 teaspoons vanilla extract
  725ml double cream
  4 lavender flowers
  2 tablespoons demerara sugar

Beat the egg yolks with the sugar and vanilla extract.

In a heavy saucepan, heat the cream with the lavender flowers and bring to simmering point. Remove the pan from the heat and allow the flavours to infuse for 10 minutes or so. Strain through a fine sieve.

Put the cream into a bowl and stand this in a shallow saucepan of simmering water. Add the egg mixture and keep stirring. Gently cook the cream until just thickened enough to coat the back of a wooden spoon.

Remove from the heat and pour into an ovenproof dish or individual ramekins and chill in the fridge for at least 4 hours.

When well chilled, carefully sprinkle the sugar on to the cold cream and either use a blowtorch to caramelise or put under a preheated grill (about 8–10cm below the heat and it must be really red-hot before you start), watching carefully, until the sugar has turned to a golden caramel.

Smoked haddock and nasturtium fish cakes

This looks and tastes marvellous. Serve it with Really rich tomato sauce (see page 277) and a green salad.

For 4:
  500g undyed smoked haddock
  About 500ml milk
  A few black peppercorns
  1 bay leaf
  Some parsley stalks
  1 onion, finely chopped
  1 garlic clove, finely chopped
  A little olive oil
  4 medium-sized potatoes
  Knob of butter
  1 egg yolk plus 1 other whole egg, beaten
  100g Parmesan cheese, grated
  Salt and black pepper
  15 nasturtium flowers, torn or roughly chopped
  Seasoned flour
  Breadcrumbs

Put the haddock in a shallow heatproof dish and cover with milk. Add the peppercorns, bay leaf and parsley, and poach until just cooked.

Lift the fish out of the liquor, reserving this for later, and carefully flake with a fork, keeping the flakes as generous as possible.

Fry the onion and garlic in a little oil until translucent.

Boil the potatoes until tender, drain and add a generous knob of butter and some of the reserved milk in which the fish was cooked. Mash, but keep the mixture quite stiff.

Add the cooked onion and garlic and the egg yolk to the potato, together with some of the Parmesan, and season well with salt and pepper.

Very carefully fold in the flaked fish and some of the torn nasturtium petals, without mixing it up too much, and then shape the mixture into small round cakes.

Have three plates ready – one with seasoned flour, a second with beaten egg and a third with breadcrumbs mixed with Parmesan and nasturtium petals. Make sure that the fishcakes are lightly covered with first seasoned flour, then egg and lastly the breadcrumb mixture.

Put into the fridge for a couple of hours and then either shallow-fry or bake in an oven preheated to 190ºC/gas mark 5 until golden.

French and runner beans

A curious and inexplicable chic hangs about French beans. If Brussels sprouts remind you of a slightly ramshackle and tweedy farmer, the French bean – the haricot vert – looks as if it's dressed for Longchamps – slim, elegant and a cool pretty green.

I think that's why French beans are almost always best on their own, but whether eaten in splendid isolation or mixed with other things, they need to be fresh. You can tell that by smelling and breaking them. They have that characteristic very clean smell and, just picked, will snap in half sharply. Unfortunately, since these beans are often sold in sealed plastic bags, you can't put them to the test. Many are, anyway, imported from Kenya and apparently doused in many chemicals as they grow.

If possible, grow your own, sowing an equal quantity of a yellow variety such as 'Roquencourt', a purple such as 'Purple Teepee' and straight green beans. I like 'Masterpiece' as a dwarf and 'Blue Lake Climbing' as a climber. All of these are slow to get stringy, have a great taste, and the three colours together look fantastic on a plate.

When you want to eat them, top and tail them, and cook them in lots of already boiling water with no lid on the pan. With the lid on, the trapped steam and acidity from the cooking beans will turn the green ones olive. You want to dilute this effect as much as you can and allow the steam to evaporate. When they are just tender, plunge them into cold water and they'll stay bright-green and firm. The yellows keep their colour on cooking, but the purples will do so only if quickly fried or steamed with the lid off.

If you go away for a week or two and come back to big stringy bean pods, don't chuck them. Shell them and boil the beans inside in plenty of water with three bay leaves. Eat them, just soft, doused in really good olive oil. Alternatively, use them like borlotti (see page 302).

Runner beans come after French beans in the garden. There is no such thing as too small a runner bean. The smaller and more tender, the nicer they are. Left to grow more than about 20cm long, they'll get that horrid toe-nail-like membrane just inside their outer skin, so pick them as often as you dare. The more you pick, the more pods will form.

There are lots of ways of preparing runner beans, but I use a sharp knife to remove the sides and then cut them across into 2cm strips. Runner beans have wonderful-tasting flowers, similar in flavour to the bean. If you grow your own runner beans, don't grow a great long line of one variety: go for a pink and a white, as well as the more usual scarlet-flowered varieties.

Summer garden tempura

If you boil purple French beans, they turn a dark grey-green. By dipping them raw and whole into tempura batter and then shallow-frying them, they stay looking fantastic and taste even better.

Mix them with mini peppers, courgette flowers, aubergines and carrots for a wonderful plate of garden vegetable tempura. Dip them into Chilli dipping sauce (see page 318) and soy sauce.

For 10–12:
  750ml sunflower or groundnut oil
  2 handfuls of French beans,
    tops and tails left on
  2 red or green sweet peppers, cut
    into strips or, if small, deseeded
    but kept whole
  3–4 mild chillies, such as
    Hungarian wax, with stems
  1 aubergine, cut into discs
  4 courgettes, cut in half or whole
    if small
  3 courgette flowers
  2 globe artichoke hearts, cooked
    (see page 116)
  Selection of green herbs: tops and
    flowers of parsley, chervil, tips
    of basil and single sage leaves,
    whole
  8 nasturtium flowers
  A few roots (beetroot, mini
    carrots, sweet potato), cooked
    briefly and sliced into bite-sized
    sections
  Sea salt and black pepper

For the tempura batter:
  225g plain flour
  Plenty of salt and black pepper
  2 eggs, beaten
  375ml iced sparkling water or
    cold lager

First make the tempura batter. Sift the flour into a bowl with the salt and pepper and make a dip in the centre. Add the eggs and, with a balloon whisk, mix in the cold water or lager to make a batter the thickness of double cream but not too smooth. Keep this in the fridge until you need it.

Pour the oil into a deep pan so that it reaches about one-third of the way up the side. Heat the oil until it reaches about 170°C. If you don't have an oil thermometer, it's easy to test the temperature. Drop a cube of bread into the oil. It should turn golden brown in less than a minute.

Dip the vegetables, herbs and flowers into the batter, a few at a time, and then into the hot oil until pale gold and crisp. Drain them on kitchen paper.

These are at their best eaten hot, sprinkled with sea salt and ground black pepper.

Spaghetti with beans and tomatoes

The River Cafe team demonstrated this at our cookery school five years ago, and I've made it many times during the summer ever since. It's an incredibly fresh-tasting and yet comforting pasta dish, perfect when the garden is full of beans and tomatoes.

For 6:
  1kg tomatoes, ideally plum
    or small beefsteak
  300g French beans, topped
    and tailed
  Salt
  150ml double cream
  1 garlic clove, whole and peeled
  Handful of basil leaves
  400g spaghetti
  50g grated Parmesan cheese,
    to serve

Skin the tomatoes, deseed with a teaspoon and chop them coarsely. Cook the beans in plenty of salted boiling water for 3 minutes until they are just tender. Cool them quickly in a bowl of cold water and drain.

Bring the cream to the boil and add the garlic. Take the pan off the heat and leave the cream to steep for 5 minutes before removing the garlic.

Then add the beans, tomatoes and torn-up basil, and toss just for a minute to warm the veg through.

Cook the pasta in salted boiling water until al dente, drain and mix with the tomatoes and beans. Serve it with freshly grated Parmesan.

Trofie with potatoes, beans and pesto

Trofie, a hard durum wheat pasta with a spiral shape, makes a delicious dish with Marcella's homemade pesto (see page 225), potatoes and beans.

For 4:

500g trofie
Salt and black pepper
4 small new potatoes
200g fine green beans
2 tablespoons pesto (preferably homemade)
Plenty of grated Parmesan cheese

Cook the trofie in plenty of salted rapidly boiling water for 18–20 minutes, until just al dente.

Cook the potatoes, peel them and cut them into 1cm slices or chunks. Cut or break the beans into short lengths and cook for 2 minutes, until tender.

Drain the pasta, leaving 3 tablespoons of the cooking water in the bottom of the pan, and add a generous amount of pesto to the water, stirring it in to make a thin sauce.

Add the drained pasta, beans and potatoes and mix together gently to combine.

Serve with plenty of grated Parmesan and black pepper.

French beans in truffle oil with fillet steak and hollandaise

This hardly needs a recipe, but is one of my favourite summer garden meals – a rare fillet steak and a big mound of French beans tossed in truffle-flavoured olive oil and topped with almonds. You also want a good dollop of tarragon hollandaise. Pick a good handful of beans for each person, harvesting them when the beans are still small and tender.

For 4:

Tarragon hollandaise (see page 233), to serve
50g almonds, quartered
4 fillet steaks, each about 150–200g, at room temperature
500g French beans
1 tablespoon white truffle oil
1 tablespoon extra virgin olive oil
Sea salt

Make the tarragon hollandaise and store it in a Thermos to keep it warm. Roast the quartered almonds in a hot oven until golden.

Preheat a hot griddle, lightly oil the steaks and cook on the hot griddle for 3 minutes on each side. Let them rest for 5 minutes, wrapped in foil.

Cook the beans in plenty of salted boiling water for 3 minutes, tasting them at this point. They should be cooked, but squeaky. Drain and drizzle the truffle oil and olive oil over them while they're still warm, and toss to coat. Add the almonds and sprinkle sea salt over the top.

Your meat should then be perfect – still warm and rested for just the right amount of time. Serve with the tarragon hollandaise.

Salad niçoise

An excellent salad which features crunchy, just-cooked beans, waxy new potatoes, salty anchovies, quails' – rather than chickens' – eggs and, if possible, fresh still-warm tuna. It feels right on a hot summer day.

For 4:
300g (2 slices) sashimi-quality fresh tuna (or tinned tuna)
Olive oil
12 quails' eggs
450g French beans
Salt
450g new potatoes (such as Belle de Fontenay, Ratte or Charlotte), cut into chunks
10 roasted cherry tomatoes (see page 278)
2 red chillies, cut into thin strips (optional)
10 radishes, halved
12 good black olives (always avoid ready-stoned ones)
12 tinned anchovies, drained
20 capers, rinsed
Basil or chervil leaves

For the dressing:
3 tablespoons olive oil
2 garlic cloves, chopped
1 teaspoon Dijon mustard
1 tablespoon red wine vinegar
Salt and black pepper

Preheat a hot griddle. Brush the tuna with olive oil on both sides and griddle for 1½ minutes on each side. Allow to rest for 5 minutes and then slice it at an angle into 5mm slices.

Boil the quails' eggs for 4 minutes and leave them under cold running water to cool sufficiently for you to peel them.

Boil the whole beans in salted water for 3 minutes before plunging them in cold water.

Cook the potatoes for about 15 minutes, until they're tender, and let them cool a bit.

Make the dressing, by combining all the ingredients and some seasoning.

On a large flat plate, make a bed with the beans. Dress and toss them. Then add the cherry tomatoes, chillies (if you want them), radishes, potatoes, olives and anchovies. Add the shelled quails' eggs, throw the capers over the top and lay the tuna on top of that.

Drizzle with the rest of the dressing and scatter over some basil or chervil leaves.

Lemon bean salad

This makes a wonderful bean salad that is particularly good with chicken.

For 4:
450g French beans (thicker ones if possible)

For the lemon dressing:
Juice of 2 lemons and grated zest of 1 lemon
1 tablespoon mascarpone cheese
1¼ teaspoons Tabasco sauce
1 garlic clove, chopped
5 tablespoons olive oil
1 teaspoon ground coriander seeds
1 teaspoon English mustard powder
2 teaspoons sugar
Salt and black pepper

First make the dressing: whisk together all the ingredients and add salt and pepper to taste.

Cook the beans in salted boiling for water 3–4 minutes until just tender. Drain and plunge them into cold water.

Mix the beans with the dressing. Serve cold or at room temperature.

Runner bean flower salad

Scatter runner bean flowers over any leaf salad or make this bean tabbouleh, where the flowers take centre stage.

For 4–6:
  2 good handfuls of small tender runner beans
  Salt and black pepper
  100g bulgar wheat
  250ml vegetable stock (enough to cover the bulgar)
  200g tomatoes, cut into small chunks
  Juice of 1 lemon
  2 tablespoons olive oil
  3 spring onions, thinly sliced
  Very large bunch of flat-leaf parsley, finely chopped, tops of stems included
  Large bunch of mint, finely chopped
  ¼ teaspoon ground cinnamon
  ½ teaspoon ground allspice
  40 runner bean flowers

String your beans and slice into thin strips at an angle. Like French beans, the best way to cook them is for 3 minutes in plenty of salted boiling water with the lid left off until just tender. Then plunge them into a bowl of cold water and drain.

Prepare the bulgar wheat by boiling the vegetable stock and covering the bulgar with it. If you don't have any homemade, use very weak organic bouillon or even water. Leave the wheat to stand for 15 minutes in a covered bowl, occasionally fluffing it up with a fork. Drain it and press with a spoon to get rid of any excess stock, then let it cool.

Add the beans, tomatoes, lemon juice, olive oil, onion and herbs. Finally add the spices and let the salad sit for half an hour for the flavours to combine. Add the flowers just before you eat.

Runner beans with cream and savory

This is a delicious soft, creamy dish that is good with roast chicken. It also makes a tasty quick pasta sauce.

For 4:
  450g runner beans
  Salt and black pepper
  150ml double cream
  1 garlic clove, peeled
  1 tablespoon chopped summer savory (or thyme), plus more to serve
  Grated Parmesan cheese, to serve

String and slice the beans and cook them uncovered in rapidly boiling salted water for 3 minutes until they are just tender. Plunge into cold water and drain.

Put the cream, garlic clove and savory (or thyme) in a saucepan. Add salt and pepper. Bring to the boil and simmer gently for 2 minutes. Remove from the heat and leave for 10 minutes for the flavours to merge. Take out the garlic.

Add the beans, put back on the heat and stir to heat them through.

Scatter more savory (or thyme) and plenty of Parmesan over the top.

Gooseberries

Gooseberries certainly don't look promising. Green, red, pink, purple, black or yellow, hairy goosegogs are just not very alluring. But appearances can be deceptive – a gooseberry is a glorious fruit. I visited the RHS fruit garden at Wisley this summer and was shown round by the maître d'. We looked at figs, grapes, kiwis, melons, as well as the more usual strawberries, raspberries, apples, pears and currants, and at the end of the day, I asked him which was the one fruit that he'd take to a desert island. It was the gooseberry – good cooked unripe, excellent for freezing, lovely in jam and his number-one top flavour when eaten fully ripe from the bush in midsummer.

Gooseberries start fruiting early and you can usually begin to pick them in late May. At this stage, they won't be ripe and will need cooking, but especially combined with elderflowers, they are delicious in tarts, fools and ice creams (see page 143), or as a sauce for grilled fish. Harvesting some will help thin the crop, so that the remaining fruit can grow and ripen. Dessert gooseberries will be ready in July and August, and can be picked and eaten straight from the bush. 'Leveller' is a good variety and was one of the gardener-cook Christopher Lloyd's favourites, as it has thin skins.

Gooseberries are easy to grow, lower maintenance than most other fruit bushes and tolerant of almost all types of soil and situation. They flower early (particularly in the case of 'Leveller'), so frost can be a problem, and they have quite brittle branches, so should be protected from strong wind. You will also need to net them when the fruit is ripening or the birds will strip the lot.

The simplest way of cooking gooseberries is to roast them in the oven sprinkled with soft muscovado sugar and a little knob of butter. This is delicious with yoghurt or cream.

To freeze, just pack them into plastic bags or boxes as they come off the bush. Top and tail them after freezing. It's much quicker when they're still rock-hard.

Gooseberry tart

A tart of sharp, delicious just-cooked gooseberries in a very light pastry.

For 6:
    450g gooseberries
    3 eggs
    100g caster sugar
    284ml double cream, plus more
       to serve
    1 teaspoon vanilla extract
    Icing sugar, for dusting

For the pastry:
    150g plain flour
    50g caster sugar
    75g very cold unsalted butter
    1 egg yolk
    A little ice-cold water

Preheat the oven to 180°C/gas mark 4.
    Make the pastry by briefly processing the flour and sugar together. Chop the cold butter into chunks and add to the flour and sugar. Pulse carefully or rub in by hand until the mixture resembles breadcrumbs, and put into a mixing bowl. Mix the egg yolk with a little ice-cold water, add to the bowl and mix with your hands until the pastry comes together in a soft ball. Roll out on to a floured surface and use to line a 25–26cm flan tin. Chill for half an hour in the fridge.
    Top and tail the gooseberries. In a bowl mix the eggs, caster sugar, double cream and vanilla extract.
    Remove the pastry from the fridge and pierce the base with a fork. Cover with greaseproof paper and baking beans or rice and bake blind for about 10–15 minutes, until golden. Take from the oven, leaving it on, remove the beans or rice and paper, and allow it to cool slightly.
    Fill with the gooseberries and pour over the egg mixture. Bake in the oven for about 35 minutes, until just firm in the centre. Dust with icing sugar and serve warm with thick cream.

Gooseberry fool

The tartness of gooseberries is wonderful with the sweetness of elderflower and plenty of whipped cream. Serve this with shortbread or Hazelnut biscotti (see page 357). Another classic gooseberry fool is made with equal parts whipped cream and egg custard (see the recipe for homemade custard on page 256). Try that too.

For 4:
    450g gooseberries (no need to
       top and tail)
    175g sugar
    3 elderflower heads or 2
       tablespoons elderflower cordial
    275ml double or whipping cream

Rinse the gooseberries and put them in a saucepan with the sugar and the elderflower heads or cordial. Bring to the boil and simmer gently until the berries are soft.
    Remove from the heat, allow to cool and then remove the elderflower heads, if using. Whip the cream to the soft-peak stage.
    If you like texture, just crush the fruit; for a smoother texture, put the berries through a mouli or push them through a sieve into a large bowl. Fold in as much of the whipped cream as you like, depending how strong a taste of gooseberry you prefer.
    Chill in the fridge.

Gooseberry and thyme jelly

This is the jelly to eat with duck or goose, and it's lovely with lamb.

For 8 jars:
  2kg gooseberries
  Large handful of thyme sprigs
  Granulated sugar (for exact quantity see below)

Put the gooseberries into a large heavy-based pan and cover with 1 litre of water.

Make a bunch of thyme and suspend in the liquid by tying it to the handle.

Bring to the boil and cook until the gooseberries are really tender.

Strain the gooseberries through a muslin or jelly bag overnight. Don't be tempted to squeeze the bag or the jelly will be cloudy.

Measure the amount that has dripped from the bag. Warm the sugar in its packets or a bowl in a very low oven for about half an hour. For every 600ml of juice add 450g sugar. Allow the sugar to dissolve completely while you stir over a gentle heat. Then bring to the boil and boil rapidly until setting point is reached (see page 170).

Leave to cool a little, then pour into warm sterilised jars. After 20 minutes, add a sprig of extra thyme to each jar. Cover with a wax disc and seal. It will keep unopened for up to a year, but refrigerate after opening.

Jane's gooseberry and elderflower sorbet

There is a gooseberry and elderflower ice cream on page 143. Here is a lighter but equally delicious sorbet recipe of my sister's.

For 6–8:
  1kg gooseberries
  4–5 elderflower heads
  225g caster sugar
  Grated zest and juice of 3–4 lemons

Stew the gooseberries and elderflower heads in a small amount of water until soft and pulpy. Take out the elderflower heads and put them aside. Then rub the rest of the mixture through a sieve or mouli.

Dissolve the caster sugar in 600ml water and then boil hard for 7 minutes to get a light syrup. Remove from the heat and add the elderflowers, plus the lemon juice and zest.

Leave the flowers in the syrup until cold, then strain and add the juice to the gooseberry mixture.

If you have an ice cream maker, freeze/churn the mixture for 20 minutes; if you don't, put it into a plastic container and freeze, breaking up the ice particles a couple of times with a fork at 2-hour intervals.

Take the sorbet out of the freezer and put in the fridge for half an hour before serving.

Baked cream with gooseberries

A delicate recipe that was given to me by a great friend, Pip Morrison.

For 4:
For the baked cream:
   100ml milk
   2 elderflower heads
   1 teaspoon vanilla extract
   400ml double cream
   5 egg yolks
   60g caster sugar
   4 tablespoons sparkling wine or
      1½ tablespoons brandy

For the gooseberries:
   400g gooseberries
   2 or 3 elderflower heads
   50g caster sugar

Top and tail the gooseberries and put them in a saucepan. Add the elderflowers and just enough water to stop the gooseberries catching on the bottom of the pan. Cook gently until the fruit is tender and then either mouli or sieve to make a purée or leave the fruit whole. Stir in the sugar. Leave to cool.

For the baked cream, preheat the oven to 150°C/gas mark 2. Put the milk into a pan with the elderflower heads and bring to the boil. Remove from the heat, stir in the vanilla and the cream and put to one side for the elderflowers to steep, ideally overnight.

Remove the elderflower heads, whisk the egg yolks with the sugar and add to the mixture. Whisk for a couple of minutes, and then stir in the sparkling wine or brandy.

Divide the mixture between 4 ramekins and sit them in a baking tin half full of water. Bake in the preheated oven for 30–40 minutes until set. Allow to cool and then cover and refrigerate.

To serve, run a knife around the edge of the moulds and turn them out into the middle of each plate. Surround them with the gooseberries.

High-summer herbs

I pick and use herbs every day. They can transform a mediocre dish into something marvellous. In the summer, it's the turn of sun-loving annuals – basil, lemon grass, oregano and dill – which join the late-cropping perennials, such as mint, fennel and tarragon, as well as the deciduous shrubby lemon verbena.

Basil is almost everyone's favourite herb, and it's easy to grow with a couple of tips up your sleeve. If you can grow basil, you'll be fine with lemon grass and oregano, as similar rules apply. If growing these herbs outside – and that's a good place to do it, with less of a risk of whitefly than in a hot contained environment – don't plant them out until you are happy to have supper in the garden. If it's warm enough for you, it's warm enough for them. If you try to put your plants out too early in summer, or leave them out too late, the foliage and stems turn black and stop growing. In the early autumn, dig up your plants with a good-sized root ball and pot them up for picking inside. Dill is a little hardier and will survive for longer in the garden, but bringing the sun-lovers under cover will keep them going for a few more weeks.

If you want to keep your plants growing fast, keep them well watered, dousing them in the morning, not in the evening. With basil in particular, if the leaves are damp, slugs and snails have a feast after dark, so plants are best left dry overnight. This will also help discourage mould.

There are many varieties of basil to choose from, but the most intense aromatic variety is 'Sweet Genovese'. I'm also addicted to 'Mrs Burns Lemon Basil'. It makes delicious herb tea, from a handful of leaves soaked in boiling water for 5 minutes. Basil is also easy to grow from cuttings. Any time during the summer, cut your plant back and wait for it to re-sprout to 3–4cm. Then take your cuttings, strip their lower leaves and put the remaining stalk with leaf tips into water. In a short time roots will appear.

With oregano, it's the annual variety you want, not the perennial marjoram form, which looks good, but has less flavour. For mint, I grow 'Bowles' mint, also called apple mint, with furry leaves, and spearmint for cooking and salads, as well as Moroccan peppermint for tea. These perennial herbs need picking hard to keep them coming. They also benefit from a potash-rich feed a couple of times during the summer and cutting to within 6–8cm of the ground in June. They will quickly re-sprout, and then provide you with plenty of fresh leaves to pick right through the summer into the autumn.

Basil ice cream

I know this sounds odd, but trust me, it's one of my favourite ever ice creams. I first had this at the wonderful Amsterdam restaurant, De Kas. There they use sweet Genovese basil, but I also love making this with Mrs Burns Lemon Basil.

For about 4 litres:
2 large bunches of fresh basil
1kg caster sugar
600g mascarpone cheese
2.5 litres natural yoghurt

Pick the leaves from the basil stems and blend them with the sugar in a food processor.

Combine with the other ingredients and pour the mixture into an ice cream maker. Freeze/churn for about 20 minutes and either serve immediately or pack into plastic containers for the freezer.

Allow the ice cream 15 minutes in the fridge before serving. This has a wonderful flavour if it is eaten as fresh as possible. Don't store it for too long in the freezer.

Basil custards

Another creamy basil dish, from *The Cook's Garden* by Lynda Brown, this is perfect for lunch or as a first course for dinner. I add pesto and a little Parmesan. The custards are best served warm, turned out on to plates, with the fresh tomato sauce and some toast or bread.

For 4:
40g basil leaves, stripped
from their stalks
2 large eggs
175ml full-fat milk
4 level tablespoons plain
whole-milk yoghurt
1 large teaspoon pesto
(see page 225)
50g grated Parmesan cheese
Salt and black pepper

For the sauce:
225g ripe tomatoes, skinned and
deseeded (see page 266)
Small knob of butter
1 garlic clove, peeled

Preheat the oven to 160°C/gas mark 3 and butter 4 ramekins.

Coarsely chop the basil and then put it with the eggs, milk, yoghurt, pesto, Parmesan and seasoning into a blender or food processor. Process until smooth.

Divide between the ramekins. Put them in a pan and add hot water to come halfway up the side of the dishes. Bake for about 20 minutes, until the centre feels just firm to the touch.

Meanwhile, prepare the tomatoes and cook them gently in the butter with the garlic for 5–7 minutes. Remove the garlic and blend.

Let the custards cool a little, run a palette knife around the edge and invert on to warm plates, giving them a gentle shake downwards.

Spoon the tomato sauce around the custards and serve.

Gravadlax

You can always buy gravadlax, but as long as you think about it well ahead, it's easy to make and a fraction of the price of ready-prepared. Serve it scattered with coarsely chopped dill, dill and mustard sauce, and Buckwheat pancakes (see right). Gravadlax is excellent with Cranberry vodka (see page 418).

For 6–8:
1kg tailpiece of salmon in two pieces, scaled, boned and filleted, but with the skin on
Large bunch of dill

For the marinade:
1 heaped tablespoon sea salt
1 heaped tablespoon caster sugar
1 teaspoon black or white peppercorns, coarsely crushed
1 tablespoon Calvados or brandy
Plenty of chopped dill

For the dill and mustard sauce:
1 egg yolk
2 tablespoons Dijon mustard
½ teaspoon sugar
1 tablespoon white wine or white wine vinegar
6 tablespoons vegetable oil
Salt and black pepper
Small bunch of chopped dill

Prepare the marinade by mixing all the ingredients together in a small bowl.

Line a shallow dish with cling film and put a quarter of the marinade into the bottom of the dish. Lay the first piece of salmon, skin side down, on the marinade. Scatter half the dill over it.

Cover the salmon with half the remaining marinade, rub the marinade into the flesh and then lay the second piece of salmon on it, with the skin side uppermost.

Cover with the remaining dill and marinade, rubbing the marinade well into the skin. Lay over some cling film and cover with a board weighed down with a heavy weight.

Chill for at least 12 hours, but 24 is even better.

Meanwhile, make the dill and mustard sauce. Beat the egg yolk with the mustard and sugar, and stir in the wine or vinegar. Slowly beat in the oil until the sauce emulsifies (see page 233). Add salt, pepper and the chopped dill. Chill.

Drain the salmon from the marinade and slice it thinly with a very sharp knife. Serve with the sauce and buckwheat pancakes.

Buckwheat pancakes

I love making real blinis with whisked egg white, but these pancakes are quicker and easier to make. If you want, you can make a huge batch and freeze them. These taste delicious with Gravadlax (see left).

For about 16–20 pancakes:
2 eggs
220ml milk
40g butter, melted and cooled
125g buckwheat flour
2½ teaspoons baking powder
½ teaspoon salt

Mix the eggs, milk and melted butter in a bowl and whisk until smooth. Sift the flour, baking powder and salt into another bowl. Make a well in the middle and gradually add the egg mixture and beat together until smooth. Leave for at least 2 hours, or overnight if possible.

Heat a non-stick frying pan and put in a tiny bit of oil or butter to coat. Use a large tablespoon as a measure and ladle 4 individual dollops of batter into the pan. Leave the pancakes to cook for a minute or two, until you see them begin to bubble on top and set. Then flip them over and cook for a slightly shorter time on the other side.

Keep warm in a napkin or tea towel while you make the rest.

Basil oil

I enjoy making a few bottles of basil oil at this time of year to give as presents at Christmas, and for adding flavour to winter salads. There are many different recipes for basil oil, but I like this one from Jane Dunn, who runs the lovely hotel near us, Stone House in Rushlake Green. Very good expensive olive oil is often recommended, but it seems wasted to me when what you're after is the flavour of the basil. This oil is a beautiful emerald green.

For 550ml:
  Large handful of basil leaves
  Iced water
  275ml sunflower oil
  275ml mild olive oil

Blanch the basil leaves briefly and put them into iced water.

Dry the leaves, using a paper towel. Put both the oils in a food processor, add the basil leaves and process for about 3 minutes.

Transfer to a jug and leave in the fridge for a week.

Strain through a muslin and then pour into a sterilised bottle and seal. This keeps for a couple of months. Once open, store in the fridge.

Ricotta al forno

This is my favourite River Cafe recipe. When I was a waitress there twenty years ago, I made this all the time and I still love it. It's rich and yet fresh – wonderful with bread and a crunchy green salad. Sometimes I make it with olives, sometimes without.

For 6:
  Knob of butter
  150g freshly grated Parmesan
    cheese, plus more for the tin
  2 handfuls of fresh basil
  Handful of mint
  Handful of flat-leaf parsley
  500g fresh ricotta cheese
  120ml double cream
  2 eggs
  Salt and black pepper
  12 black olives, stoned and
    chopped

Preheat the oven to 190°C/gas mark 5. Grease a 30cm springform cake tin using a little knob of soft butter and then coat the buttered surface with a little grated Parmesan cheese. Shake off any excess cheese.

Put the herbs into a food processor with half the ricotta and half the cream. Blend until bright green. Add the rest of the ricotta and cream, and, while blending, add the eggs one by one. Season with salt and pepper and finally fold in the 150g grated Parmesan.

Spoon the mixture into the prepared tin and spread the olives over the top.

Bake in the preheated oven for 20 minutes. It should rise and have a brown crust but the centre should be soft. Serve immediately.

Marcella's homemade pesto

I use pesto in many recipes and hugely prefer the fresher taste of homemade to the bottled variety. Mix pesto with extra cheese to stuff baked potatoes (see page 339), have a dollop of it with grilled fish and put a teaspoon on big tomatoes when you bake them in the oven. This version is based on Marcella Hazan's recipe, although she adds 40g of softened butter and I never do.

For 6:
100g fresh sweet basil
120ml extra virgin olive oil
25g pine nuts
2 garlic cloves, finely chopped
Salt
50g Parmesan cheese, grated
2 tablespoons grated pecorino cheese

Put the basil, olive oil, pine nuts, chopped garlic cloves and salt into a food processor and blend, stopping from time to time to scrape the ingredients down towards the bottom of the bowl with a rubber spatula.

When evenly blended, pour into a mixing bowl and beat in the two grated cheeses by hand. Add a little more olive oil if necessary.

If you want to store the pesto, put it into a jar, smooth off the top with the back of a teaspoon and cover completely with a thin layer of olive oil. Keep it in the fridge and it will last for several months.

After using some from the jar, make sure that there is still sufficient olive oil to cover the top completely. This will keep it fresh and prevent it from losing its colour.

Before spooning the pesto over pasta, add a tablespoon or two of the pasta water.

Verveine sorbet

This is a delicious, sparkly-fresh sorbet, ideal for supper after a hot day. To give it a real punch, you need to use a lot of lemon verbena.

For 4:
185g caster sugar
About 80 lemon verbena leaves
250ml dry white wine
Juice of 2 lemons

Make a syrup by dissolving the caster sugar in 500ml water and then boiling hard for 7 minutes.

Wash and dry the lemon verbena leaves. Put them in a saucepan with the syrup and 250ml water, and bring gently to the boil.

As soon as the mixture reaches boiling point, draw the saucepan off the heat, pour the mixture into a bowl and add the wine and lemon juice.

Cover and, when cool, put it in the fridge to steep overnight.

The next day, strain the liquid, put into an ice cream maker and freeze/churn for 20 minutes, or until it is the right consistency to scrape into containers for the freezer. If you don't have an ice cream maker, put it into a plastic container and freeze, breaking up the ice particles a couple of times with a fork at 2-hour intervals.

This sorbet needs at least 3 hours in the freezer before you use it.

Take the sorbet out of the freezer and put in the fridge for half an hour before serving.

Whole fish stuffed with fennel

This is one of my favourite dinners: whole fish – sea bream, sea bass or salmon – absolutely fresh, with the cavity crammed full of fennel leaves, barbecued over fennel stalks and served with a salsa verde. It's also lovely with Lemon grass rice (see right).

For 6–8:
1.8–2kg whole fish (see above)
1 lemon, thinly sliced
Large bunch of fennel

For the salsa verde:
150ml olive oil
Juice and grated zest of 1 lemon
About 5 stems and leaves
of fennel
2 tablespoons capers (ideally
dry-salted), rinsed
About 8 stems of flat-leaf parsley
About 6 chives
About 2 stems of summer savory
About 3 stems of coriander

Light the barbecue or heat the griddle pan until it's providing a constant gentle heat.

Stuff the cavity of the fish with the lemon slices and as much fennel as you can fit into it.

Arrange a base of thick fennel stems (with a girth the size of the base of an average thumb – they then shouldn't ignite) and lay the fish on top of that.

Barbecue or griddle it until the flesh is cooked to taste.

To make the salsa verde, put all the ingredients in a food processor and blitz for 5 seconds.

Lemon grass rice

The perfect accompaniment to barbecued or grilled fish or chicken. Just add a green salad.

For 6–8:
1 onion, chopped
2 garlic cloves, chopped
2 small red chillies, chopped
500g basmati rice
Salt and black pepper
2 lemon grass sticks, cut
lengthwise and bruised
Juice of 1 lime

Blend the onion, garlic and chillies to a paste.

Rinse the rice thoroughly under cold running water and place in a pan which has a tight-fitting lid. Add enough water to cover it by 1cm and some salt. Add the lemon grass and bring to the boil. Cover, reduce the heat and simmer gently until all the water has been absorbed.

Fluff up the rice with a fork and stir in the chilli paste. Cook over a very low heat for a further 4–5 minutes.

Before serving, adjust the seasoning and lastly squeeze over the lime juice.

Lemon grass cordial

Lemon grass makes the most wonderful tea with a few leaves steeped in boiling water for 5 minutes. It also makes a delicious, thirst-quenching summer drink.

You can make it from the base of the lemon grass stems for sale in any supermarket, but if you grow your own lemon grass (which is easy to do from seed – see page 218), use the green, grassy part as well. You can marinate any fresh fruit in it; it's particularly delicious with melon (see page 234).

For 750ml:
3 lemon grass sticks
About 5cm piece of fresh root
   ginger
450g sugar
Juice of 3 large lemons (to taste)

Chop the tips off the lemon grass and bruise the base with a heavy knife or mallet before slicing thinly. Peel the ginger and slice it. Put these into a saucepan over a gentle heat with the sugar and 600ml water. Stir until the sugar has completely dissolved before raising the heat and then allow to simmer for 5–6 minutes.

Remove from the heat, add the lemon juice and, when quite cold, strain into a screw-top bottle. Keep it in the fridge until needed, for up to about a month.

Serve as a cordial, with thin slices of lemon or lime, and topping up the glasses with water – flat or fizzy – or tonic water.

Halloumi, mint, coriander and dill pittas

Ideal for a quick lunch or supper (or even better for a picnic around the fire), these are delicious pockets of herbs and salty toasted halloumi cheese. A great friend and cook, Ivan Samarine, made this for me, having had something like it in an Uzbek café in Moscow.

For 6:
250g halloumi cheese
6 pitta breads
Good bunch of dill
Good bunch of mint
Good bunch of coriander
2 tablespoons good fruity olive oil

Cut the halloumi into slices about 1cm thick and griddle or fry the slices until warm and beginning to melt.

At the same time, warm the pittas on the griddle or fire and then cut them open lengthways. Strip the herb leaves and chop finely.

Stuff each pitta with 3–4 slices of halloumi and a good fistful of the mixed herbs, then drizzle with a little olive oil.

Mint potato cakes

We ate these fantastic potato cakes sitting in a café in the Amari valley in Crete. They were served with a sharp ewes'-milk yoghurt dressing flavoured with fresh mint leaves.

For 8 potato cakes:
500g potatoes (floury are best)
1 onion
30g butter
2 eggs
Small handful of mint, chopped
100g crumbled feta cheese
2 tablespoons plain flour
Salt and black pepper
3 tablespoons olive oil

For the mint yoghurt dressing:
Small handful of chopped mint
200g ewes'-milk yoghurt
Juice of 1 lemon
1 tablespoon fruity extra virgin olive oil

Peel and grate the potatoes (I use the grating disc of my Magimix).

Slice the onion very thinly and sweat it in a little butter to soften.

Lightly beat the eggs and mix with the mint, feta and flour, then add the potato and onion. Season and mix well.

Flour your hands and make flat patties out of good dollops (about 2 tablespoons each) of the mixture. Fry these gently in olive oil on both sides for 5–7 minutes until golden brown.

To make the dressing, crush the mint, using a pestle and mortar. Add the yoghurt and thin with the lemon juice and olive oil to the consistency of double cream.

Mint-and-gingerade

Another simple and delicious drink, based on a recipe from Bill Granger's book *Sydney Food*. This is good hot, but even better cold with lots of ice on a hot day.

For 4:
1 litre boiling water
Good handful of mint leaves, chopped, plus more to serve
Grated zest of 2 lemons
2 tablespoons peeled and grated fresh ginger
3 tablespoons sugar
Plenty of ice, to serve

In a heatproof jug, pour the boiling water over the mint, lemon zest and ginger. Add the sugar and stir until it has completely dissolved.

Allow the mixture to cool, sieve and then pour it out into glasses full of ice and a few fresh mint leaves.

Mint julep

This classic summer drink from the American south is good for a party or sipped on a porch.

For 1 glass:
12 mint leaves
Crushed ice
1 tablespoon sugar syrup (see page 225)
3 tablespoons Bourbon whiskey
Thinly pared lemon rind (use a potato peeler)

Put the mint leaves into the bottom of a tumbler and bruise with a spoon. Top up the glass with crushed ice and add the sugar syrup, Bourbon and lemon rind. Stir thoroughly. Decorate with mint leaves.

Mint and apple compote

Strong-flavoured, sharp and delicious, this compote is delicious served with cold meat. It's also lovely with Moussaka (see page 301) and simple shepherd's pie.

For 3 jars:
   1kg apples
   2 lemons, plus juice of ½ lemon, for the water
   150g peppermint leaves, chopped
   700g caster sugar

Peel and slice the apples, and then put them in a bowl of water acidulated with lemon juice.

Drain the apple slices and put them in a large pan with the zest and juice of 1 lemon, the mint leaves and 1 tablespoon of sugar. Bring this slowly to the boil, stirring from time to time, until the apples are soft. Skim the top as any scum forms.

Push the mixture through a coarse sieve or mouli to give you a green purée.

Add the rest of the sugar and juice of the other lemon.

Cook the purée, stirring until it has the consistency of marmalade.

Pour into warm sterilised pots and seal. This will keep for up to a year, but refrigerate after opening.

Mint and apple jelly

Apple forms the base of many a good herb jelly. This classic mint jelly is a lovely colour and particularly delicious with lamb.

For 4–5 jars:
   2kg cooking apples
   175ml white wine vinegar
   Bunch of mint, plus some more finely chopped mint
   Granulated sugar (for exact quantity see below)

Roughly chop the apples and put into a bowl of water acidulated with a dash of the vinegar. Keep the cores and pips.

When all the apples are chopped, drain them and put into a large preserving pan.

Cover the apples with water, tie up the cores and pips in a muslin bag and then hang the bag in the liquid from the handle.

Add the bunch of mint to the apple mixture and bring to the boil. Add the vinegar and cook until the apples are really soft.

Pour into a jelly bag and leave to drip overnight. Don't squeeze the jelly bag as this spoils the clarity of the jelly.

Measure the amount of juice and for each 570ml of juice add 450g of granulated sugar.

Put the juice in the pan and stir over a gentle heat until the sugar is completely dissolved. Then boil rapidly until the mixture reaches setting point. Keep a saucer in the fridge and to check for setting, put a teaspoonful of the jelly on the cold saucer. When it cools it should wrinkle when you push it with your finger. Pull the pan off the heat while you test.

Skim the surface with a spoon in order to get rid of any scum and then add the finely chopped mint. Let the jelly stand for 20 minutes to cool. Stir it once more, pour into warm sterilised jars and seal.

Leave for a week or two before using, to give the mint flavour time to infuse. It will keep unopened for up to a year, but refrigerate after opening.

Tarragon vinegar

There's nothing better than tarragon vinegar, with that characteristic smoky flavour, for winter salad dressings. It makes the best ever hollandaise sauce (see right).

You need:

As much tarragon as you can pick (see below)

As big a drum of good white wine vinegar as you can get your hands on

Making this is as simple as it gets. Before the plants begin to die back in late summer, pick lots of tarragon.

Blanch the tarragon instantly, by plunging the stems into a jug of boiling water, to kill any possible bugs.

Then submerge the tarragon in the vinegar and leave it to steep for a month before straining. This keeps for years.

Tarragon hollandaise

Make a bowl of hollandaise sauce using tarragon vinegar and stir in some chopped tarragon. Dip in your new baby carrots, new potatoes, beetroot and sugar snaps. There are speedier ways of making this sauce, but in my experience they are more likely to go wrong. This works.

For 6:

3 tablespoons tarragon vinegar (see left) or white wine vinegar

6 black peppercorns

1 bay leaf

2 egg yolks

175g unsalted butter, cut into small chunks

Salt and black pepper

Bunch of tarragon, chopped

Boil the vinegar and 1 tablespoon of water with the peppercorns and the bay leaf until reduced to about 1 tablespoon. Allow to cool.

Half-fill a wide shallow pan with water and bring to simmering point. Put the yolks in a heatproof bowl, sit this in the pan of water and whisk well. Add the butter bit by bit, whisking all the time. As the mixture warms, it will gradually become thick and shiny.

Remove from the heat and stir in the cooled reduced vinegar, together with salt and pepper to taste, and the chopped tarragon.

If the sauce ever looks as if it is splitting, remove it from the heat immediately and beat in a tablespoon of cold water or an ice cube.

This sauce is best served tepid but can be reheated in a bowl standing in a pan of simmering water, or it can be put into a Thermos until needed.

I prefer the taste of the reduced vinegar, but if you like you can skip this bit and just add lemon juice to taste once the sauce is ready.

Chicken in tarragon cream

This is a well-known classic chicken dish, but remains one of the very best ways of using tarragon.

For 4:

Olive oil

50g butter

1 free-range chicken, jointed into 8 pieces

1 shallot, finely chopped

200ml dry white wine or vermouth

200ml tub of crème fraîche

Bunch of tarragon, chopped

Heat the oil and butter in a large sauté pan and brown the chicken pieces all over. Cover the pan and cook over a low heat – in the oven or on the stove top – for 25–30 minutes, until the chicken is cooked through, but still tender and moist.

Remove the chicken pieces from the pan, add the shallot and cook gently for 5 minutes until softened.

Add the wine and cook for a further few minutes, scraping up the juices from the pan.

Return the chicken to the pan. Add the crème fraîche and the chopped tarragon. Season and cook for 2 minutes until the cream is bubbling and thickened.

Melons

How do you tell when a melon is ripe? It's all in the smell. If you pick it up to smell the base of the fruit and get a waft of sweet honey, it means it's perfect. This is a particularly reliable guide for 'Ogen' or 'Charentais' melons, which are often the best and most worth seeking out. If the flesh gives a little when pressing the end, that's also a good sign. Melons will ripen a bit off the plant, but the nearer they are to perfection when picked and brought out of the sun, the better the flavour. That's why fruit in Continental markets – or, even better, bought from a stall beside the road – makes you green with envy, when you compare it to what we can buy here.

You can grow some melon varieties in Britain, but they are a hassle. They thrive in lots of sun and yet need careful temperature control, liking it neither too hot nor too cold. They can only really be grown successfully under glass, with careful watering. The two varieties that are suitable for growing in cool grey Britain which should give you sweet, tasty fruit are 'Sweetheart' and 'Ogen'. Both will ripen well here in August and September, and are productive enough to make them worthwhile if you have the space. To encourage them to form plenty of fruit, you must be brutal in pinching out the growing tips as they shoot.

If melons are truly ripe and fragrant, they are lovely eaten as a first course or as a pudding. Have them just as they are, the flesh scooped out with a spoon, or cut them into segments to eat with slices of prosciutto. Eat them as they do in France, with salt and pepper or with slices of stem ginger in a fresh fruit salad. Crunchy cubes of watermelon are excellent in salads with nutty pumpkin seeds, or try filling 'Ogen' melons with a mixture of alpine strawberries and redcurrants, sprinkled with caster sugar and ginger syrup or liqueur. I love chunks marinated for an hour or two in 150ml Lemon grass cordial (see page 228). If the melon is good you can't go wrong and if the melon is disappointing this will transform it.

Try and keep melons at room temperature, not in the fridge; but if you do need to store them in the fridge, wrap them well, or everything else will catch their flavour. Bring them out of the fridge at least half an hour before you eat.

Melon, pear and rocket salad

Melon is fantastic in salad, the sweetness particularly good with the peppery taste of rocket. This is good as a light first course and it's lovely with salami, bresaola and prosciutto.

For 6:
   1 ripe melon (any variety, or
      a mixture of watermelon
      and sweet melon)
   3 ripe but still firm pears
   100g pecorino cheese
   2 tablespoons olive oil
   Juice of 3 limes and grated
      zest of 1 lime
   Salt and black pepper
   ½ teaspoon caster sugar
   Large bunch of rocket leaves
   1 red onion, very thinly sliced
   60g roasted pumpkin seeds
      (see page 372)

Peel the melon, remove the seeds and cut it into chunks. Peel and quarter the pears and make shavings of the pecorino.

   In a bowl combine the olive oil, lime juice and zest, salt and sugar to taste, and mix well together.

   Put the rocket leaves, melon, pears and thinly sliced onion into a large shallow serving bowl. Pour over just enough of the dressing to coat the leaves and fruit, and scatter over the pumpkin seeds and pecorino. Add freshly ground pepper.

Teresa's melon with blackberries

Teresa Wallace made up this simple recipe when she had a glut of blackberries in her garden in Edinburgh one summer, and she froze bagfuls of them. Throughout the year she used them in various combinations. This one was the most delicious.

For 3–4:
   1 ripe Ogen or Cantaloupe melon
   450g blackberries, fresh or frozen
   Sprinkle of sugar, depending on
      the sweetness of the melon
   3 tablespoons Cassis (see
      page 170)
   A few mint leaves, torn up

Peel and deseed the melon, and cut it into chunks. Mix gently with the blackberries. Sprinkle over a little sugar and the Cassis.

   Add the mint and put into the fridge for a few hours to chill.

   It's lovely very cold, straight from the fridge.

Melon and ginger sorbet

This is light, refreshing and very quick and easy to make.

For 4:
   450g ripe melon flesh
   110g stem ginger with
      1 tablespoon of its syrup
   150g sugar

In a food processor, purée the melon and chill well.

   Chop the ginger and add to the melon with the ginger's syrup and the sugar.

   Put into an ice cream machine and freeze/churn for about 20 minutes.

   Serve immediately or pack into a plastic container and freeze.

New summer carrots

Carrots can really be divided into two different vegetables. There are large winter maincrop carrots and there are small tender summer roots, and they suit different recipes. The large ones have less sweetness and taste, and benefit from strong-flavoured dressings or long cooking. They're delicious grated in a salad with poppy seeds (see page 430), or slow-roasted to eat with Cucumber raita (see page 196) and any roast meat.

In contrast, summer carrots are lovely just washed and eaten raw or cooked very simply. Eat them as you pull them up, or use them in a bowl of crudités with cucumber, Florence fennel and radishes. On a big plate, fill three or four bowls with a variety of dips, such as Masai mara (see page 369), Baba ghanoush (see page 299), aïoli (see page 137) and Hummus with coriander (see page 85), and surround them with raw vegetables cut to finger-size. If the carrots are very small, leave them as they are, or cut them in half, with a couple of centimetres of the leaves left on.

Young carrots are also delicious steamed. Don't bother to peel them. Cook them for 6–7 minutes so that they're still firm but not too crunchy, and eat them with lots of butter and coarsely chopped lovage or fennel, or steam them for a couple of minutes and then stir-fry them as the Chinese do with lots of other veg. With this double-cooking technique, they keep their brilliant colour and a bit of crunch.

I grow three varieties of summer carrots. 'Early Nantes', for my first batch in June, is followed by 'Sytan', which can be harvested throughout the summer. 'Sytan' has some resistance to the carrot root fly, the pest responsible for roots becoming a warren of mini holes, and it has famously good flavour. You can leave some of these in for harvesting later in the year.

Right through from late spring until the end of summer, I also try to have a row of the spherical 'Parabell' on the go. These are at their best slightly bigger than a walnut and are ideal blanched and then dipped in tempura batter (see page 207). This is also an excellent variety for those of us who garden on heavy soil. Most carrots prefer a light, sandy ground; not these – they grow happily almost anywhere.

Sally Clarke's carrots and peas

A recipe that is at its best with freshly podded peas and young carrots.

For 4–6:
- **50g unsalted butter, cut into small pieces**
- **600g young carrots, scrubbed and thinly sliced at an angle**
- **Salt and black pepper**
- **350g small podded peas**
- **2 tablespoons chopped tarragon leaves**

Choose a non-stick pan, only a little larger than is necessary to hold all the ingredients quite snugly.

Put the butter in with the carrots and a little salt and pepper, and add about 150ml water. Then add the peas and the tarragon. Cover with a circle of greaseproof paper and a lid and cook over a medium to high heat until all but a drop of water has evaporated and the vegetables are tender.

Stir the vegetables with the treacly juices. Scatter over a little more tarragon and serve immediately.

Riverford new summer carrots and turnips

Jane Baxter, Riverford Organic's cook in Devon, created this recipe. She cooks the local primary school lunch and the children love these.

For 10–12:
For the carrots:
- **1kg carrots with their tops, trimmed and cut lengthways**
- **50g butter**
- **1 teaspoon runny honey**
- **1 tablespoon balsamic vinegar**
- **1 tablespoon chopped parsley**

For the turnips:
- **600g turnips, halved**
- **1 tablespoon balsamic vinegar**
- **1 tablespoon chopped parsley**
- **50g butter**
- **1 tablespoon runny honey**

To cook the carrots, put them in a pan with the butter, honey and 3 tablespoons of water and cook them over a high heat until the mixture is simmering away.

Turn down the heat, cover and simmer for about 10 minutes, frequently checking and stirring the carrots to make sure they don't stick and burn.

When they're almost cooked, uncover and increase the heat slightly, then add the balsamic vinegar. Stir to combine, turn off the heat and add the chopped parsley.

Cook the turnips separately in the same way until just tender. Don't cook the vegetables together as they cook at different rates. When the carrots and turnips are both cooked, mix them together and serve.

Griddled or barbecued new carrots

This is a lovely way to cook many different summer vegetables – new carrots, baby Florence fennel, courgettes, French and new runner beans. Cook them all together or on their own. Griddled carrots are very good with chicken and lamb.

For 4:
    450g small new carrots
    Grated zest and juice of 1 lemon
    150ml olive oil
    2 garlic cloves, chopped
    Salt and black pepper
    Handful of flat-leaf parsley, chopped

Scrub the carrots and trim the leaves to about 2cm. If you can only find larger carrots, halve them lengthways and blanch them for a couple of minutes before you put them into the marinade.

Put the lemon zest and juice, oil, garlic, salt and pepper into a bowl, and turn the carrots in this to coat them well. Leave while you preheat the griddle or barbecue.

Griddle or barbecue the veg (reserving the dressing), turning them every few minutes, until they're just tender to the point of a sharp knife.

Transfer to a plate, pour over a little more of the dressing and add the parsley. These are lovely warm or cold.

New carrots and potatoes roasted with garlic and thyme

New summer roots are infused with the flavour of shallots, garlic, caraway, lemon and thyme in this wonderful mixed vegetable dish. If you're vegetarian, eat this with cucumber raita and a green salad. It's also the perfect all-in-one vegetable dish to eat with strong-flavoured fish or meat.

For 8–10:
    1kg new carrots
    400g shallots
    600g new potatoes
    2 tablespoons olive oil
    Bunch of thyme, plus some to serve
    Grated zest of 1 lemon
    1 teaspoon caraway seeds
    1 head of garlic
    Salt and black pepper

Preheat the oven to 180°C/gas mark 4.

If they are small, leave the carrots whole, or halve them lengthways if larger. Trim the carrot stalks to about 1cm. Peel the shallots and scrub or peel the potatoes, but leave them whole.

Heat the olive oil in an ovenproof dish and toss together all the ingredients, except the garlic, to coat with the oil.

Break up the head of garlic without peeling the cloves and add to the dish.

Put into the preheated oven for at least 45 minutes, stirring from time to time until the vegetables soften and begin to caramelise.

Season with salt and pepper, and throw over some more fresh thyme before serving.

Onions, shallots and garlic

I rarely cook a meal without reaching for one or other of these bulbs. They are some of the most versatile vegetables in terms of flavour, changing from sharp and punchy when eaten raw to incredibly sweet, treacly and mellow if cooked for ages. There is a range of tastes, too, from the sweeter, mild red onion to the strong, large white. The small, flat-topped white onions you see in Italy and France are more like red onions – like a sweet spring onion and delicious eaten raw.

The thing that can be painful with onions is the slicing. First, cut off the bottom – not the more logical top – and peel the onion, leaving the bit where the bulb joins the stem. Held intact, the onion's quicker to chop and the main gland, which releases the stuff that makes your eyes water, is at the top of the bulb not the bottom. It's there to protect the plant from being eaten by grazing animals.

Then cut down towards the top in slices as narrow as you can, before turning the onion round and slicing again at right angles to the first series of cuts, still down towards the tip. Now turn the whole thing on its side, holding the bulb so that it doesn't fall apart, and slice across in a plane at right angles to the first and second cuts.

The more you chop garlic, the stronger its taste. Chopping releases the enzymes responsible for its flavour, so if you want a mild taste, leave the garlic whole and in its skin, and remove it all together before you eat. If you want power, chop it finely and use lots. For garlic, my friend Katie Boxer has a brilliant technique. Peel a clove and – similar to the onion-chopping technique above – cut several times down vertically to the base of the clove, but leaving it intact. Then, swivel it round a little and do the same thing, still vertically. Finally, put it on its side and chop the flesh from nose to root. It should by now be almost a pulp.

Full-sized onions are widely available and cheap, so if you don't have much room in your garden, don't grow them. Similarly, with our short growing season, it's difficult to grow garlic cloves as plump as those you can buy, so unless you live in the sunny south, or you want to try the mild, huge-cloved elephant garlic, buy your garlic too.

Shallots are expensive, look fantastic in the spring garden and are easy, so I like to grow them, planting on or near the shortest day of the year and harvesting sometime around the longest. And I grow spring onions, interspersing 'White Lisbon' and a red-bulbed variety, 'North Holland Redmate', among my carrots to protect against root fly. 'Redmate' is an excellent strong tasty variety, which will fill out to a good full-sized onion if you fail to eat your whole row at the spring onion stage.

Clove and onion pasta

The secret to cooking onions so that they're sweet and delicious is long, slow, gentle frying, so that they almost melt without turning brown. With this pasta sauce, you gradually add red wine, glass by glass, waiting between each addition to let the liquid reduce right down.

For 6:
700g white onions, thinly sliced
2 garlic cloves, finely chopped
10 cloves
3 tablespoons olive oil
200ml red wine
600g spaghetti
Salt and black pepper
Small bunch of flat-leaf parsley
50g unsalted butter
150g grated Parmesan cheese

Put the thinly sliced onions, garlic and cloves in the olive oil in a heavy-based pan over a very low heat.

To cook onions safely without browning, cover the onions with a circle of greaseproof paper cut to fit inside your pan. This will keep the moisture in and allow the onions to cook until they are translucent and soft. This takes about 20 minutes on a low heat.

Once the onions are cooked, start to add the red wine, bit by bit, allowing the onions to cook more briskly until any excess liquid has evaporated. Remove the cloves.

Meanwhile cook your spaghetti in salted boiling water until al dente and drain.

Add the parsley and a chunk of unsalted butter to the sauce.

Serve with the spaghetti, plenty of grated Parmesan and some freshly ground black pepper.

French onion soup

This is a classic, and a symbol of celebration in France, often cooked for a wedding or housewarming party.

For 4:
150g butter
600g onions, very thinly sliced,
  plus 2 extra onions, thinly sliced
3 large garlic cloves, peeled
1 tablespoon sugar
1.2 litres good stock
  (any type will do)
200ml white wine
Salt and black pepper
4 slices from a baguette,
  each about 1cm thick
Gruyère or Cheddar cheese,
  to serve

Melt three-quarters of the butter in a heavy-based pan and add the very thinly sliced onions. Cover with grease-proof paper and a lid, and sweat over a gentle heat for about 10 minutes, until the onions have softened.

Remove the lid and add 2 of the garlic cloves, chopped, and the sugar. Stirring from time to time, allow the onions to become a good brown without letting them burn, which will take 10–15 minutes (the flavour of the soup depends on the onions' colour, so don't hurry this stage). Stir in the stock and wine, and season carefully. Simmer for 30 minutes.

Meanwhile, fry the 2 extra onions in the remaining butter until dark brown and slightly crisp. Put to one side. Preheat a medium-hot grill. Toast the bread and rub one side with the remaining garlic clove.

Taste the soup and adjust the seasoning. Fill some warmed earthenware bowls with the soup and float a piece of toast on the top. Grate the cheese over the toast and put the bowls under the grill until the cheese is starting to melt. Scatter the crisp onions over the cheese and serve immediately.

Pissaladière

The sharp saltiness of this classic onion tart from the south of France is the perfect thing on a hot day, eaten with a crunchy green salad. It takes more time to make than the average onion tart, but its intense flavour – with anchovies, onions, Dijon mustard, olives and tomatoes – makes it well worth the effort.

For 6:
For the pastry:
75g unsalted butter
175g plain flour
Salt
½ teaspoon ground cinnamon
1 egg, beaten
A little iced water, if necessary

For the filling:
900g onions
3 garlic cloves
6 tablespoons olive oil
450g skinned chopped
**   tomatoes (see page 266)**
**   or tinned tomatoes**
1 tablespoon tomato purée
1 teaspoon sugar
2 stems each of thyme and
**   oregano**
Dijon mustard
10 tinned anchovy fillets, drained
A few black olives

Make the pastry by rubbing the butter into the sieved flour, salt and cinnamon until it resembles breadcrumbs. This can be done by hand or by pulsing in a food processor, but make sure that the butter is cold and cut into chunks before you add it to the flour. Then add the beaten egg and just enough iced water to make a dry dough, which you can form easily into a ball.

Roll out the pastry, put into a 23–25cm ungreased tart tin and chill in the fridge for half an hour.

Preheat the oven to 180°C/gas mark 4. Prick the bottom of the tart all over with a fork, cover with a round of greaseproof paper or foil and weight it down with some baking beans or rice. Bake the tart case blind in the preheated oven for about 15 minutes, until it's cooked but not browned. Take from the oven, but leave the oven on at the same setting. Remove the beans or rice and the paper or foil and let the tart base cool.

To make the filling, slice the onions and chop the garlic. Sweat these in 6 tablespoons of oil slowly over a low heat, without allowing them to brown, for about 20 minutes until translucent and soft (see page 245).

Meanwhile, in a separate pan, cook the tomatoes, tomato purée, sugar and herbs for about 20 minutes until well reduced. Stir into the cooked onions and season.

Spread a thin layer of Dijon mustard over the base of the cooked pastry and fill with the onion and tomato mixture. Arrange the anchovy fillets in a lattice pattern over the filled tart and then place a stoned black olive in every square.

Bake in the centre of the preheated oven for about 20 minutes, brushing the top with olive oil halfway through the cooking time.

Serve warm or cold.

Onion tart from Beamish and McGlue

This is the most delicious tart from my cousin's shop in south London. It has more onions than usual – and lots and lots of nutmeg.

For 6–8:
For the pastry:
  180g flour
  Pinch of salt
  50g lard
  50g butter
  1 tablespoon grated Parmesan cheese
  1 egg yolk
  3 tablespoons cold water

For the filling:
  400g (usually 3 large) onions
  Knob of butter
  1 dessertspoon flour

For the custard:
  1 egg plus 2 extra egg yolks
  150ml cream
  150ml milk
  Salt and black pepper
  Plenty of freshly grated nutmeg
  100g grated Cheddar cheese

Make the pastry by combining the flour, salt, lard and butter, and pulsing in a processor or rubbing the flour and salt into the lard and butter by hand, until it resembles breadcrumbs. Add the grated Parmesan, and mix well. Beat the egg yolk with a little cold water, and then add this to the flour mixture. Use just enough to make a soft smooth dough that will hold together in a ball.

Roll out the pastry on a floured surface and use to line a 22cm tart tin. Put it in the fridge for 30 minutes to rest.

Preheat the oven to 200ºC/gas mark 6. Prick the bottom of the tart all over with a fork, cover with a round of greaseproof paper or foil and weight it down with some baking beans or rice. Bake the tart case blind in the preheated oven for about 15 minutes. Take from the oven. Remove the beans or rice and the paper or foil and let the tart base cool. Turn off the oven.

To make the filling, slice the onions thinly (a food processor is good for this, using the fine blade). Melt the knob of butter, add the onions and give them a good stir. Cook them gently on the lowest possible heat for as long as it takes for them to soften and caramelise a little, stirring occasionally. This can take upwards of an hour. If you want to speed things up, turn the heat up and stir them more frequently to stop them catching. When they are soft and slightly caramelised, turn off the heat and stir in a level tablespoonful of flour.

Towards the end of this process, preheat the oven again to 180–190ºC/gas mark 4–5.

Make the custard by beating or processing all the ingredients together, but leaving 30g of the grated cheese. Then stir in the cooked onions with a fork and spread the mixture over the tart case.

Scatter the reserved cheese over the top to make it lovely and brown. Bake in the preheated oven for about 30 minutes.

Shallot tatin

You can make this fantastic tart with onions, too, but the sweetness of the shallots is what makes this recipe particularly delicious.

For 6:
  450g shallots
  175g any leftover soft cheese, such as Brie or Camembert
  40g unsalted butter
  2 tablespoons olive oil
  1 tablespoon soft brown sugar
  500g puff pastry
  Salt and black pepper

Preheat the oven to 200ºC/gas mark 6.

Peel the shallots, leaving them whole, and cut the cheese into thickish slices. Bring a pan of water to the boil, add the shallots and cook them for 5–7 minutes if they are small and 10 if they are larger. Drain and put to one side.

Heat the butter and oil in an ovenproof pan or a frying pan with a detachable handle. When the butter has melted, sprinkle in the sugar and allow it to dissolve gently before adding the shallots. Season well and allow the shallots to cook until a rich golden caramel.

Remove from the heat and roll out the pastry to a circle a bit bigger than the pan.

Spread the slices of cheese over the shallots and lay the pastry over the top, pressing it down slightly all around the edge.

Bake the tart in the preheated oven for about 25 minutes, or until risen and golden.

Allow to cool a little and then put a large serving plate over the pan and invert it quickly so that the shallots are now on the top, with the pastry underneath.

Serve the tart warm with a crisp green salad.

Shallot dressing

With its perfect sharp creaminess, this is the best possible dressing for a straight tomato salad.

For 4:
 1 shallot, finely chopped
 2 tablespoons red wine vinegar
 4 tablespoons olive oil
 4 tablespoons crème fraîche
 Salt and black pepper

Combine all the ingredients together with a fork and toss with salad.

Onions baked whole in greaseproof parcels

You have to wrestle a bit with the skins of the onions as you eat them, but the flavour of the onion within is wonderful. These are lovely eaten with roast beef, venison or sausages and mash.

For 6:
 6 medium-sized onions
 A little olive oil
 60g tinned anchovies, drained and chopped
 50g butter
 6 tablespoons balsamic or cider vinegar
 Salt and black pepper

Preheat a moderate (180°C/gas mark 4) oven.

Cut the base of the onions so that they stand upright and take the tops off with a sharp knife, but leave the skins on.

Oil 6 squares of greaseproof paper and lay each on a square of foil. Sit each onion on one of these.

Rub the onions with oil, snip one or two anchovies over each onion, dot with butter and then pour over the vinegar and season with salt and black pepper.

Wrap up and squeeze the foil parcels to make money-bag shapes and put them into a shallow ovenproof dish. Cook in the preheated oven for 50 minutes.

Undo the parcels, transfer to a serving dish and spoon the liquid over the onions.

Ingrid Marsh's spring onion and coriander vichyssoise

A sharp, fragrant chilled vichyssoise which knocks the socks off the usual mix of leeks and potatoes.

For 4:
 450g potatoes
 4 spring onions, chopped (the tender green parts as well as the whites)
 ½ teaspoon freshly ground coriander seeds
 ¼ teaspoon Chinese five-spice powder
 Salt and black pepper
 1 litre good chicken stock, heated
 50g fresh green coriander leaves and stems
 250ml double or single cream
 Squeeze of lemon juice

Peel the potatoes and grate them coarsely. Put them in a heavy-based pan with the chopped spring onions.

Add the ground coriander, Chinese five-spice powder, a good pinch of salt and then a really good grinding of black pepper.

Pour on the heated stock and bring to the boil over a gentle heat, stirring to prevent the potato starch sticking to the base of the pan. Add the finely chopped coriander stalks but not the leaves.

Half-cover the pan with a lid and cook gently for about 10 minutes until everything is tender. Let it cool for a few minutes.

Whiz to a perfectly smooth purée in a liquidiser and stir the cream gradually into the purée. Allow to cool for at least 5 minutes, then chop the coriander leaves finely and stir them in. Cover and chill for several hours or overnight.

Check the seasoning before serving. A little more salt or five-spice powder or a squeeze of lemon may be a good idea. This soup will keep for 2–3 days in the fridge.

Red onion marmalade

Sweet red onion marmalade is the perfect thing to eat for lunch with bread and cheese. A good dollop also transforms Potato salad with capers and anchovies (see page 124), and it's delicious with sausages and mash.

For 3–4 jars:
**2 garlic cloves
Sea salt and black pepper
4 tablespoons olive oil
450g red onions, sliced
4 tablespoons red wine
4 tablespoons balsamic vinegar
1 tablespoon soft brown sugar
Few sprigs of thyme**

Crush the garlic with some sea salt and heat the olive oil in a heavy-based saucepan. Add the onions and garlic, and sweat gently, without allowing them to brown, for 20 minutes. To cook onions safely without browning, cover the onions with a circle of greaseproof paper cut to fit inside your pan. This will keep the moisture in and allow the onions to cook until they are translucent and soft.

Add the red wine, balsamic vinegar and brown sugar, and simmer gently until most of the liquid has evaporated, which will take about 15–20 minutes.

Add the thyme, season with salt and pepper and cook for a further 5 minutes. Put into warm sterilised jars and cover while still hot.

This keeps well in the fridge for up to a month.

Sweet onion compote

Another version of onion marmalade, with more complex tastes and textures from the added fruit.

For 3–4 jars:
**125g mixed dried fruit, such as raisins, apricots and prunes
250ml orange juice
450g white onions
1 tablespoon olive oil
or 25g butter
1 tablespoon brown sugar
225g eating apples, peeled, cored and sliced
4 tablespoons balsamic vinegar
Salt and black pepper**

Chop the mixed fruit and marinate in the orange juice for an hour or so.

Slice the onions and sweat in the olive oil or butter with the sugar over a gentle heat until they become translucent and golden brown (see left).

Add the apples, mixed fruit and vinegar, and cook for about 25 minutes until most of the liquid has gone.

Season, put into warmed sterilised jars and cover while still hot. This keeps well in the fridge for up to a month.

White beans with garlic and thyme

This is the most delicious dish – all creamy and garlicky – to eat with roast lamb. Add a good spoonful of Redcurrant or Rowan jelly (see pages 171 and 324) and some Slow-roasted winter roots (see page 424) and you've got one of my favourite meals.

Dried beans, soaked overnight, give a better, less slushy texture than tinned, but if you're cooking at the last minute, these are also fine.

For 6:
500g white cannellini or green flageolet beans, soaked overnight, or 2 x 400g tins
4 garlic cloves, thinly sliced
6 small onions or shallots, thinly sliced
3 tomatoes, halved
500ml beef or lamb stock
4 sprigs of thyme
Salt and black pepper

Preheat a medium (180°C/gas mark 4) oven. Put the beans, garlic, onions, tomatoes, stock and thyme in an ovenproof pan. Bring to the boil, then cover and transfer to the oven and cook for an hour (if using tinned beans cook for only 30 minutes.)

Add salt and pepper and cook for another 20 minutes (or 10 minutes for tinned beans).

Pizza bianca

The nicest kind of garlic bread is not that oily and soggy French garlic loaf but the type of garlic bread you get in Italy. There you have a slightly fluffier than usual pizza base, with a little garlic butter spread over the top. That's how I make mine, sometimes adding herbs, sometimes not. This is fantastic with any soup, or for eating with salad, such as Salad niçoise (see page 210), for lunch.

For 8 garlic breads:
For the topping:
110g butter
Bunch of thyme, marjoram, savory or rosemary, finely chopped, plus some to serve
2 garlic cloves, finely chopped
Salt and black pepper
Sea salt, to serve

For the bread:
600g strong white flour
1 teaspoon salt
2 teaspoons dried yeast
About 300ml tepid water
2 tablespoons extra virgin olive oil
½ teaspoon sugar

Soften the butter by leaving it out of the fridge for half an hour and then cut it into cubes and mash it up with a fork or in a food processor with the herbs and finely chopped garlic cloves. Season with salt and black pepper.

To make the bread, put the flour and salt into a large bowl. Dissolve the yeast in the warm water with the oil and sugar. Mix it and leave for a couple of minutes, and you will see bubbles start to form.

Mix the yeast with the flour. Knead the dough for 3–4 minutes and then leave it to rest underneath a damp tea towel for a couple of hours. It should at least double in size.

Preheat the oven to 200°C/ gas mark 6. Break off about a 2cm-diameter ball of dough and, on a lightly floured surface, roll it out as thinly as you can. Repeat to make 7 more.

Bake in the oven, in batches, for about 10 minutes, until the tops turn golden brown.

While still hot, cut slashes at an angle across the top of the breads and brush over the garlic and herb butter.

Scatter with sea salt and some more fresh herbs.

Roasted garlic

Roasted garlic is a crucial ingredient in many sauces and soups, giving a gentle, rich taste, rather than the sharp hit of raw garlic. By roasting it you remove sulphur compounds, making it milder and sweeter, and reducing the after-eating smell. It transforms Tomato soup and sauce (see pages 268 and 277). You'll really miss it if you don't add it to Chilled pea soup (see page 133).

You can roast several heads of garlic at once and store them in a jar of olive oil. You can then also use the flavoured oil for salad dressings and sauces.

You need:
- **1 whole head of garlic**
- **Sprig of rosemary and/or thyme**
- **1 tablespoon olive oil**
- **Salt and black pepper**

Preheat the oven to 180°C/gas mark 4.

Put the garlic in a roasting dish, sitting it on top of the thyme and/or rosemary sprigs. Add a tablespoon of oil and 2 tablespoons of water, and sprinkle with salt and pepper.

Put it in the preheated oven and cook for 45 minutes.

Microwave roasted garlic

If you're in a hurry for your roasted garlic, this technique is nifty.

You need:
- **1 whole head of garlic**
- **4 tablespoons vegetable stock or water**
- **Sprig of rosemary and/or thyme**
- **1 tablespoon olive oil**

Put the head of garlic in a ceramic or glass bowl and add the stock, herbs and olive oil. Cook in the microwave on full power for 4 minutes and leave to stand for 5 minutes before using it.

Plums and greengages

I love a plum eaten cold in the early morning straight from the branch, when the flesh is soft but not mushy. The thing about a plum is that it's much friendlier than an apple. Everything about it says 'eat me', whereas an apple says, 'I'm perfectly happy to sit here for a few days'. It's no coincidence that the English have traditionally described something at its very best as a 'real plum'.

The good news for plum lovers is that they're perfectly suited to the British climate. They thrive in our mild and moist seasons, and a plum tree is one of the easiest, lowest-maintenance fruit trees you can grow. A typical plum tree will produce top-quality fruit for twenty years.

The plum season runs from mid-July until September. Supermarkets often stock only one or two types, primarily the trusty 'Victoria'; to experience plums at their best, grow your own, or go to a good pick-your-own.

The number one rule is buy British whenever you can and avoid the horrid large imported black plums with no flavour whatsoever. In Britain, the first to crop is the delicious, early 'Opal'. This is harvested from mid-July until the middle of August. It has reddish purple skin, contrasting beautifully with its yellow flesh, and medium-sized, plump fruit. The flesh parts easily from the stone, which makes it brilliant for spectacular-looking plum tarts.

Next comes 'Czar'. This is described as a cooking plum, but when I went to Brogdale, which holds the National Fruit Collection, for a tasting, I loved the strong acidic flavour of 'Czar'. It's lovely raw or cooked. Another more recently bred, mid-season plum is 'Avalon'. It has huge, exceptionally juicy and delicious fruit.

Then comes 'Victoria', the most commonly grown and popular plum in Britain. It's a mid-season fruiter, peaking in mid-August, and is delicious eaten raw or cooked, but contrary to popular opinion, it is not the best for flavour or disease-resistance, having problems with both canker and silver leaf. Most orchards finish fruiting with the late 'Marjorie's Seedling', picked from the end of September to mid-October. It's another you can eat raw or cooked, with very sweet yellow flesh and deep-purple, blushed-blue skin. It's a vigorous grower, with late blossom that misses the frosts; so, in colder northern areas, this is the one for you.

My husband, Adam, is also passionate about greengages, which are smaller and sweeter than dessert plums, but also lower yielding and more temperamental, so increasingly rare here. They make wonderful sorbet (see page 259) and delicious tarts and jams.

Roast plums with homemade custard

Homemade custard tastes delicious with this pudding. Try it flavoured with a few scented geranium leaves steeped in the milk. It's also excellent with the addition of a bay leaf or two.

For 4:
For the roasted plums:
1kg plums
Grated zest and juice of
    1–2 oranges (depending on
    juiciness)
Grated zest of 1 lemon
2 bay leaves
1 cinnamon stick, broken into two
A few juniper berries
75–100g dark brown sugar

For the custard:
6 egg yolks
120g caster sugar
500ml milk

Halve the fruit, removing the stones, or leave whole. Preheat the oven to 180°C/gas mark 4.

Put the plums into an ovenproof dish and add the orange zest, bay leaves, cinnamon, juniper berries and sugar, and pour over the orange juice.

Bake in the preheated oven for 15–20 minutes, until the plums are tender.

Allow to cool and then cover and chill until you need them. If you want a thicker syrup, transfer the plums to a serving dish and then boil up the juice in a small pan until thick and glossy.

To make the custard, mix the egg yolks and sugar together in a large bowl. Bring the milk to the boil and pour over the eggs and sugar. Combine thoroughly and return to the pan.

Over a low heat, cook the mixture very gently, stirring constantly, until it thickens enough to coat the back of a spoon.

Remove from the heat and strain through a fine sieve.

Roast plums with bread and butter pudding

The combination of a good slice of bread and butter pudding with the treacly sauce and soft flesh of a few plums is one of the best ever late-summer puddings. One of the keys to a really good bread and butter pudding is good white bread – never use sliced – or, you can use brioche or panettone.

For 10–12:
60g unsalted butter
8 slices of good white bread,
    brioche or panettone
Sultanas, soaked in a little
    whisky, dessert wine or water
    (optional)
1 vanilla pod
500ml double cream
500ml milk
200g caster sugar
6 eggs
2kg plums, roasted (see left for
    ingredients and method)

Preheat the oven to 180°C/gas mark 4. Butter an ovenproof dish.

Butter the slices of bread and arrange them in the dish with the soaked sultanas, if using, scattered over them.

Split the vanilla pod and put into a saucepan with the cream and milk. Bring to the boil and put to one side.

Cream the sugar with the eggs until pale and thick, and add the hot cream (removing the vanilla pod) and beat together.

Strain the mixture over the bread and leave it to soak for half an hour or so, or until you are ready.

Place the ovenproof dish in a roasting tin, and fill the tin with boiling water, to come halfway up the dish. Cook in the preheated oven for 45 minutes. When set and golden, remove from the oven and allow to stand. Serve warm with the roasted plums.

Best ever plum crumble

This recipe is really good for plums, damsons, greengages and rhubarb – and, of course, wonderful with blackberry and apple. The nice thing about crumble is the sharpness of the fruit with the sweetness of the topping, so don't over-sweeten the fruit. If you are using sweet ripe plums or greengages, there is no need to add any sugar.

For 8:
  2kg plums
  Grated zest and juice of 1 lemon
  **50–75g sugar, depending on
    the sweetness of the fruit**
  Cream or Greek yoghurt, to serve

For the crumble topping:
  125g plain white flour
  **150g roughly chopped hazelnuts,
    toasted**
  25g rolled oats
  ½ teaspoon ground cinnamon
  75g soft brown sugar
  50g demerara sugar
  125g cold unsalted butter

Halve and stone the fruit, and put into a shallow ovenproof dish. Grate over the lemon zest and pour over the juice. Add 50–75g of sugar, only if the fruit is very tart. Preheat the oven to 170ºC/gas mark 3.

To make the crumble topping: put the flour, hazelnuts, oats, cinnamon, sugars and cold unsalted butter, cut into chunks, into a food processor and pulse until the mixture resembles large breadcrumbs. This can be kept in the fridge until you want it, or put straight over the prepared fruit. Bake in the preheated oven for 30 minutes, until the topping is pale gold.

Crumble is much better served warm rather than hot, with lashings of cream or Greek yoghurt.

Darina Allen's Tuscan plum tart

We tried many plum tarts and upside-down cakes, and this one of Darina Allen's was exceptional. She cooked it for us when she came to the school. Serve it with crème fraîche or softly whipped cream.

For 10–12:
  450g sugar
  900g plums
  150g soft butter
  200g self-raising flour
  3 eggs
  **Vanilla ice cream, crème fraîche
    or softly whipped cream,
    to serve**

Use a 25cm sauté pan or a cast-iron frying pan, or one with a removable handle. Preheat the oven to 170ºC/gas mark 3.

Put 275g sugar and 150ml water into the pan and stir over a medium heat until the sugar dissolves, then cook without stirring until the sugar caramelises to a rich golden brown.

Meanwhile, halve and stone the plums and then arrange, cut side down, in a single layer over the caramel in the pan.

Put the butter, remaining sugar and flour into the bowl of a food processor and whiz for a second or two. Add the eggs and stop whizzing as soon as the mixture comes together. Spoon over the plums and spread gently in as even a layer as possible.

Bake in the preheated oven for about 1 hour. The centre should be firm to the touch and the edges slightly shrunk from the sides of the pan.

Allow to rest in the pan for 4–5 minutes before flipping over.

Serve with vanilla ice cream, crème fraîche or softly whipped cream.

Plum sauce

This intense plum sauce can be used to brush on lamb, beef, pork and fish before barbecuing or grilling. Use it too to enrich the juices of pork, duck and goose, adding a lovely sweet-and-sour taste. Thinned a little with a light oil, it is also wonderful as a dipping sauce.

For 500ml:
  450g ripe plums
  2–3 garlic cloves
  2 dried chillies or 1 fresh red chilli
  **3 heaped tablespoons soft
    brown sugar**
  1 tablespoon grated fresh ginger
  4 tablespoons soy sauce
  Salt

Halve the plums and remove their stones.

Chop the garlic and the chilli; or, if you are using dried chillies, crush using a pestle and mortar.

Put all the ingredients into a heavy-based saucepan and simmer for at least half an hour until rich and thick and most of the liquid has evaporated.

Pour into warm sterilised jars, seal and cover. This keeps very well in the fridge for 3–4 weeks and freezes for up to a year.

Savoury plum jam

I prefer plum jam that is not too set or too sweet, so that I can use it in a sandwich with Cheddar cheese or as a compote with yoghurt, crème fraîche or ice cream. If you prefer a traditional set, very sweet jam, allow equal weights of sugar to fruit.

For 3–4 jars:
  1kg plums (stoned weight)
  750g granulated sugar
  300ml warm water
  25g finely chopped stem ginger

Depending on the size of the fruit, halve or quarter your plums and remove the stones.

Put all the ingredients into a thick-bottomed preserving pan. Stir it all together and then allow to stand for an hour.

Warm the mixture slowly to dissolve the sugar completely, stirring regularly for the first 10 minutes.

Turn up the heat to bring the fruit to a rolling boil. Keep stirring if it's catching on the bottom and cook for about another 15 minutes until setting point is reached (see page 170).

Pour into clean sterilised jars, cover and seal. This jam stores for at least a year. Once opened, it should be kept in a fridge.

Greengage sorbet

An utterly delicious sorbet which is easy to make and tastes intensely of greengage.

For 6:
  150g sugar
  Juice of 1 lemon
  675g greengages

Bring 150ml water and the sugar to the boil, and cook for 3 minutes. Allow to cool and add the lemon juice.

Preheat a moderate (180°/gas mark 4) oven.

Either halve the greengages and remove the stones or just leave them, stones, skins and all, put them in an ovenproof dish and cover with foil. They need no extra liquid.

Bake in the preheated oven until they are really soft and, if you have left the stones in, just pick them out with a knife and fork. Put the whole lot into a food processor and process until you have a thick, smooth purée.

Add the cooled sugar syrup, process to combine and put into a bowl. Cool and cover until you are ready to make the sorbet.

If you have an ice cream machine, empty the contents of the bowl into the machine and freeze/churn for about 15–20 minutes, until the mixture is thick but still easy to transfer into plastic containers for the freezer.

If you don't have a machine, pour the mixture into a plastic container, making sure that you have a depth of about 4–5cm at least. Cover and freeze. After an hour or so, beat or process the mixture and put back into the freezer. Repeat a couple more times over the next 4 hours and then cover and freeze until you want it.

Allow the sorbet to thaw for about 20 minutes in the fridge before eating.

Raspberries, tayberries and loganberries

When picking raspberries, there's that great moment when you lift a branch and find a perfect colony, missed by the person before, stiff with ripe fruit that drops easily into the palm of your hand. I love going with the children to a pick-your–own and gathering bowl after bowl of them. But rather than a pick-your-own, why not grow your own? You need space to grow raspberries, but not much time. They're one of the best low-maintenance, generally healthy fruit crops there are. The star performer amongst all current raspberry varieties is 'Glen Ample', which fruits throughout July. Its fruit is vast – almost twice the size of a normal raspberry – so you can pick a meal of these in half the time. But it also has great flavour – slightly tart and strong.

If you love raspberries, you may want to add an autumn-fruiting variety to extend the season. I've put in 'Autumn Bliss'. Despite new varieties arriving on the scene, this is still the autumn mainstay. It fruits – admittedly at quite a low level – from early August to mid-to-late-September, even sometimes into October, and the good thing about autumn raspberries is that you don't have to net. With so many berries and fruit around, the birds aren't usually interested.

To freeze raspberries, lay them out individually in one layer on a tray and put them in the freezer for a couple of hours. You can then bag them up and they will stay as single fruit, rather than disintegrate into a mush (as strawberries do).

Raspberries are wonderful, but I also want to grow loganberries. These have large, juicy fruit, plump and soft, about twice the size of a standard raspberry, with a tart flavour that reminds me of kiwi fruit. They are excellent cooked or raw, and have very good disease-resistance, making them perfect for gardens. Plants will carry on fruiting for twenty-five years or more.

Tayberries and loganberries are close relations, both the result of a cross between a blackberry and a raspberry. Tayberries also have good flavour and disease-resistance, but without quite the intensity of flavour of the loganberry. They do, however, produce massive yields, twice the weight of fruit per plant. There is now also a thornless variety available, which makes picking and pruning much easier.

Both of these fruits make superb jam and you can freeze them by the bagful to use in the winter. I make syrupy purées to go with vanilla ice cream and use them instead of blackberries mixed with Bramleys in fruit crumbles and tarts. There is one big disadvantage to the tayberry: each berry has a large central core which usually remains attached to the calyx as you pick. The berries need to be picked through to remove this before eating or jamming, and that's a pain!

Meringue roulade with raspberries

Caroline Davenport-Thomas, who has cooked for our garden openings, makes this delicious pudding, ideal for feeding lots of people.

For 8:
  Sunflower oil, for the tin
  6 egg whites
  300g caster sugar
  50g flaked almonds
  350ml double cream
  400g fresh raspberries

Preheat the oven to 200°C/gas mark 6.

Line a Swiss roll baking tin (or any shallow baking tray) with greaseproof paper and brush with a trace of sunflower oil.

Whisk the egg whites in a clean, dry bowl until very stiff. Gradually add the sugar, one tablespoon at a time and whisking between each spoonful. Once all the sugar has been added, continue whisking until the mixture is very thick and glossy.

Spread this meringue mixture into the prepared tin and scatter with flaked almonds. Place the tin fairly near the top of the preheated oven and bake for 8 minutes. Then lower the oven temperature to 160°C/gas mark 3 and bake until golden brown. Don't cook the meringue too long, or else it will be difficult to roll up.

Remove it from the oven and turn it almond side down on to a sheet of greaseproof paper. Peel off the paper from the base of the cooked meringue and allow to cool for 10–15 minutes.

Whisk the cream until it stands in stiff peaks and gently mix in half the raspberries. Spread the cream and raspberries evenly over the meringue. Letting the greaseproof paper help you, roll the long side fairly tightly until it is all rolled up like a roulade. Wrap in non-stick baking paper and chill before serving. Scatter the rest of the raspberries over the top to serve.

Juicy summer pudding

As with bread and butter pudding, the best summer pudding is made with panettone or brioche, not cheap sliced white bread. It must also be juicy, with no white showing anywhere. You can use any combination of summer fruit, even gooseberries, but don't use too many blackcurrants, as they will dominate the flavour.

For 8–10:
  6–8 slices of brioche or good
    (not ready-sliced) white bread
  900g mixed soft fruit, such
    as raspberries, redcurrants
    and loganberries
  100–175g caster sugar, depending
    on taste
  Cream, to serve

Rinse (but don't dry) a 900ml pudding basin or soufflé dish with cold water. This makes it easier to turn out and helps spread the juice evenly. Cover the base and sides of the dish with the sliced brioche or bread, reserving some to cover the top.

Top and tail the fruit, and put in a pan over a gentle heat. Sprinkle the sugar over the fruit and simmer for just 2–3 minutes until the juice begins to run and the fruit is softened. Remove it from the heat and spoon the fruit mixture into the lined bowl.

Put in three-quarters of the juice and cover the top with a lid of brioche or bread. Put the remaining juice to one side.

Put a plate that fits the inside of the bowl on top. Place a weight on this and leave in the fridge overnight.

Remove the weight and plate and invert on to a flat dish. Pour the saved juice over the top of the pudding and serve with a bowl of cream.

Raspberry and redcurrant jam

This is the most fantastic colour and hardly cooked, so the fruit stays almost whole. The redcurrants counter the sweetness of the raspberries, making the best ever raspberry jam. It doesn't set firm, and has a runny consistency.

For 5 jars:
  500g granulated sugar
  500g raspberries
  200g redcurrants, topped
    and tailed

Warm the sugar in its packet or a bowl in a very low oven for half an hour.

Gently crush the fruit and warm it in a saucepan over a low heat. Bring just to the boil and add the warmed sugar. Stir over a low heat until dissolved and then boil fast for 3–4 minutes.

Pour into warm sterilised jars. Cover with a wax disc and seal.

Once open, store in the fridge.

Spectacular rice pudding with raspberry and redcurrant jam

Rice pudding is one of the best British puddings, particularly topped with Raspberry and redcurrant jam (see left). You need to prepare it a couple of hours before you want to eat, but it only takes 5 minutes to combine the ingredients.

For 4:
  Large knob of unsalted butter
  1 vanilla pod
  570ml whole milk
  40g round-grain rice
  Freshly grated nutmeg
  2 tablespoons caster sugar
  Double cream
  Raspberry and redcurrant jam,
    to serve

Preheat the oven to 150ºC/gas mark 2. Butter an ovenproof dish.

Split the vanilla pod, put it in a saucepan with the milk and bring this to the boil.

Rinse the rice and put it in the dish with some flakes of butter, grated nutmeg and the sugar.

Remove the vanilla pod from the hot milk, pour the milk over the rice and stir.

Put the ovenproof dish into the preheated oven and take out to stir two or three times over the next hour. After about an hour, stir in a good dollop of double cream and leave in the oven until the rice is quite cooked, but before all the liquid has been absorbed; this will take about 20 minutes. Keep checking, as you don't want it to be dry.

Serve with the Raspberry and redcurrant jam.

Tiramisu with red berries

Molly, my ten-year-old daughter, makes this pudding. It's also Adam's favourite, and my middle stepson William chose it for his eighteenth birthday party, so it's popular here! Strictly speaking, a true tiramisu has alcohol in it and no fruit, but I leave out the alcohol – so that younger children can eat it – and add plenty of raspberries or, even better, tart loganberries to cut through the gooey creaminess.

For 12:
  100g caster sugar
  4 eggs, separated
  400g mascarpone cheese
  400g raspberries, loganberries
    or tayberries
  400g sponge fingers
  About 500ml strong cold coffee
  Cocoa powder

Cream together the caster sugar and egg yolks. Add the mascarpone, and then beat the egg whites until stiff and fold into the mixture.

Put a layer of fruit in the bottom of a shallow dish and then prepare the sponge fingers. Douse these in the strong cold coffee by dipping rather than soaking them and arrange them in a layer over the top of the fruit.

Cover this with about half an inch of the mascarpone, making sure you cover the sponge fingers completely. Repeat these layers until you reach the top. With a sieve, dust the top with cocoa powder.

Put the tiramisu in the fridge for 3–4 hours for the tastes to amalgamate.

Tomatoes

Good tomatoes are the defining taste of summer, when their round, juicy softness comes into its own. The more of that just-picked, slightly acrid – almost poisonous – smell that they have the better. They are, after all, related to deadly nightshade.

When you're shopping, pick them up and sniff them. If they have a strong smell, they're likely to taste good. Tomatoes sold 'on the vine' look lovely, but they're more expensive than those off the stem and they don't have better flavour. I picked a truss of 'Sungold' and left them on the stem and another that I stored as separate fruit. I tasted them both after three days and there was no difference at all. The ones still attached had a stronger tomato scent, but that came from the stem, not the fruit. It's the variety, if anything, that makes the difference and it may be that growers take more trouble with varieties they choose for selling 'on the vine', because they can charge more.

For eating raw, choose sweet cherry tomatoes or big juicy varieties. For stuffing and cooking, the dryer-textured, almost seedless plum tomatoes are best. They keep their shape and when long-cooked reduce to a sweet and intense tomato sauce. Whenever you can, select a mix of varieties with different colours, shapes and sizes – you'll usually find several different types at farmers' markets. If you grow your own, go for an interesting range.

My top cherry tomato is the yellowy-orange 'Sungold', a heavy-cropping, healthy variety with small, very sweet fruit. My favourite large beefsteak is 'Costoluto Fiorentino', as well as the stalwart Russian variety 'Black Krim'. These are both full of flavour, and more prolific and easier to grow than the foodie favourite 'Brandywine'. Unless it's a very hot summer, 'Brandywine' tends to get end rot in the base of the fruit before it's ripe. I also like two heavy-producing plums: 'Harlequin', with small to medium-sized fruit that need to be cooked; and the larger 'San Marzano'.

Don't store tomatoes in the fridge; it changes their texture and diminishes their taste. Keep them in a bowl somewhere warm. Skin tomatoes by pricking each one lightly with a sharp knife, then dropping them in a bowl of boiling water and leaving for 20–30 seconds. Scoop them out of the water with a perforated spoon and strip off the skin. If they're to be used raw, don't be tempted to leave them in the water too long or they'll start to cook. If the skins are difficult to remove, drop them back for another stint. On the whole, try not to deseed tomatoes. There's lots of flavour in the jelly around the seed, so process the whole fruit and then press through a mouli or sieve; the mouli removes seeds but allows the jelly to get pushed through.

Baked tomatoes with cream

A friend of mine, Belinda Eade, first cooked this for me when we were at university. It's real comfort food – creamy and slightly sweet – and delicious eaten with new potatoes and a green salad, but I love it most with mash or rice.

For 6:
  30g butter
  2kg tomatoes
  3 tablespoons thyme leaves, chopped
  2 teaspoons sugar
  Salt and black pepper
  2 garlic cloves, finely chopped
  200ml double cream
  75g anchovies
  75g grated Parmesan cheese

Preheat the oven to 190°C/gas mark 5. Lightly butter an ovenproof dish.

Skin and chop the large tomatoes, but leave the small ones whole and lay half of them out, tightly packed, in the buttered ovenproof dish.

Scatter 1 tablespoon of thyme, 1 teaspoon of sugar, some salt, pepper and half the garlic over the tomatoes. Add another layer of tomatoes and scatter the same amount of thyme, sugar, salt, pepper and garlic over the top. Pour over the cream.

Add the remaining thyme, chopped anchovy fillets and oil from their tin. Season with salt and pepper, and spread this mixture over the top. Finish by scattering little bits of the remaining butter and add the grated Parmesan.

Bake in the preheated oven for 20 minutes, until the top is turning a nice brown.

Tomato soup

This recipe comes from Teresa Wallace, via Mary Contini at Valvona and Crolla in Edinburgh, who in turn got it from La Potinière restaurant in Gullane, East Lothian.

The soup is hugely tomatoey and fresh. It's ideal for making when you can buy huge quantities of rather battered, very ripe tomatoes cheaply. Make lots and freeze it. You can use port or Marsala (to add sweetness if the tomatoes are not tip-top quality) instead of sherry.

For 4–6:
  200g onions, chopped
  50g unsalted butter
  900g tomatoes
  5 tablespoons dry sherry
  1 tablespoon sugar (optional, according to the quality of the tomatoes)
  3 tablespoons torn basil, plus some to serve
  Salt and black pepper
  Vegetable stock (optional)
  A little cream, to serve

Sweat the onions very slowly in the butter. You don't want them to brown, but they should be cooked through. Add everything else except the cream and cook for about 10 minutes until the tomatoes are softened.

Whiz the soup in a blender and sieve, or push through a mouli. It will be fairly thick, but can be thinned, if necessary, with some stock.

Serve with a dribble of cream and more fresh basil.

Cleopatra's tomato soup

This is a South African recipe which makes a delicious rich tomato soup. It comes from Cleopatra's Mountain Farmhouse in the Drakensberg Mountains, the hotel belonging to Richard Poynton, a passionate cook. The ingredients list looks long, but it's very easy to make and it's as good cold as it is hot.

For 8:

1.5kg ripe tomatoes
2 large onions, quartered
Generous drizzle of olive oil
Salt and black pepper
3 garlic cloves, crushed
2 teaspoons grated ginger
½ small red chilli, chopped, or 1 dried chilli, crumbled
Bunch of coriander, leaves and stems chopped, plus more to serve
300ml tomato juice
2 x 400g tins of coconut milk
1 rounded tablespoon soft brown sugar
2 tablespoons Thai fish sauce
Bunch of fresh coriander, to serve

Preheat the oven to 180°C/gas mark 4 and roast the tomatoes – you don't need to skin them – and onions with olive oil, salt and black pepper for about 30–40 minutes until slightly browned on the edges.

Meanwhile, heat a little olive oil in a saucepan and cook the garlic, ginger, chilli and coriander (leaves and stems) for 3–4 minutes.

Add the tomato juice and coconut milk, and cook for a few minutes. Cover, remove from the heat and allow the flavours to infuse.

Add the tomatoes, onions, sugar, fish sauce and seasoning. Cover and simmer for 10 minutes.

Blend in a food processor and serve with plenty of fresh coriander.

Gazpacho

This punchy garlicky soup, served very, very cold on a hot day, is absolutely delicious. The flavour improves if it is made the day before. You can use tinned tomatoes, but the taste isn't the same as fresh.

For 6–8:

3–4 thick slices of good white bread, preferably a day old
2 garlic cloves
Generous drizzle of olive oil or equal parts olive oil and sunflower oil
1½ tablespoons red wine vinegar
675g tomatoes
2 sweet red peppers, bottled or fresh, grilled/roasted and skinned (see page 369)
1 large mild onion
1 cucumber
425ml tomato juice
Salt and black pepper
Iced water (optional)
A few fresh chives or a couple of ice cubes, to serve

Cut the crusts off the bread and discard. Tear the bread into small pieces in a large bowl.

Crush the garlic and add it to the bread. Add just enough oil for the bread to absorb and then stir in the vinegar. Skin, deseed and chop up the tomatoes.

Chop the roasted skinned peppers and roughly chop or grate the onion. Deseed and chop the cucumber. Add these to the bowl and mix well. Add the tomato juice and season with salt and pepper.

Blitz the whole thing with a wand whizzer, or put the mixture into a food processor and process, until it becomes quite smooth.

Check the seasoning and add iced water to get the consistency you want. Chill and serve very cold, with a few fresh chives or ice cubes.

Sungold tomato focaccia

This is a garden version of a focaccia recipe given to me by our local organic bakery – Judges in Hastings. It tastes deliciously of olive oil, which you slurp over and then press into the bread just before it goes into the oven. As Emmanuel Hadjiandreou from Judges says, this pressing action is like playing the piano, just using the tips of your fingers.

For 6–8:
- **1 teaspoon dried yeast**
- **300ml warm water**
- **1 level teaspoon sea salt, and a little more for topping**
- **400g strong white bread flour**
- **8 tablespoons olive oil**
- **20 cherry tomatoes, such as Sungold, left whole**
- **1 teaspoon rosemary leaves**

In a large mixing bowl, dissolve the yeast in the warm water. Stir in the salt and all the flour to make a fairly sticky dough. If the dough is very soft it makes the yeast work more quickly and then you get the characteristic holes forming in the bread, so try not to add extra flour.

Cover it with cling film and leave to rise for 30–45 minutes. When it has doubled its volume, add 2 tablespoons of the olive oil. Fold the dough in the bowl to integrate the oil and then cover again with cling film and leave the dough to rise as before.

Repeat this whole process twice, each time adding another 2 tablespoons of the olive oil and folding the dough.

When the dough has risen for the fourth time, place it on a baking tray (35 x 20cm-ish) lined with paper or greased with olive oil. Push the dough out to the corners (it should be about 2cm thick) and then slurp on another couple of tablespoons of olive oil and press it into the bread. You're aiming to make 1cm-ish dents.

Cover the dough with a cloth and leave to rise again for another hour or so until it has doubled in volume and begun to bubble.

Preheat a fairly hot (200°C/gas mark 6) oven. Sprinkle the dough lightly with sea salt, scatter over the tomatoes and rosemary, and bake in the preheated oven. Place a heatproof bowl of water in the bottom of the oven. This creates steam which gives a lighter, fluffier texture to the bread.

Bake until the focaccia has a nice golden colour. Allow to cool for half an hour and then place on a wire rack to cool further.

Andalusian soup-salad

My mother found this recipe in a 1970s copy of *Vogue*. It's a kind of coarse gazpacho, with many of the same punchy raw ingredients. It is just as good the next day and even the day after that. If I'm making this for the children, I add less onion and leave out the chilli. You can use tomato juice instead of tomatoes.

For 4–6:

1kg tomatoes (should give you about 1 litre tomato juice, but the quantity varies according to the ripeness and juiciness of the tomatoes), plus an extra 2–3 tomatoes
4 eggs, hard-boiled
1 teaspoon Dijon mustard
4 tablespoons extra virgin olive oil
2 tablespoons red wine vinegar
2 garlic cloves, crushed
1 slice of good white bread that is a couple of days old, crusts removed, torn up
½ large cucumber, deseeded and chopped
1 red pepper, roasted, peeled, deseeded and chopped (see page 369) or 1 bottled pimento, drained and chopped
4 spring onions, thinly sliced
1 mild chilli, thinly sliced
Salt and black pepper

Start making this soup at least a couple of hours before you want to eat. Like gazpacho, it's best eaten really cold and so, once assembled, needs an hour or two in the fridge.

Skin the 2–3 extra tomatoes (see page 266) and coarsely chop them.

Purée the rest of the tomatoes in a food processor and sieve or mouli them to get rid of the skin and seeds.

Shell the hard-boiled eggs and separate the whites from the yolks.

In the bottom of a large bowl, mix the mustard, olive oil, vinegar, garlic, broken-up bread and egg yolks to make a paste. Add all the chopped vegetables and then the tomato juice. Stir it all together.

Season with plenty of salt and pepper, and add the coarsely chopped egg whites before putting the soup in the fridge to chill.

Tabbouleh

I love tabbouleh made with only a little bulgar wheat, but lots of tomatoes, mint and parsley. As in the fresh tabboulehs of Lebanese restaurants, the herbs and tomatoes should be flecked with bulgar, not the other way round. This is good with a plate of different meze – hummus (see pages 85 and 305), falafels and Baba ghanoush (see page 299) – or serve it with roast or barbecued lamb.

Peeled chopped cucumber or chopped melon make delicious additions to this recipe. If you don't have homemade stock, use very weak organic bouillon or plain water.

For 4–6:

100g bulgar wheat
250ml boiling vegetable stock (enough to cover the bulgar)
500g tomatoes, skinned (see page 266), deseeded and cut into 1cm chunks
Juice of 1 lemon
2 tablespoons olive oil
3 spring onions, thinly sliced
Large bunch of flat-leaf parsley, finely chopped, tops of stems included
Bunch of mint, finely chopped
¼ teaspoon ground cinnamon
½ teaspoon ground allspice
Salt and black pepper

Prepare the bulgar first, by covering it with boiling vegetable stock. Leave the wheat to stand for 15 minutes in a covered bowl. Drain it, press with a spoon to get rid of any excess liquid and let it cool.

Add the tomatoes, lemon juice, olive oil, onions and herbs. Finally add the spices and seasoning, then let it sit for half an hour to allow the flavours to meld before you eat.

Fattoush

This is a Lebanese dish similar to
tabbouleh, but made with toasted flat
bread not bulgar wheat. This is
a crunchier and more textured salad.
You can make a robust and extra-
delicious fattoush with olive and thyme
tapenade (see page 49) spread over
the flat bread before it goes into the
salad. This is also good eaten with
hummus (see pages 85 and 305) or
Baba ghanoush (see page 299) and
more hot pitta bread.

For 4:
   250g pitta breads
   250g cucumber
   350g tomatoes
   2 handfuls of flat-leaf parsley,
      finely chopped
   2 handfuls of mint, finely chopped
   100g radishes
   3 spring onions
   2 tablespoons olive oil
   Juice of 1 lemon
   Salt and black pepper

Toast the pitta breads in a single layer
in a hot oven for 10 minutes until
they're crisp. You may need to cook
them for 10 minutes and then split the
two sides, break them into bits and
put them back into the oven for
another couple of minutes to get them
properly crunchy.

   Peel the cucumber, halve and
deseed it, then cut it into 1–2cm
chunks. Skin the tomatoes (see page
266), then thinly slice the radishes and
spring onions.

   Break up the toasted pitta into
small chunks and combine these with
the vegetables, herbs, oil, lemon juice
and seasoning in a shallow bowl.

   If you want to add tapenade,
spread this on to the pitta after you've
toasted it, before breaking it up into
chunks and adding to the salad.

Saganaki

This Cretan shepherd's dish of baked
feta with tomatoes is simple and
delicious, its salty flavour offset by the
odd sweet burst of tomato. You can
cook it in foil parcels on a griddle or
in a fire, or bake it quickly in a shallow
heatproof dish. A warm flat bread,
straight from the oven, works well with
this dish (see page 46).

For 6:
   600g (3 packs) feta cheese,
      broken into rough 2cm pieces
   20 large or 30 small cherry
      tomatoes
   20 capers
   15 Kalamata olives, halved and
      stoned
   2 tablespoons olive oil
   6 sprigs of thyme or marjoram

To make the saganaki as individual
parcels for cooking on an open fire,
place about 100g feta on a square
of foil. Add a few cherry tomatoes, a
teaspoon of capers and 3 olives, and
drizzle with a little olive oil. If using
larger tomatoes, cut them up into
cherry-tomato-sized cubes.

   Put a sprig of the herbs on top
and fold up the parcel loosely. Cook in
the fire for 10–15 minutes.

   If you want a communal dish
in the middle of the table, preheat the
oven to 200°C/gas mark 6, put the
cheese into a shallow ovenproof dish
with everything else and bake it in the
hot oven for about 15 minutes until the
cheese is bubbling and browning on
top. This must be eaten hot or warm.

Panzanella

When I worked as a waitress at the River Cafe, this was one of the first recipes I learnt. Using bread in a salad may seem odd, and you might think it would be heavy, but this is one of the best summer tomato salads.

For 4 as a main course, 8 as a starter:

1kg ripe tomatoes
2 thick slices of coarse white bread, such as Pugliese or ciabatta
2 garlic cloves, crushed
Salt and black pepper
3 tablespoons extra virgin olive oil
2 tablespoons red wine vinegar
1 generous tablespoon capers, roughly chopped
75g tin of anchovies, drained and roughly chopped
1 small red onion, very thinly sliced
12 black olives, pitted
Large bunch of basil (sweet and purple if you can find it), roughly chopped
Large bunch of flat-leaf parsley, roughly chopped
2 mild fresh red chillies, thinly sliced (optional)

Skin the tomatoes (see page 266). Put one large tomato aside and deseed and roughly chop the rest. Place the chopped tomatoes in a sieve over a bowl to catch any juices.

Tear the slices of bread into small chunks and put them in a large bowl. Season the collected tomato juice with garlic, pepper, oil and vinegar, and pour this over the bread. Add the tomatoes and then stir a little. If the bread still looks dry, add more oil.

Put a layer of the bread and tomato mix on a large plate and add some capers, anchovies, onions, olives, herbs and, if you want them, chillies. Then add another layer of bread and tomatoes, then more capers, anchovies, olives, etc.

Leave the panzanella for at least an hour to let the different tastes soak into the bread before you eat. Add a few more leaves of fresh basil and one freshly chopped tomato just before serving.

Raw tomato pasta

This is one of the simplest things you can do with tomatoes, but they need to be really tip-top. We eat this at least once a week in July and August, when the greenhouse is full of varieties like Black Krim and Costoluto Fiorentino. It's worth using a good oil: you'll really taste the fruity flavour.

For 4:
1kg tomatoes
1 tablespoon coarse rock salt
100ml extra virgin, cold pressed olive oil
2 garlic cloves, finely chopped
Juice and zest of 1 lemon
350g pasta
Small bunch of basil leaves, torn
Grated Parmesan cheese, to serve

Peel (see page 266) and halve the tomatoes, then deseed with a teaspoon and chop them into chunks. Scatter the rock salt over them and leave them to drain in a colander for half an hour to get rid of some of their juice.

Move the tomatoes to a pan and mix them with the olive oil, garlic, lemon zest and juice, and heat just to warm the sauce but not cook it.

Cook the pasta in salted boiling water until al dente, drain and stir in the tomato mixture along with the torn basil leaves.

Serve with plenty of freshly grated Parmesan.

Really rich tomato sauce

This is an excellent tomato sauce, which forms the basis of many different dishes. Spread it on your Pizza (see page 281), use it for Moussaka (see page 301), or serve it as it is with pasta.

For 8–10:
1kg tomatoes
1 large onion
2 garlic cloves
2 tablespoons olive oil
1 tablespoon tomato purée
1 heaped tablespoon chopped oregano
1 large teaspoon sugar
200ml red wine
Salt and black pepper

Skin the tomatoes (see page 266) and chop them roughly.

Chop the onion and the garlic. Heat the olive oil and sweat the onion over a low heat until it begins to soften, but don't let it brown. If the onion begins to catch, place a lid on the pan.

Add the chopped tomato, tomato purée, garlic, oregano, sugar and wine, and simmer gently over a low heat for at least for 40 minutes until it has reduced and thickened.

Season well. This is excellent for freezing, but leave out the garlic (freezing garlic makes it taste mouldy) and add it when you reheat.

Pasta with roasted tomatoes and garlic

This sauce can be eaten fresh, or frozen to use in the winter and spring, when tomatoes with any taste are hard to find. There's a lot of garlic in this dish, but it's not overwhelming. Once garlic is roasted, it becomes sweet and mild. Enrich the sauce at the end with a knob of butter to give a creamier taste. Eat with a mixed leaf and herb salad.

Removing cherry tomato skins after you've roasted them is easier than the usual boiling water technique. Once they've cooled enough to handle, gently squeeze each fruit until it pops out of its skin.

For 4:
  500g cherry tomatoes
  3 tablespoons olive oil
  1 tablespoon balsamic vinegar
  1 level dessertspoon sugar or
     honey (exclude with sweet
     cherry tomatoes)
  Salt and black pepper
  350–400g spaghetti
  3–4 cloves of Roasted garlic
     (see page 253)
  100g butter
  1½ tablespoons fresh herbs,
     such as marjoram, oregano,
     basil or thyme
  Grated Parmesan cheese,
     to serve

Preheat the oven to 180°C/gas mark 4.

Prick the cherry tomatoes several times with a sharp knife and lay them out in an ovenproof dish. Add the oil, vinegar and sugar or honey. Season well with salt and pepper, and put the dish in the preheated oven for 20 minutes. Skin them when they come out of the oven.

Meanwhile cook the pasta in salted boiling water until al dente.

Add the roasted garlic to the tomatoes by squeezing out the creamy flesh of each clove into the mixture. Put the dish back into the oven for another 5 minutes to allow the flavours to combine.

Remove the sauce from the oven and add the butter and the fresh herbs, with the leaves torn or chopped at the last minute.

Drain the pasta and serve lots of freshly grated Parmesan with the sauce. If you want to freeze the sauce, leave the garlic out (freezing garlic makes it taste mouldy) and add it when you reheat.

Tomato bruschetta

A mix of yellow and red cherry tomatoes works well on bruschetta, as do juicy beefsteaks. Use white bread: a robust white Italian bread like Pugliese makes the best crostini.

For 4:
  1kg tomatoes
  Salt
  1 teaspoon white sugar
  2 tablespoons olive oil
  20 basil leaves, plus more for
     scattering
  2 teaspoons red wine vinegar
  8 finger-thick slices of white bread
     (see above), cut at an angle
  2 garlic cloves (optional)
  Extra virgin olive oil
  Black pepper

If you're using cherry tomatoes, chop them in half, scatter with salt and leave them to bleed for half an hour in a colander. You don't need to skin cherry tomatoes, but if you're using full-sized ones, skin them before chopping (see page 266).

In a bowl, mix the tomatoes with the sugar, oil, basil and vinegar. If you're using very sweet cherry tomatoes such as Sungold, leave out the sugar and double the red wine vinegar to make them sharper. Try to keep the basil leaves whole. Once cut or torn, basil blackens quickly. If the leaves are too big and you need to halve them, just add at the last minute.

To make the crostini, preheat the oven to 180°C/gas mark 4. Drizzle the olive oil over the bread. Toast the bread in the oven for 10 minutes, but don't let it become too hard. You can also cook it on a preheated medium-hot barbecue or griddle pan until brown and crispy.

Lightly scrape one side with fresh garlic, if you are using it, and then add the tomatoes. Sprinkle with salt and black pepper, and scatter over some extra basil.

Quick tomato tart

This tomato tart is special because you can throw it together very quickly and it needs few ingredients. You can use any old tomato, bar cherry varieties. I always make mine in a frying pan with a metal or removable handle – a tarte tatin pan – so that I can slot the whole thing into the oven for final cooking.

For 6–8:

10 medium-sized tomatoes (800g)
2 red onions, thinly sliced
Slurp of olive oil
2 garlic cloves, finely chopped
½ tablespoon coarsely chopped fresh thyme
1 teaspoon sugar
Salt and black pepper
30g (drained weight) anchovies
20 capers
500g packet of puff pastry

Preheat the oven to 200°C/gas mark 6. Skin the tomatoes (see page 266) and cut them in half horizontally.

Sauté the onions gently in a little olive oil with the garlic, thyme, sugar, salt and pepper for about 10 minutes. If you are planning to freeze, leave out the garlic (freezing garlic makes it taste mouldy).

Lay out the anchovies on top of the onion mix and sprinkle on the capers. Add the tomatoes, placing them cut side down and pushing them into the mix, and cook gently for a further 3–4 minutes.

Roll out the pastry to a thickness of about 5mm. If you're using bought pastry, it's often pre-rolled to about this size. Put the pastry over the pan, cutting away any excess, and push it down gently on to the tomatoes.

Put the pan into the preheated oven for 15–20 minutes, until the puff pastry has risen and is golden brown.

Remove it from the oven and allow the tart to rest and cool slightly. It tastes much better warm or cold rather than hot and it's easier to turn out when slightly cooler. Before you turn the tart, check there's not too much juice. Tip the pan on its side and drain any excess before turning.

Place a large flat plate – the ideal size is one that sits perfectly just inside the pan – over the top and flip the whole tart. Scatter a few extra sprigs of thyme over it.

Pizza

The secret of a good pizza is a crisp wafer-thin base and the keys to that are in the dough recipe and in rolling it very thinly. You'll need to use a good solid baking sheet on the bottom of a very hot oven.

If you don't have time to make Really rich tomato sauce (see page 277), use tinned tomatoes cooked with a good 3 tablespoons of olive oil and 2 whole garlic cloves, which I later take out, and reduce.

We've done taste trials of different types of mozzarella and, once your pizza is cooked, you really can't tell the difference between the uninviting Danish blocks and the more expensive buffalo spheres. Use the ordinary mozzarella for cooked toppings and save the delicious buffalo for eating fresh, sliced on top of the cooked pizza base with a handful of rocket and slices of juicy fresh tomato drizzled with olive oil.

For 8 medium-sized pizzas:
For the bases:
  600g strong white flour, plus more for dusting
  1 teaspoon salt
  1½ teaspoons dried yeast
  About 300ml tepid water
  2 tablespoons extra virgin olive oil
  ½ teaspoon sugar
  Sunflower oil for the baking sheet

For the pizza topping:
  Really rich tomato sauce (see page 277)
  600g mozzarella cheese, grated
  2 tins of anchovies, drained
  100g capers, rinsed
  100g pine nuts
  12 slices of prosciutto
  24 thin slices of chorizo
  12 asparagus spears
  6 artichoke hearts
  250g spinach
  A few eggs

To make the dough, put the flour with the salt into a large bowl. Dissolve the yeast in a cup with the warm water, oil and sugar, and leave to froth. It's worth doing this, rather than just adding the yeast straight into the flour, so that you know that the yeast is working. If it is active, you'll see bubbles starting to form within a couple of minutes.

Mix the yeast with the flour. If your mix is too dry, add a little more water. A moist, sticky dough makes a light pizza base with a crisp crust, so don't be put off by the mess.

Once the dough is well mixed, there's no need to knead if you don't have time. Leave it to rest under a damp tea towel for a couple of hours. It should at least double in size, but even if it hasn't, it will still make fine dough. This is not a precise science.

To make your bases, break off a ball of dough about 3cm in diameter – depending on the base size required – and roll it out as thinly as you can on a lightly floured surface, then transfer to a lightly oiled baking sheet.

To make the topping, you need to spread only a thin coating of tomato sauce – really ladling it on makes for a soggy base. Top the sauce with a light, even covering of grated cheese. Let people construct their own toppings. As well as cheese and tomato – the straight Margherita – I put out a couple of tins of anchovies, capers, pine nuts, a plate of prosciutto and thinly sliced chorizo, and maybe some asparagus spears or artichoke hearts. My husband, Adam, loves the classic Fiorentina with wilted spinach and an egg broken over the top.

The temperature of the oven should be at least 250°C/gas mark 9 (the maximum on conventional ovens) – in which case 5 minutes is all a pizza will take.

De Kas tomato jam

This is my adaptation of a recipe from one of my favourite restaurants, De Kas in Amsterdam. A delicious sweet tomato pickle with a fragrant taste from the spices, it is fantastic on crostini and lovely with bread and cheese, sausages, pork or thinly sliced cured and dried ham.

For 1 litre:
- **1.5kg tomatoes (use lots of different varieties for a good structure and taste)**
- **2 star anise**
- **3 cardamom pods**
- **1 teaspoon coriander seeds**
- **1 teaspoon juniper berries**
- **3 cloves**
- **1 teaspoon black peppercorns**
- **1 vanilla pod**
- **1 orange**
- **1 lemon**
- **Salt**
- **300g white sugar**

Put a small saucer into the fridge to cool. Halve the tomatoes and scrape out the seeds. Roughly chop the halves into pieces and put into a large heavy-based pan.

Cook the spices in a small frying pan over a moderate heat until they begin to pop and smoke. Allow them to cool and then grind them quite finely using a pestle and mortar or in an electric grinder.

Split the vanilla pod and add the whole pod to the pan with the spices. Grate the zest from the orange and lemon, and squeeze the juice. Add these, together with the salt and sugar, to the rest of the ingredients in the pan and heat slowly until the sugar has dissolved completely.

Simmer for at least 30 minutes to thicken and reduce, stirring regularly. Test for a set by putting a teaspoonful on the chilled saucer – it should just hold its shape and be the consistency of soft jam.

Remove from the heat and put into warm sterilised jars. Cover with greaseproof discs and lids. Allow to mature for a few days before using it. This will keep well in the cool and dark for a couple of months, but refrigerate after opening.

Stuffed tomatoes
with roast potatoes

Last spring I had a fantastic cooking lesson from two Greek women, Efi Polis and her sister Marina, in the town of Stavros on Ithaca. This is one of Efi's favourite vegetable-based recipes. The rice grains need to have a bit of a crunch and the tomatoes must be slightly charred for the texture to be as good as the taste.

It is delicious for lunch served with a lemony-dressed crunchy green salad or the typical Greek mix of one part coarsely grated carrot with two parts thinly sliced white cabbage, dressed with plenty of salt, lemon juice and olive oil.

For 6:
**10 large beefsteak tomatoes,
 or 12 large plum tomatoes
1 large onion, finely chopped
1 garlic clove, finely chopped
150ml olive oil
3 serving spoons of white rice
3 serving spoons of brown rice
Generous bunch of herbs (a mix
 of one or all of fresh basil,
 oregano, dill, mint and
 marjoram)
1 teaspoon sugar
Salt and black pepper
500g medium-sized to large
 waxy potatoes, such as Belle
 de Fontenay or Charlotte**

Preheat a medium (180°C/gas mark 4) oven.

Take the roof off the tomatoes, scoop the seeds and central flesh out with a teaspoon and put them in a colander over a bowl.

Cook the onions and garlic in the oil until they're soft. Add the tomato seeds and flesh, but keep the juice that's dripped out into the bowl separate, then add the rice and most of the herbs, the sugar, and the salt and pepper.

Stuff the tomatoes three-quarters full with the mix (as the rice cooks, it swells a bit). Arrange the tomatoes in a baking tray.

Parboil the potatoes for a few minutes in salted boiling water and then halve or quarter them longways. Add these to the tray full of tomatoes, poking them into any gaps.

Add a couple of tablespoons of olive oil to the tomato juice and pour this over the top of everything in the tray. Sprinkle over more salt and the remaining herbs, and cook the potatoes and tomatoes together in the preheated oven, uncovered, for about an hour.

'Sun-blushed' tomatoes

This soft, succulent way of preserving tomatoes – admittedly for only a couple of weeks – is totally delicious. These tomatoes are expensive to buy but inexpensive to make. Made without vinegar, they're not long-term preserved, but taste all the sweeter for that. Eat them straight with a slice of bread, or as part of an antipasti with mint and crumbled feta cheese, or mix them with mozzarella and basil-flavoured olive oil (see page 224).

For 1kg:
  3kg small tomatoes or large cherry varieties about 3cm in size, such as Sultan's Jewel, Harlequin or Principe Borghese
  1 teaspoon salt
  Black pepper
  1 tablespoon fresh or dried oregano
  1 teaspoon muscovado sugar (optional)
  1–2 garlic cloves, peeled but left whole (optional)
  Organic sunflower oil

Don't slice the tomatoes completely in half, but cut them almost through from the apex to the stem end and open them out into a figure of eight. Lay them out in a single layer on a wire rack in a baking tray.

Sprinkle the tomatoes with the salt, pepper and oregano – and if you like things sweet, you can add one teaspoon of muscovado or caster sugar. Put them in a tray in a very cool oven. About 3kg on a rack tightly covers an oven tray for a standard-sized oven. Fan ovens are ideal and you want to cook them at about 80°C, leaving the door slightly open, for 4–5 hours. The length of time they take will depend on their size and texture. Look at and taste them after 3 hours. Their flavour should have intensified hugely and their skin should be a bit wrinkly, but not collapsed.

Put them in a sterilised jar, add the garlic, if using, and cover them with sunflower oil. One's instinct is to use olive oil, but lighter good organic sunflower oil allows the flavour of the tomatoes and herbs to come through fully. It's also less heavy and gloopy.

Properly covered in oil, these should last in the fridge for a couple of weeks. If you want to keep them longer, put them in the freezer.

Green tomato chutney

Some people are sniffy about this chutney, but the truth is that if you grow your own tomatoes, particularly outside, they won't ripen much after mid-September. Bring them inside before they blacken during a cold night and ripen them in a paper bag or in a drawer with a banana. There will be some tomatoes which refuse to turn, so it's good to have a recipe up your sleeve for using them.

For 10 jars:
  About 7cm piece of root ginger
  2–3 red chillies, halved
  1.5kg green tomatoes
  900g cooking apples
  450g shallots, chopped
  450g sultanas
  1.75 litres wine vinegar
  450g demerara sugar
  Juice of 2 lemons
  25g mustard seeds
  50g salt

Bruise the ginger by whacking it with a rolling pin and then tie it in a muslin bag with the halved chillies. Slice the tomatoes. Peel, core and chop the apples. Put all these and the remaining ingredients into a large preserving pan.

Tie the muslin bag to the handle and let it dangle into the pan to release the flavour of the ginger and the chillies while the mixture is cooking. Stir over a low heat to dissolve the sugar and then simmer for 2 hours, uncovered, until the consistency is rich and thick.

Remove the muslin bag and put the chutney into warm sterilised jars, cover and seal. It's worth leaving the taste to mature for a couple of months before you eat this chutney.

September | October

Apples

When I think of paradise, it's an orchard full of apple trees in full pink-flushed flower, with a carpet of cow parsley and the occasional sheep grazing below. Amongst British fruit blossom, apple comes last, flowering in May, and is arguably the most beautiful, with its simple single flowers and bright golden anthers.

We grow plenty of good apples in Britain, ranging from early dessert varieties, such as 'Discovery', to the late cooker 'Bramley'. I love 'Discovery', one of the first native apples ready for picking in early August. It's delicious, with small slightly sharp-flavoured fruit and lovely crunchy flesh, creamy-white with a beautiful pink flush below the skin. It needs to be eaten within a few days.

'Egremont Russet' and 'Rosemary Russet' come next, both ready in September. They will store until Christmas. They have that classic acidic, russet flavour and are an acquired taste, but are often the favourites of the apple connoisseur. Then there are the Cox varieties such as the traditional 'Cox's Orange Pippin'. These are all late dessert apples with an aromatic, almost pineapple flavour. If kept cool, they will last well into the new year.

My daughters love 'Estival', another mid-to-late-season apple. This has vast fruit, with a sweet flavour and excellent crunchy flesh. You'll only find these at a good pick-your-own fruit farm.

The outstanding British cooking apple is 'Bramley's Seedling', with its characteristic large irregular, flat fruit. When you cook this variety, the released acids break down the flesh, giving the perfect fluff-ball texture and tangy taste. 'Bramley' is a late-flowering and harvesting variety that stores brilliantly.

'Orleans Reinette' is another cooker, bred by the French to make tarte tatin. It keeps its structure perfectly when cooked and is the variety to use for perfect crescent-shaped slices.

In addition to the full-sized apples, there are many varieties of the smaller crabs. The fruit of the crab apple ranges from gobstopper to golf-ball size, and all are superb for jelly. They have a high pectin level, so you won't need to add much sugar for setting, and many of them produce a beautiful warm coral-pink jelly.

It's important to store only perfect fruit. Put it on slatted wooden trays (the slats help with air circulation). Keep each variety separate, as storing times vary. They are best kept in cool, dry dark conditions, individually wrapped in newspaper. If you have a barn or tool shed, put them there, or line a drawer with newspaper in the coolest room in the house.

Baked apples

Jane's apple hotpot

A British classic which should be eaten at least once during the apple season. Serve it with thick cream. The apples are also lovely filled with mincemeat.

For 4:
- **4 medium-sized Bramley or other cooking apples**
- **75g soft butter, plus more for the dish**
- **75g soft brown sugar**
- **Grated zest of 1 whole lemon and juice of ½ lemon**
- **100g sultanas**
- **1 tablespoon brandy or Calvados (optional)**
- **1 tablespoon slivered almonds or pine nuts, toasted**

Preheat the oven to 180°C/gas mark 4.

Core your apples and, with a sharp knife, score a line just through the apple skin round each apple two-thirds of the way up. This will stop them from exploding in the oven as they expand during cooking. Place in a buttered shallow open dish.

Mix together the butter, sugar, sultanas, lemon zest and juice. Stir in the brandy or Calvados, if you are including it. Fill the cavities of the apples with the mixture, piling it up on top on the apples.

Bake in the preheated oven for about half an hour. Spoon the remaining syrup over the apples and scatter with the toasted almonds or pine nuts.

This, my sister's recipe, is a quick and easy way of using up extra apples and mincemeat. It is lovely for breakfast or supper, served with Greek yoghurt or ice cream.

For 8:
- **1kg mixed Bramley and eating apples**
- **200ml orange juice**
- **200g mincemeat, preferably homemade**
- **Butter for the dish**
- **100g soft brown sugar (optional)**
- **Grated zest of 1 lemon**

Preheat the oven to 180°C/gas mark 4.

Peel, core and thinly slice the apples. Mix the orange juice into the mincemeat.

Butter a deep ovenproof dish and lay half the apples in the bottom. Sprinkle with half the brown sugar, if necessary, and some of the lemon zest. Cover this with half the mincemeat and on that layer the remaining apples, then sprinkle them with the rest of sugar, if you are using it, and the rest of the lemon zest. Top with the remaining mincemeat, cover with foil and cook in the preheated oven for 30 minutes.

This will make a lot of juice, so leave it until it is lukewarm to serve, when the liquid will have been partially absorbed and thickened to a syrup.

Pheasant with Calvados, apple and chestnut

As we all know, pheasant can be dull and dry, but with this recipe the flesh remains succulent and full of flavour.

For 6:
- 2 pheasants
- 2 tablespoons seasoned flour
- 50g butter
- About 5 tablespoons Calvados
- 4–6 apples (depending on size), plus a few slices for caramelising
- 4 onions, quartered
- 150ml dry white wine
- 1 dessertspoon soft brown sugar
- Salt and black pepper
- 200g chestnuts
- 2 tablespoons crème fraîche
- 1 tablespoon caster sugar

Preheat the oven to 180°C/gas mark 4.

This recipe works equally well either with each bird jointed into four or kept whole. Roll the joints or the birds in a light coating of seasoned flour and brown them well in hot foaming butter. When they are golden, pour in the Calvados and carefully ignite. Wait until the flames subside and allow to bubble up for a few seconds. Stir well.

While the pheasant is browning, peel, core and quarter the apples. Put both the onions and apples in an ovenproof dish. Lay the browned pheasant on top of them and pour over the pan juices and white wine. Sprinkle with the sugar and season well.

Cover and cook in the preheated oven for about an hour (50 minutes if the pheasant is jointed). Then add the chestnuts and cook for a further 10–15 minutes.

While the pheasant is cooking, make the caramelised apple slices. Sauté a few thin slices of apple in butter and caster sugar.

With a slotted spoon, lift out the pheasant, apples, onions and chestnuts, and place on a serving dish. Cover and keep warm.

Scrape up the juices from the pan and simmer over a medium heat until the liquid has reduced by one-third and thickened slightly.

Take off the heat and stir in the crème fraîche. Adjust the seasoning and pour a little of this sauce over the pheasant, and serve the rest separately.

Decorate with a few of the caramelised apple slices on each plate as you serve the pheasant.

Crab apple and herb jelly

A good jelly to make when there are plenty of crab apples around, though it also works well with Bramleys. The apples provide the pectin and sweetness, and you can use almost any herb. Thyme and mint are my favourites. It's good to eat with red meat and poultry, and delicious whisked into sauces and gravies.

For 5–6 jars:
- 1.4kg cooking or crab apples
- Small bunch of thyme or mint, plus 3 tablespoons chopped fresh thyme or mint
- 150ml white wine vinegar
- Granulated sugar (for exact quantity see below)

Chop the apples in half – unpeeled – and put them into a large heavy-based pan with 900ml water.

Tie the bunch of whichever herb you're using to the saucepan handle, letting it sit in the mixture of apples and water. Simmer until the fruit is really tender. Add the vinegar and cook for a few more minutes.

Put the fruit into a jelly bag (or muslin) and allow it to drip into a china bowl overnight or for several hours. Don't be tempted to squeeze the bag or the jelly will be cloudy.

Warm the packets or bowl of sugar in a very low oven. When the fruit has stopped dripping, measure the juice in the bowl and pour it back into the pan. For every 600ml of liquid add 450g of warmed granulated sugar.

Over a gentle heat, dissolve the sugar, making sure it is completely melted before raising the heat and boiling rapidly to setting point (see page 170). Always take the saucepan off the heat while checking for setting.

Skim the scum off the surface. Once the jelly has rested for 10–15 minutes, stir in the freshly chopped herbs. Then pour into warm sterilised jars and cover.

Apple juice

Freshly pressed apple juice is really worth making. We have a juicer, which turns two apples into an extraordinarily good drink that bears little resemblance to the urine-like pasteurised filtered apple juice you find in the supermarket.

My favourite juice is apple with pineapple and lime – bright, sharp and delicious. If you want a sweet juice, choose Discovery or James Grieve or for something more tart, use a Russet or a mix of two – a sweet and a sour, such as Cox and Bramley. Try adding other things instead of the pineapple, such as watercress or rocket.

For a jug for 4:
600ml apple juice from Bramley and Cox apples
100ml pineapple juice
Juice of 1 lemon or lime
Crushed ice

Mix all the ingredients in a jug. If you're not drinking it straight away, a little lemon or lime juice will stop the apple oxidising and turning brown so quickly.

Kentish apple cake

Living on the Kent/Sussex border and being surrounded by orchards, I'm obliged to have a quick and simple apple cake recipe up my sleeve. This is a lovely one, with plenty of cinnamon and sultanas. It makes a good cake for tea or you can serve it warm as a pudding with lots of thick cream.

For 8–10:
225g unsalted butter, plus a little extra for the tin
350g self-raising flour
1 teaspoon ground cinnamon
Pinch of salt
110g sultanas or raisins, soaked for an hour or two in water or fruit juice
175g caster sugar
75g toasted hazelnuts, roughly chopped or halved (optional)
450g cooking apples, such as Bramley
Grated zest of 1 lemon
3 large eggs
Plenty of demerara sugar for dusting

Preheat a medium (180°C/gas mark 4) oven. Grease or line a 20cm loose-bottomed cake tin.

Pulse the sifted flour, cinnamon, salt and butter in a food processor until it looks like fine breadcrumbs. Put this mixture in a bowl and stir in the sultanas, sugar and toasted nuts, if using.

Peel, core and chop the apples roughly, and add to the other ingredients with the lemon zest. Lightly beat the eggs and stir them in.

Spoon the mixture into the prepared cake tin and bake in the preheated oven for about 1–1¼ hours, or until firm to the touch. You may need to cover the cake lightly with foil to prevent it becoming too brown on the top. While it's still hot, sift over plenty of demerara sugar. Let it cool in the tin on a wire rack.

Toffee apples

Bonfire Night coincides with the apple season. Make plenty of these for it.

For 6:
6 small dessert apples (small is best here)
225g demerara sugar
1 tablespoon golden syrup
30g butter
2 teaspoons lemon juice
You will need 6 x 15cm pieces of wooden dowel (or use lolly sticks if you can find them)

Wash the apples in very hot water to remove any oils from the skin that would otherwise prevent the toffee sticking. Remove the stalks and dry them well. Push a piece of dowel or a lolly stick into the centre of each apple.

Put all the other ingredients into a heavy-based pan with 4 tablespoons water. Cook over a gentle heat until the sugar has completely dissolved and then bring to the boil and boil rapidly for 5–10 minutes.

Line a baking tray with non-stick paper to stand the apples on once they've been dipped. Have a jug of cold water with you at this stage and, every minute or so, test the toffee by dribbling some into the water – gradually you will see it form thick threads that will become increasingly brittle. When you have a toffee that hardens instantly into a crisp thread, remove the pan from the heat and stir to cool a little – this helps prevent the toffee from overcooking and burning.

Dip the apples into the toffee one at a time – swirling as you go – until they are evenly coated. Lift them up and let the excess toffee drip back into the pan. Immediately dip the coated apples in a bowl of iced water so that the toffee sets quickly, and put them on the lined baking tray until they are needed. If the toffee hardens or thickens too much as you dip, put it back on the heat to allow it to soften.

Uncooked autumn chutney

As this chutney is uncooked it is very quick and easy to make. It's wonderful with cheese and ham, and try it under grated cheese on a piece of toast to make the best ever Welsh rarebit.

For 7–8 jars:
900g apples, peeled and cored
450g onions, quartered
450g stoned dates
450g sultanas
450g demerara sugar
1 teaspoon ground ginger
1 teaspoon salt
Cayenne pepper, to taste
450ml white wine vinegar

Chop the apples, onions and dates or pulse them carefully in a food processor. Don't over-do it, as you don't want a purée. Put the mixture into a large china bowl and add the sultanas, sugar, ginger, salt, cayenne and white wine vinegar.

Leave for 36 hours, stirring occasionally, and then put into warm sterilised jars. It keeps for months, if not years.

Apple and plum chutney

Another chutney that is delicious in great dollops with bread and Cheddar cheese. Windfall apples are fine for it.

For 7–8 jars:
450g soft light brown or
**   unbleached cane sugar**
900g plums
900g apples
570ml cider vinegar
450g onions, chopped
450g sultanas
2 level teaspoons salt
1 teaspoon whole cloves
1 teaspoon whole allspice
1 teaspoon black peppercorns
1 medium-sized piece of
**   root ginger**

Put the packets or bowl of sugar into a very low oven to warm for about half an hour. Halve and stone the plums and peel, core and chop the apples. Put the fruit into a large saucepan and add the cider vinegar, onions, sultanas, salt and spices. Bruise the ginger, tie it in a muslin bag and let it dangle from the handle into the mixture.

Bring the pan to the boil and simmer gently for about 30 minutes, until the fruit has softened.

Remove from the heat, discard the ginger and stir in the warmed sugar. Stir over a low heat until the sugar has completely dissolved and then bring to the boil and simmer. Stir the mixture from time to time and make sure that it is not sticking to the bottom of the pan – use a heat diffuser if necessary. Cook until the mixture has reduced considerably to a thick mass, with only a little excess liquid in the pan. (The mixture will thicken even more as it cools.)

Once the chutney has reduced and thickened, stir well, pour into warm sterilised jars and cover with a disc of greaseproof or wax paper. Seal and leave for 6 weeks before using. This keeps for ages.

Aubergines

Aubergines are one of the most beautiful fruits of the edible plant world, ranging from small, tomato-sized varieties such as 'Slim Jim' to the handsome glossy fat 'Violetta'. If you want to grow them, choose early-ripening varieties such as 'Moneymaker' or little ones, which, like cherry tomatoes, ripen more easily in our cool climate. They will continue to fruit outside until the end of October, and keep even longer on the plant in a greenhouse.

Whether you're buying or growing aubergines, you can tell if they are ripe by looking under the calyx – the greeny-purple star where the fruit joins the stem. If the skin there is pure white, the fruit is ripe; if it is tinged green, wait a few days before you use the fruit. It will ripen on and off the plant. In a perfect state, the skin at the apex should be soft and have a slight give as you squeeze. Over-ripe fruit is easy to spot too: when you cut it open, the flesh is full of seeds.

Unripe or over-ripe, you can still eat aubergines, but they won't be as nice. They'll have a chewy texture, so will need a longer cooking time. They can also be bitter, so if you have to use them unripe or over-ripe, scatter some salt over the sliced flesh to draw out the juices for half an hour before you start to cook. You won't need to use this old-fashioned technique with perfectly ripe fruit. Modern hybrids – and almost all you come across to buy will be – have been bred specifically to get rid of the bitter juice.

There are many great recipes for aubergines, but sometimes simple is best. One of my favourite ways of eating them is in slices, dipped into Cucumber raita (see page 196). Slice the aubergine into discs about 2cm thick. Fry these on both sides until they are golden and dry them on kitchen paper. Alternatively, slice the aubergine and cut shallow diagonal cuts into the flesh. Rub fennel seed, a little salt and extra virgin olive oil into the cuts, and griddle them for a few minutes on each side until they're slightly charred and tender. Eat them on their own or dipped into crème fraîche flavoured with fresh dill or fennel leaf.

Spiced aubergine salad

This fragrant salad is lovely served warm as a first course, with Cucumber raita (see page 196) and flat or naan bread (see page 46 and right).

For 6–8:

3 large to medium-sized aubergines (about 1kg)
3 tablespoons good extra virgin olive oil
1 large onion, finely chopped
1 tablespoon cumin seeds
1 tablespoon coriander seeds
1 teaspoon allspice berries
1 star anise
1 teaspoon ground cinnamon
1 teaspoon paprika
5 medium-sized tomatoes, skinned (see page 266), or a 400g tin of chopped tomatoes
Generous handful of coriander, coarsely chopped
Generous handful of mint, coarsely chopped
Juice and grated zest of 1 lemon

Preheat a medium-hot (200°C/gas mark 6) oven. Dice the aubergines into 1cm chunks. Drizzle 2 tablespoons of the oil over the top and roast in the preheated oven for about 30 minutes. Cook until the edges start to char.

Meanwhile, fry the onion gently in the rest of the oil until it's glassy and soft. In a separate pan, toast the cumin and coriander seeds, allspice and star anise for a couple of minutes until they begin to smoke and then grind them to a coarse powder in a spice grinder or using a pestle and mortar. Add the toasted spices to the onion, together with the cinnamon and paprika, and then add the cooked aubergines and tomatoes. Cook the mixture over a gentle heat for 20–30 minutes.

Once the tomato juice has reduced so that there's little liquid left, take the pan off the heat and stir in the fresh herbs and add the lemon juice and zest.

Baba ghanoush with naan bread

I have tried lots of baba ghanoush recipes and this is my favourite, from the *Moro Cookbook* by Sam and Sam Clark. It has a nutty, lemony taste and the texture is light and creamy.

For 6:

3 large to medium-sized aubergines (about 1kg)
2 garlic cloves, crushed to a paste with 2 teaspoons salt
Juice and grated zest of 1 lemon
3 tablespoons tahini
4 tablespoons olive oil
Salt and black pepper

For the naan bread:

450g strong white bread flour
1 teaspoon dried yeast
2 teaspoons salt
½ teaspoon baking powder
4 tablespoons milk
60g butter, plus a little extra for brushing
4 tablespoons natural yoghurt
¼ teaspoon bicarbonate of soda
1 egg
Plenty of poppy seeds

Pierce the skins of the aubergines and grill or barbecue them whole, turning them until they are cooked and the skin is charred and crisp all over. Or you can cook them in a very hot oven (220°C/gas mark 7) for about 45 minutes.

Let the aubergines cool, and then cut them in half lengthways and scrape away the skin from the flesh. Put the flesh and juices in a food processor and whiz until nearly smooth. Add the garlic, lemon zest and juice, tahini and olive oil. You may need to thin with a little water – you are aiming for a hummus-like consistency. Season.

To make the naan bread, put the flour, yeast, salt and baking powder into a food processor. Warm the milk, butter and yoghurt, and add

the bicarbonate of soda and egg. Add this to the flour in the processor. (This saves a lot of time and washing up.)

Whiz to a bread dough consistency – you may need a little more milk. Let the dough rise in the container for about an hour, covered with a damp cloth in a warm room.

Whiz again to break it down, and shape it into 12 balls. Roll these into teardrop shapes and leave for 10 minutes (you can start cooking the first one by the time you've rolled the last one). Brush one side with melted butter and sprinkle with poppy seeds. It's nice to have different textures on each side, so don't be tempted to butter and poppy seed both sides.

Flip on to a large hot griddle, a thick frying pan or the right-hand simmering plate (cool) of an Aga. You can do 4 at a time. They swell brilliantly. When they colour, flip them over to cook on the other side.

Aubergine and feta salad

Another, much sharper-tasting aubergine salad which you can eat warm or cold. The smoky flavours of roasted aubergine work well with the acidity of lemon and saltiness of feta.

The finishing touch to this salad is a good handful of any green herb, and coarsely chopped flat-leaf parsley is ideal.

For 8:
**3 large to medium-sized
    aubergines (about 1kg)
2 tablespoons olive oil
200g feta cheese
2 tablespoons extra virgin olive oil
Juice and grated zest of 1 lemon
Salt and black pepper
Handful of coarsely chopped
    parsley**

Cut the aubergine into large chunks and roast them in oil as in the Spiced aubergine salad on page 299. Meanwhile, break up the feta into small lumps.

Take the aubergine out of the oven and, while it is still hot, stir in the extra virgin olive oil, lemon juice, lemon zest and feta. Season with salt and pepper to taste. Once it has cooled down a little, add plenty of parsley.

Caponata

This classic Italian dish is a good way of storing aubergine. The balsamic vinegar preserves it, so it can be kept in a jar in the fridge for at least 2 weeks. Serve this cold, as a starter. It is lovely with prosciutto and cold meats and cheeses. Salted capers have the best flavour, so find these if you can. Drain and rinse them under cold running water and then dry on kitchen towel.

For about 750ml:
**1 large or 2 small aubergines
    (about 500g)
2–3 tablespoons olive oil
1 large onion, sliced
2 garlic cloves, finely chopped
A few basil leaves
2 tablespoons capers
5 tomatoes, skinned (see page
    266) and roughly chopped, or
    a 400g tin of chopped tomatoes
2 tablespoons balsamic vinegar
1 tablespoon brown sugar
1 teaspoon cocoa powder
Handful of black olives, stoned
    and quartered
Salt and black pepper**

Preheat a moderate (180°C/gas mark 4) oven. Peel and chop the aubergines. In a pan, heat the olive oil and sauté the aubergine until it begins to brown. Add the onion and garlic, and cook for a further 5 minutes.

Tear up the basil leaves and add these to the aubergine and onions, together with all the other ingredients, and cook gently over a moderate heat or in the preheated oven for about 40 minutes. Check to make sure that the mixture is not catching on the bottom of the pan and add a little water if necessary.

When the caponata has finished cooking, the mixture should look dark and rich, with most of the excess liquid absorbed.

Baked aubergines with mozzarella

Aubergines and mozzarella – *Melanzane Parmigiano* – is an Italian classic and the ultimate comfort food – ideal for a chilly autumn night, eaten with a spicy green salad. It's good then and there, and even better reheated. Don't compromise with anything but the best mozzarella. You really taste the difference.

For 4:

3 large to medium-sized aubergines (about 1kg)
Olive oil
Salt and black pepper
200g freshly grated Parmesan cheese
500ml Really rich tomato sauce (see page 277)
700g buffalo mozzarella
Handful of flat-leaf parsley
Handful of basil, torn up

Preheat the oven to 175°C/gas mark 3–4.

Slice the aubergines lengthways into slices about 1cm thick. Brush the surface of each side with a little olive oil and sprinkle with salt. Bake or griddle until they are tender. (Make sure, if you are baking them, that they don't dry out or brown too much. You can cover them with foil.)

Oil an ovenproof dish and cover the bottom with a layer of aubergine. Season with black pepper and a scattering of Parmesan. Spread a layer of tomato sauce over the aubergine and top that with thick slices of mozzarella and a scattering of herbs. Add another layer of aubergine and continue as before. Make sure you finish with a layer of tomato and a generous amount of Parmesan.

Cook in the preheated oven for an hour, then allow to rest for at least 20 minutes. It will hold its heat well. As with so many recipes, this tastes far better warm rather than piping hot.

Moussaka

For years Tam has been trying to recreate the best moussaka ever, which she had in a back-street restaurant in Heraklion years ago. This is pretty faithful to the original. The key ingredients are feta, yoghurt, cinnamon, nutmeg and allspice. Unlike many English adaptations of this dish, it does not contain Parmesan, Cheddar or Gruyère.

For 4–6:

3 large to medium-sized aubergines (about 1kg)
Olive oil
1 large onion, chopped
450g minced lamb or beef
½ teaspoon freshly ground allspice
½ teaspoon freshly ground cinnamon
Salt and black pepper
500ml Really rich tomato sauce (see page 277)
20g chopped thyme

For the béchamel sauce:

500ml milk
3 bay leaves
80g butter
80g plain flour
1 heaped teaspoon nutmeg, freshly grated
1 level teaspoon cinnamon, freshly ground
200g feta cheese, finely crumbled
250g Greek yoghurt
2 egg yolks
Salt and black pepper

Preheat a medium (180°C/gas mark 4) oven or a griddle.

Cut the aubergines lengthways into slices about 1cm thick and brush them on both sides with a little olive oil. Bake the aubergines in the preheated oven or griddle them until they are soft but not charred.

Keep the oven on if using or preheat as above if not. Over a moderate heat, sweat the onion in a little olive oil and, when it has softened, add the meat, allspice, cinnamon, salt and pepper. When the meat begins to brown, add the tomato sauce and the chopped thyme. Cover and simmer gently for half an hour, checking from time to time. If the mixture begins to stick, add a little water. When the meat is ready, there should be no extra liquid in the pan. Put the meat to one side.

For the béchamel sauce, bring the milk and bay leaves to the boil, take off the heat and allow to infuse. Melt the butter in a saucepan, stir in the flour, freshly grated nutmeg and cinnamon, and cook for 2 minutes. Using a balloon whisk, gradually add the strained hot milk and keep stirring until you have a perfectly smooth sauce. Cook gently for a couple of minutes and put to one side. When the sauce has cooled for a few minutes, add the feta, Greek yoghurt and egg yolks. Season with a little salt and plenty of black pepper. Whisk gently until the mixture is smooth.

Lightly oil an ovenproof dish and cover the bottom with a layer of the aubergine slices. Spread over a layer of the meat and tomato mixture, then another layer of aubergine, another layer of meat and finally a thick layer of the béchamel sauce.

Bake for an hour in the preheated moderate oven, covering the moussaka with foil if it colours too much on the top. Allow to stand for at least 20 minutes before serving.

Again, this is much better eaten warm rather than hot.

Borlotti beans

The eau de nil and crimson-stippled borlotti bean is a beautiful thing. Climbing up a tepee or sprawling over a frame, they look so handsome you'd want them in your garden even if they didn't taste so good, but they do. They have a creamy flavour and a meaty, hearty texture which is just what you need as the weather gets colder at this time of year.

You can grow borlotti beans quite successfully in this country, but they are difficult to buy. If you can't get hold of them fresh, use dried. Tinned don't have the flavour or the texture, but they'll do as a last resort.

'Lingua de Fuoco 2' is the most widely available variety here. The key to growing the perfect borlotti is climate. In Italy, it is said that their ideal conditions are high altitude, poor soil, heat in the day and cool moisture at night. To grow them here, sow in late spring with your runner beans, although, unlike runners, you don't need to add lots of organic material to their planting soil. They'll do fine on any soil, but they particularly love chalk.

In my garden, borlotti crop best in a sunny, sheltered spot out of the wind, and in soil which is not enriched. If over-fed, they produce lots of lush green growth and fewer flowers and beans. For this reason, borlotti are ideal for growing in a large pot with a tepee of canes. Pick them as the bean pods turn from green to cream. This is when the beans inside are ripe. Or you can pick them earlier and dry them somewhere bright and warm inside: lay the pods out over a greenhouse bench for a couple of weeks and they should ripen well. You can use them at this stage, or shell them and dry them out of their pods in the same place for another week or so, then store them in a jar for use in the winter.

Borlotti ratatouille

This is my absolute favourite recipe for borlotti. It's good as a starter, but can also be eaten as a main course, with a green salad and perhaps some roasted or griddled aubergine.

For 6–8 as a starter or a side dish:
1 large onion, finely chopped
2 garlic cloves, finely chopped
15 medium-sized tomatoes, skins removed (see page 266) and roughly chopped, or 3 x 400g tins of chopped tomatoes
Splash of olive oil, plus a little extra for drizzling
500g fresh borlotti beans (or, if using dried beans, use 250g soaked overnight in cold water)
Salt and black pepper
Really generous bunch of fresh coriander, coarsely chopped
Fine slivers of Parmesan cheese

Cook the onion and garlic gently in the oil until it's soft. Add the tomatoes and the beans, and stew gently for about 45 minutes. Add a little water if they become too dry at any time.

When the beans are tender but not mushy, remove them from the heat and leave for 15 minutes to cool. Season with salt and black pepper.

Just before you eat, add the coriander, a drizzle of olive oil and the slivers of Parmesan.

Sweet-and-sour borlotti beans

This is a classic northern Italian antipasto, eaten speared on a cocktail stick, or as a dollop on a plate with ham and salami. In this country you may not find enough fresh borlotti to want to preserve them, but you can make this with dried. It's good pre-party food.

For 2 litres:
1.3kg fresh borlotti beans (or, if using dried beans, use 650g soaked overnight in cold water)
Salt
2 white onions, sliced
2 red peppers, deseeded and cut into slim matchsticks
3 small glasses of white wine vinegar
3 level dessertspoons sugar
750ml extra virgin olive oil

Boil the beans in salted water until they're tender, but retaining their shape. This will take about half an hour. Drain and let them cool.

Put them into a large pan with the onions, red peppers, vinegar, sugar and oil. Bring them to the boil again and bottle them in warm sterilised jars, filled right to the top. Seal well.

Turn the jars upside down immediately and wrap them in a wool blanket or jersey. Leave them wrapped up for a couple of days, so that the liquor cools very slowly, preserving the borlotti beans. They will keep for at least a year.

Borlotti hummus

Borlotti also make a delicious lighter-than-chickpea hummus. If you don't have any borlotti, cannellini beans, soaked overnight, work well. Eat this hummus with black olives and Rosemary flat bread (see page 46).

For 6:
   250g fresh borlotti beans (or, if using dried beans, use 125g soaked overnight in cold water)
   50g tin of anchovies
   1 garlic clove
   Juice and grated zest of lemon, to taste
   2 tablespoons extra virgin olive oil
   2 tablespoons yoghurt
   Salt and black pepper
   Handful of chopped coriander

Cook the beans for half an hour or until tender in plenty of salted water. Strain, reserving the cooking liquid, allow to cool and then purée them with the drained anchovies, garlic, lemon juice and zest to taste, yoghurt and a little of the cooking liquid and olive oil. Season well and add the chopped coriander.

Cannellini, borlotti or white butter bean soup

This soup is filling, so serve it in small bowls, with a dollop of Greek yoghurt or a splash of a good fruity extra virgin olive oil over the top. There's no need for bread.

For 8:
   3 garlic cloves, finely chopped
   1 teaspoon ground cumin seeds
   2 small Preserved lemons (see page 35), pith removed (or you can use strips of lemon rind)
   ½ hot chilli (left in one piece so that you can remove it)
   Olive oil
   1kg fresh or tinned cannellini, borlotti or white butter beans (or, if using dried beans, use 500g soaked overnight in cold water)
   1 litre chicken stock
   Juice of ½ lemon
   Good handful of coriander leaves, coarsely chopped
   Salt and black pepper

Sweat the garlic, cumin, lemons or lemon rind and chilli in a splash of olive oil for a couple of minutes. Then add the beans and stock, and cook them for about 40 minutes until the beans are soft. Remove the chilli.

Purée the mixture with a wand whizzer or in a food processor. You may want to dilute the soup with stock or water and a little lemon juice to taste.

Stir in the coriander, season with salt and pepper and serve.

Borlotti beans with sage

I first had this simple dish in the Madonna restaurant in Venice to accompany slow-roasted belly of pork. The River Cafe in London serves a similar borlotti recipe as a first course with lots of rocket.

Fresh borlotti beans make this extra delicious as they have a softer, creamier texture than dried.

For 6 as a starter, 8 as a side dish:
500g fresh borlotti beans (or, if using dried beans, use 250g soaked overnight in cold water)
1 garlic clove, peeled
10g sage leaves, chopped, plus plenty extra for scattering
3 tablespoons extra virgin olive oil, plus a little extra for drizzling
100g pancetta, chopped
Slurp of red wine vinegar
2 tablespoons Dijon mustard
Salt and black pepper
3 handfuls of rocket or young spinach leaves (optional)

Put the beans, garlic and chopped sage into a pan, bring them to the boil and simmer for 30–40 minutes until the beans are soft. Drain them and, while still warm, add 1 tablespoon of oil and put aside.

Meanwhile, fry the pancetta in a very little olive oil until crisp and add to the beans. Mix together the vinegar, mustard, salt and pepper, and slowly add the rest of the olive oil to give a very creamy dressing. Pour this over the still-warm beans, keeping a third back if you are using the salad leaves. Scatter plenty of chopped sage leaves over the top.

If using the salad leaves, dress the leaves and divide between the plates, and spoon the beans over the leaves. Drizzle with a little extra virgin olive oil.

Borlotti bean brandade

Marseilles is the home of this dish, which is served as an accompaniment to lamb. The French eat it topped with croutons fried in olive oil. It is rich, robust and delicious, and also lovely spread on crostini.

For 4:
250g fresh borlotti beans (or, if using dried beans, use 125g soaked overnight in cold water)
1 onion, halved
1 carrot
2 bay leaves
6 cloves
½ head of garlic
5 anchovies
100ml milk
75ml extra virgin olive oil
1–2 tablespoons lemon juice
Sea salt and black pepper

Cook the beans in a saucepan filled with lots of water, along with the onion halves, carrot, bay leaves and cloves for 30–40 minutes until tender.

Roast the garlic in the oven until soft (see page 253).

Rinse the anchovies if they are salted and chop finely.

Bring the milk to the boil in a small saucepan.

Drain the beans and remove the vegetables, bay leaves and cloves. Squeeze the roasted garlic to reveal the soft, sweet cloves and purée with the beans. Return the mixture to a low heat and stir constantly while gradually adding the oil.

Stir in the boiled milk, anchovies and lemon juice to taste and season with a little sea salt and plenty of ground black pepper. Keep warm and serve as soon as possible.

Bulb fennel

It's the gentle aniseedy flavour as well as the texture of bulb – or so-called Florence – fennel that makes it such a great vegetable. The texture can change from a delicious water-filled crunch when raw to soft squidgy caramel when cooked. Florence fennel – very fresh – makes a good addition to a green salad and very thinly sliced, it is delicious on its own. I also love the everyday French way of preparing fennel – blanching thick slices of it for a couple of minutes in salted water and then cooling it quickly in cold water before dressing with a little warm olive oil, black pepper and topping with halved black olives. Try griddling slices too, and then dress them with lemon juice, olive oil and a thinly sliced chilli. This is lovely hot or cold the next day.

If you're going to cook whole bulbs, they benefit from a long slow roast. This softens any fibres – even of the outer layers – and brings out the sweet treacly flavour. Always keep them covered in the oven, so that they steam and roast at the same time and don't start to char. They're perfect eaten with chicken, and they also taste fantastic with fish.

Growing bulb fennel is worthwhile if you avoid sowing from mid-May to late July. Sown early in the year under cover, or outside in August or early September, it will bulb up well before it tries to flower. The most reliable variety of all I've tried is the late-season 'Romanesco'. It's slow to bolt and forms huge bulbs. If you get a few bulbs that flower, use the beautiful acid green umbels in salad, or dip them in tempura batter (see page 207) and shallow-fry them. They are delicious.

Braised fennel

Slow-cooking bulb fennel makes it one of the best vegetables to eat with any meat or poultry.

For 4:
  1kg fennel bulbs
  1 whole head of garlic
  4 tablespoons olive oil
  5 tablespoons white wine (or 150ml if not using Pernod)
  5 tablespoons Pernod (optional)
  Salt and black pepper

Trim the fennel bulbs, removing any damaged outer leaves and the stalks. Keep some of the feathery tops to one side. Split the bulbs in half. Separate the garlic cloves but leave the skins on.

In a heavy-based pan, heat the olive oil, add the fennel bulbs, cut side down. Put in all the garlic cloves and season with salt. Cover and cook the fennel very gently until the undersides are golden. Turn and allow the other sides to colour – this takes about half an hour. (This can also be done in the oven, preheated to 160°C/gas mark 3.) Squash the garlic flesh out of the skins and mix it in.

Add half the white wine and the Pernod, if using, turn the fennel once more, cover and continue to cook very gently for about an hour. Add a little more wine or Pernod from time to time if necessary. Pernod, with its higher sugar and alcohol content, gives a creamier flavour.

When the fennel is tender and a rich gold, season and serve with some of the reserved, chopped fennel leaves on the top.

Bulb fennel and grape salad

One of the best salads for eating at this time of year – refreshing with a hint of aniseed.

For 2–3:
  2 fennel bulbs, plus 1 tablespoon chopped fennel tops and a little extra to garnish
  Extra virgin olive oil
  Black pepper
  Grated zest of ½ lemon
  1 teaspoon toasted crushed fennel seeds
  2 dessertspoons crème fraîche or fromage frais
  Small bunch of seedless green grapes

Take off any tough or discoloured outer layers from the fennel bulb. Slice the fennel as thinly as you possibly can – a mandoline is the best tool for this – and finely chop the ferny top. Arrange in a deep bowl with a little extra virgin olive oil, black pepper, lemon zest and fennel seeds. Fold in the crème fraîche.

Halve the grapes and add them to the ingredients in the bowl. Stir to combine and decorate with more chopped fennel tops.

Sage, Florence fennel and Pernod pasta

The wonderful smoky taste of sage and aniseed infuses this pasta sauce.

For 4:

   6 shallots, peeled and roughly
      sliced
   3 medium-sized fennel bulbs,
      outer leaves removed and
      roughly chopped
   20 sage leaves, coarsely chopped
   5 tablespoons Pernod
   50g butter
   3 tablespoons olive oil
   50g pine nuts
   150g pasta (tagliatelle is ideal)
   100ml crème fraîche
   Salt and black pepper
   Freshly grated Parmesan cheese,
      to serve

Preheat a slow (150°C/gas mark 2) oven.

   Put the shallots, fennel bulbs, sage leaves, Pernod, butter and olive oil in a covered ovenproof dish with some seasoning. Braise gently in the preheated oven for an hour, until the fennel bulbs are soft. Check every so often to make sure that they are not sticking and, if the liquid has been absorbed, add more Pernod or water.

   Chop or pulse once in a food processor to combine the ingredients, but do not reduce to a purée.

   Towards the end of the braising time, toast the pine nuts for 3–4 minutes and cook your pasta in salted boiling water until al dente.

   Drain the cooked pasta, leaving in about 3 tablespoons of water, and fold in the sauce. Add the crème fraîche.

   Scatter with plenty of Parmesan and more salt and pepper to taste.

Fennel and prawn risotto

For this, it's really worth finding fresh prawns, not frozen shelled ones. The quickest and best fish stock is made from the cooking liquid, reduced after you have removed the cooked prawns.

For 4:

   Pinch of salt
   400g uncooked tiger prawns,
      shell on
   40g butter
   1 tablespoon extra virgin olive oil
   1 large onion, thinly sliced
   1 large or 2 medium-sized fennel
      bulb(s), cut into 1cm-ish slices
   250g Arborio rice
   135ml white wine
   Grated zest and juice of 1 lemon
   Black pepper
   Chopped parsley, to finish
   A few fennel tops, chopped,
      to serve

In a saucepan, bring 1 litre of water to the boil, adding a generous pinch of salt. Throw in the prawns and, when the water comes back to the boil, remove from the heat. Allow to stand for a couple of minutes.

   Remove the prawns with a draining spoon, leaving the liquid in the saucepan, and plunge them into cold water. When the prawns are cool enough to handle, peel them, put them to one side and put the shells back into the saucepan. Boil up the shells in the water to make the stock.

   While the shells are boiling, melt half the butter in a large saucepan and add a generous glug of olive oil. Sweat the onion and fennel together in the saucepan and then cover with a circle of greaseproof paper, so that they don't colour.

   After a few minutes, add the Arborio rice and stir to make sure the rice is well coated before adding the white wine. Bubble up and wait until the wine has evaporated before adding the hot stock gradually in

strained ladlefuls. Before each addition keep stirring until the stock has been absorbed. (You will need to add about three-quarters of the stock.)

   It will take about 15–20 minutes for the rice to become al dente and, when it reaches this stage, add the lemon zest, lemon juice to taste and the cooked prawns. Stir over the heat for a few seconds to warm the prawns.

   Season with black pepper and take the pan off the heat. Stir in the chopped parsley and the remaining butter.

   Cover and leave for a few minutes. Check the seasoning and serve with some of the chopped feathery fennel tops.

Celery

Celery is good raw when it's crunchy and fresh, ideal for eating with strong cheese or in a tall glass of Bloody Mary. It's also delicious cooked, a fundamental flavour for a good stock, and excellent sliced and slowly braised.

When you're buying it, look out for the huge blanched heads with really black soil at the base. These are grown in the peaty fens and have fantastic flavour. A lot of commercially mass-produced celery is now grown hydroponically (mostly in Holland) and, in my experience, has almost no taste, and has among the highest pesticide residues you'll find in any vegetable.

Whether you're eating celery raw or cooked, choose a good head and remove the damaged outside branches. With a potato peeler, strip away the fibrous strings of the outer layer. This will stop you wasting the outer sticks, which are usually the tastiest. Remove the top branches at the joints and rinse the prepared celery under cold running water.

I grow 'Mammoth Pink', which needs blanching (excluding the light) to make the stems more tender and less bitter. You can blanch with earth, newspaper, cardboard or roofing felt, but earth seems to work the best. You dig a celery trench – a beautiful thing – adding as much compost as you would for hungry runner beans. As soon as the last frosts are over, plant your young celery seedlings in the bottom of the trench in a double row (20cm between each) and cover with soil. When the tops of the plants rise above soil level, earth them up and continue to do so as often as you can. To grow well, celery benefits from a steady water supply and a rich soil.

Another good thing about celery is that the leaves are useful, too. They are an excellent addition to soups and stews, and the young heart leaves are lovely in salad.

Braised celery

The intensified flavour of the braised celery stems is delicious and, like bulb fennel, perfect with the gentle flavours of chicken and fish. Another version of braised celery is to finish it off with cream. After braising, warm through 200g of crème fraîche. Add 1 tablespoon Madeira and pour over the celery. Season and serve with plenty of chopped parsley.

For 6:
  3 celery heads
  Salt and black pepper
  30g butter
  3 shallots, thinly sliced
  500ml good vegetable or chicken stock
  Juice of 1 lemon
  1 tablespoon sugar
  Bunch of parsley, finely chopped

Tie some string around the top of the celery branches to hold the hearts together as they cook. Bring a large saucepan of salted water to the boil and add the celery. Simmer gently for 10 minutes and then cool the celery quickly by plunging it into cold water. Dry on a tea towel. Remove the strings from the celery stalks and then trim the ends.

Melt the butter in a pan. Add the celery, shallots, stock, lemon juice, sugar and a little salt. Simmer for about 30 minutes over a low heat without covering, making sure that it doesn't boil dry.

When the celery is tender, lift out on to a serving plate and add some freshly ground pepper and plenty of chopped parsley. If there is more than a little liquid in the pan, boil to reduce it and pour over the celery.

Braised beans and celery

I had a wonderful lunch this summer in a simple restaurant outside Asolo in the Veneto. We had roast rabbit with chard, mashed potato and these very delicious borlotti beans. The beans – boiled in vegetable stock – were braised quickly with finely cut celery. The crunch of the celery made a perfect contrast to the softness of the beans.

For 4–6:
  250g dried borlotti beans (or any other dried beans)
  1 litre vegetable or chicken stock
  30g butter
  Olive oil
  ½ onion, finely chopped
  275g celery, finely chopped
  1 garlic clove, finely chopped
  Large glass of white wine
  1 teaspoon sugar
  Several sprigs of thyme
  Salt and black pepper

Soak the beans for about 6 hours and then drain and cook in the stock for about half an hour, until tender but still holding their shape.

Heat the butter with a little olive oil in a pan and sweat the onion, celery and garlic, covering them with a circle of greaseproof paper and a lid to prevent them from colouring. Cook for about 10 minutes until they become just translucent and the celery is still a little crisp.

Add the wine, sugar and thyme, and cover and simmer gently for another 5 minutes. Add the cooked beans. Warm them through and season.

Celery and cucumber salad in mustard dressing

The tastes and textures of cucumber and celery make a very good salad with a punchy, mustard dressing. This is good with any cold meat – beef, chicken, turkey or ham – and is an excellent salad for Boxing Day.

For 6:
1 cucumber
Salt and black pepper
1 celery head
1 tablespoon Dijon mustard
1 teaspoon Colman's English mustard
1 tablespoon red wine vinegar
Juice of 1 lemon
4 tablespoons sunflower oil
Bunch of parsley or winter savory, finely chopped

Peel and deseed the cucumber (cut in half and use a teaspoon). Slice the halves into 1cm-thick half-moons, put in a colander and sprinkle with salt. Leave to drain for half an hour.

Meanwhile, prepare the celery as described on page 312, and then slice it into similar-sized chunks.

Put the mustards in a bowl. Add the vinegar and lemon juice, and then slowly add the oil to make a thick mustard dressing.

Pour the dressing over the celery and cucumber, and mix in plenty of salt and pepper and finely chopped parsley or winter savory, if available.

Bottled celery

The Italians have a glorious tradition of spreading out various bowls of different antipasti to dip into before lunch or supper. Eat this celery antipasto with salami, prosciutto, salted almonds, sweet roasted peppers, griddled aubergine slices and olives. The lovely thing about bottled celery is not just its flavour, but also its texture – crunchy but not raw.

For about 6 jars:
2 celery heads, stringy outer stems removed
Plenty of fine salt
1 large white onion, chopped
4 tablespoons olive oil
100ml white wine vinegar
Freshly ground white pepper

Slice the celery into 2cm chunks and put in a colander. Cover in a dusting of fine salt and leave to drain for about an hour. Then rinse off the salt and pat the chunks dry.

Sweat the chopped onion gently in plenty of olive oil for 10 minutes without browning and then add the celery, vinegar, freshly ground white pepper and a little salt, cooking it enough to soften the celery slightly, but keeping its crunch.

Fill about 6 warm sterilised jars right to the top, topping up with oil so that the celery is completely covered.

Seal the jars and turn them upside down straight away. Wrap in wool blankets or jerseys, and leave them wrapped up for a couple of days, so that the liquor cools very slowly. The celery will last for at least a year.

Chillies

Once you've had one or two sessions of tasting and eating chillies, you'll find that they are addictive. They contain an oil, capsaicin, that sends a burning sensation from the nerve endings in the mouth to the brain. The body defends itself against this 'pain' by secreting endorphins, natural painkillers, which cause a physical 'rush' in the same way as the opium-derived drug morphine. As a result, you feel good and the high keeps you coming back for more.

The highest concentration of capsaicin is in the seeds and the 'ribs' attaching them to the fruit walls. If you've got mild chillies such as 'Hungarian Hot Wax' in their unripe green stage and want to maximise their heat, chop them whole, leaving the seeds in. If you've a hot variety, such as the pretty tangerine-coloured 'Habanera', you may want to cut the chillies open and discard the seeds.

A chilli's heat is measured on the Scoville Scale, named after the chemist Wilbur Scoville. A number was assigned to each chilli, based on how much it needed to be diluted before you could taste no heat. The Scoville grade of 'Hungarian Hot Wax' is 5,000 to 10,000, a similar range to that of the popular 'Jalapeño' (2,500 to 8,000). 'Scotch Bonnet', which you'll see in many African and Arabic vegetable stalls, is considerably hotter (100,000 to 325,000). The heat varies according to how and where it's grown. Grown harder, outside in the garden, chillies tend to be noticeably hotter.

When you're preparing chillies, wear rubber gloves and don't touch your eyes until you've taken the gloves off. Capsaicin is not water-soluble, so you can't just wash it off and, if you burn your mouth eating chillies, drinking water won't help. Dairy products are very effective in cooling you off. They contain the protein casein, which breaks the bond between the pain receptors and the capsaicin.

You can buy your chillies, but most of the interesting varieties are not widely available. Source these from specialist mail order suppliers, or grow your own. 'Hungarian Hot Wax' crops heavily over a long season, and is excellent if you like a mild to medium chilli. 'Jalapeño' is of similar heat, with chunky, fleshy fruits and fantastic productivity. If you like them hot, there's 'Habanera', but this needs more attention and higher temperatures than others, or 'Twilight', a beautiful chilli with multicoloured cream, green, red and purple fruit, which makes ideal house plants.

With all the following recipes, the amount of chilli you use will depend on the heat of that particular crop and your tolerance of it. The quantities given are just a guide – make sure you taste as you go.

Pickled chillies

Long thin chillies like the Hungarian Hot Wax are best for this, with a strength that is slightly surprising but doesn't burn. If you like things a bit hotter, Jalapeño are also good. These pickled chillies are lovely with a glass of wine before supper. They are also excellent with a char-grilled burger and chips, and are one of my favourite things for lunch with bread and Cheddar cheese.

For a small jar:
  6 mild to medium-hot chillies
  5 tablespoons white wine vinegar
  1 teaspoon sugar
  1 teaspoon mustard seeds
  ½ teaspoon salt

You can leave the chillies whole and pickle them, but they're easier to eat, and more versatile, when sliced into quite thick rings. If you want to maximise the heat, leave the seeds in; if you want them mild, remove them. Meanwhile bring the pickling mix of sugar, mustard seeds, salt, vinegar and 1 tablespoon of water up to the boil.

Stuff the chilli rings tightly into a warm, sterilised jar and pour on the hot pickling mix. Seal and cover.

These are best left for a few weeks to mature. The longer you leave them, the hotter they get. They'll keep for a year.

Chilli dipping sauce

A wonderfully simple dip that is delicious for any tempura (see page 207). Have a bowl of this and one of good soy sauce so you can alternate from sweet to salty. This one has some punch, but it's not too fiery. Many commercial varieties have too much sugar and contain unnecessary preservatives, so it's worth making your own.

For 2 jars:
  400g white sugar
  2 chopped red Jalapeño or Cherry Bomb chillies, seeds left in
  5 garlic cloves, chopped
  250ml cider vinegar
  250ml orange juice

Put the packets or bowl of sugar into a very low oven to warm up for about half an hour.

Put all the ingredients, including the warmed sugar and chillies, into a saucepan over a low heat to dissolve the sugar. Simmer for about 15 minutes – until it's syrupy – and then pour into sterilised bottles or jars and seal. The vinegar in the sauce acts as a preservative and so, kept cool, this lasts for months.

Chilli jam

Chilli jam is fantastically versatile stuff. Try it spread on corn cobs instead of butter, or on top of cream cheese on a crostini. I use it instead of mint jelly with lamb or red meat and it's famously good with fish cakes or calamari rings. I have taken to having it on toast on top of cream cheese for a late breakfast!

For about 6 jars:
  500g very ripe tomatoes
  4 garlic cloves, peeled
  4 large red chillies (seeds left in if you want your jam hot)
  6–7cm piece of ginger root, sliced
  300g golden caster sugar
  2 tablespoons Thai fish sauce
  100ml red wine vinegar

Blitz half the tomatoes with all the garlic, chillies and ginger in a food processor. Pour into a heavy-based saucepan. Add the sugar, fish sauce and vinegar, and bring to the boil, stirring slowly. Reduce to a simmer.

Dice the remaining tomatoes finely and add them to the pan. Simmer for 30–40 minutes, stirring from time to time. The mixture will turn slightly darker and sticky.

Store in warm dry sterilised jars and seal while the mixture is still warm. The longer you keep this jam the hotter it gets. It keeps for about 3 months in the fridge.

Plum, apple and chilli jelly

There are many chilli jellies, but I particularly like the colour and flavour of this one, which has the taste of plum and apple, and the heat of the chillies. It tastes excellent with any meat or cheese.

For about 2kg:
- **900g Bramley or crab apples**
- **900g plums (any variety), stoned**
- **175ml cider vinegar**
- **Sugar (for exact quantity see below)**
- **3 Jalapeño or medium-hot chillies, sliced into rings, deseeded if you don't want it hot**

Roughly chop the unpeeled apples and put them into a large preserving pan with the plums and 1.7 litres water. Bring to the boil, cover and simmer for one hour. Add the cider vinegar and boil for 5 minutes.

Strain overnight through a jelly bag or muslin. Don't be tempted to squeeze the bag as this will make the jelly cloudy.

Put the packets or bowl of sugar into a very low oven to warm up for about half an hour. Measure the juice and for every 570ml of juice use 450g of warmed sugar. Pour the juice into the preserving pan and add the sugar. Dissolve the sugar completely, while stirring over a gentle heat, and add the chillies.

When the sugar has dissolved, raise the heat and boil vigorously until setting point is reached (see page 170). Leave the jelly to stand for at least 20 minutes and stir once more to ensure the chillies are distributed evenly through the jelly.

Pour into warm sterilised jars and seal. Keeps for up to a year.

Barbecued stuffed chillies

The two best varieties for barbecuing are the mild Hungarian Hot Wax and the medium-hot Cherry Bomb. They have a decent-sized cavity for you to stuff and don't collapse when cooked. It's good to have a variety of heat and flavour, so also think of using the mini red pepper Jingle Bells.

These are delicious served with barbecued meat, or as part of a mix of starters with Barbecued sweetcorn (see page 384).

For 20 chillies/mini peppers:
- **200g cream cheese or goats' curd cheese**
- **50g pine nuts, dry roasted for 3–4 minutes**
- **4 basil leaves, chopped**
- **Juice of ½ lemon**
- **Salt and black pepper**

For the long, horn-shaped chillies, slice them in two lengthways and scrape out the seeds. For the round ones, slice off the top, trying to keep as much of the globe as you can, and scrape out the seeds.

Mix your stuffing ingredients together and scoop them into the chillies with a teaspoon.

Put them on a hot griddle or barbecue and cook them, skin side down, for 5 minutes. They may pop and jump slightly on the heat, so you need to watch them. Cook them until the undersides just begin to char.

Chilli chocolate

You may think this recipe, given to me by the South Devon Chilli Farm, sounds revolting, but it's extraordinary and delicious. It will make all the difference if you make it with top-grade chocolate, and it is the perfect thing for eating after dinner. It also makes a lovely Christmas present.

The amount of chilli will vary, depending on which variety you use and the amount of heat you want, so the quantities given here are only a rough guideline.

For 100g:
- **2 red chillies, fresh or dried**
- **100g really good dark chocolate**

If you're using fresh chillies, remove the seeds and chop very finely. If you're using dried ones, grind them to a powder using a pestle and mortar.

Melt the chocolate in a bain-marie and add the chilli bit by bit – and keep tasting.

Cool quickly by sitting the bowl in iced water and, before the chocolate sets, pour on to baking parchment. Leave to cool for 10 minutes, and score into squares with a knife. Once it's cooled completely, cut it up and bag it. Store it somewhere cool.

Damsons, sloes, rowans, blackberries, mulberries and elderberries

Every one of these fruits – which you're unlikely to find in a supermarket – is worth seeking out. They make some of the most delicious puddings, as well as jams and jellies that you can eat through the year. You may have to make an early autumn visit to a good fruit pick-your-own or, in the case of rowans, elderberries, blackberries and sloes – the fruit of the blackthorn tree – search them out in the hedgerows or woods. The ideal conditions for a bumper fruit harvest from any of these bushes and trees is a long mild autumn the previous year, so that the fruiting wood has plenty of time to grow and develop, followed by a cold old-fashioned winter and a rain-drenched August, to blow up the fruit.

Blackberries and elderberries are great baked or stewed with apple and they, as well as rowan berries and sloes, make fantastic jelly. These last two are excellent for serving with game, particularly venison. Damsons make one of the best ice creams (see page 322), and a damson compote made with lots of spices (see page 322) is superb to eat with cheese. Mulberries used to flavour vinegar (see page 324) make a wonderful aromatic sauce to drizzle over almost any fresh fruit. Mulberries are often the connoisseur's favourite fruit, rich and full of flavour, with the right balance of sugar and acidity, at their best when very black. I've never seen them for sale, so to eat this delicacy you've got to know someone with a tree in their garden, or plant your own.

Mulberries are the bloodiest and juiciest of all fruits, which is why they feature in a Greek myth. The handsome youth Pyramus, thinking that his lover Thisbe was dead, lay under a white mulberry tree and plunged his sword into his heart. His blood spurted all over the tree and sank into its roots, so that the tree became the black mulberry. If you want a fruiting mulberry, it's the black, not the white – silk worm – mulberry that you want.

Damson compote

There are various preserves that you can make with damsons – damson cheese, damson chutney and jelly – but this is my favourite. Tart from the fruit and spicy from the cinnamon, star anise and cloves, this compote is wonderful with cheese and with meat.

For about 6 jars:
    900g damsons
    400ml malt vinegar
    2 cinnamon sticks
    12 cloves
    4 star anise
    600g granulated sugar

Pick over the damsons and remove the stalks. Put the vinegar, spices and sugar into a saucepan and over a gentle heat stir gently to dissolve. Add the damsons and simmer until the fruit is softened but still whole. Carefully lift out the fruit and put into a bowl.

Boil the poaching liquid for 10 minutes and pour over the fruit. Leave overnight or for a few hours. Strain and boil the liquid once more for a further 10 minutes and then add the damsons and simmer for 1 minute.

Remove the cinnamon sticks. Divide the fruit between warm sterilised jars and top up with the liquid. Put a disc of greaseproof paper into each jar and seal. It keeps for 3 months. Once open, store in the fridge.

Damson chutney

My sister Anna makes and sells lots of jams, jellies and chutneys. This is her favourite and most popular recipe. She recommends it for when the Spanish would serve quince jelly, with cheese, and with cold meat – the leftovers of ham, beef or game.

For 10–12 jars:
    675g soft brown muscovado sugar
    225g apples
    900g damsons
    850ml vinegar (cider or wine vinegar, or a mixture of dark brown malt and one of these)
    450g raisins
    2 onions
    1 tablespoon sea salt
    2 garlic cloves, crushed
    A few chillies, fresh or dried
    15g ground allspice
    15g ground ginger

Place the packets or bowl of sugar in a very low oven to warm up for about half an hour.

Peel, core and chop the apples. Add to the damsons in a large pan with the vinegar and all the remaining ingredients, except the sugar, and simmer until soft. (Stir the pan regularly to prevent the chutney sticking.) Remove from the heat. After this you can don your rubber gloves and pick out the stones if you want to.

Add the warmed sugar, put back on the heat and stir constantly over a low heat until the sugar has completely dissolved. Simmer until the volume is sufficiently reduced to a thick mass. This may take some time and it will be necessary to stir it regularly to keep it from sticking. (Use a heat diffuser if necessary.) The mixture will thicken even more when it is cold, but there should not be much excess liquid at the end of the cooking time. Spoon into warm sterilised jars, seal and store for a month before use. This chutney keeps really well for up to 2 years.

Damson ice cream

A delicious ice cream which is tart and packed with flavour.

For about 1.5 litres:
    525g damsons
    375ml double cream
    5 egg yolks
    300g granulated sugar
    375ml natural yoghurt

Put the whole damsons into a medium-sized saucepan with 5 tablespoons water and poach over a gentle heat until the fruit is soft. Rub through a sieve to extract the stones and chill the purée in the fridge.

Bring the cream to boiling point and pull off the heat while you whisk the egg yolks and sugar together in a heatproof bowl until pale in colour. Pour the scalded cream over the egg mixture and stir to combine.

At this point you can return the mixture to the rinsed saucepan and very carefully thicken the custard over a gentle heat (preferably with a heat diffuser under the pan). Do not allow it to simmer. Alternatively, sit the saucepan in a wide shallow pan containing 4cm of simmering water.

For either of these methods, stir the mixture until it thickens enough to coat the back of a wooden spoon. If you are worried that the mixture has overheated, plunge the base of the bowl or saucepan into very cold water and keep stirring until it loses some of its heat. Strain the custard into a bowl, cover with a sheet of greaseproof paper and chill in the fridge.

Combine the custard with the yoghurt and fruit purée and freeze/churn for 20 minutes in an ice-cream machine, or put into a plastic container in the freezer and, after an hour or two, whisk with a hand mixer and return to the freezer, repeating this twice at intervals of about 1½ to 2 hours.

Remove from the freezer to the fridge about 20 minutes before serving.

Damson and almond pudding

This is a really old-fashioned pudding, with very sharp damsons contrasting with the sweet almond top.

For 8:
**75g cold unsalted butter, plus
   a little extra for the dish
900g damsons
110g caster sugar
75g light muscovado sugar, plus
   an extra dessertspoonful for
   sprinkling
110g plain flour
100g ground almonds
3 level teaspoons baking powder
Salt
175ml buttermilk (or 175ml whole
   milk with 1 teaspoon lemon
   juice and a pinch of salt)
2 drops of natural almond essence
25g flaked almonds**

Preheat the oven to 200°C/gas mark 6. Lightly butter a 2-litre ovenproof dish.

Pile the washed damsons (unstoned) into the buttered dish and sprinkle over the caster and muscovado sugars.

Combine the flour, ground almonds, baking powder and a pinch of salt, and blend for a few seconds by hand in a bowl or in a food processor. Chop the butter into chunks and add to the flour mixture, pulsing until it looks like breadcrumbs. Add the milk and almond essence and mix again.

Spoon the mixture in mounds on top of the damsons. Stick the flaked almonds into the mounds and sprinkle with an extra dessertspoon of muscovado.

Cook in the preheated oven for 25 minutes until risen and golden. Keep an eye on the almonds as they tend to brown quickly.

Sloe or damson vodka or gin

This makes good Christmas presents and is perfect for drinking after dinner over Christmas. If you use damsons, when you strain them from the vodka, eat them with ice cream or yoghurt.

For about 800ml:
**450g sloes or damsons
710ml vodka or gin
350g caster sugar**

Make sure that the sloes or damsons are really dry and remove any stems. Prick the fruit with a fork and put them into a large sterilised kilner jar with the vodka or gin and sugar. If you're doing a large batch and can't face pricking every one, shove the sloes or damsons in the freezer over night. This will have the effect of breaking the skins, but doesn't affect the flavour.

If you prefer things less sweet, add less sugar (250g). You can then add a little more once you have tasted it, when re-bottling.

Close the jar tightly and put in a dark place for three months, turning it as often as you remember – ideally every few days – until the sugar has completely dissolved.

After 3 months, strain off the sloes or damsons, pour the alcohol through a funnel into a dry warm sterilised bottle and seal.

Sloe and apple jelly

A lovely jelly with a tart taste and beautiful colour. It tends to be a bit sticky, so put it in the jars when it is a little runnier than most jellies. It will firm up anyway after a few months.

For 2 jars:
   Granulated sugar (for exact quantity see below)
   1.35kg apples, chopped but not peeled or cored
   1.35kg sloes

Put the packets or bowl of sugar in a very low oven to warm up for about half an hour.
   Cook the apples and sloes, adding just enough water to cover the fruit. Simmer gently until tender. Strain the juices and then measure how much you have.
   Add 450g warmed sugar for each 570ml of juice, stir until dissolved and then boil rapidly until setting point is reached (see page 170). Pour into warm sterilised jars, cover and seal. You can eat this straight away or store for up to a year.

Rowan jelly

This is a recipe from my brother-in-law, Norrie MacLaren, who has made this jelly every year for twenty years. It's smoky and tart, perfect with venison or any game.

For about 8 jars:
   2kg rowan berries (or however many you can pick)
   Granulated sugar (for exact quantity see below)
   Peeled rind of 1 lemon and juice of ½ lemon
   2 cloves
   Chilli and mint to taste (optional – use both or neither)

Pick the berries from the stalks and wash out any earwigs. Put the rowans in a pan and just cover with cold water. Simmer them until they're pulpy. This takes about an hour.
   Strain through a jelly bag, ideally overnight.
   Put the packets or bowl of sugar in a very low oven to warm up for about half an hour. Measure the juice and add 450g warmed sugar to 600ml of liquid and the lemon juice. Add the lemon rind and cloves, tied in a muslin bag so that you can fish them out later.
   Heat until the sugar has dissolved and then boil briskly to setting point (see page 170). This usually takes about 20 minutes, but test every 10 minutes until you get a set on a saucer in the fridge.
   Let the mixture cool for half an hour before stirring in the chopped herbs, if using. Pour into warm sterilised jars and seal. You can eat this straight away, but it will keep unopened for up to a year.

Sweet black mulberry vinegar

Try splashing this over fresh fruit, particularly blueberries, melon and pineapple. It's a wonderful way of storing away the extraordinary flavour of mulberries for a rainy day. I have bought this in the past from Stratta (see page 35), but when I can get my hands on mulberries, I make my own.
   Try it also as part of a salad dressing or as a marinade for red meats and game. Again, the exact amounts depend on how many mulberries you can lay your hands on.

You need:
   Black mulberries
   White wine vinegar
   Caster sugar (for exact quantity see below)

Cover the mulberries in vinegar – with liquid about one and a half times the volume of the fruit. Cover and leave somewhere cool and dark for 2 weeks.
   Strain, measure the liquid and add 500g sugar for each litre. Dissolve the sugar in the juice and slowly bring to the boil, simmering very gently, for 15 minutes.
   Decant into warm sterilised bottles and seal immediately. You can use this immediately but unopened it will keep for up to 2 years and more.

Bramble jelly

This jelly is lovely on toast for breakfast and good with lamb.

For about 5 jars:
  **Granulated sugar (for exact
    quantity see below)**
  900g blackberries
  Juice of 1 large lemon

Put the blackberries and 100ml water into a pan and simmer until they are soft. Allow the juice to drip through a jelly bag overnight (don't be tempted to squeeze the bag).

Put the packets or bowl of sugar in a very low oven to warm up for about half an hour. Measure the juice and add 450g warmed sugar for every 570ml of juice.

Put the juice into a large preserving pan with the lemon juice and warmed sugar, and stir over a gentle heat until the sugar has completely dissolved. The pectin in the lemon is critical to get the jelly to set.

Bring to a rolling boil until setting point (see page 170) is reached. Pour into clean warm jars, cover and seal. Keeps for up to a year.

Baked blackberries and mascarpone

Rose Gray demonstrated this recipe at our cookery school recently, and I've made it several times since.

Blackberries are excellent when quickly cooked. A bit of heat releases their strange, sweet mellow flavour and yet – unlike raspberries – the fruit does not collapse.

For 6:
  1kg blackberries
  2 vanilla pods
  3 egg yolks
  500g mascarpone cheese
  30g icing sugar

Preheat the oven to 200°C/gas mark 6. Wash the blackberries and pick them over. Scrape the seeds from the vanilla pods.

Mix the mascarpone, egg yolks, vanilla seeds and icing sugar together.

Put the blackberries in a small baking dish. Spoon the mascarpone over and bake in the preheated oven for about 5 minutes, until the mascarpone begins to brown.

Cranachan

This is a child-friendly version of a Scottish classic of whisky, cream, raspberries and oatmeal. In this one, I add pudding wine instead of whisky, and I make a sweet granola with toasted oats. This is excellent with blackberries, or you can use autumn raspberries.

For 6:
300ml double cream
300ml natural yoghurt
Grated zest of 1 lemon and a little lemon juice, to taste
Caster sugar, to taste
Beaumes-de-Venise, or any sweet white wine, to taste
450g blackberries or raspberries

For the oat and seed granola:
2 tablespoons sunflower oil, plus more for the tray
2 tablespoons honey
125g light brown sugar
Pinch of ground cinnamon
Pinch of freshly grated nutmeg
125g pinhead oatmeal
125g porridge oats
125g sesame seeds
About 300g mixture of chopped nuts (pecans, hazelnuts, almonds)

First make the granola. Preheat the oven to 180°C/gas mark 4. Warm the oil, honey, sugar and spices together in a small saucepan. Mix together the remaining ingredients and put on a lightly oiled baking tray. Pour over the warmed honey mixture and toss really well together, making sure everything is coated. Roast in the preheated oven for about 15–20 minutes, checking the mixture often to see that it is not burning. Remove from the oven and leave to stand. The mixture will crisp up.

When it's cool, break it up into small pieces and store in a screw-top jar. This is delicious for breakfast, sprinkled on porridge or with yoghurt or added to cereal. It keeps for a month in a screw-top jar.

Then whip your cream to the soft-peak stage and fold in the yoghurt. Add the lemon zest, lemon juice, sugar and Beaumes-de-Venise to taste.

Layer the cream with the fruit and scatter the toasted oats and seeds over the top.

I think of figs and grapes under the same umbrella, both ready at this time of year and at their best eaten plain and simple, just as they come off the vine or tree. When they're perfect, they're perfect – you need do nothing to them.

Having said that, it's still worth having a few ideas up your sleeve for when you've got an enviable glut, when they're abundant and cheap in a market, or when the fruit is slightly over- or under-ripe. You can then use them to make some delicious things.

Grapes make wonderful jelly and, mixed with oranges, they make a good pudding (see page 330). The fresh leaves from a vine are also delicious stuffed. As far as grape varieties go, 'Phoenix' and 'Orion' (both white grape varieties) grow and fruit well outside in this country. They have been specially selected for their suitability to cold climates, have good mildew resistance and are sweet enough to eat just as they are. The delicious fat, sweet 'Muscat' fruits best in a greenhouse.

If you have room, plant a fig and, if you want it to fruit, restrict its roots in a container – submerged or ornamental. Left to get on with it, figs grow huge and barely fruit. Pruned and their roots restricted, they make a good small tree and produce well. To get the maximum fruit, protect the fruit buds from frost. Site a fig tree against a south-facing wall or, if you have anywhere frost-free under cover, grow it in a large pot and bring it in for the winter.

White gazpacho with grapes

This is delicious, but very rich, so don't be tempted to serve large portions of this autumn gazpacho.

For 6 as a starter:
- **110g blanched almonds, plus some toasted for scattering**
- **2 garlic cloves, peeled**
- **110g stale white bread, crusts removed**
- **Salt**
- **4 tablespoons sunflower oil**
- **2 tablespoons extra virgin olive oil**
- **3 tablespoons sherry vinegar**
- **800ml iced water**
- **225g seedless white grapes, halved**

Blend the almonds, garlic, bread and salt in a food processor until you have a smooth mixture. Gradually add the oils, vinegar and half the iced water.

Pour into a bowl and, with a balloon whisk, mix in enough of the remaining iced water to give you the exact consistency you want – something rather like a granular double cream. Adjust the seasoning, stir in the grapes and chill.

Serve very cold, with toasted almonds scattered over the top of each bowl.

Black and white grape salad

This is originally from Marcella Hazan's *Classic Italian Cookbook* and it is not only beautiful but light, refreshing and utterly delicious. It is perfect on its own after a large meal.

For 6–8:
- **450g black or red grapes, seedless if possible**
- **450g seedless green grapes**
- **Grated zest of 1 lemon**
- **60g caster sugar**
- **3 oranges**

Detach the grapes from their stems and cut the black grapes around the middle. If they have seeds, make sure you slice not right through them but just until you can feel the seeds: then twist the two halves, and you will easily be able to remove the seeds. If the green grapes are small, leave them whole; if not, slice them in half lengthways.

Put the grapes into a bowl and add the lemon zest and the sugar. Squeeze the juice from the oranges. There should be just enough to cover the grapes – add a little more if not.

Mix thoroughly, cover and chill for at least 2 hours before serving.

Grapes with caramel

Another quick, easy and delicious pudding with grapes.

For 6:
- **800g white cane sugar**
- **1.3kg grapes, ideally mixed green, red and Muscat**
- **100ml green ginger wine or other sweet wine**
- **350ml crème fraîche**
- **Grated zest and juice of ½ lemon**
- **350ml Greek yoghurt or mild natural yoghurt**
- **Caster sugar, to taste**

Put the sugar into a heavy-based saucepan with 350ml water and stir over a gentle heat so that the sugar dissolves completely. Place a silicon mat or a layer of greaseproof paper on a baking tray. Boil the syrup until it becomes a rich caramel colour and then carefully pour into the lined tray and allow to cool.

Halve the grapes, or at least half of them, and put them into a large glass dish. Spoon over the wine. Mix the crème fraîche, lemon zest and yoghurt together, and add a little caster sugar and lemon juice to taste. Pile on to the grapes, cover the dish and chill.

Just before serving, break up the caramel into shards and pile on to the cream.

Grape jelly

Home-grown grapes in this country tend to be small, not all of them ripen and they can be thick with pips. You can eat a few with cheese and make jelly with the rest. This is lovely on bread or toast and wonderful whisked into a sauce with meat or game.

You need:
Granulated sugar (for exact quantity see below)
Juicy grapes
Juice of ½ lemon

Take the grapes off the stalks and put them into a preserving pan. Put enough cold water into the pan just to cover them and bring them to the boil. Simmer the grapes over a moderate heat until they are tender. Pour through a jelly bag and allow to drip overnight into a china bowl. Don't be tempted to squeeze the bag.

Put the packets or bowl of sugar in a very cool oven to warm up for about half an hour. Measure and then warm the grape juice in the preserving pan and add 450g warmed sugar for every 570ml of juice and the lemon juice. Dissolve gently over a low heat and, when the sugar is completely dissolved, raise the heat and bring to a rolling boil. Boil until it reaches setting point (see page 170).

Take off the heat, skim the surface to remove any scum and pour into warm sterilised jars and seal.

Jude's stuffed vine leaves

I love dolmades – hot as well as cold. This is a vegetarian recipe of Jude Maynard, who cooked in our school for several years. Serve with yoghurt.

For 4–6:
250g young vine leaves, or preserved ones
2 large onions, chopped
150ml olive oil
2 tablespoons pine nuts
½ teaspoon tomato purée
2 tablespoons currants
200g risotto rice
1 teaspoon ground allspice
Handful of dill, chopped
Handful of mint, chopped
400g tin of chopped tomatoes
1 teaspoon sugar
Juice of 1 lemon
Salt and pepper
750ml vegetable stock

If you are using fresh vine leaves, remove the tough part of the stem and blanch for about 3 or 4 minutes in salted boiling water. Drain and refresh in cold water. If you are using preserved vine leaves, soak them in hot water for about 20 minutes, rinse and drain.

Fry the onions in 3 tablespoons of olive oil until they are soft. Add the pine nuts and stir until they are golden. Add the tomato purée and stir in the currants, rice, allspice and herbs – but do not cook. Season to taste.

Place a small mound of the filling on to the vine leaf and roll up tightly, folding in the sides as you go, to make a secure parcel. Pour the tinned tomatoes into a heavy pan and pack the rolled leaves on top. Mix the remaining oil, the sugar and the lemon juice together and pour over the vine leaves. Cover these with the stock and then a plate to weight them down and simmer gently for an hour, adding a small amount of water if necessary.

Roast stuffed figs with Gorgonzola and walnuts

This is good eaten as a first course or for lunch, served with slices of Parma ham and a pile of mixed watercress and rocket leaves.

For 4 as a starter:
8 ripe figs
150g Gorgonzola cheese
200g chopped walnuts, toasted
Black pepper
1 dessertspoon honey
1 dessertspoon balsamic vinegar
2 tablespoons extra virgin olive oil

Preheat a medium (180°C/gas mark 4) oven and place the figs in an ovenproof dish. Mix together the Gorgonzola and the toasted chopped walnuts, and season with black pepper. Cut a cross shape in the top of each fig, but leave 2cm at the bottom intact.

Squeeze the centres to open the figs out a little and then pile in the cheese and walnut mixture. Warm the honey, balsamic vinegar and a little extra virgin olive oil and then pour over the figs.

Bake in the preheated oven for about 8 minutes and serve.

Fresh fig tart

This is a really wonderful tart, with that characteristic taste of figs only just cooked. It looks good too.

For 6:
  150g plain flour
  Pinch of salt
  70g unsalted butter
  4 eggs
  2 level dessertspoons
    caster sugar
  275ml double cream or
    crème fraîche
  1 tablespoon green ginger wine
    or other sweet wine
  40g toasted flaked almonds
  7 fresh figs

Sieve the flour and salt together and rub in the butter, or pulse in a processor, until the mixture resembles breadcrumbs. Mix 1 egg with a little very cold water and add just enough of this to be able to pull the pastry together into a ball. Roll the pastry out and use to line a 22cm tart tin. Chill for 30 minutes.

Preheat a medium (180°C/gas mark 4) oven. Prick the bottom of the tart with a fork, cover with a round of greaseproof paper or foil and weight this down with some baking beans or rice. Bake the pastry case blind for about 20–25 minutes. Take it out of the oven, but leave the oven on, and let it cool, then remove the beans or rice and the lining paper.

Mix together the caster sugar, cream, remaining eggs, beaten, and wine. Scatter the toasted almonds over the base of the tart. Quarter the figs, arrange them on the almonds and pour over the cream mixture.

Put into the preheated oven and cook until the custard has set and is just beginning to brown on the top. This should take about 15 minutes. Serve the tart warm.

Quail with figs

A simple dish full of the sweet flavour of figs. I think that one quail per person is plenty, but just double the quantities if you want two each.

For 4:
  4 quails
  Salt and black pepper
  50g butter
  4 slices of smoked bacon or
    pancetta
  2 tablespoons extra virgin olive oil
  3 shallots, finely chopped
  175ml (a small wine glass)
    dry white wine
  16 figs

Preheat the oven to 180°C/gas mark 4.

Season the quail with salt and pepper. Put a generous knob of butter inside the cavity and wrap each bird with the bacon or pancetta. Secure with a cocktail stick. Heat the olive oil and sweat the shallots until softened but not brown and put them in a casserole dish. Brown the quail and add them to the shallots. Pour over the white wine, cover and then either simmer or cook in the preheated oven for 30 minutes.

Remove the quail from the casserole dish and keep warm. Quarter the figs without cutting through the base and then put them into the casserole dish with the juices etc. Cook for 10 minutes.

Remove the bacon or pancetta from the quail and serve them surrounded by the figs. Pour over the juices and, with scissors, snip the bacon or pancetta over the top.

Fig confit

The most delicious fig preserve I've tasted. Unlike some versions, where the fruit has been stewed for too long, this does not feel like a waste of precious figs. It is fresh and chunky, delicious served chilled with game or cheese, as well as lovely on toast.

For a jar:
  200ml Marsala wine
  100g sugar
  300g figs
  Sprig of rosemary
  2 small bay leaves
  Piece of thinly pared lemon rind
    and juice of ½ lemon

Put the Marsala into a saucepan with 100ml water and the sugar. The Marsala will preserve the figs. Over a gentle heat, stir to dissolve the sugar completely. Trim the stalks from the figs, quarter them lengthwise and add them to the pan with the rosemary, bay and lemon rind. Simmer until the figs are tender but not over-soft.

Remove them with a draining spoon and put them into a warm sterilised jar, leaving enough space for the liquid.

Remove the rosemary, bay and lemon rind. Add the lemon juice and bring the syrup to a fast boil to reduce for 5 minutes. Pour the hot syrup over the figs in the jar and cover. You can and should use this straight away – it will only last a couple of weeks. To store it, keep in the fridge.

Maincrop/floury potatoes

Maincrop potatoes – the ones that are stored in a sack through the winter – could not be more different from newly lifted, waxy new potatoes. Many maincrops, the fluffy ones with a high starch and low water content, make good baked potatoes and mash, as well as crunchy roast potatoes, chips and rösti. We have a huge range of floury varieties available in Britain, from the white-skinned, long-storing 'Maris Piper' to the pinky-red-skinned 'Red Duke of York'. There are also waxy types such as 'Pink Fir Apple' and 'Ratte' that perform a different culinary role. With a high water, low dry-weight content, these don't collapse when boiled and so make the best salad potato (see pages 122–127).

Here is how you make delicious roast potatoes: preheat the oven to 200°C/gas mark 6 and put in a baking tray, with a thin layer of oil covering the bottom of the tray. Meanwhile, parboil your potatoes for 5 minutes in salted water. Drain them, dry them off over a low heat and bash them around a bit to break up the outside flesh, or use a fork. Season with salt and put them into the hot oil. You can scatter thyme, rosemary or sage over them, ensuring that the herbs as well as the potatoes are well coated with oil. After 30 minutes, you could scatter finely chopped garlic over them, then put them back in the oven to finish cooking. After 45 minutes, they should be perfect.

You'll need to bear the following in mind if you want to make the best chips. After cutting the potatoes into chips, they need to be soaked in water for a good hour before frying (dry them thoroughly beforehand). Use groundnut oil and fill the oil to only one-third of the depth of the chip pan. Have the oil very hot (take care) and fry them in small batches. Lastly, the secret is to cook them twice. Fry them in hot oil for 5 minutes until cooked but not brown; drain them on paper towel, leave them to rest and then re-heat the oil to 170°C, giving them a re-frying to make them perfectly crisp.

Finally, don't forget sweet potatoes. These can be grown in this country, but they really need a longer growing season than we can give them here. I love the colour of the pink-fleshed ones and seek these out in preference to the white (though the taste is the same).

Rösti potatoes

Rösti potatoes might be fattening, but no more so than chips, and they have infinitely more flavour.

For 6 large rösti:
3 or 4 potatoes (Desiree is ideal)
2 tablespoons chopped onion
Handful of chopped flat-leaf parsley
1 tablespoon flour
Salt and black pepper
2 tablespoons vegetable oil
50g butter

Preheat a medium (180°C/gas mark 4) oven.

Grate the potatoes on a coarse grating disc and twist them in a tea towel to squeeze out the moisture. Once the potatoes are dryish, put them into a bowl with the onion, parsley and flour, and season them well with salt and pepper.

Heat the oil and butter in a heavy-based pan and spread the potato mixture over the pan. Push it down hard with the back of a spoon. Cook until the bottom is brown and crisp – it will then hold together better – and turn to cook the underside until golden brown.

Allow to cool and cut into either wedges or rounds. Reheat them in the preheated oven for a few minutes to make them really crunchy.

Nutmeg mashed potato

I first had this with my brother-in-law, Andrew Wallace, and now almost always add nutmeg to my mash. If you want to try something different, add 3 bay leaves to the potato cooking water and another couple of bay leaves when you heat the milk.

Many chefs are keen on using baked potatoes, scooped out, for mash, claiming this method gives better flavour and creamier texture. I've done a taste and texture comparison between the baking and boiling techniques, and I don't think it makes any difference.

For 4:
6 large potatoes (Maris Piper makes great mash)
Salt and black pepper
150g butter
150ml milk (or cream)
Freshly grated nutmeg, to taste

Cut the potatoes in half (not into small chunks, as this makes them watery) and boil in salted water for about 15 minutes until they're soft, but not overcooked.

Drain and mash thoroughly with butter, salt, pepper and some milk or cream with grated nutmeg.

You can keep this warm in the oven, covered in little knobs of butter and some foil, for up to an hour, or dot with butter and brown.

Rosemary saddleback potatoes

These are delicious and quicker to cook than roast potatoes, and you really get the taste of rosemary. While they are raw the potatoes are sliced, but not quite to the bottom, so that they fan out slightly when they're cooked. The flavours of the herbs and oil – it's worth using extra virgin olive oil – soak right into the potatoes. If you can find them, Edzell Blue potatoes make the showiest-looking saddlebacks. Pesto is a good alternative to rosemary, and try them with garlic and anchovies pounded in a mortar with black pepper.

For 8:
750g potatoes
6 tablespoons extra virgin olive oil
Leaves from 5 sprigs of rosemary
Salt and black pepper

Preheat the oven to 190°C/gas mark 5. Peel the potatoes, or keep the skins on if you prefer. Cut them in slices just under 1cm thick, stopping just before the bottom of the potato.

Put them on to an oiled baking tray and scatter over the rosemary, pushing the herbs right down into the slices. Douse with olive oil and season with salt and pepper.

Put them in the oven and roast for about 1 hour until they're golden brown.

Stuffed baked potatoes with pesto

My children love these. In the autumn, I make them with basil pesto (see page 225), while in the spring I make them with Wild garlic pesto (see page 95).

For 4:
 4 baking potatoes
 200ml crème fraîche
 175g grated cheese (Wensleydale or another crumbly hard cheese; Parmesan is also good, but halve the amount)
 150ml pesto (homemade or bought)
 2 garlic cloves, peeled and crushed
 Salt and black pepper

Preheat a medium (180°C/gas mark 4) oven.

Wash the potatoes and score round the full diameter of the potato with a sharp knife, only just piercing the skin. This makes it easier to cut them precisely, so that you get two perfect halves.

Bake the potatoes for about an hour, until they're cooked all the way through. Remove them from the oven, keeping it on, and cut them in half. Carefully scoop out the potato from the skins and put it into a bowl.

Add all the other ingredients to the potato flesh and mix thoroughly with a fork. Spoon the mixture back into the potato skins, piling them up above the edges so that they look generously filled. You may need to sacrifice a couple of skins to get enough filling to do this. Return them to the oven for about 15 minutes, until the tops become golden.

Stuffed baked potatoes can be made in advance and kept in the fridge for up to two days to cook when needed. They are also suitable for freezing at the just-stuffed stage.

Warm potato and lentil salad

This is lovely for lunch with a mixed leaf salad or as a side dish to accompany meat or fish. If you want something more substantial, add chunks of curd cheese – either goats' or sheep's.

For 8 as a starter or a side dish:
  250g Puy lentils
  2 tablespoons extra virgin olive oil, plus a little more for finishing
  2 garlic cloves, peeled but not chopped
  ½ onion, chopped
  Handful of coarsely chopped parsley and some parsley stalks
  1 bay leaf
  Plenty of salt and black pepper
  450g potatoes
  Plenty of mint leaves
  Juice and grated zest of 2 lemons

Cook the lentils in enough water to cover together with the olive oil, garlic, onion, parsley stalks, bay leaf and salt. For a richer taste, use half water, half white wine. Simmer gently for about 15 minutes, until the lentils are soft but not collapsing. Drain.

Boil the potatoes in salted water with most of the mint. When they are cooked and after they have cooled slightly, peel and cut them into chunks.

Add the potatoes to the lentils with more olive oil, the lemon zest and juice, and plenty of chopped parsley and mint.

Season well and eat while the salad's still warm.

Bubble and squeak cakes

This is a great way of eating leftover mash and veg, but the best bubble and squeak is made from floury potatoes that are broken up, not mashed. These cakes are good with bacon and baked beans for brunch, or with griddled salmon and chilli jelly or chilli jam for lunch or dinner. Bacon fat or dripping, if you have some, is excellent for frying the onions and then the potato cakes.

For 16 cakes (enough for 8):
  1 onion, sliced
  1 leek, thinly sliced
  Olive oil (or butter, bacon fat or dripping), for frying
  1.5kg potatoes
  1 small Savoy cabbage
  Small bunch of spinach (about 250g), stems removed
  4 tablespoons seasoned flour

Gently fry the onion and leek in olive oil. Peel and cook the potatoes until they're soft. Drain them and put aside. Meanwhile, cut up the cabbage into ribbons and boil it for 3 minutes in salted water. Cook the spinach for 5 minutes and coarsely chop. Add plenty of salt and pepper to the potato, and then mash roughly.

Combine everything well. Shape the mixture into palm-sized cakes, roll them in seasoned flour and fry them gently in olive oil, until they are brown and crunchy on the outside but heated through to the middle.

You can keep the unfried mixture in the fridge for a couple of days.

Sweet potato gratin

Sweet potatoes have some of the densest flesh of any root vegetable and so take some cooking. Slice them thinly to get the best texture and taste. This is filling and good with a green salad on its own or as a side dish to eat with any red meat.

For 4:
  2 sweet potatoes, peeled and thinly sliced
  2 tablespoons extra virgin olive oil
  2 red chillies, deseeded and finely chopped
  4cm piece of fresh ginger, peeled and chopped
  2 garlic cloves, chopped
  Salt and black pepper

Preheat a medium (180°C/gas mark 4) oven.

Oil an ovenproof dish and layer the sweet potato, with a scattering of chilli, ginger, garlic, seasoning and a little olive oil on every second or third layer. Cover with foil and bake in the preheated oven for 1 hour.

Griddled sweet potato with ginger, chilli and lime

I love the look and the taste of these griddled pink sweet potatoes.

For 8–10:
  4 medium-sized sweet potatoes
  200ml extra virgin olive oil

For the dressing:
  5 tablespoons lime juice
  3 tablespoons chopped fresh coriander
  2 tablespoons runny honey
  4 teaspoons grated fresh ginger
  1 red chilli, deseeded and finely chopped
  2 garlic cloves, crushed
  Salt and black pepper

Peel the sweet potatoes and cut into thin slices, about 3mm thick. Blanch the slices in boiling water for a couple of minutes. Drain them and allow to dry. Put the slices in a bowl and smother with the olive oil.

Heat a griddle and cook the potato slices for 3–4 minutes on each side. This is fine when you're cooking for a few, but for this sort of number, it's quite a few batches to griddle. It's quicker, but produces less handsome striping, if you put the whole lot in a baking tray and do it under the grill.

Make the dressing by mixing all the ingredients together and drizzle over the sweet potatoes while still warm. This is delicious hot or cold.

Roasted sweet potato and feta salad

An excellent salad that is ideal as a first course with crusty bread.

For 8:
  8 good-quality tomatoes
  Salt and black pepper
  Pinch of sugar
  3 tablespoons extra virgin olive oil, plus more for drizzling
  2 red onions
  4 sweet potatoes
  500g baby leaf spinach
  1 tablespoon balsamic vinegar
  300g feta cheese

Preheat the oven to 110°C/gas mark ¼. Halve the tomatoes, sprinkle with salt, pepper and a pinch of sugar, and drizzle with olive oil. Place on a baking tray and put in the oven for 4 hours. Remove, and cover to keep warm.

Increase the oven setting to 180°C/gas mark 4. Peel and quarter the red onions. Put them on a baking tray and roast for 45 minutes.

Peel the sweet potatoes and chop them into 2cm rounds, and add them to the roasting tray with the onions after 15 minutes, giving them 30 minutes' cooking time. The onions should be well cooked and caramelised and the sweet potato starting to brown around the edges.

Arrange the spinach in a shallow bowl or plate, and dress with the extra virgin olive oil and balsamic vinegar and some pepper. Scatter the still-warm roasted tomatoes, onions and sweet potatoes over the dressed spinach (if the spinach wilts a bit, that is all to the good) and throw the juices from the roasting pan over the vegetables.

Dice the feta into small cubes and arrange over the top. Grind some pepper over the top and serve immediately.

Mushrooms

Strictly speaking, mushrooms aren't garden vegetables, but you couldn't have a garden cookbook without them. The British are traditionally fearful about eating fungi, anxious that they'll pick the wrong one when foraging for them in the wild. We can abandon a lawnful of the most perfect mushrooms to the slugs just because we're not sure. We're unique in this and, unlike most other Europeans, we miss out.

All you need is a good book that clearly tells you the ten or fifteen best wild mushrooms to search for, and which are the non-edible or poisonous ones that look similar. It will take you a couple of seasons to feel confident. I learnt from Antonio Carluccio's mushroom book. He has the good, the less good and the dangerous close together on the page, so it's difficult to make a mistake. Roger Phillips has also written a definitive guide.

My favourites, which are all quite common in the late summer and autumn around Perch Hill and easy to identify, are field mushrooms, parasols, shaggy ink caps (when they've just emerged from the ground), chanterelle (beware of the false ones: not deadly, but disappointing), cep (porcini or penny bun) and hedgehog fungus. Chicken of the wood – the sulphur polyphose – is also good and so much like chicken that some will be completely fooled by its long-grained meaty texture. It requires longer cooking than the others I've mentioned, but is equally delicious.

With lots of these recipes, a mixed basket will give you a range of colour and texture and make for a more interesting dish, so when you're out foraging, try to find a few of several different types. There is now a wide range of interesting mushrooms available in good greengrocers. I don't often buy tight button mushrooms, but the big flat ones have fantastic flavour and my local farm shop now almost always has tasty oyster mushrooms as well. Just a couple of thin slices of each with a splosh of cream and a sprinkle of nutmeg transforms a simple baked egg into a wonderful quick supper dish. And of course mushrooms – wild or bought – make a great omelette.

Jane's chanterelles

My twin sister, Jane, is a great fungi enthusiast and a fantastic cook. She lives in Scotland, where there are lots of chanterelles. If you're lucky enough to find them, this wine-rich sauce with garlic is the best way to eat them. It's good with rice – brown gives an extra crunch – and any pasta. This recipe also works well with a mix of mushrooms – ceps and hedgehogs, as well as chanterelles.

For 6:

- **1 medium-sized onion (preferably red), finely chopped**
- **1 tablespoon olive oil**
- **100g smoked streaky bacon or pancetta, cut into matchsticks**
- **1 large garlic clove, finely chopped**
- **750g chanterelles (and some cep and hedgehog fungus, if possible)**
- **1 glass of white wine**
- **A little cream (optional)**
- **Handful of chopped parsley**
- **Salt and black pepper**
- **75g grated Parmesan cheese**

Fry the onion in olive oil gently for 10 minutes until just soft. Add the bacon or pancetta and cook for another 5 minutes until browned. Add the garlic and cook for 1 minute. Add the mushrooms, breaking up the large ones so that they cook consistently.

Cook for about 5 minutes – after a couple of minutes they will exude water, which you want to evaporate (a wide pan helps with this). Before the mushrooms become mushy, add the white wine and cook until there is just a little sauce left. Add the cream (if using), parsley, salt and pepper and heat for another couple of minutes. Add the Parmesan cheese.

Raw mushroom salad

A mix of wild mushrooms is the most interesting fungi to use for this salad, but they must be very young or closed bought ones. These stay firm, not going soggy in the marinade.

This is perfect for eating before a rich main course. It's good with homemade brown bread and butter. If you cannot find hazelnut oil, you could use walnut oil and warm chopped walnuts.

For 4:

- **280g very young wild or closed-cup bought mushrooms**
- **Bunch of flat-leaf parsley**
- **A little hazelnut oil**
- **1 teaspoon freshly grated nutmeg**
- **Squeeze of lemon juice**
- **Salt and black pepper**
- **30g skinned hazelnuts**
- **Warm brown bread or toast, to serve**

Trim the mushroom stalks and slice them thinly.

Chop the parsley and add to the bowl with the mushrooms. Pour over just enough hazelnut oil to coat the mushrooms – don't drown them – and stir in the nutmeg and a little lemon juice. Stir to combine and season carefully with salt and black pepper.

Leave this to one side to marinate for 20 minutes or so, stirring from time to time.

Just before serving, toast the hazelnuts, chop them into halves and serve warm on top of the mushrooms with a little more hazelnut oil if you wish. Season.

Serve with warm brown bread or toast.

Mushroom soup

You can practically stand your spoon up in this soup, it is packed so full of mushrooms.

For 6:

- **600ml good chicken stock**
- **1 large onion, finely chopped**
- **1 garlic clove, finely chopped**
- **75g butter**
- **450g mushrooms (a mixture of mushrooms is delicious, including some button or closed-cup)**
- **50g flour**
- **Generous pinch of ground mace or freshly grated nutmeg**
- **600ml whole milk**
- **150ml single cream**
- **1–2 teaspoon(s) lemon juice**
- **Handful of parsley, finely chopped**
- **Salt and black pepper**

Warm the stock and put to one side. Fry the onion and garlic in the butter to soften. Roughly chop half the mushrooms and add to the onion. Cook until the mushrooms are soft. Stir in the flour and mace or nutmeg, and cook for a couple of minutes.

Using a large balloon whisk, gradually add the hot stock and bring to the boil. Cover and allow to simmer for 15–20 minutes. Liquidise the soup and return to a clean pan.

Season well. You can freeze the mixture at this point in batches.

Finely chop the rest of the mushrooms and add to the pan with the milk. Bring to the boil and simmer for a further 10 minutes. Take off the heat and add the cream and lemon juice and seasoning to taste. Scatter some parsley on each bowl.

The soup can be reheated gently, but do not bring to the boil once the cream and lemon juice have been added.

Porcini and prosciutto pasticcio

Another of my sister Jane's recipes. This is a dish that she made with Hugh Fearnley-Whittingstall. She still remembers it as one of the best feasts she's ever had. They found so many ceps in Morayshire that they had to think of different ways to cook them. If you have a glut of ceps, cook this.

For 8:

400g ceps or mix of wild and farm-grown mushrooms
½ onion
1 garlic clove
6 tablespoons extra virgin olive oil, plus a little more for the dish
250g lasagne sheets, either homemade or the no-pre-cook packet variety
10 slices of Parma ham (prosciutto)
100g grated Parmesan cheese
Salt and black pepper
A few knobs of butter to finish

For the béchamel sauce:

1 litre milk
80g butter
80g flour
1 egg yolk
250g tub of mascarpone cheese
Freshly grated nutmeg, to taste, plus a bit extra to finish
Plenty of salt and black pepper

Preheat a medium (180°C/gas mark 4) oven.

Slice the mushrooms and onion, and peel the garlic clove, crushing it with the side of a knife but ensuring you leave it whole.

Heat the olive oil in a deep saucepan and cook the onion and garlic on a gentle heat until golden-brown. Remove the garlic and add the mushrooms to the pan. Cook for 10 minutes until the fungi are soft.

While the mushrooms are cooking, make the béchamel sauce. Bring the milk to the boil and, in a separate pan, melt the butter. Stir the flour into the butter, allow it to cook for a couple of minutes and then gradually add the hot milk. Add the egg yolk, then the mascarpone and plenty of nutmeg, stirring continuously. Season with plenty of salt and pepper. Add almost all the grated cheese and stir until it melts.

If your pasta needs pre-cooking, boil the sheets in plenty of salted water and allow them to dry flat on a clean cloth.

In an oiled ovenproof dish, build up thin layers of mushroom, ham, béchamel and pasta, repeating in this order. Finish with the remaining béchamel, then the rest of the grated cheese and dot the top with the butter and a bit of extra nutmeg. Cook in the preheated oven for 35–40 minutes.

Mushroom pasta

This is a more everyday way of eating mushrooms, and makes a good quick weekday supper.

For 4:
    300–400g pasta
    Salt and pepper

For the sauce:
    1 large onion, finely chopped
    1 tablespoon olive oil
    50g butter
    1 garlic clove, finely chopped
    6 large flat field or mixed
        mushrooms, sliced
    1 glass of white wine
    Juice and grated zest of 1 lemon
    1/6 nutmeg, freshly grated
    250ml crème fraîche
    2 tablespoons finely chopped
        parsley or 1 tablespoon finely
        chopped thyme
    Parmesan cheese, grated

To make the sauce, gently fry the onion in the olive oil and a knob of butter for 10 minutes and then add the garlic and mushrooms.

Just stir enough to combine everything, as you don't want to knock mushrooms about too much or they'll bleed lots of black juice. Add the white wine, lemon juice and zest, and then nutmeg, salt and pepper to taste. Continue to cook for 10 minutes. Pour in the crème fraîche and three-quarters of the parsley, and just heat through without boiling.

Meanwhile, boil the pasta in salted boiling water until just al dente. Drain the pasta. Mix with the sauce and scatter the rest of the parsley and the Parmesan on top.

Mushrooms with polenta

Anything with a strong flavour and a gunky soft texture is good with polenta. I love polenta with Braised chicory (see page 25) and it's wonderful with garlicky mushrooms. You can use a real old mix of mushrooms for this – cep, field mushrooms, parasols and very fresh shaggy ink caps.

For 8:
    140g quick-cook polenta
    50g butter
    75g grated Parmesan cheese,
        plus a bit extra for scattering
    Plenty of salt and black pepper
    Double quantity of Mushroom
        pasta sauce (see left)
    Extra virgin olive oil, for drizzling
    A bunch of parsley, coarsely
        chopped, for adding at
        the end

To cook the polenta, bring 1.5 litres of salted water to the boil and then remove from the heat while you whisk in the polenta.

Keep whisking until the mixture is quite smooth and then put the pan back on the heat. It will start to bubble furiously, but keep stirring and turn the heat down. Cook the polenta for a few minutes, until it becomes thick and creamy. Add the butter and Parmesan, and season well. This dish really does benefit from plenty of salt and pepper.

To griddle or fry the polenta, turn it out on a large shallow plate or dish (ideally, the depth of the polenta should be about 1.5cm) and allow it to cool completely while you cook the mushrooms. When the polenta is cold, cut it into triangles or fish-finger-sized slices ready for cooking.

Make sure the griddle is really hot and put the wedges of polenta on to char-grill them for about 5 minutes on either side. For a richer option, fry the slices in butter or olive oil.

To serve, heat the mushroom sauce and put a slice of polenta and a good dollop of sauce on each plate. Drizzle with a little olive oil and scatter over the parsley and grated Parmesan.

Nuts

My husband's family has a brilliant tool for roasting chestnuts. It's a small iron pot, with a few holes punctured through the base and sides, and a well-fitting lid. You can fit fifteen or twenty chestnuts in one go – each one first pierced with the tip of a sharp knife – and then you poke the pot into the middle of the fire to roast. After five minutes, tipped out to cool, they're perfect.

That's one of the best ways to eat chestnuts – hot, smoky, soft and sweet – but there are other delicious things to do. They are good in puddings (with meringue) and savoury dishes – mixed with Brussels sprouts (see page 391), added as invaluable texture in a terrine or used as a rich centre for stuffed meat (see page 350) or soup. Either buy your chestnuts vacuum-packed or cook and skin them yourself. This takes time and is a fiddle, but it can be done. Make a decent-sized nick in the skin on the flat side of each chestnut and then put them in a pan of boiling water for 10–12 minutes. Try one and see if it's soft after 10. If you overdo them, they fall apart. Drain them and let them cool a bit before you peel them. They are very rich and full of protein, so a few chestnuts go a long way.

This spring I spent a morning in a hazel plat, an orchard full of 100-year-old trees. It was a beautiful place on a slope overlooking Plaxtol in Kent. At the top end of the field was a large wooden shed, standing half a metre high on stone stilts. The shed floor was lined with sheets of tin, which were bent to a third of the way up its walls. This was a hazel store, armoured against squirrels and mice. There aren't many of these buildings left and there aren't many plats either. In 1900, there were 7,000 acres of hazelnut orchards in Britain; now there are only 250. Let's all start growing and eating more. Like chestnuts, they're incredibly good for you and have a unique and wonderful taste. Eat them green – fresh, straight off the tree – with cheese, or use them dried in ice cream (see page 357), salads, biscuits (see page 357) and cakes.

Walnuts are another nut that we grow and eat lots of in Britain, and picking green walnuts, leaving one's hands black for days, is an activity that immediately makes me feel eight years old. That acrid yet oddly addictive smell is a powerful memory press. Dried walnuts are a big part of Christmas. Cut up and toasted, they make a good addition to salads (see page 26), while green, they are wonderful to eat with cheese. Instead of non-native pecans, they also make an excellent toffee walnut tart (see page 355).

Chestnut-stuffed pork fillet

Stuffing things often feels a step too far, but once you've made this, you'll realise how quick and easy it is to do, and that the chestnut filling makes an ordinary bit of meat into something very delicious.

For 4:

1 pork fillet
1 onion, finely chopped
2 tablespoons olive oil
150g pancetta or streaky bacon
Several garlic cloves, finely chopped
225g spinach, chopped
Freshly grated nutmeg
Bunch of sage leaves, finely chopped
1 tablespoon breadcrumbs
Salt and black pepper
15 prunes, stoned and roughly chopped
15–20 chestnuts
6 full slices of prosciutto for wrapping the fillet
8–10 baby onions or shallots
2 glasses of white wine
1 tablespoon redcurrant jelly
2 tablespoons crème fraîche

Preheat a medium (180°C/gas mark 4) oven.

Make a cut along the length of the pork fillet, without cutting it in two, and open it out. Put the pork between 2 sheets of cling film and beat it out until it is at least twice the size.

Chop the onion and sauté it in the olive oil with the pancetta or bacon and garlic for a few minutes until the onion is softened. Add the spinach, nutmeg, sage and enough breadcrumbs to absorb any liquid given off by the spinach. Season and take off the heat.

Stuff the length of the pork fillet with this mixture. Add the prunes and chestnuts, scattered through, and roll it up. Wrap the roll with the prosciutto and tie at intervals with string.

Brown this for a couple of minutes all over in the pan in which the stuffing was made and then put it in a shallow ovenproof dish with the baby onions or shallots – whole if small, cut in half if large – and cover with the white wine.

Roast in the preheated oven for 40 minutes and then remove the meat from the roasting dish and keep it warm. Scrape up the juices from the dish, add the wine (or some stock) and allow to bubble up and reduce a little before adding a little redcurrant jelly and the crème fraîche. You can add more chestnuts at this stage. Pour this sauce over the meat.

Chestnut pavlova with caramelised Bramleys

The nuttiness of this chestnut meringue with the tartness of the Bramleys is wonderful. This is a fantastic party pudding for autumn.

For 8:
For the meringue:
110g granulated sugar
110g caster sugar
4 egg whites
1 teaspoon cornflour
1 teaspoon vinegar

For the filling and topping:
300g cooked chestnuts,
fresh or tinned
275ml double cream
Splash of brandy
Caster sugar, to taste
2 Bramley apples
25g unsalted butter
Icing sugar for sifting

Preheat a cool (160°C/gas mark 3) oven.

To make the meringue, mix the two sugars together. Whisk the egg whites until they are really stiff and continue whisking while you add three-quarters of the sugar, one tablespoon at a time. Make sure that the mixture regains its former stiffness and finally, carefully fold in the remaining sugar with a metal spoon. Add the cornflour and vinegar. Sparsely oil 2 circles of greaseproof paper (or use silicon mats) and divide the mixture between the two, spreading it out as lightly as possible.

Cook in the preheated oven for about 45 minutes until the meringue is crisp and has turned coffee-coloured. Turn off the heat and allow the meringue to cool completely in the oven before removing from the baking sheet.

To make the filling, first purée 200g of the chestnuts in a food processor. Then whip the cream with a tot of brandy and sugar to taste, and carefully fold into the chestnut purée to combine the two.

Peel and core the apples, and cut into thickish slices. Toss these in melted butter and a little sugar over a high heat until they begin to go brown, but remove them to a bowl before they become soft, and keep warm.

Add the remaining whole chestnuts to the pan in which you heated the apple and toss them until they are glazed with the sugar and butter mixture. Add to the apples.

Sandwich the 2 meringue layers together with the chestnut cream and a layer of caramelised apples and chestnuts, sift icing sugar over the top and serve with the rest of the apples and chestnuts.

Pickled walnuts

These are good just as they are with smoked meats and cheese, and also lovely added to hot game or beef dishes. You really need freshly picked nuts for this treatment.

For 1kg:
1kg freshly picked green walnuts,
shelled weight
Salt
1 cinnamon stick
1 litre malt or wine vinegar
1 teaspoon freshly grated ginger
1 teaspoon ground allspice
1 teaspoon cloves
12 black peppercorns
400g soft brown sugar

Prick the walnuts with a sharp fork or needle. Put them into a china bowl, cover them with water and add a handful of salt. Leave this for 5 or 6 days, stirring from time to time.

After this time, drain them and cover with fresh water and salt again, and leave for another few days.

Drain and lay the walnuts out in a dry place. They will turn black after 2 or 3 days.

Crumble the cinnamon and put it into a pan with the remaining ingredients and put over a gentle heat until the sugar has completely dissolved. Bring to the boil and simmer for 10 minutes. Add the blackened walnuts and simmer for a further 10 minutes. Lift out the walnuts with a slotted spoon and divide between 3 or 4 large jars, filling the jars about two-thirds full. Pour over the strained syrup and cover.

Leave the walnuts for at least 6–8 weeks before using them. They will last for ages.

Parmesan and walnut crisps

You can eat these as a snack before supper with a glass of wine, or they are lovely with a salad and make a wonderful autumn starter with Poached pears (see page 361).

For 12 crisps:
50g grated Parmesan cheese
20g chopped walnuts
½ teaspoon crushed peppercorns (ideally Szechuan for their aromatic flavour)

Preheat a medium (180°C/gas mark 4) oven.

Mix the grated Parmesan with the chopped walnuts and peppercorns and, using a tablespoon, put little circular heaps of the mixture on to either a silicone baking mat or a sheet of greaseproof paper on a baking tray. Press the mixture down with the back of a wooden spoon or your fingers and bake in the preheated oven for a few minutes until just beginning to colour. Allow to cool a little before using a metal palette knife to transfer them a wire rack. (As they cool, they will crisp up and are much less likely to break.)

Pappardelle with walnuts

This classic Italian dish is great as it is, and also good with the addition of whole walnuts and sliced meaty chestnut mushrooms.

For 4:
20g unsalted butter
120g walnuts, plus a few more for adding at the end
2 tablespoons extra virgin olive oil
2 shallots, finely chopped
1 garlic clove, chopped
3 tablespoons white wine
Generous grating of nutmeg
5 tablespoons double cream
Salt and pepper
400g pappardelle
Grated Parmesan cheese (optional)

Put 10g of butter into a pan and cook the walnuts for 3–4 minutes (or roast in a moderate oven). Be careful not to overcook them as they will turn bitter.

Put them to one side and add 1 tablespoon of oil and the shallots to the pan and gently sweat the shallots until they have softened but not browned. Add the garlic and cook for a couple of minutes.

Remove the shallot and garlic and put them into a food processor with the cooked walnuts. Add the remaining oil, the wine and a generous grating of nutmeg. Then pulse only briefly to combine the ingredients. Do not purée. Add the cream and season.

Cook the pasta in plenty of salted rapidly boiling water until al dente. Drain all but 2 tablespoons of the cooking liquid and keep the pasta warm. Combine the cooking liquid with the walnut sauce and warm gently.

Toss a few more walnut halves in butter. Combine the sauce with the pasta, pile on to warm plates and serve with the walnut halves and a bowl of freshly grated Parmesan if you wish – I don't think it is necessary!

Walnut tart

Rather like a toffee pecan tart, this recipe replaces pecans with our native walnuts. It is rich and delicious, a little going a long way. Serve it with crème fraîche or, even better, vanilla ice cream.

For 10–12:
For the pastry:
   275g plain flour
   Salt
   Grated zest and juice of 1 orange
   175g unsalted butter

For the filling:
   8 eggs
   350g caster sugar
   275ml runny honey
   275ml maple syrup
   1 teaspoon vanilla extract
   Salt
   450g walnuts, halved

To make the pastry, sift the flour and a pinch of salt into a bowl, mix in the orange zest and rub in the butter until the mix resembles breadcrumbs. This can be done by pulsing in a food processor. Add just enough orange juice to make the pastry hold together in a ball, roll out and use to line a 30cm loose-bottomed flan tin. Chill for half an hour in the fridge.

Preheat the oven to 200°C/gas mark 6. Prick the bottom of the tart with a fork, cover with a round of greaseproof paper or foil and weight this down with some baking beans or rice. Bake the pastry case blind for about 10 minutes, or until the pastry is cooked but not coloured. Take it out of the oven, but leave the oven on, and let it cool slightly, then remove the beans or rice and the lining paper.

To make the filling, beat the eggs together in a bowl, adding the sugar, honey, syrup, vanilla and a pinch of salt. Place the halved walnuts over the base of the cooked flan case and pour over the egg mixture. Cook the tart for 20 minutes and then reduce the oven setting to 180°C/gas mark 4 and cook for a further 30 minutes until the filling has set. Cover the tart with foil if it begins to brown too much.

Allow to cool a little before removing from the tin. This is best eaten warm.

Hazelnut biscotti

A delicious crunchy hazelnut biscuit, traditionally served in Italy after dinner. The biscuit is baked hard so that it will hold its shape when dipped into a glass of vin santo. They are also lovely with poached fruit or ice cream.

For about 24 biscuits:
  200g plain flour
  Salt
  1 teaspoon cream of tartar
  ½ teaspoon bicarbonate of soda
  200g demerara sugar
  **2 eggs, beaten, and 1 extra
    egg white**
  40g pine nuts
  80g skinned hazelnuts (see right)
  40g raisins

Preheat a medium (180°C/gas mark 4) oven and line a baking sheet with baking parchment.

Sift the flour with a pinch of salt, the cream of tartar and the bicarbonate of soda. Add the sugar and the beaten eggs and extra white, and mix well together. Fold in the nuts and fruit. As the mixture will be sticky, flour your hands and make it into 3 or 4 rolls about 18cm long and 4–5cm in diameter. Space them out well on the baking parchment and bake for about 25 minutes in the preheated oven until firm. Remove from the oven, turning the oven setting down to 140°C/gas mark 1, and allow the biscuits to cool for 10–15 minutes.

Cut the rolls at an angle into slices about 2cm thick and then put them back into the oven for another 10 minutes.

After that time, turn them over and cook them for another 10 minutes or until they are golden.

These biscuits will become very crisp and will keep very well in an airtight container.

Hazelnut ice cream and praline

In our family we're obsessed with this creamy-textured nocciola ice cream.

For 6–8:
  425g hazelnuts
  100g caster sugar
  875ml milk
  8 egg yolks
  225g soft brown sugar
  ½ teaspoon vanilla essence
  425ml double cream

Preheat a medium (180°C/gas mark 4) oven and roast 375g of the hazelnuts in it for 5 minutes until golden brown, but watch them, as they burn readily. While they are hot, skin them by rubbing them in a dry cloth. Blend in a food processor until very fine.

To make the hazelnut praline, put the caster sugar in a pan over a low heat and let it dissolve very slowly. Add the remaining hazelnuts, some halved, and keep on the heat until the liquid is a rich brown. Pour the mixture on to an oiled marble slab or baking tray and, when it is cool, break it into shards or crush it with a rolling pin.

To make the ice cream, bring the milk to the boil, remove from the heat, add the ground hazelnuts and allow to cool completely. Line a sieve with muslin, or use a very fine-meshed sieve, and push through as much of the mixture as you can.

Whisk the eggs and brown sugar together and add the vanilla essence and the hazelnut mixture. Put this over a gentle heat or in a bowl over simmering water, and keep stirring until the mixture is thick enough to coat the back of a spoon. Do not allow it to boil. Strain into a bowl and, when it is cool, mix in the cream. Then put it into an ice cream machine to freeze/churn for 25 minutes.

Remove the ice cream from the freezer and put it in the fridge about 20 minutes before serving. Scatter with the praline.

Pears

One of the best things I've ever eaten is a 'Doyenne du Comice' pear with a slice of Gorgonzola, sitting in the Madonna restaurant next to the Rialto Bridge in Venice. Once peeled, the pear was pouring juice and the flesh so ripe it was collapsing. The sweetness of the pear was perfect in contrast to the creamy yet punchy taste of the cheese. It made me want to rush home and plant a tree.

'Conference' appears on the shelves first, at the end of summer. It's one of the best storers, and an excellent cooker, the best for poaching, as well as being good straight from the tree. I love its characteristic long, odd-shaped narrow fruits. They look unpromising, but they are, in fact, delicious and juicy once peeled. 'Williams' is around early too, with more elegant plump, oval smooth-skinned fruit. These are beauties, as lovely to look at as they are to eat. A plate of these yellow-skinned, streaked and stippled red pears makes a wonderful still life. But 'Williams' pears don't store – you need to eat them good and quick before the flesh gets furry. They are too often picked very unripe and then cold-stored for ages. They then lose their scent and their true sweet flavour.

After 'Williams' and 'Conference' come 'Beurre Hardy' and 'Doyenne du Comice'. 'Beurre Hardy' is less widely available (find a good pick-your-own) but is one of the finest dessert pears, with tender, juicy sweet flesh which, as the name suggests, has a buttery texture that melts in the mouth. The foodie's favourite, 'Comice', comes next, in September/October. Grab it whenever you see it – it's tops for flavour and texture, but doesn't travel well, so is often sold unripe.

One of the last to ripen is 'Concorde', which is not ready until mid-October. Its parents are 'Conference' and 'Comice', a fantastic pedigree. It is shaped like the nose of an aeroplane, and has melting, juicy flesh.

Pears in this country can be disappointing when bought. You'll get the best if you grow your own or find them at a pick-your-own fruit farm. Then store them carefully, in a cool and dark place – checking on them almost every day to catch them when they're just right.

Darina Allen's pears poached in saffron syrup

A fragrant recipe for poached pears that is fresher and lighter than the more wintry dish of pears poached in port (see right). It is good eaten with almost any ice cream.

For 4:
- **200g caster or granulated sugar**
- **6 whole cardamom pods, lightly crushed**
- **¼ teaspoon good-quality saffron threads**
- **3 tablespoons freshly squeezed lemon juice**
- **4 firm pears**

Put the sugar, cardamom pods, saffron and lemon juice in a wide shallow pan with 425ml water. Stir to dissolve the sugar and bring to a simmer.

Meanwhile, peel the pears, halve and core them, and immediately put them into the simmering syrup, cut side uppermost. Cover with greaseproof paper and the lid of the pan and cook gently for 20–30 minutes, spooning the syrup over the pears every now and then.

Carefully remove the pears and arrange in a single layer in a serving dish, cut side down. Pour the syrup over them and allow to cool.

Chill in the fridge and serve very cold. These keep for several weeks, covered, in the fridge.

Poached pears

These make an excellent easy pudding with Parmesan and walnut crisps (see page 354), which make a good savoury contrast to the sweetness of the treacly poached pears. These pears are also good with crème fraîche or vanilla ice cream.

For 6:
- **6 firm pears**
- **600ml port (or wine, see below)**
- **50g sugar**
- **1 star anise**
- **Rind of 1 lemon, cut into strips**
- **1 cinnamon stick**

Choose a saucepan that will hold the pears snugly. Peel the pears with a potato peeler, leaving the stalks on the fruit, and cut a thin slice off the bottom so that the pears will sit upright.

Put the port into a saucepan with 200ml water, the sugar, star anise, lemon rind and cinnamon, and stir to dissolve the sugar. You can substitute red wine for the port, but the flavour is less interesting. Poached in dessert wine, the pears are delicious, but you'll need less sugar.

Add the pears and simmer, covered, until the pears are tender but not soft. Remove the pears to a bowl and return the liquid to the heat. Reduce, by simmering, until the mixture is slightly thicker and the taste intense.

Pour over the pears and leave for several hours, turning the pears occasionally, until they have taken on the rich colour of the liquor. Chill.

Pears, bananas and grapes with fudge sauce

A wonderful standby for unexpected visitors, this is always loved by adults and children alike. Make some of the fudge sauce and have it at the ready in the fridge. It keeps well. Dried apricots are a lovely possible addition to this, and toasted flaked almonds are delicious scattered on the top. Serve with vanilla ice cream.

For 6:
For the fudge sauce:
- **50g butter**
- **75g soft light brown sugar**
- **150ml golden syrup**
- **120ml double cream**
- **1 teaspoon vanilla extract**

For the fruit:
- **6 just-ripe pears, peeled and quartered**
- **3 bananas, sliced**
- **400g green or black grapes**

First make the fudge sauce. Heat the butter, sugar and syrup gently until the sugar has completely dissolved. Turn off the heat and allow the mixture to cool for a few minutes before adding the cream and vanilla extract. This sauce is delicious hot or cold.

Put the fruit into a dish and generously pour the sauce over it.

Toffee pear tart

This is my standard quick-to-rustle-up pudding, using pastry that is kept in the freezer.

For 6–8:
    4–5 firm pears
    Juice and grated zest of 1 lemon
    110g unsalted butter
    110g caster sugar
    500g packet of puff pastry
    Cream or ice cream, to serve

Preheat the oven to 190°C/gas mark 5. Peel, halve and core the pears, and cover them with lemon juice to prevent them turning brown.

Melt the butter in a non-stick frying pan with a metal or removable handle and add the sugar. Cook the two together gently until the sugar has dissolved completely. Add the pear halves and lemon zest and continue to cook until the sugar mixture deepens to a dark brown, but take care not to burn the sugar at this stage. Take off the heat.

Roll out the pastry to a circle a little bigger than the pan and press it down gently on the pears. Bake for 20 minutes in the preheated oven or until the puff pastry has risen and is golden. If you don't have a frying pan with a metal handle, cook the pears in an ordinary frying pan. Let the butter and sugar mixture become well caramelised and tip into an ovenproof dish. Cover with the pastry and then bake in the oven.

Allow the tart to cool slightly. Run a knife around the edge of the pan, and invert on to a plate. Serve warm with cream or ice cream. If you need to prepare this tart a few hours ahead, leave the cooked tart in the pan and warm through thoroughly before turning it out on a plate.

Pear and almond tart

Another classic pear tart, with a wonderfully sweet and nutty taste.

For 6–8:
    4–5 ripe (but not soft) pears
    100g unsalted butter
    25g plain flour
    100g granulated sugar
    3 eggs
    150g ground almonds
    1 teaspoon vanilla extract
    30g flaked almonds
    2 tablespoons apricot jam,
        warmed and sieved
    Icing sugar, for dusting

For the pastry:
    250g plain flour
    Pinch of salt
    1 tablespoon caster sugar
    150g unsalted butter
    1 egg yolk mixed with
        a little very cold water

To make the pastry, sift the flour with the salt and sugar. Either by hand, or with a food processor, work the butter into the flour until it resembles breadcrumbs. Add just enough of the egg and water mixture to hold the pastry together. Wrap in cling film and chill for 30 minutes.

Preheat the oven to 190°C/gas mark 5. Roll out the pastry and press into a 25cm flan tin. Prick the base with a fork and bake blind by covering the pastry with greaseproof paper weighted down with baking beans or rice and placing in the oven for 12–15 minutes. Remove the baking beans or rice and paper and allow to cool.

To make the filling, peel and core the pears and then slice them up or leave them in halves. Beat the butter, flour, sugar, eggs, almonds and vanilla extract together and pour over the pastry. Arrange the pears on top, scatter with flaked almonds and brush with the apricot jam.

Bake in the preheated oven for 15–20 minutes, until set and golden. Serve warm, dusted with icing sugar.

Spiced preserved pears

These pears are delicious cold with Parma ham and are a good addition to a cheese board. Warmed slightly, they are wonderful with roast duck or goose. If you have a pear tree in your garden, this is one of the best ways of preserving the pears. They make a great Christmas present.

For 1 litre:
350g light brown sugar
275ml white wine vinegar
275ml cider vinegar
3 cinnamon sticks
½ lemon, cut into slices
½ teaspoon whole cloves
1 level teaspoon juniper berries
1 level dessertspoon mixed peppercorns
900g firm pears (Conference are best, but any hard pear will do)

Put the packet or bowl of sugar in a very low oven to warm up for about half an hour.

Put all the ingredients, except for the pears, into a saucepan over a low heat and bring slowly to the boil, making sure the sugar dissolves.

Peel the pears, but leave the stalks on them. Quarter and core them, trying to keep the stalks, or leave them whole. Add the pears to the pan, bring up to a gentle simmer and let the pears cook for about 20 minutes until just tender but not soft.

Using a draining spoon, transfer the pears and slices of lemon to a warm sterilised preserving jar. Boil the syrup hard for about 5 minutes to reduce it and pour in enough to fill the jar to its neck and completely cover the pears. Scoop out the spices from the pan and add them to the jar.

Cover, seal and store for a month before using. The pears will keep for up to a year.

Pear, apple and quince Charlotte

I like apple Charlotte, the crunchy buttery bread a good contrast to the soft sweet apple inside. It's even better when the apple is mixed with quince and pear, more interesting and less sweet.

If you want to prepare this in advance for a party, allow it to become completely cold, run a knife around the edge to loosen it and invert on to a board. With a round cutter, cut rounds of the Charlotte and put on a lightly greased baking tray. Bake at 180°C/gas mark 4 just to heat through and to crisp up the top.

For 6–8:
3 large apples
3 firm pears
2 quinces
Juice of ½ lemon
90g sugar
A loaf of white bread, cut into slices (don't be tempted to use cheap white sliced bread)
200g butter, melted
Crème fraîche or Greek yoghurt, to serve

Preheat a medium (180°C/gas mark 4) oven.

Peel, core and quarter the apples and pears, and cut the quinces into smaller slices, as they take longer to soften. Poach the fruit gently in 100ml water and the lemon juice, adding a little more water if the fruit begins to stick. When the fruit is soft, add the sugar. Mash the fruit to break up any large pieces, but do not purée.

Choose an ovenproof dish about 30 x 22cm. Cut the crusts off the bread and, with a pair of scissors, cut the slices into shapes that will completely cover the bottom and sides of the dish. Put some for the top to one side. Using a pastry brush, brush a layer of melted butter over the bottom and sides of the dish. Sprinkle with a little sugar and shake the dish to distribute it over the sides and base. Brush each side of all the pieces of bread with melted butter and lay them in and round the dish. Spoon over the fruit mixture and cover with the remaining bread, then brush the top generously with melted butter.

Bake in the oven for at least 40 minutes, until the top is golden brown.

Serve with crème fraîche or Greek yoghurt.

Peppers

Dutch red and yellow peppers can be very bland. You're more likely to find them sweet and tasty if you eat them during their natural cropping season, from the middle of August right through the autumn. Buy Italian or Spanish ones if you can, as the sun brings out the flavour.

Green peppers are quicker to produce and therefore cheaper, but they aren't nearly as sweet. This sharper taste suits some Oriental dishes and they're an essential ingredient in Jambalaya (see page 370). As a general rule, they taste better when fully matured to red or yellow. Look out for the less uniform, more unusually shaped reds. These are rare in supermarkets, but they have the most flavour.

Peppers grow best under cover and require regular care, and many don't – in my view – give enough in return. I grow only three that seem to be uncharacteristically prolific varieties. 'Unicorn' is a large red pepper, in the classic bell shape. This is ideal for filling with capers, anchovies and cherry tomatoes (see page 370), and delicious with mozzarella. I also grow the medium-sized, highly productive 'Marconi Rosso', with a narrower, horn-like shape and an excellent sweet flavour. 'Jingle Bells' is another good one, with miniature fruit right through the summer and into the autumn, that gradually turn from green to red. This variety looks good enough for long enough to make ideal house plants. The fruit is small, 5 x 4cm – the perfect size for eating whole, stuffed and barbecued alongside mild chillies (see page 319) or eaten as tempura (see page 207).

I rarely eat peppers raw. They have a reverberating taste, but cooked – roasted, grilled or fried – they can be magnificent. Removing the skin makes them more digestible.

To peel, roast them in a medium (190°C/gas mark 5) oven for 30–40 minutes until they begin to char and the flesh is soft to the point of a knife. Put them in a plastic bag, or in a bowl covered with cling film, and leave them to steam for another 15 minutes. They will taste deliciously sweet – warm and almost treacly – and the peel comes off easily in your fingers.

Roasted pepper soup

A lovely rich soup. Serve it warm with a dollop of Greek yoghurt and some just-torn-up basil leaves; or, if it's a beautiful warm autumn day, serve it cold with a floating ice cube.

For 6–8:
  4–5 red peppers (about 600g)
  600g ripe tomatoes
  1 red onion
  3 garlic cloves
  ½ red chilli
  1 tablespoon balsamic vinegar
  3 tablespoons extra virgin olive oil
  Handful of basil leaves
  1.2 litres good chicken or
    vegetable stock
  Salt and black pepper
  200g Greek yoghurt, to serve

Preheat a medium (180°C/gas mark 4) oven.

Quarter the peppers and deseed them. Halve the tomatoes and roughly chop the onion, garlic and chilli. Put all the vegetables and basil on a roasting tray, mix the vinegar and oil, and pour it over the vegetables, making sure everything is well coated.

Roast them in the preheated medium oven, turning them from time to time, for 45 minutes. Put everything through a mouli or sieve to get rid of the skins. If you pulse it in a food processor the flavour will be less mellow, as it will include that of the skins, but it will still be delicious.

Thin the soup with the stock to the consistency you want and season with salt and freshly milled pepper. Tip into a saucepan and warm for a couple of minutes, or put it in the fridge to cool. Before serving, add a dollop of Greek yoghurt.

Pheasant soup

Matthew Rice gave me this recipe for a light, elegant Oriental-tasting soup, with a subtle flavour of red peppers. Matthew is a keen shot and inventive cook. Pheasants, in season, are cheap, and this is an excellent way of eating them. Ideally, you want to start making this recipe the day before.

For 4:
  2 pheasants
  2 red peppers, deseeded
  1 onion, chopped
  3 lemon grass sticks, chopped
  2 garlic cloves, chopped
  6cm piece of root ginger, peeled
    and chopped
  1 teaspoon Chinese five-spice
    powder
  8 spring onions
  2 tablespoons sherry
  Salt and black pepper
  Small bunch of coriander,
    roughly chopped

Cut the breasts from the pheasants and put them to one side. Chop one of the red peppers and put with the rest of the pheasants, the onion, lemon grass, garlic, ginger and the Chinese five-spice powder in 2 litres of water in a pan.

Cook these together, simmering gently, for an hour. Strain and leave to cool overnight.

Skim any fat off the surface of the stock. Measure out 6 medium-sized ladlefuls of stock (i.e. 1½ per person) into a saucepan and bring it up to a rolling boil.

Cut the raw pheasant breasts into fine slivers. Slice the spring onion and the other red pepper into equally fine strips. Put the vegetables and pheasant breast strips into the hot stock and cook them gently for 5 minutes. Add the sherry and season.

Add the chopped coriander to each bowl.

Masai mara

This is from *The African Kitchen* by Josie Stow and Jan Baldwin and it is by far the most interesting and delicious way of using red peppers as a dip. It beats all the comparable Greek, Italian and Spanish recipes. Have it as part of a selection of starters and dip into it with strips of Rosemary flat bread (see page 46).

For 8:
  4 large red peppers
  250ml extra virgin olive oil
  6 garlic cloves, thinly sliced
  75g pecans or walnuts, toasted
    for a few minutes
  75g white breadcrumbs
  Juice of 2 lemons
  2 teaspoons freshly ground
    cumin seeds
  2 teaspoons sugar
  1 teaspoon finely chopped red
    chilli (or to taste)
  Salt and black pepper

Preheat the oven to 200°C/gas mark 6.

Cut the peppers in half and remove the ribs and seeds. Coat them with a little of the oil and bake them in the preheated oven until they begin to blacken. Then flip them and do the same on the other side. Remove the skins that come off easily, but don't worry about getting every last bit.

Put the roasted peppers, garlic, pecans, breadcrumbs, lemon juice, cumin, sugar, chilli and some salt and pepper into a food processor and whiz until smooth. Pour in the rest of the oil and continue processing until the mixture is glossy. Season.

This is good warm or cold.

Roasted red peppers with mozzarella

A brilliant easy starter, this is ideal if you're cooking for lots of people and have little time. You can use goats' cheese instead of mozzarella for a stronger taste. Anchovies packed in salt have the best flavour: rinse them carefully in cold water. If you use anchovies in oil, use the oil from the tins, plus a bit more. For lunch, serve two stuffed pepper halves, a few slices of mozzarella, a dollop of Caponata (see page 300) or Spiced aubergine salad (see page 299), some rocket and plenty of bread for dipping.

For 6 as a starter:
3 red peppers
12 cherry tomatoes, cut in half
2 garlic cloves, chopped
12 anchovy fillets, salted or in oil, chopped (see above)
24 capers
3–4 sprigs of thyme
Salt and black pepper
Extra virgin olive oil
2 mozzarella or goats' cheeses, sliced
Small bunch of basil leaves

Preheat a medium (180°C/gas mark 4) oven. Cut through the peppers, including the stem, and remove the ribs and seeds. Put the halved peppers on a baking tray and, starting with the tomatoes, add the different filling ingredients. Bright 'Sungold' cherry tomatoes, cut in half, look best. Then add the garlic, anchovies, capers, thyme, a little salt and pepper, and a drizzle of olive oil.

Bake the peppers in the preheated medium oven for 30 minutes, until the edges are beginning to char. Take them out, put the slices of cheese over the top and cook for a further 10 minutes.

Finally, before you eat, scatter the basil leaves – freshly torn – on top. These peppers are best eaten just warm.

Jambalaya

This recipe involves more ingredients than many, but jambalaya is a great Caribbean family dish. Make it when you have lots of people to feed. Prawns – still in their shells – added at the end are a good extra. Serve the jambalaya with a big mixed salad.

For 6–8:
2 tablespoons olive oil
2 skinless chicken breasts, each cut into 3 pieces
350g pork, shoulder or loin, cut into pieces
2 onions, roughly chopped
3 green peppers, sliced into strips
2 garlic cloves, finely chopped
1 tablespoon tomato purée
6 tomatoes, skinned (see page 266) and roughly chopped, or a 400g tin of chopped tomatoes
100g chorizo, cut into chunks
½ teaspoon cayenne pepper
½ teaspoon ground cloves
½ teaspoon ground mace
1–2 red chillies, finely chopped
4 bay leaves
Salt and black pepper
200g good-quality long-grain rice, rinsed
330ml good vegetable or chicken stock
Large glass of white wine
Good handful of flat-leaf parsley

Preheat a medium (180°C/gas mark 4) oven.

Heat some olive oil in a sauté pan and brown the pieces of chicken and pork. Put them in an ovenproof dish. Then fry the onions and pepper until the onions are just beginning to soften. Add the garlic, tomato purée, tomatoes, chorizo, spices, chillies, bay leaves, salt and pepper.

After a couple of minutes, mix in the uncooked rice. Stir to make sure the rice is well coated with oil. Transfer everything into the ovenproof dish with the chicken and pork. Add the stock and wine and cover with a lid. Cook in the preheated oven for about an hour, stirring 2 or 3 times during the process. Remove from the oven and stir in plenty of parsley.

Peperonata

Peperonata is as simple and delicious as it comes: ribbons of pepper, preserved in oil and vinegar, to eat then and there or bottle and store away. The vinegar preserves the peppers and the sugar softens the flavour. This takes a lot of peppers for just one jar, so this recipe is one for when they're cheap in a market or you have more than you can eat from the garden. Peperonata is lovely eaten with hot or cold meat and excellent with cheese.

For a jar:
4 red peppers
2 yellow peppers
2 tablespoons caster sugar
200ml white wine vinegar
200ml extra virgin olive oil

Roast the red and yellow peppers whole for half an hour in a medium (180°C/gas mark 4) oven. Put them in a plastic bag or covered bowl for 5 minutes and then skin, deseed and cut into thin strips about 5cm long. Put them in a pan. Add the sugar and vinegar and cook over a medium heat for 5 more minutes.

Put the mixture into a warm sterilised preserving jar, filling it right to the very top, and cover the peppers with olive oil. Secure the lid, turn it upside down and wrap it in a wool blanket or jersey. Leave it wrapped up for a couple of days so that the liquor cools very slowly. It will then be safely preserved. This is the traditional bottling technique used all over Italy and the peperonata should keep for up to a year. Once open, keep it in the fridge.

Red pepper frittata with prosciutto

The peppers are the dominant flavour in this Spanish omelette, which is delicious either warm or cold, when the flavours of the peppers and herbs really come to the fore. This is ideal outdoor food; wrap it up and take it on a picnic. Serve with crusty bread and a green salad.

For 6–8:
3 medium-sized potatoes, chopped
4 red peppers
2 tablespoons olive oil
25g butter
1 onion, sliced
1 garlic clove, crushed and chopped
6 eggs
200ml double cream
Salt and black pepper
Freshly grated nutmeg
50g prosciutto, sliced into strips
75–100g goats' cheese
30g grated Parmesan cheese
Bunch of chives, chopped

Preheat the oven to 200°C/gas mark 6. Rinse the potatoes under cold water and dry.

Roast the peppers whole until the skins are well charred – this will take about half an hour – and then put them into a plastic bag to sweat for a few minutes. Skin and cut the peppers into strips and lower the oven setting to 180°C/gas mark 4.

Heat the olive oil and butter in an ovenproof pan (preferably with a removable handle or one which has a metal handle). When the oil and butter are foaming, add the chopped potato. After a few minutes, add the onion and garlic, and cook until the potatoes are tender. This will take about 15 minutes. Remove from the heat.

Whisk the eggs with the cream and season with plenty of salt, pepper and nutmeg. Add the prosciutto, goats' cheese, most of the Parmesan, the chopped chives and the peppers, and pour over the onion and potato in the pan, stirring gently to combine. Put the pan back on the heat and cook for just a couple of minutes until the bottom of the frittata is beginning to set. Put into the preheated oven and cook for 10 minutes, until just firm to the touch.

Invert the frittata on to a large plate. I think the top looks nicer, so tend to flip it back again. Allow it to rest. It has far less flavour when it's piping hot. Scatter with more Parmesan and cut into wedges.

Pumpkins and squashes

Pumpkins and squashes are fantastically buttocky and bosomy, and generous of form. Their sheer pregnancy makes you want to gather them up like a flock of expectant mothers. Get out the biggest bowl you can find and put it on your kitchen table. Don't just buy or pick one squash or pumpkin: find lots in different shapes and sizes and pile them up in a great multicoloured mass – amber-oranges, golds and vermilion, as well as the subtler bottle-green, lichen grey-greens, clear cream and faded apricot. They come small and large, ribbed and warty, knobbly and perfectly smooth. Admire them, and cook and eat them from the bowl. Most will last for months.

Squash will give you a huge range of flavours and textures, from soft and sweet ('Butternut' or 'Crown Prince') to parsnip ('Sweet Dumpling') and chestnut ('Red Kuri' or onion squash). Some are tasteless and boring, such as the widely available 'Jack-O-Lantern', but you'll find delicious giant varieties ('Giant Pink Banana'), ideal for making a huge batch of soup, and small ones that can be eaten easily in one sitting ('Baby Blue', 'Red Kuri' or onion squash). You can use either pumpkins or squash, but on the whole squash have better flavour and texture.

Save the seeds of the ones you like for growing next year and, whenever you scrape decent-sized seeds from your pumpkin or squash, keep a few and clean the stringy flesh from them. These are rich in good oils and make a delicious snack. For every 400g pumpkin seeds, you want 2 teaspoons of salt and 5 tablespoons of water. Roast the seeds for 5 minutes in a preheated medium (180°C/ gas mark 4) oven until they are slightly brown. Dissolve the salt in the water and sprinkle over the hot seeds. Stir them around to make sure that they're evenly coated and return them to the oven for a couple more minutes.

Many squash or pumpkin varieties are hugely prolific growers and put out shoots in every direction. If you're growing your own, once one arm gets to about 2 metres, it's a good idea to pinch out the tip. This stops the vegetative growth and encourages the plant to flower and fruit. These growth tips are delicious. Boil them in salted water for about 5 minutes and dress them in olive oil or a little butter. They have an unusual taste, not unlike spinach but more fragrant.

Stuffed butternut squash

Sage and squash soufflé

This is a simple butternut squash recipe that we often cook for lunch in the autumn, when there are lots of them about. You can use any squash, but with butternut, it's perfect.

For 2:

1 medium-sized butternut squash
Generous drizzle of olive oil
Salt and black pepper
1 teaspoon cumin seeds, freshly ground
3 tablespoons crème fraîche
3 tablespoons chopped sage (or chives)
2 tablespoons grated Parmesan cheese

Preheat the oven to 200°C/gas mark 6. Cut the squash in half lengthways. Drizzle the cut flesh with olive oil and sprinkle with salt, pepper and cumin. Bake, cut side upwards and covered in foil, on a baking tray in the preheated oven for about 45 minutes. Prick it with a fork to check that the flesh is soft. If not, give it 10 minutes more.

Take the squash out of the oven, lower the oven setting to medium (180°C/gas mark 4) and leave the squash until it is cool enough for you to handle.

Scoop out the seeds and stringy bits, and discard, then scoop out most of the flesh with a tablespoon into a bowl and mix this with the crème fraîche and 2½ tablespoons of the sage (chives are good in the summer). It is best to do this with a fork, or give the mixture a quick zap in the processor to get rid of any lumps of squash. Check the seasoning. Spoon the squash back into the empty skins.

Scatter the Parmesan and remaining herbs over the top and then bake in the oven for 15 minutes, or until the top starts to look brown and crunchy.

These twice-cooked soufflés are a lovely orangey colour and – with the goats' cheese and sage – have a fantastic flavour. They can be prepared ahead and will rise again when you bake them a second time, which makes them ideal for a party.

For 4:

Oil, for the ramekins
Large knob of butter, plus more for the ramekins
1 small butternut squash
1 tablespoon light soft brown sugar
225ml full-cream milk
1 bay leaf
Blade of mace
25g butter
25g self-raising flour
1 teaspoon finely chopped red chilli
1 tablespoon finely chopped sage
120g grated goats' cheese
2 large eggs, separated, and 1 extra egg white
Salt and black pepper
Freshly grated Parmesan cheese, for dusting

Preheat the oven to 200°C/gas mark 6. Butter or oil 4 ramekins.

Cut the squash into 2 halves, scrape out the seeds, add the butter and sugar to each half and season well. Cover lightly with foil and bake in the preheated oven for about 40 minutes, until the squash is really tender. Spoon out the flesh and blend to a purée. Leave the oven on.

Bring the milk to the boil with the bay leaf and the mace, and leave to infuse for a few minutes off the heat. In another pan, melt the butter and stir in the flour. Allow to cook for a couple of minutes and then gradually add the hot milk, stirring continuously. Allow to simmer very gently for another minute or two. Transfer this mixture to a bowl and add the squash purée,

chopped chilli, sage and goats' cheese. Mix well. Add the egg yolks and mix thoroughly to combine. Check the seasoning.

In another bowl, whisk the 3 egg whites until stiff and dry, and fold very carefully into the squash mixture with a large metal spoon. You must retain the lightness of the egg white.

Spoon into the ramekins and place in a baking tin. Add about 2cm boiling water to the tin and bake the soufflés in the oven for about 15 minutes, until they are puffed up and just firm but not too brown. Remove from the oven and allow to cool.

They can now be left, covered, in the fridge until you need them.

Again, preheat the oven to 200°C/gas mark 6. With a sharp knife, ease the cold soufflés out of the ramekins and put them on a lightly oiled baking sheet. Dust the tops with freshly grated Parmesan and re-bake until they have risen and browned.

Squash and cumin soup with squash chips

One of the most flavourful autumn soups for pumpkin or squash. The flavour improves if you cook it some time before eating. It also freezes well.

For 6:

- 3 teaspoons cumin seeds
- 1 teaspoon coriander seeds
- 1 teaspoon caraway seeds
- ½ teaspoon cayenne pepper
- 1 medium-sized onion squash or butternut squash (at least 1kg)
- Generous drizzle of olive oil
- 3 medium-sized onions
- 2 garlic cloves
- 50g butter
- 750ml vegetable or chicken stock
- Salt and black pepper
- 220ml crème fraîche
- Groundnut oil, for frying the chips

Preheat the oven to 190°C/gas mark 5. Toast the seeds in a dry frying pan for a couple of minutes and grind to a powder with the cayenne.

Take a small slice off your squash and put aside for making chips. Then cut your squash in half, remove the seeds, drizzle with the olive oil and bake in the preheated oven for 45 minutes to 1 hour, or until it is soft. Scrape the flesh from the skin and put to one side.

Finely chop the onions and garlic and sweat them gently in the butter for about 10 minutes until they are soft but not browned. Add the spices, squash and stock, and simmer gently for a few minutes.

Blend if you want a very smooth soup. Season well and whisk in the crème fraîche.

To make the chips, slice thin strips of squash from the reserved piece with a potato peeler and shallow-fry them in very hot groundnut oil until they begin to brown. Drain on kitchen towel and serve them scattered over the top of the soup.

Squash and rocket salad with pears and rosemary

Without the rocket, this is a great side dish to eat with almost anything, and it's good on its own as a first-course warm salad, with rocket tossed in at the last minute.

For 6:

- 1 medium-sized pumpkin or squash, such as onion squash or butternut (about 1kg)
- 2 tablespoons olive oil
- Salt and black pepper
- 2 firm pears, cored and sliced longways into 4
- 50g butter
- 1 teaspoon finely chopped rosemary
- 4 handfuls of rocket
- Slivers of Parmesan cheese

Preheat a medium (180°C/gas mark 4) oven.

Peel the pumpkin and cut it into large chunks. Drizzle with olive oil, salt and pepper, and roast in the preheated oven for 35 minutes until the outside of the chunks begin to char.

Sauté the pears quickly in foaming butter with a teaspoon of finely chopped rosemary until the pears are slightly brown but still with a good bite.

Lay out a base of rocket leaves on one large or several smaller plates. When the pumpkin and pears are cool, scatter them over the top and finish with slivers of Parmesan.

Pumpkin, sage and pecorino ravioli

This sounds a palaver to make, but it's so delicious that it's worth having a go. Sadly, the widely available fresh lasagne sheets are too thick to use, but if you have a good Italian deli near you, you can order the ready-made ravioli sheets from them, and then it's a doddle.

For 6–8:
For the pasta:
500g hard wheat pasta flour (De Cecco semola di grano duro rimacinata 176 is a good flour)
2 good pinches of fine salt
5 eggs

For the filling:
1 pumpkin or squash (about 1kg)
Olive oil
Salt and black pepper
150g pecorino or Parmesan cheese, plus extra for serving
2 tablespoons finely chopped sage, plus 36 whole sage leaves, to serve
100g butter, melted

To make the pasta, tip the flour and salt into a round pile in the middle of a table. Make a dip in the centre, break the eggs into that and then mix. Work the dough, kneading it with your hands until it becomes elastic and soft. Every now and then throw the ball down from a height. The force of this knocks the air out and helps the dough to soften.

Work it for about 10 minutes until it has a really smooth texture. Allow the dough to rest, covered with a damp tea towel, for half an hour or so. You will end up with a mound of smooth dough.

Cut the dough into 5 chunks. Flatten these with the palm of your hand and start to feed the first one into a pasta machine. To begin with the roller must be on the widest setting (1), then progress through 2, 3, 4, 5 and 6. With every rolling, the dough becomes silkier. If it begins to get a bit sticky, dust it with a little flour. If the sheets break at any time, just roll them up into a ball and start again.

When you reach setting 6, lay the long, thin smooth sheets on clean tea towels dusted with flour. Space them well, so they can dry out for half an hour. You can freeze the pasta at this stage, rolled carefully in a tea towel or greaseproof paper to keep the sheets apart. You may have a little pasta left over from the sheets – freeze it, or put it through the cutting disc on the pasta machine to make fettucine.

To make the filling, preheat a hot (200°C/gas mark 6) oven, peel the pumpkin or squash and cut it into small chunks. Remove the seeds. Drizzle with olive oil and season well. Cover it with foil and roast in the preheated hot oven for about 30 minutes, until tender. When cooled a little, mix it with the freshly grated pecorino and chopped sage. Check the seasoning. The pecorino is salty, but you'll want plenty of black pepper. Mash it or pulse it in a food processor.

For 6, you will use 4 sheets of pasta. Put teaspoon mounds of the filling at intervals and brush with water between the mounds. Then cover with another sheet of dough, and press the top piece down gently to seal each mound of filling, starting at one end and working to the other, ensuring that all the air is released around the dollops of mix. Cut into squares or rounds with a pasta cutter or knife.

Poach the ravioli, a few at a time, in a wide shallow pan in plenty of salted gently boiling water for 8–10 minutes until al dente, then drain and dry on a clean tea towel.

Serve the pasta with melted butter and freshly ground pepper. Sprinkle generously with grated pecorino and scatter over the whole sage leaves quickly fried in a little bit of olive oil.

Pumpkin pie

The best pumpkin pie I – and, with a bit of luck, you – have ever tasted.

For 6:
For the pastry:
50g butter
100g plain flour
1 egg yolk, beaten
Icing sugar, for dusting

For the filling:
450g pumpkin flesh, cut in chunks
100g soft brown sugar
Pinch of salt
½ teaspoon ground cinnamon
½ teaspoon ground ginger
½ teaspoon freshly grated nutmeg
1 tablespoon honey
Grated zest of 1 lemon and juice of ½ lemon
Grated zest of 1 orange and juice of ½ orange
3 eggs, beaten

To make the pastry, rub the butter into the flour until the mixture resembles breadcrumbs. Add the egg yolk and just enough very cold water to gather it into a ball. Roll out the pastry and line a 20cm loose-bottomed flan tin. Chill in the fridge for 30 minutes.

Preheat the oven to 180°C/gas mark 4. Prick the bottom of the tart with a fork, cover with greaseproof paper and weight this down with some rice or baking beans. Bake the pastry case blind for about 20–25 minutes. Take it out of the oven, but leave the oven on, and let it cool slightly, then remove the rice or beans and paper.

To make the filling, having removed its seeds, steam the pumpkin until tender. Put the pumpkin and all the remaining ingredients, except the eggs, into a food processor and purée until smooth. Add the eggs and blend.

Pour into the pastry case and bake for 55 minutes, until a skewer comes out of the centre clean. Allow to cool and dust with icing sugar.

The quince is a handsome yellow-green fruit, like an irregular, furry-skinned pear with a fragrant, fruity-rose smell that reminds me of Turkish delight. If you can bear not to eat them all straight away, put a bowl of quinces somewhere warm – near a fireplace or radiator – and they'll look good and scent the room for several weeks. They are currently fashionable with chefs, so let's hope they become more widely available, as they are a very delicious fruit. At the moment they can be difficult to find.

Quinces are good eaten in savoury dishes as well as puddings. They're invaluable added to almost any stew – just include a few peeled pieces as an odd but pleasant surprise. And there's the Spanish classic *membrillo* – quince paste – eaten with manchego cheese (see page 380). I also love quinces as jelly: make this just as you would Medlar jelly (see page 381). Spread it on toast, or mix up a couple of tablespoons with Greek yoghurt or crème fraîche to eat with fresh fruit. It's lovely with pineapple and blueberries.

Medlars aren't as good to eat as quinces, but they make a lovely fragrant jelly. This is delicious eaten on toast for breakfast and is perfect with pork and gentle-tasting spring lamb. Medlars have odd-looking fruits, like a cross between a russet apple and a rose hip, traditionally eaten on the high tables of Cambridge and Oxford colleges, where they were said to be a great delicacy. You can only eat them uncooked once soft, or 'bletted', but I think that at this stage they're like a rotten pear and revolting!

Quinces and medlars both make good trees for a smaller garden, with large single pink (quince) or white (medlar) flowers in late spring. If you have room, plant your own. Medlars have wonderful autumn colour and an interesting bark and shape that look good even in the winter. In late autumn they're covered in fruit.

Membrillo

A classic way to eat quince. It is easy to make and stores well. Eat it with cheese, on its own, or add a little to flavour casseroles and sauces.

For 2kg:
  Granulated sugar (for exact quantity see below)
  2kg quince (or quince and cooking apples if you are short of quince)
  A little ground cinnamon

Put the packets or bowl of sugar in a very low oven to warm up for about half an hour.

Roughly chop the unpeeled quinces and put into a pan with 300ml water. Cover and stew gently until the fruit is soft. Sieve or mouli the fruit and measure the purée. For each 600ml of purée, add 350g of sugar. Gently heat in a deep saucepan until the sugar has completely dissolved. Raise the heat and bring to the boil, stirring continuously to prevent it catching. As it reduces, it will spit and splatter, so cover your hand with a cloth.

After about 45 minutes the mixture will have turned a lovely reddish brown and will begin to come away from the side of the pan as you stir. Pour into baking trays lined with non-stick paper or an oiled mould. Leave, uncovered, at room temperature for 2–3 days before cutting into blocks or chunks.

Baked quinces in orange syrup

This takes a couple of hours to bake, but it is very easy to do and is delicious with yoghurt or cream.

For 6:
  1.2kg (3 large) quinces
  1 large orange
  275g caster sugar
  5 tablespoons orange juice
  ½ teaspoon orange flower water

Preheat the oven to 190°C/gas mark 5.

Wipe the quinces with a damp cloth and then prick them all over with a skewer. Wrap each one individually in foil and stand them close together, upright, in an ovenproof dish. Bake in the preheated oven for about an hour, until they are just tender. Remove from the oven and allow to cool sufficiently for you to be able to handle them. Reduce the oven setting to 180°C/gas mark 4.

Cut the quinces in half, core them and put them, cut side down, in the same ovenproof dish.

With a vegetable peeler, pare the orange rind in thin strands. Put this in a small pan with the sugar, 250ml water, the orange juice and the orange flower water. Stir over the heat, without boiling, until the sugar dissolves. Bring to the boil and simmer for 5 minutes, not stirring.

Remove the orange rind and reserve, pour the syrup over the quinces and bake uncovered in the preheated oven for about an hour, until the fruit is soft and everything is treacly.

Add a few strands of orange rind over the top as you serve.

Windfall apple and quince cake

This is a brilliant recipe given to me by Montagu and Sarah Don, and one of the richest and fruitiest of autumn cakes. It's wonderfully gooey with cream or ice cream.

For 6:
  1 quince
  2–3 large apples
  2 lemons
  225g brown sugar
  180g unsalted butter
  2 eggs
  85g self-raising flour
  ½ teaspoon baking powder
  100g whole blanched almonds, ground to breadcrumb consistency
  50g flaked almonds

Preheat a medium (180°C/gas mark 4) oven. Line a 26cm round springform baking tin with greaseproof paper.

Peel, core and roughly chop the quince and apples, and place them in an ovenproof dish. Grate the zest from one lemon and squeeze the juice, pouring it over the fruit with the zest. Sprinkle over 50g of the sugar, cover with greaseproof or baking parchment and bake for 20 minutes in the preheated oven until the fruit is soft.

Cream 150g of the butter and 150g of the sugar in a food processor. Add the eggs one at a time, mixing each in. Fold in the flour, baking powder and ground almonds. Add the cooked apple and quince, and lightly mix it in. Spoon the cake mixture into the prepared baking tin and bake in the preheated oven for 30 minutes.

Grate the zest from the remaining lemon and squeeze the juice. Melt the remaining 30g butter and 25g sugar in a small saucepan, stir in the zest and juice and mix in the flaked almonds. Take the cake out of the oven and spread this mixture on top. Bake for another 10–15 minutes until golden brown. Cool it in the tin.

Greek pork with quince

The nutmeg, lemon and quince give the pork in this recipe a fabulous flavour. It is good when you eat it hot and just as good cold, when the different flavours really emerge. This is a traditional Greek dish taken from *The Real Greek* by Theodore Kyriakou and Charles Campion.

Shoulder of pork is the best cut to use, as it doesn't harden with long-cooking and the fat in the joint keeps the texture good. The difficulty is that it makes a ragged joint, so it is tricky to roll yourself. Ask your butcher to roll it loosely for you, so that you can push in the lemon rind yourself later and then tie it up more firmly.

For 6:
2 lemons
1.5kg boned shoulder of pork (rolled and tied by your butcher, see above)
Salt and black pepper
75g unsalted butter
1kg quinces
3 tablespoons olive oil
1 dessertspoon freshly grated nutmeg
2 tablespoons honey
1 tablespoon sugar

Preheat a medium (180°C/gas mark 4) oven. Pare the lemon rind in long strips from the 2 lemons and then squeeze the juice. Poke the lemon rind into the joint and season well.

Weigh the joint to calculate the cooking time. Allow 25 minutes per 450g for the oven cooking, plus 30 minutes on top of the stove.

In a heavy-based casserole dish, heat a little oil and brown the joint well to seal it, then add 300ml water, the lemon juice and the butter. Cover and simmer gently for 30 minutes.

Peel and quarter the quinces, and warm the olive oil in a frying pan. Cook the quinces gently in the oil for a few minutes. Put them into a bowl and mix thoroughly with the freshly grated nutmeg, honey and sugar.

Spoon the quince mixture over the top of the pork joint and add a little more water if necessary. Cover and bake in the preheated oven according to the weight of the joint as above.

When the meat is ready, remove it with the quinces, cover and allow it to rest while you prepare the sauce.

Boil the juices rapidly to reduce by at least a quarter, until slightly thickened and syrupy. Skim with a spoon if there is too much oil on the surface. Season and serve separately.

Medlar or quince jelly

Medlar jelly is sweet and mellow, with a fragrant taste, rather like quince, that is lovely with meat and game. Gather the fruit so that some of it is ripe and soft and some still hard; such a mixture is best for this recipe. The amounts all depend on how many medlars or quinces you can get.

You need:
Medlars or quinces
Juice of 1 lemon (optional)
Granulated sugar (for exact quantity see below)

Put the medlars or quinces into a large pan and just cover with water. You can add the juice of a lemon if you want the flavour sharper, but it is not necessary from the setting point of view. Boil gently until the fruit breaks. Do not be tempted to break up the fruit yourself.

When the fruit is soft, strain off the liquid through a jelly bag and allow to drip overnight or for several hours.

Put the packets or bowl of sugar in a very low oven to warm up for about half an hour. Without squeezing the jelly bag (as this will make the jelly cloudy), measure the amount of juice in the bowl and return the juice to the pan. For each 600ml of juice add 450g of warmed granulated cane sugar.

Over a gentle heat, make sure that the sugar is completely dissolved before bringing it to a rolling boil. Continue to boil until setting point is reached (see page 170). Both medlars and quinces have a very high pectin content, so the jelly will set easily.

Remove from the heat and take off any scum with a spoon. Pour into warm sterilised jars and seal.

Sweetcorn

Sweetcorn gets sweeter and sweeter, with new breeding programmes forever aiming at a higher sugar content. Try to get the cobs as fresh as you can and, if possible, grow your own. As soon as the cobs are picked, the sugar starts turning to starch and noticeably loses some of its taste.

Don't put salt in the water when cooking them. It turns the kernels hard – better to serve with Maldon sea salt as you eat them. If you have very fresh sweetcorn, cook it briefly in strongly boiling water for 3 or 4 minutes. This heats the corn through and softens it, but you still get a good crunch. If you've bought the corn, it may need boiling for longer – about 10 minutes. The flavour and texture are better if you leave the outer husks on while the corn cooks; let them act as insulation until you eat. Only remove them when they have cooled enough to handle. When you're ready to eat, smother the cobs in butter, olive oil or Chilli jam (see page 318), and plenty of salt and pepper.

Try roasting corn on the cob too, in the oven with the husks on, or wrap the cobs in foil if you've bought them with no husks.

Corn is more fun chewed straight from the cob, but you can remove the kernels with a very sharp knife and toss them in butter or olive oil with plenty of black pepper and salt. If you can't find fresh, the next best is frozen. As with peas, most frozen corn is processed rapidly enough after harvest to keep its sugar content. Even tinned corn can be used for many of these recipes, but the taste and texture is less good.

Barbecued sweetcorn with thyme butter or chilli jam

Barbecuing corn concentrates its sweetness. You get a delicious smoky, treacly taste. This is also good with garlic butter.

For 8:
8 corn cobs
Thyme butter (see page 80) or
Chilli jam (see page 318)

Cook the corn in salted boiling water for 10 minutes – or less if home-grown (see page 382) – with the husks on, but silks removed before cooking. Plunge into cold water and then dry them as much as you can. Peeling back the husks, smear the herb butter or chilli jam over the corn and then fold the casing back. Put on a slow-burning barbecue, turning occasionally. When the husks are charred, they're ready.

Smoked haddock and sweetcorn chowder

This is comforting, filling and delicious. It is enough as a meal on its own.

For 4:
1 bay leaf
A few peppercorns
A blade of mace
2 cloves
750ml whole milk
450g undyed lightly smoked haddock
50g butter
1 onion or leek, chopped
1 teaspoon plain flour
6 small new potatoes, cut into quarters
Kernels from 2 corn cobs, removed with a sharp knife (or 250g if using frozen)
Good bunch of flat-leaf parsley, chopped
150ml cream
Salt and pepper
Juice of ½ lemon

Put the bay leaf, peppercorns, mace and cloves into a saucepan with the milk. Bring just to the boil, add the haddock (cut into 2 pieces, if it is too long) and simmer for a further 2 minutes. Take off the heat, cover and allow to cool in the liquid.

Strain, reserving the liquid, and lift out the fish. Gently flake the haddock, discarding the skin and bones, and cover until you're ready.

Put a knob of butter into a saucepan and sweat the onion or leek until soft but not brown. Stir in the flour and cook for a couple of minutes. Gradually whisk in the reserved liquid until the mixture is quite smooth. Add the potatoes and cook gently until just tender, adding the corn for the last 3 or 4 minutes. (If the soup seems to be a little thick, you can add some water at this stage.)

Turn down the heat and add the chopped parsley, the flaked fish and the cream, and make sure that everything is heated through without boiling. Remove from the heat and season with salt and pepper and a little lemon juice.

Smoked haddock and sweetcorn soufflé

The cheesy taste, fluffy soufflé top and crunch of the sweetcorn make this one of our family favourites. It is from my aunt Fortune Stanley's cookbook *English Country House Cooking*. It goes down well with children, including those who do not normally like fish.

For 4–5:
  400g undyed smoked haddock
  400ml milk
  35g butter
  2 heaped tablespoons plain flour
  200g mature Cheddar or Gruyère
    cheese, grated
  Kernels from 2 corn cobs,
    removed with a sharp knife
    (or 250g if using frozen
    or tinned)
  Salt and black pepper
  3 whole eggs and 1 extra
    egg white

Preheat a medium (180°C/gas mark 4) oven. Poach the fish in the milk gently for 3 or 4 minutes. Strain and reserve the milk. Skin the haddock and separate it into pieces.

Melt the butter in a largish saucepan. Add the flour and cook gently for a minute. Using a balloon whisk, add the warm milk gradually while stirring. Carefully fold in the cheese, fish and corn, and season.

Separate the eggs. Add the yolks to the slightly cooled soufflé base. Whisk the whites to stiff peaks and then fold them into the mixture as carefully as you can, to avoid losing the volume.

Butter a deep ovenproof (ideally soufflé) dish. Pour the mixture into the dish and bake in the preheated oven for 20 minutes. The outside and top will be well risen, browned and slightly crunchy, and the middle a little gooey and soft.

Sweetcorn blinis

These blinis are lighter than fritters, with a better texture and more flavour. My children like making these with tinned sweetcorn at any time, but they are more delicious when they're made from newly picked corn. Serve them with griddled salmon or tuna, some sour cream and a dollop of Chilli jam (see page 318). This is good with a peppery mixed leaf salad.

For 6:
  100g ricotta cheese
  2 eggs, beaten
  Kernels from 2 corn cobs,
    removed with a sharp knife
    (or 250g if using frozen
    or tinned)
  50g self-raising flour, sieved
  1 red chilli, finely chopped
    (optional)
  2 good handfuls of chopped
    coriander
  Salt and black pepper
  Butter or olive oil, for frying

Put the ricotta into a bowl with the eggs, corn, flour, chilli (if using), coriander, salt and pepper. Mix well and leave to stand for 15–20 minutes.

Melt the butter or oil in a heavy-based pan and, when it's hot, add spoonfuls of the mixture to the pan. Turn when the blinis are browned and cook the other sides.

Brussels sprouts

Brussels sprouts are not something I want to eat every day, but I love them once in a while. Well cooked, sprouts are not the grey-blue-green blobs I remember from school but a brilliant cheery green. I also grow a crimson variety, 'Red Rubine'. It is smaller than green varieties, with a mild flavour and a nutty taste.

Brussels sprouts, like many winter veg, occupy their ground from early summer until you harvest, and require lots of space, so unless you have a large vegetable patch, they're not first choice. Keys to success are a good variety (I grow 'Fortress' for green) and staking each plant firmly with a stout stake from the moment you plant it out. Wind rock will weaken the root and compromise growth.

Don't start to harvest until the cold weather sets in. They then become sweeter and have more taste. November and December are their best months. Pick from the bottom upwards, choosing the largest sprouts first.

To keep the clarity of either colour, put your Brussels sprouts in a pan with a couple of inches of salted water, bring to the boil and don't cover them with a lid. They'll take about 8 minutes, but you can poke them to see that they're cooked – they should be firm, but not mushy or losing their outer leaves.

If you have Brussels sprouts growing in the garden or allotment and have just picked them, all you need do is remove any damaged outer leaves. If they've been picked for a while, re-cut the base – they develop a nasty greyish heel – but you don't need to make that traditional cross cut. It's meant to help the centre cook at the same pace as the outer leaves, but I've experimented with cut and uncut sprouts and, as long as they are not huge, cutting doesn't make any difference.

Brussels sprouts are good with almost any meat and in order to get the colours on the plate to sing, have them with something bright orange – carrots, squash or sweet potato – and crunchy roast potatoes. If I have crimson Brussels sprouts such as 'Red Rubine', I tend to sauté them with a little chilli and toasted almonds (see page 391). They look as good as they taste. Once you've eaten all the sprouts, eat the sprouting tops too. These are rather like more tender spring greens and are best cooked in the same way (see page 62).

Sauté of red Brussels sprouts with almonds

Sautéed with a dash of vinegar, these amazing crimson Brussels sprouts keep their colour.

For 6:
   750g small red Brussels sprouts
   30g unsalted butter
   1 tablespoon olive oil
   ½ red chilli or a few dried chilli flakes, to taste
   1 tablespoon white wine vinegar
   50g whole almonds, cut in half lengthwise and toasted
   Salt and black pepper

Trim the Brussels sprouts. Melt the butter with the olive oil in a sauté pan. Add the sprouts, sliced chilli (or flakes) and vinegar, and cook over a moderate heat.

Keep shaking the pan to avoid the sprouts cooking too much and losing their colour. While still crunchy, take off the heat and stir in the toasted almonds. Sprinkle generously with salt and freshly ground pepper.

Puréed Brussels sprouts in nutmeg cream

I remember having this as a teenager when we went to lunch with friends of my parents and, having always hated Brussels sprouts, I was converted. The sprouts are best lightly cooked and then pulsed quickly in a food processor, so that you're left with some texture. Stir in a few chestnuts for extra crunch and flavour. This is fantastic with Christmas turkey and any roast meat.

For 8:
   1kg Brussels sprouts
   150ml crème fraîche
   Freshly grated nutmeg, to taste
   250g (10–15) chestnuts, roasted or vacuum-packed

Halve the sprouts and cook them for 5 minutes so that they're still quite firm. Drain them, and coarsely mash, in a food processor, adding the crème fraîche and nutmeg before you blitz.

Add the chestnuts, roughly chopped, to the sprout purée and heat in a heavy open pan for a couple of minutes.

Professor Van Mons's Brussels sprouts

This is a recipe from *Jane Grigson's Vegetable Book*, which I first cooked twenty years ago and have done countless times since. It's straight up, old-fashioned and delicious, best with chicken or game.

For 8:
   1kg Brussels sprouts
   100g butter
   3 tablespoons white wine vinegar
   Handful of chopped green herbs, such as parsley, fennel, thyme, chives and tarragon
   Salt and black pepper

Steam or boil the Brussels sprouts for about 8 minutes, drain and keep them covered so that they stay warm.

Heat the butter in a frying pan until it turns nut brown (not dark brown or black). Quickly stir in the wine vinegar and let the mixture sizzle for a few seconds.

Mix in the herbs, pour the sauce over the sprouts and season with salt and pepper.

Chard

Chard is a rarity in the greengrocer's, so it's good to grow your own – and easy too. The American variety 'Fordhook Giant' is the one I grow. If you keep picking it, preventing it running to flower and seed, one sowing should crop for four or five months.

Here in the south of England, from a July or August sowing, I can grow and pick it right the way through the winter. The outer leaves may get a bit frost- and wind-frazzled, but they are usually protecting a blemish-free heart. Space your plants well, allowing at least 30cm (and ideally 45cm) between them.

In my cooking I use white-stemmed Swiss chard (or silver beet) rather than the decorative varieties such as 'Rainbow', 'Bright Lights' or 'Ruby'. It's much more productive and the flavour is better, with a cleaner less muddy taste.

The key to cooking chard is to realise you have two vegetables in one. The white stems take 2–3 minutes longer to cook than the green, so strip the leaf from the stem before you cook and use the two parts separately. The whites need about 8 minutes; the green only 5–6. Or cook together: start off with just the whites, giving them a head start before adding the greens. The cut stems brown quickly left uncovered in the air so, after slicing, drop them into a bowl of acidulated water.

In the summer, you can just slice off the whole plant with a sharp knife and within a couple of weeks it will be ready to be picked again. To get the best out of chard when it's truly cold, use a different picking technique. In the winter, you want to do what's called 'picking round', harvesting only the outer leaves, leaving the heart to continue to grow. This gradually creates a trunk, with the leaves sprouting at the top, and makes the plant much hardier, lifted away from the cold wet soil.

Many of the recipes for chard are also good with spinach but, particularly in the winter, chard is more prolific and easier to grow. Chard has a stronger taste and a coarser texture. It takes more cooking and is not good raw, but it suits slow-cooked gratins, pasta and pies (see Ithaca pie, page 74) and is delicious in a nutmeg béchamel with roast meat.

Chard and feta parcels

These delicious cheesy parcels freeze well, so you can make them in large batches when you have lots of chard or spinach. Just heat them through, straight from the freezer.

For 12 parcels:
- **1 leek, finely chopped**
- **25g butter**
- **200g chard (greens only), chopped**
- **200g feta cheese, half grated, half in small lumps**
- **100g Parmesan cheese, grated**
- **1 egg, beaten**
- **Salt and black pepper**
- **1 packet of filo pastry in sheets of about 45 x 20cm**
- **A little melted butter**
- **A few sesame seeds**

Fry the leek in the butter until soft. Wash and dry the chard so that there is very little water and sweat it with the leek for a few minutes. Take the pan off the heat and add the grated feta, Parmesan, egg and seasoning, mixing all together.

Take one sheet of filo pastry and cut into 10cm-wide strips. Brush this strip on one side with melted butter. Put 1 tablespoon of the mixture in the top right-hand corner. Fold this over, making a triangle, and then keep folding the triangle down the length of the strip, ending up with a triangular parcel, several layers thick. You can freeze at this stage.

Preheat the oven to 200°C/gas mark 6. The parcels look good finished with a dusting of sesame seeds. With a pastry brush, brush on a light coating of butter and dip into a plate of sesame seeds.

Cook the parcels in the hot oven for 10–15 minutes, until golden brown.

Chard and coconut soup

A wonderful sweet and earthy soup. It is best served warm, rather than piping hot.

For 6:
- **250g chard**
- **125g Red Giant mustard, kale or more chard**
- **2 medium-sized onions, finely chopped**
- **1 garlic clove, finely chopped**
- **2 tablespoons olive oil**
- **1.5 litres vegetable stock**
- **400ml tin of coconut milk**
- **Salt and black pepper**

Prepare the chard and/or Red Giant mustard or kale, stripping the green from the stem and shredding it into ribbons.

Sweat the onion and garlic gently in olive oil for about 10 minutes until they're soft. Add the greens, stock and coconut milk, and bring to the boil. Simmer for 10 minutes and then whiz everything up together with a wand or food processor. Season to taste, and serve.

Horta

This is an adaptation of the wilted wild greens you'll find in almost every Greek household and restaurant, particularly in the spring. Among many different leaves, the Greeks use wild rocket, dandelion, wild beet, chicory and herbs, such as savory, marjoram and mint. This dish feels virtuous and yet delicious. Particularly in the early spring, it's what our bodies are craving – iron- and vitamin-rich leaves.

For 8 as a side dish:
- **3 handfuls of chard stems and leaves**
- **2 handfuls of spinach stems and leaves**
- **1 handful of wild bitter leaves (as above, if you can find them)**
- **2 garlic cloves, peeled**
- **Bunch of parsley, winter savory or mint (whichever green herb you can find), coarsely chopped**
- **Grated zest and juice of 1 lemon**
- **3 tablespoons olive oil**
- **Salt and black pepper**

Boil the chard, spinach and mixed leaves with the whole garlic cloves in salted water for about 7–8 minutes, until the leaves are tender but not mushy.

Drain the leaves in a sieve or colander and press them down gently with the back of the spoon to get rid of any excess water, but without mashing them. Add the herbs.

In a bowl, whisk the lemon juice and zest into the olive oil.

Pour this over the leaves, adding salt and pepper as you eat.

Chard and nutmeg farfalle

This is an excellent quick family supper, popular with everyone. We eat it all the time in winter.

For 6:

500g pasta, such as farfalle
400g chard
Salt and black pepper
30g butter
2 tablespoons extra virgin olive oil
200ml crème fraîche
¼ nutmeg, freshly grated
100g Parmesan cheese, plus
   more for serving

Put the pasta on to cook in a large pan of salted boiling water.

Strip the green chard from the leaves. Put the stems aside into a bowl of acidulated water to cook another time. Coarsely chop the greens.

Put a sprinkling of salt in the bottom of a saucepan, together with a knob of butter or slosh of olive oil, and add the chard. The water caught in the washed leaves is plenty to cook with.

Cook gently for 6–7 minutes until the chard is tender and then strain in a sieve or colander, and squeeze out as much water as you can with the back of the spoon. When the pasta is al dente, drain well.

Add the crème fraîche, nutmeg, Parmesan, pepper and, if needed, a pinch more salt to the chard, and heat through for a minute or two. Then whiz the mixture up with a wand or food processor and add it to your pasta.

Serve with more Parmesan.

Chard and risotto balls

It's good to make too much risotto so that you can fry up balls of it again the next day, as in this recipe. This is made more delicious by putting a lump of melting mozzarella in the middle and wrapping it in chard. There's no point giving quantities for this recipe. Just use up all you have left over.

You need:

Chard
Leftover risotto
Mozzarella cheese
Parmesan cheese, grated

Lay the largest leaves of chard you can find on a board. Cut out the thickest two-thirds of the midrib of each of the leaves.

Bring a frying pan of water to the boil and blanch the ribless chard for 2 minutes.

Lay the leaf out on the board and place on it a tablespoon-sized ball of risotto folded around a small lump of mozzarella. Wrap the leaf around the rice ball as though it is a present. It will hold in place.

When you want to eat them, fry the balls carefully on both sides and scatter with grated Parmesan.

Chard gratin

A fantastic meal-in-one recipe, which is delicious just as it is, served with a few potatoes. It's also lovely with good olives cut in half and added to the chard. Or you can add mussels cooked in white wine – a Provençal version – which we had as the first course of our wedding dinner.

For 6–8:
1.5kg Swiss chard
Salt and black pepper
3 garlic cloves
3 tablespoons olive oil
10 anchovies in olive oil,
  drained (or rinsed salted),
  finely chopped
50–75g butter
A few stems of fresh marjoram
  (if available)
Plenty of grated nutmeg
275ml double cream
Parmesan cheese, to grate
  over the top

For the mussels (optional):
1kg mussels
30g butter, plus some for the dish
1 tablespoon olive oil
1 onion, finely chopped
1 garlic clove, finely chopped
250ml white wine

Preheat the oven to 180°C/gas mark 4. Put a pan of salted water on to boil.

Strip the green leaves from the chard stalks and cut the stalks about 1cm wide across. Wash both leaves and stalks in a colander. Cook the stalks in the boiling salted water. When they're just cooked (no longer resistant to the point of a knife), remove with a slotted spoon and drain on a tea towel.

Blanch the greens for about 2–3 minutes, remove and drain any excess water, pushing with the back of a spoon in a colander or sieve, or twist in a tea towel. Then coarsely chop.

Chop the garlic finely and heat in a pan with the olive oil. When the garlic begins to colour, add the finely chopped anchovies. Add the chard stalks and cook gently until the anchovies start to dissolve. Remove from the heat.

To cook the mussels, if you are using them, debeard and clean them, discarding any open ones that don't close when tapped. Melt the butter and 1 tablespoon of olive oil in a large pan. Add the finely chopped onion and garlic, and sweat until translucent.

Add the mussels with the wine and cook them for 3 minutes until they open, but no more.

Drain the mussels and allow to cool enough for you to be able to handle them, then remove from the shells.

Roughly butter a baking dish and spoon in the chard stalks and anchovy to cover the base of the dish, then scatter over half the shelled mussels, if you are using them. Lay the green chard leaves lightly over the top. Scatter the marjoram, grated nutmeg and remaining shelled mussels over them. Pour over the cream. Season with salt and pepper and grate some Parmesan over the top. Some of the chard will be uncovered and some submerged. Cook the gratin in the preheated oven for 25–30 minutes.

Chard stems in a mustardy dressing

Many chard recipes are quite substantial. You may want something plainer and lighter. This recipe – using the stems with a mustardy dressing – is ideal. The stalks are also good with lemon butter and toasted pine nuts.

For 4:
400g chard stems
Salt
1 garlic clove, peeled
Bunch of flat-leaf parsley,
  chopped

For the dressing:
2 tablespoons Dijon mustard
Juice and grated zest of 1 lemon
4 tablespoons extra virgin olive oil
Salt and black pepper

Cut the chard stems into long fingers and cook them in a frying pan of salted water, with the garlic clove, for 8 minutes.

Make the dressing by mixing the mustard, lemon juice and zest, then slowly adding the oil. Season.

Drain the chard and, while still warm, pour over the dressing and scatter over plenty of parsley.

Kale

I'm obsessed with kale. When you buy it, all too often it's tough and leathery, and, once cooked, it makes you feel like a giraffe eating old leaves. The flavour may be good, but there's too much fibre in the way. The other extreme is the sopping-wet, overcooked kale that many of us ate through the winter at school. This mushy stuff, with a nasty bitter aftertaste, is not worth bothering with.

I promise that this isn't the full story. If you grow your own, or can find the right varieties to buy, there is another side to kale. As Harold McGee relates in his book *On Food and Cooking*, growing conditions affect the strength of flavour and the bitterness in the leaves. What happens is the opposite of what one might think. In the summer, high temperatures and lack of water give kale a very strong, sometimes bitter, taste, whereas the cold and damp and dim sunlight of autumn and winter make for a milder flavour and creamier texture. The flavour is said to improve after the first frost.

'Redbor' is the most impressive-looking, with statuesque, deep-red, trunk-like stems covered in crimson crinkly leaves. This makes the best deep-fried 'seaweed' (see page 403). It's easy and quick to shallow-fry and, once crisped up, it will stay so even when cold.

I love the soft-textured 'Red Russian' kale, another beautiful plant with a strong purple wash over greyish leaves. The purple deepens as the weather gets colder. Stir-fry it, or it is wonderful just as steamed leaves, washed and shaken by hand with the central stems removed. Throw it into a pan with only the water left in the creases, a chopped garlic clove and a good slurp of olive oil. Cook on a high heat for 2–3 minutes, with the lid off, stirring it around as it cooks. I sometimes add a splash of soy sauce. 'Pentland Brig' and cavolo nero are also ornamental and tasty, with the leaves at their best quite young.

Kales will grow almost anywhere, in any month of the year. They are the easiest to grow and hardiest productive plants. They can be used as a cut-and-come-again crop, continuing to grow strongly right through the depths of winter and providing countless meals.

With all varieties, before you cook remove the stems with all but the youngest leaves. These are tough and need a much longer cooking time.

Kale and chickpea curry

My sister Jane gave me this very good Oriental-tasting and healthy curry recipe. She discovered it while on a detox, but now cooks it all the time. It's one of my children's favourite meals. The mushrooms and chickpeas make it taste meaty. Serve with basmati rice and Cucumber raita (see page 196).

For 8:

1 large onion, finely chopped
3 garlic cloves, finely chopped
A little vegetable oil
1 heaped teaspoon medium curry powder
25g grated fresh ginger
2 green chillies, or 1 red, finely chopped
Salt and black pepper
250g chickpeas, soaked overnight and cooked (see page 44), or 2 x 400g tins
400ml tin of coconut milk
250g button mushrooms, halved
Juice of 1 lime
2 lemon grass sticks
15 medium cavolo nero leaves
2 tablespoons soy sauce
2 tablespoons Thai fish sauce
Large bunch of coriander

Fry the onion and garlic gently in the oil until soft. Add the curry powder, fresh ginger, chilli, salt and pepper, and stir.

Next, add the cooked chickpeas, coconut milk, mushrooms, lime juice and lemon grass sticks, and simmer for 30 minutes.

Remove the stems from the kale and chop the leaves into strips. Steam them for 5 minutes and then add them to the chickpea mixture. Add the soy and fish sauces.

Scatter with coarsely chopped coriander. This is best served warm, when all the flavours seem to sing out.

Quick-fried kale

A quick and delicious vegetable dish that can be easily rustled up.

For 4:
  2 garlic cloves, very thinly sliced
  125g pancetta chunks
  30g butter
  1 tablespoon olive oil
  300g kale, roughly chopped
  1 tablespoon white sugar
  Salt and black pepper

Fry the garlic with the pancetta in the butter and olive oil until the pancetta is crisp.

Add the kale and scatter over the sugar and seasoning. Cook on a low heat for 10 minutes.

Ribollita

Ribollita is an amazing meal in a soup. It is good hearty stuff and one of my favourite winter recipes. You can put almost any winter vegetable into it, but kale is an essential.

For 8–10:
  200g borlotti or other beans, fresh or dried and soaked
  1.5kg kale
  500g chard (or just more kale)
  3 tablespoons olive oil
  2 onions, chopped
  2 garlic cloves, chopped
  2 carrots, diced
  Bunch of flat-leaf parsley, chopped
  1 head of celery or 2 Florence fennel bulbs
  5 slices of good white bread, crusts removed and bread torn up
  Salt and black pepper
  Grated Parmesan cheese, to serve

Cook the beans until they're soft, which usually takes about 40 minutes, and leave them in their liquid. You can use tinned, but the texture is better with fresh or pre-soaked dried beans.

Prepare the kale and chard, removing stalks and chopping the leaves.

Cover the base of a big saucepan with olive oil and sweat the onion, garlic, carrot, parsley and celery or bulb fennel gently for about 15 minutes, until they are all soft.

Add half the beans, together with the kale and chard, cover everything with 1.5 litres of water and cook for half an hour.

Put the other half of the beans in a food processor and purée them with their cooking liquid. Add the purée and the bread to the soup, also adding a little water if the soup is too dry.

Drizzle on a little olive oil. Season and have plenty of Parmesan on the table for scattering over the top.

Kale seaweed

One of my favourite snacks for a winter party – a big plate of kale seaweed, with everyone dipping in. Because of the amount of oil in the cooking, a little goes a long way. Redbor is the best variety for seaweed, but any kale will do. You can scatter cashew nuts or toasted flaked almonds over the top. You want one kale leaf per person if you're making it for a party, or one and a half leaves per person for a first course.

For 8–10:
  Groundnut oil for deep-frying
  500g kale leaves, with midrib removed, torn or cut into strips
  1 teaspoon soft brown sugar
  2 good pinches of salt
  25g crushed cashew nuts or toasted flaked almonds (optional)

Heat some oil to 170ºC. Use a deep-fat fryer if you have one; if not, the oil should fill only a third of the pan, so use a wide heavy-based saucepan rather than a frying pan. You can use an oil thermometer or the more basic technique of dropping a strand or two of kale into the oil. If it sizzles immediately, but doesn't burn, the oil is at the right temperature.

Before you cook a batch, dry the kale thoroughly in a clean tea towel or lettuce spinner.

Carefully drop a handful of kale into the hot oil. Don't try to cook it all at once as the oil temperature will drop and it won't crisp up the kale.

Fry for about a minute until the colour darkens. It will crisp up as it cools. Drain it on kitchen paper.

Scatter soft brown sugar and salt over the top, and add the crushed cashew nuts or flaked toasted almonds, if using.

Always serve this immediately; it's far nicer hot.

Kale bruschetta

This recipe is akin to a robust winter salsa verde, with plenty of olive oil and parsley. It's good spread on bruschetta as a first course and I also love it as a pasta sauce. Add plenty of Parmesan and more olive oil, and eat it with tagliatelle or spaghetti. The softer-textured kale varieties – cavolo nero or Red Russian – are best for this dish.

For 8:
  200g kale
  Salt and black pepper
  2 garlic cloves, peeled
  Juice and grated zest of 1 lemon
  3 tablespoons chopped capers
  3 tablespoons chopped gherkins
  3 tablespoons chopped shallots
  3 tablespoons chopped black or green olives
  3 tablespoons chopped flat-leaf parsley
  1 small tub of mascarpone cheese (optional)

For the bruschetta:
  Fresh good-quality white bread
  1 garlic clove
  Extra virgin olive oil

Prepare the kale by discarding the outer leaves and removing the stalks.

Bring 2 litres of water to the boil and add some salt. Add the kale and whole garlic cloves. Cook for 3–4 minutes, until the kale is tender, and drain, squeezing out as much water as you can from the leaves with the back of a spoon in a colander or sieve, or twist in a tea towel.

Chop the kale and garlic (ideally by hand so that you have a coarsely textured mix).

Add the lemon juice and zest, capers, gherkins, shallots, black or green olives and flat-leaf parsley, and check the seasoning.

To make the bruschetta, cut the bread into finger-thick slices and drizzle over olive oil. Grill, griddle or roast the bread in the oven at about 180ºC/gas mark 4 for 10 minutes. Keep an eye on it, to make sure it doesn't turn too hard.

Lightly scrape one side of the bread slices with fresh garlic and sprinkle with salt. Once they've cooled a bit, spread a little mascarpone (if using) on the bread and add the kale topping. Sprinkle with olive oil.

Leeks

I love leeks when they're finely chopped; left in large chunks or whole, they can be stringy and slimy. You so often see them left on the side of a plate. As well as improving the texture, slicing leeks thinly makes cleaning them much easier. If they're bought, they won't be, but if they're home-grown, your leeks may be particularly dirty. Cut across the flesh all the way down the shaft of each leek, dividing it into four sections attached at the bulb. Then soak the whole thing in a sink of cold water for half an hour. This will get out any soil and dirt between the layers. If the leeks already look quite clean, just slice them into thin discs, whoosh them around in a sink of water and roughly dry them on a tea towel.

Leeks are good as a side vegetable, gently fried in a good knob of butter, lemon juice, lemon zest and a few sage leaves. They are invaluable in soups and stews, and will transform a fish, chicken or pheasant pie (see page 407).

Leeks are also easy and reliable to grow, and look great, giving a good vertical spire in the vegetable garden amidst all those fat, round-leaved cabbages and kales. I plant strips of a green leek such as 'Hannibal' (which has exceptionally long white stems) next to a panel of the silver, washed-purple French leek 'St Victor'. Out in the frosty garden, they look superb.

You can, of course, grow leeks at almost any time of the year, but they have less of a problem with disfiguring rust when it's cold. The fungal spores are wiped out by frost, so as long as your crop is relatively clean in the autumn, it will remain so right the way through the winter.

It's a good idea to leave a few unharvested leeks lining your paths, or on the outside of your beds in an ornamental vegetable patch. Remaining there in the garden from the previous year, they will bud and flower in the late spring. They always look fantastic in full flower, and you can easily harvest your own seeds to sow the next winter crop straight away.

Potato and leek soup

A standard quick-to-make soup, and one of my favourites in the winter. An added bonus is that the taste improves after a day or two in the fridge. Just before you eat, add the herbs and cream.

Unlike many recipes for this soup, this one uses loads of leeks and few potatoes, making the soup full of flavour and not too stodgy, with a lovely colour.

For 8:
- **1 onion, thinly sliced**
- **1 tablespoon olive oil**
- **25g butter**
- **6 large leeks, cut into 1cm slices**
- **3 medium-sized waxy potatoes, such as Charlotte or Pink Fir Apple, very thinly sliced**
- **1 litre vegetable or chicken stock**
- **500ml milk**
- **Handful of fresh basil or chervil, chopped**
- **Freshly grated nutmeg, to taste**
- **5–6 tablespoons single cream or crème fraîche**
- **Salt and black pepper**

In a large heavy-based pan, sauté the onion in olive oil and butter until soft. Add the leeks and potatoes, and cook for 6–7 minutes. Add the stock, which should just cover the vegetables, and simmer until the veg are tender. If you cut the potatoes very thinly, 10 minutes is plenty of cooking time.

Liquidise and add enough milk for the consistency you want, then bring to the boil.

Remove from the heat, add the herbs, nutmeg and cream, and warm through on a low heat.

Season with plenty of salt and pepper.

Creamed leek and haddock

Mitch Tonks is a really wonderful fishmonger and cook. One of his basic recommendations is to serve creamed leek with almost any fish, especially haddock or turbot, but also salmon, hake, brill or scallops.

For 4:
- **2 medium-sized leeks**
- **30g butter**
- **1 tablespoon olive oil**
- **200ml double cream**
- **Salt and black pepper**
- **1 teaspoon English mustard**
- **Vegetable oil for frying**
- **300g skinless haddock fillets**
- **Bunch of chervil, coarsely chopped (or parsley if chervil not available)**

Preheat the oven to its maximum.

Chop the leeks as finely as you can and fry them gently in the butter and olive oil. Add the cream, salt, pepper and mustard and continue to cook for a few more minutes. Only add the chervil as you are about to serve.

Put some vegetable oil into a hot frying pan with an ovenproof handle. Season the fish fillets with a little salt and fry, flesh side down, for about 5 minutes, until golden. Put the pan in the oven for another 3–4 minutes.

Put a spoonful of leeks on each plate and place the fish on top.

Ray Smith's pheasant and leek pie

This is a recipe from the River Cottage team. It is perfect for when you have lots of people around at a weekend. It's good warm or cold.

At River Cottage they make the pie with a pastry base, but I prefer putting the pastry on the top only.

For 6:
Breasts of 4 hen pheasants
475ml ruby port
2 teaspoons crushed juniper berries
Ground black pepper
A little olive oil
110g butter
900g white part of leeks, finely chopped
275ml double cream
350g puff pastry, ready-made or homemade (see below)

For the puff pastry:
350g plain flour
A pinch of salt
175g butter (cold and diced into small pieces)
A little lemon juice
Beaten egg, to brush

Marinate the pheasant breasts in a deep bowl with the port, juniper berries and pepper overnight.

If you are making the pastry, sift the flour with the salt and work the butter into the flour, or pulse in a food processor until the mixture resembles breadcrumbs. Drizzle in the lemon juice and just enough cold water to bind, and bring together to form a ball of dough.

Flour a surface and roll out to an oblong. Fold over into three, turn the pastry by 90 degrees and repeat the whole process another couple of times. Cover with cling film, chill and rest for 30 minutes.

Take the pheasant breasts from the marinade and fry in a little oil over a medium heat until just coloured on both sides but not cooked through, and put to one side.

Melt the butter in a pan, add the leeks and cook gently until they are tender. Stir in the cream, season and leave to cool. Preheat the oven to 200°C/gas mark 6.

Transfer the marinade to a pan and, over a low heat, simmer to reduce it by half.

Put a layer of the leek mixture into the pie dish, then add the pheasant, cut into thick slices, over the top. Add the reduced marinade and put the remaining leek mixture on top.

Roll out the pastry and moisten the upper edge of the dish with water. Place the pastry over the top of the dish, gently indenting the pastry at the edges with your finger to seal. Brush with an egg wash and bake in the preheated oven for 30 minutes, until the pastry is crisp and golden.

This pie can be difficult to serve neatly. Allow it to cool and it will be easier to slice, or serve it with a spatula and a spoon.

Leek and goats' cheese tart

This stands out from the plethora of recipes for this tart. It's adapted from a Claire Macdonald recipe, with very short pastry and the addition of Dijon mustard.

For 6–8:
2 tablespoons Dijon mustard
2 large eggs plus 2 extra large egg yolks
285ml single cream
Salt and black pepper
4 leeks, thinly sliced
2 tablespoons olive oil
200g soft goats' cheese

For the pastry:
120g butter
½ teaspoon salt
200g plain flour

First make the pastry. Sift the flour with the salt and work the butter into the flour, or pulse in a food processor, until the mixture resembles breadcrumbs. Add just enough cold water for it to bind together as a dough. Roll out and use to line a 23cm flan dish. Put this in the fridge for at least an hour.

Preheat the oven to 180°C/gas mark 4. Prick the base of the pastry case with a fork and bake blind by covering the pastry with greaseproof paper weighted down with baking beans or rice and placing in the oven for 20–25 minutes. Remove the baking beans or rice and paper and allow to cool. Leave the oven on at the same setting.

Allow the pastry to cool a little, then spread Dijon mustard all over the base. Beat together the eggs, extra yolks, cream and seasoning.

Fry the leeks in the oil gently until they're soft and put them in the pastry case. Crumble the goats' cheese over the leeks and pour over the egg mixture.

Bake in the oven for 20 minutes until the tart is set.

Boiled chicken with leeks and salsa verde

Buy a really good chicken – slow-reared, organic, free-range. Put it in a pot with a mound of leeks and carrots, some white wine and herbs, and eat it with creamy mash and a winter salsa verde. It makes one of the best Sunday lunches for this time of year. It's also lovely if you extract some stock halfway through and cook a simple risotto as a change from mash.

For 6:
**1 medium-sized organic,
   free-range chicken
250ml dry white wine
Salt and black pepper
A few parsley stalks
8 large carrots, peeled and
   chopped into thumb-length
   chunks
8 large leeks, chopped into
   thumb-length chunks
Mashed potato, to serve**

For the salsa verde:
**Large bunch of flat-leaf parsley
Small bunch of winter savory
   or thyme
4 gherkins
30 capers
250ml olive oil
Juice of ½ lemon**

Preheat the oven to 180°C/gas mark 6.
   Half-cover the chicken with equal parts wine and water. Season, add a few parsley stalks and half the carrots and leeks, and bring to the boil. Cover and cook in the preheated oven (or leave gently simmering on the top) for about an hour, depending on size. The good thing about cooking chicken in liquid is that it doesn't matter if it's slightly overcooked. It won't be dry, but it will start to fall apart if you really overdo it.
   Take the bird out and put it on a warmed plate, then cover it with foil and a thick cloth to rest. It will retain its heat for 20 minutes at least.

Strain the liquid and discard the herbs and vegetables (which will have lost most of their flavour). Put the stock back in the pan. Turn the heat up so that the liquid is boiling strongly and add the other half of the carrots and leeks. Boil for 5 minutes, until the stock has reduced and the vegetables are just tender.
   To make the salsa verde, whiz all the ingredients together in a food processor with some seasoning. Do this only briefly, or chop by hand to give a coarse texture.
   Carve the chicken and serve it with a few carrots and leeks, a dollop of mashed potato and good spoonful of salsa verde on each plate.

Pomegranates and cranberries

Make the most of pomegranates and cranberries over the Christmas season. They don't just look festive and beautiful: they can be used in all sorts of wonderful recipes.

There are few stronger contenders for the fruit beauty parade than a pomegranate cut in half. If you just want to admire them, smear the cut surfaces in Vaseline, and they'll look good for twice as long as they would if left open to the air. Make a jumble of them all over your Christmas table.

To extract the seeds, whack the pomegranates against the table, or hit them hard on all sides with a rolling pin or meat mallet. Then slice the fruit and the seeds will tumble out. Or cut the fruit in half and bang the back with a wooden spoon until the seeds fall into a bowl.

The tart flavour and crunchy texture of pomegranates are lovely in salads and with couscous and rice, and they make a good contrast to creamy puddings. Eat them scattered over vanilla ice cream or try them with Panna cotta (see page 416) or Frozen mocha and ginger meringue cake (see page 415).

Cranberries have a versatile and sharp taste. They make a good smoothie with bananas, an excellent uncooked relish and, of course, good old cranberry sauce.

It's worth remembering that both pomegranates and cranberries are superfoods. Pomegranates are packed with vitamins and antioxidants. They're said to be the most anti-ageing food you can eat, and the juice, used as a mouthwash, is brilliant for healing mouth ulcers. Also, current research is focusing on a study that suggests that a glass of pomegranate juice a day improves the function of blood vessels, reduces hardening of the arteries and improves heart health. Cranberry juice should be the drink of choice for those prone to urinary tract infections: the juice is said to be the best thing for mild urinary tract disease – both bacterial and viral.

Jewelled couscous

You can eat this to accompany anything and it looks beautiful. It's delicious on its own with a salad and is perfect for stuffing quail (see right).

For 6:
375g couscous
150g chopped dried apricots
150g raisins
100g pomegranate seeds (about 3 fruits)
3 shallots, finely chopped
2 level tablespoons ground cumin seeds
1½ teaspoons ground coriander seeds
Grated zest and juice of 2 oranges
75g toasted pine kernels
75g pistachios
Plenty of flat-leaf parsley, chopped
Salt and black pepper

Put the couscous in a bowl with the fruit (except the pomegranate seeds), the shallots and the spices. Add enough boiling water to make up the orange juice to 600ml of liquid and pour over the couscous, stirring in the orange zest. Cover and leave for 10–15 minutes.

Add the nuts, pomegranate seeds and parsley. Season well, stir and serve.

Stuffed roast quail with jewelled couscous and spiced citrus sauce

This is wonderful for a party, easy to do for large numbers and not too filling, so you'll have room for pudding.

For 6–8:
8 boned quail
Jewelled couscous (see left)
8 thin slices of Parma ham or pancetta

For the spiced citrus sauce:
200ml honey
125ml lemon juice
125ml orange juice
750ml good stock
Freshly grated nutmeg
2–3 cloves
4 star anise
½ teaspoon ground ginger
250g butter
Salt and black pepper

Preheat the oven to 180°C/gas mark 4.

Stuff the quail with the jewelled couscous. Wrap the whole stuffed quail with a slice of Parma ham and secure with a cocktail stick. Roast the quail in the preheated oven for 25 minutes.

To make the sauce, place the honey in a medium-sized saucepan and caramelise. Deglaze the roasting tin with the lemon and orange juices, pour them into the saucepan and cook gently for 10 minutes. Add the stock and spices and reduce by a third. Whisk in the butter, season and set aside.

When the quail are ready, warm the sauce and either pour over the birds or serve separately.

Game salad with pomegranate

If you've had game over Christmas, this salad is ideal for Boxing Day, and it's always handy to have some good-looking salads up your sleeve for the winter. You can use a pheasant, as here, or the remains of partridge, grouse, duck or any game bird. This is the recipe of a friend of mine, Lucy Boyd, who is a wonderful cook.

For 6:
1 whole cooked pheasant
1 fennel bulb
Handful of mixed winter leaves, such as dandelion, the small young tips of cavolo nero, mizuna and mâche, leaves separated
1 head of Treviso, radicchio or Belgian chicory
100g Parmesan cheese, cut into rough slivers
12 whole fresh chestnuts, roasted
Seeds of 1 pomegranate
3 tablespoons aged balsamic vinegar

For the dressing:
6 tablespoons extra virgin olive oil
Juice of 1 lemon
Salt and black pepper

Pull the meat off the bird's bones in rough pieces.

Thinly slice the fennel (this is easiest done on a mandoline). Cut the larger salad leaves and the chicory lengthways down their spine.

Make a simple dressing by mixing the olive oil and lemon juice, salt and pepper. Toss the salad leaves in the dressing, then add the pheasant pieces. Add some Parmesan slivers and roasted chestnuts and scatter over a few pomegranate seeds.

Drizzle a little of the aged balsamic over and season.

Frozen mocha and ginger meringue cake with pomegranate sauce

I love this pudding and it's very easy to make. Serve it with pomegranates in winter and raspberries in summer. To save time, you can buy the meringues – it doesn't matter if they are powdery and dry.

For 8–10:
  2 tablespoons strong instant coffee powder or granules
  1 tablespoon boiling water
  750ml double cream
  1 tablespoon caster sugar
  1 tablespoon coffee liqueur, such as Tia Maria or Kahlúa
  3 pieces of stem ginger, thinly sliced, plus 1 tablespoon of the ginger syrup

For the meringues:
  6 egg whites
  180g granulated sugar
  180g caster sugar
  Sunflower oil

For the pomegranate sauce:
  3 tablespoons redcurrant jelly
  275ml pomegranate juice (bought or fresh)
  Juice of 1 lime
  1 heaped tablespoon arrowroot
  Seeds of 2 pomegranates

Preheat the oven to 110°C/gas mark ¼.
    To make the meringues, whisk the egg whites until very stiff and dry, and slowly add the granulated sugar bit by bit, whisking until the egg white regains its former stiffness. Fold in the caster sugar with a large metal spoon. Spoon on to greaseproof paper rubbed with a trace of sunflower oil, or 'Lift-Off' paper, or a silicone mat, and bake in the preheated oven for about 3 hours until crisp. Remove and break the meringues into pieces.
    Mix the instant coffee with the boiling water, then chill it well. Whip the cream to the soft-peak stage and mix in the sugar, Tia Maria or Kahlúa and half the coffee. Fold the mixture with the sliced ginger, ginger syrup and meringue pieces. Spoon the mixture into a deep (8cm) straight-sided round cake tin, 22cm in diameter, or a loaf tin, lined with non-stick paper, and marble the top with the remaining coffee. Freeze for at least 24 hours.
    To make the sauce, melt the redcurrant jelly in the pomegranate juice over a low heat until dissolved. Add the lime juice. Bring to the boil, remove from the heat and add the arrowroot (which thickens clear), already mixed with a little cold water. Put back on the heat and simmer gently, while whisking, for a couple of minutes. Then let the sauce cool. When it's completely cold, add the pomegranate seeds.
    Serve the cake straight from the freezer, drizzled with the sauce.

Panna cotta with marinated pomegranate

This is quite alcoholic, so it may be better for dinner than lunch!

For 4:
For the panna cotta:
  3 leaves of gelatine or 1½
    teaspoons powdered gelatine
  250ml double cream
  185ml whole milk
  55g caster sugar, plus 2 extra
    teaspoons
  1 vanilla pod
  1 long piece of lemon zest
    (pared with a potato peeler)

For the marinated pomegranate:
  3 ripe pomegranates
  Juice of 1 lemon
  85g caster sugar
  85ml Grand Marnier or brandy

Cut the pomegranates in half and knock out the seeds. Place in a bowl and add the lemon juice, sugar and liqueur and mix carefully. Cover and chill for at least an hour in the fridge.

Soak the gelatine leaves, if using, in a little water for a few minutes to soften. Heat the cream and the milk with the sugar, vanilla pod and lemon zest in a heavy saucepan over a medium heat.

When the cream and milk reaches the boil, remove the vanilla pod and zest. Add the softened gelatine leaves or powder. Stir well to dissolve the gelatine and strain into 4 lightly oiled ramekin dishes.

Tap them to release any air bubbles and chill until set. To serve, dip the moulds quickly into very hot water and tip out. Surround the mounds with a good spoonful of the marinated pomegranate seeds.

Cranberry tart with hot toffee sauce

An excellent Christmas pudding for eating at any time when you have lots of people to feed. It has a good balance of sweet and sour.

For 6:
  500g cranberries, fresh or frozen
  Juice and grated zest of 1 orange
  200g caster sugar
  150g shelled pecan nuts, chopped
  1–2 eggs, beaten well
  60g plain flour, sifted
  75g butter, melted
  Crème fraîche, to serve

For the toffee sauce:
  180g dark brown sugar
  120g butter
  120ml double cream

Preheat the oven to 180°C/gas mark 4. Grease a 20cm-diameter springform cake tin.

Put the cranberries in a non-stick pan with the orange juice and zest and mix well. Cook them for about 3–4 minutes, until the cranberries pop.

Put the just-cooked cranberries into the prepared cake tin. Sprinkle with half the sugar and the pecans, and mix well.

In a bowl, beat the remaining sugar with the egg until well mixed. Add the flour and melted butter to make a smooth batter. Pour this over the cranberries in the tin and bake for 40–45 minutes.

To make the toffee sauce, heat the sugar, butter and cream together until the sugar has dissolved and the sauce is bubbling. Take off the heat and serve warm. This makes generous quantities of sauce and you may have some left over for ice cream the following day.

Serve the tart warm with the hot toffee sauce and crème fraîche.

Orange and cranberry pies

Make these as a refreshing change from mince pies.

For 36 pies:
300g soft brown sugar
350g cranberries
Juice of 1 orange
4 cloves, crushed

For the orange pastry:
450g plain flour
200g icing sugar
Grated zest and juice of ½ orange
Pinch of salt
350g butter

To make the pastry, sift the flour with the icing sugar, orange zest and salt, and rub in the butter (or pulse in a processor) until the mixture resembles breadcrumbs. Add just enough orange juice to bring the mixture together in a ball and chill for 30 minutes.

Meanwhile, mix the filling ingredients together in a pan and cook over a gentle heat for 10 minutes.

Roll out the pastry and cut out equal numbers of circles and slightly smaller circles. Grease and line a mince pie tin with the circles, and spoon the filling into them. Top each pie with a smaller pastry circle. Brush the edge with a little water. Pinch the bottom and tops together. Chill for about 10 minutes to firm up the pastry.

Preheat the oven to 180ºC/gas mark 4. Brush the pies with milk and cook in the preheated oven until brown. This should take about 20 minutes.

Cranberry vodka

An excellent drink for a shot or two at Christmas, this vodka is fantastic with blinis and smoked salmon and eel.

For 20 small glasses:
100g fresh cranberries
75cl bottle of vodka
1 tablespoon clear honey

Crush the cranberries and add them to the bottle of vodka with the honey. Infuse at room temperature for 24 hours and then strain.

Cranberry cocktail

A sharp, limey cranberry cocktail that is good for Christmas.

For 1 glass:
4 tablespoons cranberry juice
1½ tablespoons Grand Marnier
2½ tablespoons Tequila
1cm piece of ginger, crushed
Dash of lime juice
Dash of sugar syrup
  (see page 225)
Crushed ice

Shake all the ingredients with crushed ice and strain into cocktail glasses.

Venison, cranberry and chestnut casserole

This dish is based on a recipe by Philippa Vine. Its taste is much improved if made at least a day in advance and carefully reheated, as this allows the flavours to deepen. Serve with Nutmeg mashed potato (see page 336) and Quick braised red cabbage (see page 21).

For 6:
 1kg lean shoulder of venison
 2 tablespoons plain flour
 Salt and black pepper
 18 shallots
 110g smoked streaky bacon
 1 tablespoon olive oil
 ¾ bottle of red wine
 2 bay leaves
 3 sprigs of fresh rosemary
 3 sprigs of fresh thyme
 1 tablespoon dried wild
    mushrooms (any type or
    a mixture), soaked in hot water
    or warm milk for 10 minutes,
    then drained and chopped
 1 tablespoon redcurrant jelly
 10g tomato purée
 ½ teaspoon ground juniper
    berries
 ½ teaspoon ground coriander
    seeds
 ½ teaspoon freshly grated nutmeg
 200g fresh or frozen cranberries
 200g peeled chestnuts

Preheat the oven to 170°C/gas mark 3. Cut the venison into large chunks and toss in the seasoned flour to coat lightly. Peel the shallots and cut the bacon into lardons.

Fry the bacon and shallots until golden and put into a casserole dish. Seal the venison, in batches, in the hot pan in a little oil and add to the casserole dish. Deglaze the pan with the red wine and add with all the other ingredients, except the cranberries and chestnuts, to the dish. Taste and adjust the seasoning if necessary. Cover with a lid and put in the oven.

After an hour, add the cranberries and chestnuts to the casserole.

After another half hour, start testing to see if the meat is really tender: the cooking time will vary, depending on the age of the animal and how long it has been hung.

Kate's cranberry and macadamia flapjacks

This was a chance invention of Kate Dawson, who had lots of leftover cranberries after one Christmas. They're so good you'll eat them all year round. Fresh cranberries give a sharper taste than dried, delicious in contrast to the sweetness of the other ingredients.

For 12 flapjacks:
 250g butter, plus more for the tin
 75g fresh (or dried) cranberries
 175g demerara sugar
    (halve this amount if you're
    using dried cranberries as they
    are sweeter)
 2 tablespoons golden syrup
 ½ teaspoon ground ginger
 275g rolled oats
 75g macadamia nuts, some
    cut in half

Preheat the oven to 180°C/gas mark 4. Butter a shallow baking tin.

Put the butter, demerara sugar and syrup into a heavy-based saucepan and stir over a gentle heat until the sugar has completely dissolved. Add the ground ginger and take the pan off the heat. Stir in the oats, nuts and cranberries, and press the mixture into a greased tin.

Cook in the preheated oven for 25–30 minutes. The mixture will still be soft at this stage but it will harden as it cools.

When it has cooled a little, cut it into squares.

Winter roots

Winter roots are enjoying a renaissance, with great restaurants such as the River Cafe and De Kas in Amsterdam putting parsnips, celeriac, swede and turnips centre stage. We're all familiar with the common roots, but people are wary of celeriac, Jerusalem artichoke, salsify and kohlrabi. What do we do with these?

Celeriac has a slightly aniseedy, nutty flavour and it stores well, lasting for over two weeks in the vegetable basket. It's good raw in salads such as Celeriac rémoulade (see page 434) and makes an excellent winter mash or soup (see page 432). Try it in a soufflé, cooking it in the scraped-out root (see page 432). On my heavy soil, celeriac is tricky to grow; it needs so much space – 45cm between each root to maximise its health and growth – from spring until winter that I tend to buy mine. If you do grow it, don't harvest the roots until after a mild frost, which will improve their flavour. On the other hand, don't leave them in the ground too long, as they will not stand hard frost.

Jerusalem artichokes are sweeter than celeriac, but share the nuttiness. They're a cinch to grow – almost too much so. If you leave a few un-dug from one winter to the next, they'll start to invade your vegetable patch. Jerusalem artichokes are tubers, spread by runners, and left to romp, they can become a pest. I love them, and they're always there when you're running out of other things to eat from the garden. Don't peel your artichokes: just scrub them. This makes them easier to prepare and the flavour is better. If they are encrusted with soil, leave them to soak in cold water for a while before you scrub.

Kohlrabis aren't strictly speaking a root but a swollen stem base. They have a gentle turnipy flavour and are good raw, thinly sliced or cooked. I love them as a first course with hollandaise sauce (see page 440). They are easy to grow and, like many brassicas, extremely hardy.

My mother is very keen on salsify and scorzonera – twin sisters with thong-like taproots that are coming back into fashion. Salsify has pale skin and pink-purple flowers, scorzonera black skin and yellow flowers. The flowers of both are edible and good to scatter over a salad. People divide sharply as to whether they think these two roots are deliciously unique or deadly boring. I like the flavour, which is not unlike a sweeter Jerusalem artichoke, but the roots feel a bit measly for the amount of preparation involved.

Winter bagna cauda

There are lots of different versions of this recipe, but many of them are a hassle, with the milk curdling at the drop of a hat. With this one, the cooking of the garlic is easy and works every time. You can make bagna cauda (garlic and anchovy dip) in the summer using courgettes, peppers, fennel and carrots to dip. In winter, use lots of different roots. I like eating them raw, but sometimes you may prefer to have them warm and lightly steamed.

For 6–8:
- **1 celeriac, peeled and cut into julienne strips (then doused in lemon juice to stop them discolouring)**
- **3 Jerusalem artichokes, sliced**
- **½ cauliflower, broken into small florets**
- **2 carrots, cut into batons**
- **2 Florence fennel bulbs, cut into chunks**
- **1 celery head, broken into sticks**
- **Selection of crunchy-stemmed salad leaves, such as Red Giant mustard, rocket, komatsuna**

For the bagna cauda:
- **16 garlic cloves, peeled**
- **Milk, to cover**
- **300g anchovy fillets (preferably salted and rinsed; if in oil, drained)**
- **200ml extra virgin olive oil**
- **300g butter, cut into pieces**
- **100ml double cream**

First make the bagna cauda. Preheat the oven to 150°C/gas mark 2.

Put the garlic cloves into a small loaf tin, cover with milk and then with a layer of greaseproof paper and a layer of foil. Cook in the oven for about 30–40 minutes, until the garlic is soft. Make sure that the garlic remains covered by the milk and doesn't dry out. Lift out the garlic and discard the milk.

Put the anchovies into a bowl over a pan of simmering water and add the soft garlic cloves. Mash them together with a fork to a paste. Using a hand whisk, gradually add the oil and butter, whisking to combine. Finally add the cream.

Pour the bagna cauda into a bowl or, even better, into a fondue dish so it is kept warm. Then dip the vegetable pieces into it.

Vegetable stock

It's winter roots that give much of the flavour to a good vegetable stock. Use leftovers and the clean peel or tops and bottoms of any of these roots – whatever you have. Homemade stock is really worth having; leave bought stock cubes for emergencies.

For about 1.5 litres :
   1 onion, unpeeled and cut in half
   2 carrots
   1 small celeriac, swede or turnip root – whichever you have around
   Bunch of parsley, including the stems
   6 celery sticks
   2 bay leaves
   6 black peppercorns

Coarsely chop all the vegetables and simmer them gently in 2 litres of water with the bay and peppercorns for 40 minutes. Strain the liquid and use, or boil for a further 30 minutes until it's reduced right down, pour into ice trays and freeze. Use for soup, risotto, sauces and stews.

Slow-roasted winter roots and herb couscous

This makes an excellent vegetarian dish, and you can also serve it with harissa or Cucumber raita (see page 196) as well as the couscous.

For 6:
For the roasted vegetables:
   2 beetroot
   2 carrots
   1 sweet potato
   2 parsnips
   2 onions or shallots
   2 whole heads of garlic
   2 tablespoons olive oil
   Bunch of thyme
   Sprinkling of balsamic vinegar
   150ml good vegetable stock
   Salt and black pepper

For the herb couscous:
   275g couscous
   500ml good vegetable stock, brought to the boil
   Salt and black pepper
   Handful of mint or coriander, chopped
   Handful of parsley, chopped
   Juice and grated zest of ½ lemon or lime
   Extra virgin olive oil (optional)

Preheat the oven to 160°C/gas mark 3.
   Scrub the beetroot, removing any blemishes, but leave the skin on. Cut in half if they're large. Peel the carrots, sweet potato and parsnips, and cut into wedges. Quarter the onions (unless using shallots) and leave the heads of garlic whole. Lightly oil a baking tray and put in all the vegetables, except the onions, together with the thyme. Turn them so that they are covered with the oil and sprinkle with balsamic vinegar.
   Put the veg in the preheated oven for about 40 minutes and then add the onion, together with the stock (if you add only this amount, it stops them burning on the bottom, but still allows them to crisp up). Roast for a

further 35–40 minutes, until they are crisp and golden, and all the liquid has been absorbed.
   Fifteen minutes before the vegetables come out of the oven, make the couscous. Put the couscous into a deep bowl, pour over the boiling stock, stir, cover and then leave for 5–10 minutes for the grains to soften.
   Season well and stir in the chopped herbs, lemon zest and juice, and a dash of olive oil if you wish. Season the roasted vegetables with salt and black pepper before serving.

Venison fillet with root vegetable chips

I love fillet of venison with root vegetable chips, and the gamier and stronger the venison the better. The vegetable chips go well with any red meat or game. A mix of beetroot, sweet potato and parsnip looks wonderfully colourful.

For 6:
For the venison:
  Salt and black pepper
  2 garlic cloves, crushed with salt
  15 juniper berries, crushed
  1 venison fillet (about 1kg)
  30g butter
  1 tablespoon olive oil
  Rowan jelly (see page 324),
    to serve

For the root vegetable chips:
  3 parsnips
  3 beetroot (ideally 2 stripy,
    1 purple)
  1 sweet potato
  Salt
  Groundnut oil, for frying

First, prepare the vegetables for the root vegetable chips. Peel and slice them into thin slices or chips (use a mandoline if you have one) and soak them in cold water for about an hour.

Next prepare the venison. Mix the garlic with the crushed juniper berries and black pepper. Roll the venison fillet in the mixture. Leave for at least half an hour to allow the juniper flavour to penetrate.

Preheat a medium (180°C/gas mark 4) oven. Fry the fillet in a mix of olive oil and butter for 5 minutes over a high heat, turning it every so often, until all sides of the meat are browned.

Cover the venison with foil and put it in the preheated oven for 15 minutes. With a small fillet this will be sufficent to cook it through. If you have a larger one then it will need a longer spell in the oven. Remove from the oven and leave to rest for at least 10 minutes, still wrapped in its foil. Turn up the oven to 220°C/gas mark 7.

While the venison is cooking and resting, cook the vegetable chips. Preheat the oil for deep-frying to 170°C. Drain the vegetable slices and dry them carefully, then deep-fry them in the very hot oil in small batches, not more than a handful at a time, until they just begin to brown.

If you don't have a deep-fryer, shallow-fry them until golden, taking care not to fill the pan more than a third full with oil. To test the temperature, throw one chip in the oil and it should cook within a minute if the oil is hot enough.

Whether deep- or shallow-fried, as you cook the chips batch by batch, once they begin to brown take them out and put them aside.

Once you've fried the lot, spread them out on a baking tray and blast them in the oven for 5 minutes, until they are crisp. Keep an eye on them, as they can burn quickly.

Take the rested venison out of its foil and serve with the chips as soon as they are all cooked, accompanied by rowan jelly.

Roast parsnips rolled in Parmesan

These are crunchy and sweet, and great with any meat or stew, to eat with an aperitif, or as a first course dipped into crème fraîche flavoured with dill and/or Chilli jam (see page 318).

For 6:
   Olive oil, for the tin
   600g parsnips
   100g Parmesan cheese, grated
   100g fresh brown or white
      breadcrumbs
   Seasoned flour
   2 eggs, beaten

Preheat the oven to 190°C/gas mark 5 and put an oiled baking tin in it to get really hot.

Peel the parsnips and cut them into wedges, then steam them for 10 minutes.

Mix the breadcrumbs with the Parmesan. Dip the hot parsnips in the seasoned flour, then into the beaten egg and lastly roll them in the breadcrumb mixture.

Put the parsnips into the preheated oven in the oiled baking tin and roast for about 35 minutes, until tender and golden brown.

Spiced parsnip soup

A deservedly well-known recipe. You'll need only a bowl of it – with some bread – for a filling and delicious lunch.

For 6:
   30g butter
   1 tablespoon sunflower oil
   1 onion, chopped
   675g parsnips, chopped
   1 teaspoon ground coriander
      seeds
   1 teaspoon ground cumin seeds
   ½ teaspoon ground turmeric
   ¼ teaspoon chilli powder
   1.2 litres good vegetable stock
   Salt and black pepper
   A little milk (optional)
   150ml single cream
   Yoghurt, to serve
   Chopped coriander, to serve

Melt the butter with the oil in a large heavy-based pan and add the chopped onion and parsnips. Sweat them for 5 minutes, without allowing them to colour. Stir in the spices and cook gently for another 2 minutes.

Add the stock and bring to the boil. Reduce the heat, cover and simmer for about 30 minutes or until the parsnips are quite tender. Allow to cool slightly, season carefully and purée in a food processor.

Return the soup to a clean pan, adding a little milk if necessary, depending how thick you would like the soup.

Add the cream and warm through gently without allowing the soup to boil. Serve with a dollop of yoghurt and some chopped coriander.

Parsnip purée with Bourbon

A very rich purée, so you'll need only a little. It's wonderful under a piece of rare fillet of beef and very good with venison or goose.

For 6:
   1.5kg parsnips
   Salt and black pepper
   30g butter
   100ml double cream
   Freshly grated nutmeg
   50ml Bourbon or Irish whiskey
   Breadcrumbs (optional)

Peel the parsnips and cut them into wedges. Boil or steam with salt until they are tender. Drain well.

Add the butter to the parsnips and mash well or pulse carefully in a food processor, but don't over-blend or the purée will be too smooth.

Stir in the cream and nutmeg to taste, followed by the whiskey. Season.

Serve straight away or put the purée into an ovenproof dish, cover with a layer of breadcrumbs and bake in an oven preheated to 180°C/gas mark 4 for 20 minutes.

Smoked haddock and parsnip fishcakes

These parsnip fishcakes are delicious – sweet and smoky – and very good with a sharp tartare sauce or mustard mayonnaise. They freeze well, so you can make lots in one go.

For 8 fishcakes:
½ **onion, chopped**
75g streaky bacon or pancetta, thinly cut and chopped
300g smoked haddock
1 bay leaf
6 cloves
275ml milk
150g parsnips, chopped
150g potatoes, chopped
10g butter
Chopped parsley
1 red chilli, finely chopped (optional)
Salt and black pepper
Seasoned flour
1 egg, beaten
80g white breadcrumbs
Olive oil, for frying

Cook the onion with the bacon or pancetta over a moderate heat for 10 minutes and put to one side.

Put the smoked haddock into a pan, together with the bay leaf and cloves. Pour over the milk, cover and bring to the boil. As soon as the milk boils, remove from the heat and allow the fish to cool in the liquid.

Boil or steam the parsnips and potatoes together until they are tender. Mash them with the butter and a dash of the boiled milk and season well.

Combine the onions, bacon, mashed potatoes and parsnips, parsley and chilli, if using. Barely flake the fish, and fold carefully into the vegetable mixture. The fishcakes are far nicer if the flakes of fish are intact. Adjust the seasoning.

Dust your hands with seasoned flour and shape balls of the mixture into cakes. Dip these into the beaten egg and coat with the breadcrumbs.

Shallow-fry in the olive oil until golden or bake for 15–20 minutes in an oven preheated to 180ºC/gas mark 4. They can be made in advance and kept on a baking tray in the fridge until you want to cook them.

Vichy carrots

This is very good for cooking winter carrots, which have less taste than summer-harvested ones. Lengthy cooking intensifies the flavour.

For 6:
1kg carrots
50g butter
Pinch of salt and black pepper
1 teaspoon sugar
Plenty of chopped parsley
Juice of 1 lemon

Peel the carrots and slice them. Put them in a saucepan with the butter, salt, pepper and sugar. Just cover with cold water and let them boil until the water has evaporated and they are tender and glazed.

Stir in masses of chopped parsley and the lemon juice to taste.

Grated carrot and poppy seed salad

A good salad for when you've got a few maincrop carrots that are a bit on the old side in mid-winter. It has a delicious sharp and nutty taste. Make it a few hours in advance so that the carrot gets a chance to marinate in the lime and oil. The texture of grated carrot is quite dense, so a little of this salad goes a long way.

For 6:
 3 large carrots
 1 tablespoon extra virgin olive oil
 Juice and grated zest of 1 lime
 Salt and black pepper
 1 tablespoon poppy seeds, toasted

Peel the carrots and grate on a medium-grade grater.

Mix the oil with the lime zest and juice, and salt and pepper, in the base of a large salad bowl. Put the carrot in on top, followed by the hot seeds, straight from the pan.

Stir everything together and leave for a couple of hours. Actually, this is surprisingly good the next day.

Bejuja carrots

This robust carrot dish is from Jude Maynard, who cooked here in the school for several years. It is good for a vegetarian lunch, eaten with a dollop of yoghurt and rice, and also as a side vegetable.

For 4:
 4 tablespoons vegetable oil
 675g carrots, sliced
 4 garlic cloves, chopped
 5cm piece of root ginger
 1 teaspoon poppy seeds
 1 teaspoon ground turmeric
 2 teaspoons ground cumin seeds
 2 teaspoons ground coriander seeds
 1 chilli, deseeded and chopped
 1 teaspoon salt
 Large handful of chopped coriander
 Natural yoghurt, to serve

Heat the oil in a frying pan and gently fry the carrots for 10 minutes. Stir in the garlic, ginger and poppy seeds, and fry for a couple of minutes.

Stir in the turmeric, cumin, coriander, chilli and salt, and cook until the carrots are tender. Cook them very slowly so that they don't catch.

Finally, stir in the chopped coriander and serve the carrots with a bowl of yoghurt.

Carrot cake with grapes and honey

The good thing about any carrot cake is that it lasts well and, in this recipe, the grapes make a lovely addition. It makes a good pudding, and can also be served with a good vanilla ice cream.

For 6–8:
 275g plain flour
 1 teaspoon bicarbonate of soda
 2 teaspoons baking powder
 175g grated carrot
 4 tablespoons honey
 100ml orange juice
 3 eggs, beaten
 175ml sunflower oil
 1 teaspoon poppy seeds
 ½ teaspoon ground cinnamon
 ½ teaspoon salt
 Small bunch (about 110g) of seedless green grapes, halved if large

For the mascarpone cream:
 250g tub of mascarpone cheese
 1 tablespoon icing sugar
 A few drops of vanilla essence

Preheat the oven to 180°C/gas mark 4. Line the bottom and sides of a 22–23cm springform cake tin with greaseproof paper.

Sift the flour, bicarbonate of soda and baking powder into a large bowl. Then add all the remaining ingredients, except for the grapes, and mix thoroughly. Fold in the grapes and pour the mixture into the prepared tin.

Cook in the preheated oven for about 1½ hours, covering the top with foil after one hour. The cake is ready when a skewer inserted into the middle comes out clean.

To make the mascarpone cream, sweeten the mascarpone with sieved icing sugar. Add the vanilla and beat together. Serve each slice of cake with a generous dollop of the cream.

Carrot and Jerusalem artichoke soup

The problem with artichoke soup is that it's one of the most wind-producing things that you can eat. If you mix artichokes with the same amount of carrot, you still enjoy the artichoke's lovely sweet flavour, but without the same effect. This is a recipe from *Gardener Cook* by Christopher Lloyd.

For 6–8:
1 small onion, chopped
1 tablespoon olive oil
30g butter
750g Jerusalem artichokes
500g carrots
250g celeriac
1.5 litres vegetable stock
Salt and black pepper
Bunch of parsley, finely chopped
Dollop of natural yoghurt or crème fraîche

Fry the onion in the oil and the butter until soft.

Peel the artichokes (this is not essential), discarding the knobbles, and chop them. Peel the carrots and celeriac and cut them into slices. Sweat all the vegetables together with the onion for 5 minutes. Add the stock and simmer for 20 minutes.

Purée in a blender or with a wand whizzer and season carefully.

Add plenty of finely chopped parsley and a dollop of crème fraîche or natural yoghurt.

Jerusalem artichoke gratin

I prefer this gratin to one made only with potato. It has a richer, more interesting taste. You could add cheese – any grated hard cheese – on the top.

For 4:
300g Jerusalem artichokes
300g potatoes
Butter, for the dish and dotting the top
570ml good vegetable stock
75g pancetta or prosciutto
Freshly grated nutmeg
Salt and black pepper
Hard salty ewes' cheese, grated (optional)

Preheat a moderate (180°C/gas mark 4) oven.

Peel the artichokes and potatoes, and slice them thinly (the slicing disc of a food processor is ideal for this).

Butter an ovenproof dish and put a layer of mixed artichokes and potatoes at the bottom. Snip over some strips of pancetta or prosciutto, then some grated nutmeg and season.

Crumble over some of the cheese, if you are using it, and dot with a little butter.

Repeat the layers, pour in the stock and finish with a layer of cheese. Cover and bake in the preheated oven for 1 hour. Remove the cover, dot with butter if you omitted the cheese and increase the temperature to 200°C/gas mark 6 to brown the top for about 10 minutes.

Allow to cool for 10–15 minutes before serving.

Grated celeriac with lime

As with carrot, celeriac with lime is a good combination. This is an excellent way of serving celeriac as a vegetable, or side salad (preparation for both is shown below).

For 6:
300g celeriac
1 teaspoon caraway seeds
150g carrots
20g butter
Juice of 1 lime
1 dessertspoon honey
2 tablespoons sour cream
Salt and black pepper
1 teaspoon Dijon mustard
   (optional)

Peel the celeriac and use it immediately to avoid it discolouring. Toast the caraway seeds.

To prepare as a vegetable side dish, grate the celeriac and carrots on the largest grating, or julienne, disc of a food processor. Heat the butter in a sauté pan and toss the celeriac and carrots in it for 2 minutes. Add the lime juice, honey and caraway seeds, and take the pan off the heat. Stir in the sour cream, season and serve immediately. This is delicious with grilled chicken.

If you want instead to prepare this as a salad, once you have grated the celeriac and carrots (or use celeriac on its own, if you prefer), pour over the lime juice, mixed with the honey. Stir in the sour cream, Dijon mustard (if you like) and caraway seeds, and season with sea salt and black pepper.

Celeriac and apple soup

I love the sweetness of the celeriac, the sharpness of the apple and the richness of the cheese in this recipe. Celeriac as a soup on its own is, I think, too soft a flavour.

For 6–8:
1 litre good chicken or
   vegetable stock, hot
1 celeriac
2 onions
2 celery sticks
25g butter
2 garlic cloves, crushed
   or chopped
1 Bramley apple, peeled
   and chopped
1 dessert apple, peeled
   and chopped
Salt and black pepper
75g blue cheese, such as Stilton
   or Cashel Blue, crumbled
2 tablespoons single cream
   (optional)

Warm the stock, and peel and chop the vegetables.

Melt the butter in a large pan. Add the vegetables and sweat them for several minutes without allowing them to colour. Add the garlic and pour over the hot stock. Bring to a simmer.

Simmer for 10 minutes, then add the peeled chopped apples. Season, then cover and simmer for another 20 minutes.

Purée with a hand blender or in a food processor, and season with salt and black pepper.

Just before serving, stir in the crumbled cheese and the cream if you are using it.

Celeriac soufflé

I first saw this in a pretentious French cookbook, and I loved the idea – the contrast of a frothy soufflé in a knobbly old root. A soufflé dish is fine if you can't face scraping out the root.

For 4 as a starter, 2 as a main course:
1 large celeriac
30g butter
2 egg yolks and 5 egg whites
1 tablespoon Dijon mustard
Plenty of freshly grated nutmeg
Salt and black pepper
Chopped parsley

Preheat a moderate (180°C/gas mark 4) oven.

Take a slice off the bottom of the celeriac so that it stands upright, and cut off the top. Scoop out the flesh with a strong pointed spoon (or melon baller), leaving about 1cm of shell.

Steam the flesh until tender and put it into a food processor. Process while adding the butter, chopped into small cubes, egg yolks, mustard, nutmeg and seasoning.

Beat the egg whites into stiff peaks and carefully fold them into the celeriac mixture.

Spoon the mixture back into the celeriac shell and bake in the preheated oven for 35–40 minutes.

Scatter with chopped parsley and serve immediately.

Apple and celeriac salad

A good sharp-tasting and crunchy winter salad.

For 4 as a starter, 6 as a side dish:
- **75g walnuts**
- **2 crisp eating apples, such as Discovery, Cox or Spartan**
- **½ celeriac root**
- **Plenty of flat-leaf parsley**

For the dressing:
- **1 tablespoon cider vinegar**
- **1 shallot, finely chopped**
- **2 teaspoons Dijon mustard**
- **Grated zest and juice of ½ lemon**
- **1 dessertspoon runny honey**
- **85ml walnut oil**
- **Salt and black pepper**

Make the dressing by mixing together the vinegar, shallot, mustard, lemon juice and honey in a food processor. Add the oil in a stream while processing and check the seasoning. Toast the walnuts.

Peel, core and slice the apples. Grate the celeriac, using a food processor fitted with a large grating disc, or cut into fine matchsticks. You must use both apples and celeriac immediately before they start to turn brown. Toss the apples and celeriac together and pour over just enough dressing to coat.

Scatter the toasted walnuts, lemon zest and plenty of flat-leaf parsley over the salad.

Celeriac rémoulade

I like the texture of raw celeriac. There are recipes for this dish that tell you to blanch it briefly first, but I think that's unnecessary. Eat this as a first course on its own, or serve it with a plate of Parma ham.

For 6:
- **1 medium-sized celeriac**
- **Lemon juice, for acidulation**
- **1 tin of anchovies in oil, drained and chopped**
- **3 tablespoons capers**
- **Large bunch of parsley, coarsely chopped**

For the homemade mayonnaise:
- **1 whole egg and 1 extra yolk**
- **1 level teaspoon mustard powder**
- **1 garlic clove (optional)**
- **Good pinch of salt and black pepper**
- **200ml good sunflower oil**
- **100ml olive oil**
- **Lemon juice or white wine vinegar, to taste**
- **150ml whipped cream (optional)**

To make the mayonnaise, put the egg and yolk, mustard powder, garlic (if using), salt and pepper into a liquidiser or bowl. Whisk until the mixture becomes frothy. Add the oils in a stream while processing or whisking, until it thickens. Add the lemon juice or vinegar to taste and then season. If you prefer a milder taste, you can add some whipped cream.

If the mayonnaise curdles at any point, start the whole process again with a third egg yolk, whisking it in a clean bowl and adding the curdled mixture in a slow stream while processing or whisking. This makes about 400ml and can be stored in the fridge for a few days.

Peel the celeriac root and slice it as thinly as you can into big round discs. Then slice these into julienne (matchsticks). You can use a food processor for this, but I like the mix of shapes and sizes that you get when doing it by hand. As you cut them, put the matchsticks into a bowl of water acidulated with a good squeeze of lemon juice to stop them turning brown.

Drain them, pat them dry with a tea towel and put into a bowl. Stir in just enough mayonnaise to coat them. Mix in the chopped anchovies, capers and parsley. This adds to the texture and gives some strong taste highlights.

Caramelised celeriac with pancetta

I had this when I went to the wonderful Amsterdam restaurant De Kas. The sugars caramelise and the taste, mixed with the smoky saltiness of the bacon, is fantastic.

For 4–5:
1 large celeriac, peeled and sliced
into 10 pieces
Salt and black pepper
½ tablespoon chopped lemon
thyme
½ tablespoon chopped rosemary
2 garlic cloves, chopped
2 tablespoons olive oil
20 slices of pancetta

Preheat the oven to 160°C/gas mark 3.
Steam the raw chunks of celeriac for 10 minutes. Dry them and put them into a large bowl. Season with salt, pepper, chopped herbs, garlic and olive oil, and mix well. Leave for at least 10 minutes.
Wrap each chunk in 2 slices of pancetta and then roast them in the preheated oven until the pancetta is crisp and the celeriac is soft in the middle.

Purée of swede

A deluxe version of that Scottish classic, mashed neeps.

For 4:
900g swede
Salt and black pepper
4 garlic cloves
50g butter
2 heaped teaspoons finely
chopped root ginger
4 tablespoons double cream
A little ground cinnamon, to taste

Peel and chop the swede into large chunks and steam or boil in salted water until tender.
Crush and chop the garlic. Melt the butter in a small saucepan and cook the garlic and ginger gently for 3–4 minutes, without allowing them to brown.
Purée the swede in a food processor, adding the garlic and ginger, then pour in the cream.
Season with salt, cinnamon and black pepper.

Roast swede with maple syrup

You can roast swede as you would celeriac, wrapped in pancetta (see left), or douse it with maple syrup, as here, for a lovely caramelised taste. Serve this with any roast meat.

For 4:
700g swede
2 tablespoons olive oil
3 tablespoons maple syrup
Salt and black pepper

Preheat the oven to 200°C/gas mark 6.
Peel and cut the swede into large pieces, about the size of a roast potato. Heat the olive oil in a baking tray and, when it is hot, add the pieces of swede and toss in the oil.
Using a pastry brush, coat the swede with the maple syrup and season with salt and pepper. This prevents a pool of maple syrup forming in the tray, which would burn easily.
Bake in the preheated oven, turning from time to time, for 45 minutes until crisp and golden.

Braised turnips

I'm not a massive fan of the turnip. They can be good when small, grated or finely sliced in a salad – but this is probably my favourite way of eating them cooked.

For 6–8:
  600g small to medium-sized
    turnips
  50g butter
  Salt and black pepper
  1 teaspoon sugar
  4 teaspoons white wine vinegar

Peel and cut the turnips into segments, then heat the butter and sweat these in it over a very gentle heat for 5 minutes. Season with salt and pepper and add the sugar.

Pour in the vinegar and turn up the heat to reduce the liquid by about two-thirds. Add 100ml water, cover with greaseproof paper and cook gently for 10 minutes.

Scotch broth

When you're in Scotland, you'll see neeps (swede) in even the smallest shop. The Scots often use them as mash with haggis, and in soup. Swede is one of the essential tastes in a good Scotch broth.

For 8–10:
  Leftover roast leg of lamb and
    vegetables
  1 onion, thinly sliced
  1 leek, thinly sliced
  2 tablespoons olive oil
  ½ mug of pearl barley
  1 small swede, diced
  2 small turnips, diced
  1 carrot, diced
  3 celery sticks, thinly sliced
  200g cabbage, cut into strips
  Large bunch of parsley, coarsely
    chopped
  Plenty of salt and black pepper

If you've had a leg of lamb for supper, boil up the bone with any leftover veg. Drain, reserving the stock, and allow to cool. Cut up the remaining meat.

In a large pan, sweat the onion and leek in the oil. Pour over the stock, add the pearl barley and the chopped meat, and cook gently for half an hour.

Then add the swede, turnip, carrot and celery, and cook in the pan for a further half an hour.

Throw in the cabbage for the last 2 minutes and finally the parsley. Season generously and serve.

Roast salsify

Salsify used to be more widely available, but today it isn't around so much. However, many chefs are now seeking it out. It has an unusual rich taste to which many become addicted after just one tasting. Cook the roots and simply turn them in crème fraîche with nutmeg, or add them to a lemon béchamel. This roast salsify with thyme is quick, simple and delicious, and particularly good with lamb or beef.

For 3–4:
450g salsify
Lemon juice or vinegar,
   for acidulation
2 tablespoons extra virgin olive oil
1 tablespoon chopped thyme
Salt and black pepper

Preheat the oven to 190°C/gas mark 5.
   Scrub and scrape the salsify (a stiff veg brush will get rid of all the whiskery roots), and cut it at an angle into 5cm lengths. Put them straight into a bowl of water acidulated with a good squeeze of lemon juice to keep them from going brown. When you are ready to cook them, dry them on kitchen paper and put them into a roasting tray.
   Turn the roots over in a little olive oil, scatter with the thyme and season.
   Roast for about half an hour until the salsify is tender.

Fried salsify in breadcrumbs

Fried salsify is good served as a first course, with melted butter, a wedge of lemon and some chopped parsley. Serve this dish as a first course or a side vegetable.

For 4:
700g salsify
Lemon juice, for acidulation
Seasoned flour
1 egg, beaten
100g fresh white breadcrumbs
Sunflower oil, for deep- or
   shallow-frying

Scrub the salsify and scrape or peel the roots, then immediately put them into cold water with a good squeeze of lemon juice to stop them turning brown.
   Steam the roots, or boil until they are just tender but still have a bite.
   Dip the roots first in well-seasoned flour, then into the beaten egg and lastly into the breadcrumbs.
   Either heat oil in a pan and deep- or shallow-fry until the roots are golden and crisp, or roast in an oiled baking tin in an oven preheated to 170°C/gas mark 3½ until tender and golden.

Marni's salsify

This is my godmother Marni Hodgkin's favourite recipe for salsify, which came originally from Rosamund Richardson's book *Definitely Different*. Small chunks of the cooked root are tossed in a mix of garlic and parsley, and served sizzling-hot.

For 4:
675g salsify or scorzonera
Salt and black pepper
50g butter
4 tablespoons good olive oil
2 garlic cloves, crushed
2 tablespoons finely chopped
   flat-leaf parsley

Clean and scrub the salsify and cut into chunks. Cook them unpeeled in a little boiling salted water in a covered pan for about 10 minutes, until just tender. Salsify has a waxy bite and is better soft than al dente. Rinse the salsify under cold running water, as this makes peeling easier, and peel.
   Melt the butter with the olive oil and gently fry the garlic for a couple of minutes.
   Add the salsify roots and toss them in the garlic butter mix. Sprinkle with lots of parsley and serve.

Scorzonera salad

Scorzonera was much more widely eaten in our parents' generation. The dressing peps it up nicely.

For 4:
700g scorzonera
Lemon juice, for acidulation
1 teaspoon salt
Bunch of flat-leaf parsley, finely chopped, to serve

For the dressing:
1 shallot, finely chopped
1 teaspoon Dijon mustard
1 egg yolk
1 tablespoon lemon juice
1 teaspoon caster sugar, or to taste
3 tablespoons extra virgin olive oil
3 tablespoons sunflower oil

Scrape or peel the scorzonera and cut at an angle into large pieces. Immediately put them into a pan with cold water (enough to cover the roots), a squeeze of lemon and a teaspoon of salt. Bring to the boil and simmer until just tender.

While the roots are cooking, combine all the ingredients for the dressing, except the oil, and whisk with a wand or in a processor. Add the oil in a stream while you are whisking. Season carefully.

When the scorzonera is ready, drain and let it cool slightly. When it is lukewarm, pour over the dressing.

Serve with plenty of chopped flat-leaf parsley.

Kohlrabi and hollandaise

The simple earthy, cabbage-tasting vegetable is lovely in contrast to the creamy richness of hollandaise sauce. The combination makes an excellent winter first course.

For 6:
5–6 kohlrabi

For the hollandaise sauce:
3 tablespoons white wine vinegar
6 black peppercorns
1 bay leaf
2 egg yolks
175g unsalted butter, cut into small chunks
Salt and black pepper

Cut the kohlrabi into chunks like the segments of a chocolate orange. Steam them for about 10 minutes, until tender. Keep them warm.

To make the sauce, boil the vinegar and 1 tablespoon of water with the peppercorns and bay leaf until reduced to one tablespoon.

Half-fill a wide shallow pan with water and bring to a simmer. Put the yolks in a heatproof bowl, sit this in the pan of water and whisk well. Add the butter, bit by bit, whisking all the time. As it warms, the mixture will gradually become thick and shiny. Remove from the heat and stir in the cooled reduced vinegar, salt and pepper. (See page 233 for more hollandaise tips.)

Serve with the hollandaise in a bowl in the middle of a large plate of the kohlrabi chunks.

Horseradish sauce

Horseradish sauce is, of course, the best thing to eat with roast beef, and it's also lovely with smoked fish – such as trout, eel and mackerel – and other root vegetables, such as potatoes, celeriac and beetroot.

You can't be precise about quantities for this recipe, as the root varies hugely in strength according to when you dig it. It's at its strongest in October and November, and best when freshly dug, but will keep without drying out too much for 2–3 months. Scrub it and wrap it in very slightly dampened kitchen paper, then store it in a plastic bag in the fridge until it is needed.

You need:
Grated horseradish
Double cream or crème fraîche
A little mustard powder
Lemon juice, to taste
Pinch of white pepper
Salt

Peel and grate the horseradish. If you want it very strong, grate it when you eat. It has highly volatile essential oils and so its strength will quickly fade – which is why you never want to cook it. It also discolours quickly, so mix it with the other ingredients immediately.

Add enough double cream (or crème fraîche) to the grated horseradish to give you a creamy consistency. Add a little mustard powder, white pepper and salt, and finish by adding lemon juice to taste.

Horseradish cheese on toast

A tasty twist on cheese on toast.

For 4:
30g grated Gruyère cheese
30g Parmesan cheese, grated
1 tablespoon double cream
2 teaspoons freshly grated horseradish
Few drops of tarragon vinegar
Pinch of paprika
4 slices of toast or fried bread

Preheat a hot (230°C/gas mark 8) oven or grill. Mix all the ingredients together and pile on to the fried or toasted bread.

Put in the preheated oven or under the grill for 5 minutes until the cheese is melting and brown.

Horseradish dumplings

These are excellent in any beef or game stew and they're lovely with pork chops. This recipe comes from Lynda Brown's book *The Cook's Garden*.

For 12 dumplings:
½ teaspoon baking powder
60g plain flour
1 egg, beaten
60g grated suet
60g breadcrumbs
1 heaped tablespoon freshly grated horseradish
Salt and black pepper

Sift the baking powder and flour into a bowl, and then mix in the egg. Then add all the other ingredients and mix together.

Using wetted hands, pinch off the dough into 12 portions and roll each one into a ball. Add these to a casserole – if you're eating them with one – for the last 20 minutes of the cooking time. Make sure they sit on top of the stew and are not submerged.

Continue to cook your casserole, covered. About 10 minutes before the end, if cooking in the oven, remove the lid and allow the dumplings to brown a little on top. If cooking on the hob, take the lid off and place the casserole in a hot oven (200°C/gas mark 6) for the final 10 minutes.

If you're eating the dumplings with pork chops, poach them in barely simmering salted water for 15 minutes. They should double in size and be light and cooked through.

S

Acknowledgements

This book was long in the making and Adam, Rosie and Molly have lived with it as much as I have, trying all the recipes and being immensely supportive. My friend and colleague Louise Farman has also put up with my long-term distraction.

Warm thanks go to my agent Caroline Michel, who has always been hugely enthusiastic about the idea, and to Richard Atkinson, my commissioning editor at Bloomsbury, who from the word go understood the concept of such a large book on this simple subject and like me wanted to make it beautiful. That absolute support and mutuality has been invaluable. I would like to thank Natalie Hunt who coordinated the whole project, Lisa Fiske in the production department, and everyone at Bloomsbury who has been involved with the book. As soon as I met Karl Shanahan, the designer, I knew he would create the book I hoped for – and he did. And thanks too, to Lewis Esson and Anne Askwith, who did wonderful work neatening up the text.

There have been many different inspirations for this book. The first was from my childhood, when holidays at Asolo in the Veneto introduced me to the colourful spectrum of Mediterranean vegetables and to the practice of shopping and cooking every day according to what the market could provide. I think this more than anything has made me love the food I do. I owe enormous thanks to my mother for introducing me to that world.

I greatly value the real and direct way of cooking that Nigel Slater has championed for so long. Rose Gray and Ruth Rogers, Antonio Carluccio, the Clarks from Moro and the chefs from the great Dutch restaurant in Amsterdam, De Kas, have all been sources of enthusiasm and inspiration. I am indebted to them all.

I've always had fun cooking and, of course, eating with friends. Many of the recipes here have been taught to me by my friends: Ivan and Pots Samarine, Aurea Carpenter and Andrew Palmer, Hugh Fearnley-Whittingstall, Kate and Charlie Boxer, Flora McDonnell, Kate Hubbard, Sarah and Montagu Don, Caroline Owen-Lloyd, Pip Morrison, John Keeling, Jane Sackville West, Jude Maynard, Jo Clark, Tessa and Simon Bishop and Sofka Zinovieff. I have loved cooking with Matthew Rice, a man who is as committed to beautiful vegetables as I am, and learning from my sister, Jane Raven, who now has an allotment, and from her mother-in-law, Teresa Wallace. Clare Smith, Pip Morrison, Jane Raven, Teresa Wallace, Kate Hubbard and Matthew Rice have been a terrific help with the unwieldy manuscript. All thanks to them!

I am very grateful for the meticulous work done by the recipe testers: Debbie Staples, Liz Wood and Caroline Davenport Thomas. Bea Burke and Colin Pilbeam have grown all the vegetables at Perch Hill. Warm, heartfelt thanks goes to them. They make the whole process of cooking from the garden a joy, with a harvesting walk one of the greatest pleasures in my life.

I have worked with Jonathan Buckley photographing plants and gardens for ten years, but this was the first time we photographed food together, and I love the results. We often had very long days, starting at dawn and having to keep going until long into the evening, but Jonathan was always extremely patient. At the end of one day in May I ran over his camera case in the Land Rover! It still contained two cameras and all but one of his lenses – I think he wanted to cry, but he laughed instead. I hope that we continue doing gardening books together, and that this is the first of many on food.

The person who has influenced me most in recent years is Tam Lawson. She has taught me that it is sometimes best to follow a plan. She is a wonderful cook, light on her feet, ocean-like in her knowledge and vastly generous in sharing her expertise. Many of the recipes included here are originally hers. We've spent days, months, years chatting about food, and it's to her that I dedicate this book.

Many thanks for specific recipes also go to: Carolyn Agius (Double pepper broccoli, page 65); Emma Ainslie (Onions baked whole, page 248); Lucy Baring (orange firelighters, page 30); Caroline Beamish (Onion tart from Beamish and McGlue, page 247); Cathy Bevan (Strawberry and black pepper ice cream, page 147); Lucy Boyd (Chard gratin, page 397); Ruth Bradley (Pumpkin pie, page 377); Lynda Brown (Spring greens risotto, page 65); William Buckingham (Naan bread, page 299); Virginia Chapman (Puréed Brussels sprouts in nutmeg cream, page 391); Jo Clark (Quick tomato tart, page 279, Stuffed baked potatoes with pesto, page 339 and Stuffed butternut squash, page 374); Harold Costello (Braised beans and celery, page 314); Sue Culley (Cranberry tart with hot toffee sauce, page 416); Adrian and Michael Daniel, *The Gate Vegetarian* (adaptation of their Spinach and tomato dhal, page 74); Caroline Davenport Thomas (Smoked salmon pâté with chervil, page 85); Kate Dawson (Watercress and smoked trout salad with horseradish, page 95); Jane Dunn (Griddled mini globe artichokes, page 118); Hugh Van Dusen (Parsnip purée with Bourbon, page 427); Kate Gattaker (Baked cream with gooseberries, page 217); Laurie Graizeau (French onion soup, page 245); Annie de la Grange Sury (Roast beetroot soup, page 164);

Michael Hobbs (Grated carrot and poppy seed salad, page 430); Sue Kennedy (Baked quinces in orange syrup, page 380); Michael Lawson or 'Judge Jam' (French strawberry jam, page 150, French apricot jam, page 157, Peach zabaglione, page 158, Savoury plum jam, page 259, Mushroom soup, page 345 and Fried salsify in breadcrumbs, page 438); Sophia Lawson (White gazpacho with grapes, page 330 and Panna cotta with marinated pomegranate, page 416); Ingrid Marsh (Tunisian orange and almond cake, page 34); Fiona Mates (onion cutting technique, page 242); Rebecca Nicolson (Borlotti ratatouille, page 304); Andrew Palmer (Smashed roast new potatoes with garlic and rosemary, page 127); Emmanuela Palú (Tiramisu with red berries, page 265 and Pumpkin, sage and pecorino tortellini, page 377); Daniela Piccolotto (Sweet-and-sour borlotti beans, page 304, Bottled celery, page 315 and Peperonata, page 371); Efi Pollis (Greek courgette pie, page 186); Anna Raven (Rosemary saddleback potatoes, page 336); Faith Raven (Celeriac rémoulade, page 434); Jane Raven ('Sun-blushed' tomatoes, page 285); Anne Revell (Chilli jam, page 318); Matthew Rice (Chard and risotto balls, page 396 and Quick-fried kale, page 402); Mary Samarine (orange slices, page 33); South Devon Chilli Farm (Pickled chillies, page 318, Chilli dipping sauce, page 318 and Chilli chocolate, page 319); Debbie Staples (Grated beetroot salad with toasted mustard seeds and orange, page 163, Warm potato and lentil salad, page 340 and Chard and feta parcels, page 395); Alice Stobart (Roasted sweet potato and feta salad, page 341); Josie Stow and Jan Baldwin, *The African Kitchen* (Griddled sweet potato with ginger, chilli and lime, page 341 and Masai mara, page 369); Teresa Wallace (adaptation of her Lemon soufflé, page 36); Janet Wilson (Sloe and apple jelly, page 324); Wendy Wolf (Peaches with Bourbon, page 158); Liz Wood (Toffee apples, page 294); Sofka Zinovieff (Spinach with split peas or lentils, page 78).

Suppliers

Many of the vegetable, herb, salad and fruit varieties in this book are available from my mail order company. If you'd like a catalogue, please contact:

Sarah Raven's Kitchen and Garden
www.sarahraven.com
Telephone: 0844 884 6474

Excellent box schemes:
Riverford Organic Vegetables Ltd
Wash Barn, Buckfastleigh, Devon TQ11 0LD
www.riverford.co.uk
Telephone: 0845 6002311

Abel and Cole Ltd
16 Waterside Way, Plough Lane, Wimbledon, Surrey SW17 0HB
www.abel-cole.co.uk
Email: organics@abel-cole.co.uk

My favourite pick-your-own fruit farm:
Maynards
Windmill Hill, Ticehurst, East Sussex TN5 7HQ
www.maynardsfruit.co.uk
Telephone: 01580 200619

Other suppliers:
South Devon Chilli Farm
Wigford Cross, Loddiswell, Kingsbridge, Devon TQ7 4DX
www.southdevonchillifarm.co.uk
Telephone: 01548 550782

Stratta Oils
33 Vicarage Drive, Eastbourne, East Sussex BN20 8AP
www.stratta.org
Telephone: 01323 732505

About the author

Sarah Raven is an expert on all things to grow, cut and eat from your garden. In her last book, *The Great Vegetable Plot*, Sarah wrote: 'A vegetable garden is a beautiful thing to make, with the bonus of producing the best possible things to eat. If you get it right, the whole place can become your market, your haven and your playground.' This enthusiasm bubbles through all of her books, including *The Cutting Garden*, which won the Garden Writers' Guild Award for Best Specialist Gardening Book, and *The Bold and Brilliant Garden*.

Sarah is a passionate teacher, running cooking, flower arranging and gardening courses at her East Sussex farm. She is also a presenter on BBC's *Gardeners' World* and writes for the *Daily Telegraph* as well as several leading magazines. Sarah is married to the writer Adam Nicolson and has two daughters and three stepsons.

About the photographer

Jonathan Buckley specialises in garden and plant photography and his work has been widely published in books, magazines and newspapers worldwide. He has been collaborating with Sarah Raven, taking photographs at Perch Hill, for ten years. He was named Photographer of the Year and Features Photographer of the Year by the Garden Writers' Guild in 2006.

First published in Great Britain in 2007

Text © Sarah Raven 2007
Photography © Jonathan Buckley 2007

The moral right of the author has
been asserted.

Bloomsbury Publishing Plc,
36 Soho Square,
London W1D 3QY

A CIP catalogue record for this book
is available from the British Library.

Designer: SMITH, Karl Shanahan
www.smith-design.com
Photographer: Jonathan Buckley

The text of this book is set in
Neue Helvetica.

ISBN 9780747588702

10 9 8 7 6 5 4 3

Printed and bound in Italy
by Graphicom

All papers used by Bloomsbury
Publishing are natural, recyclable
products made from wood grown
in well-managed forests. The
manufacturing processes conform
to the environmental regulations
of the country of origin.

www.bloomsbury.com
www.sarahraven.com